DEADPOOL

CLASSIC

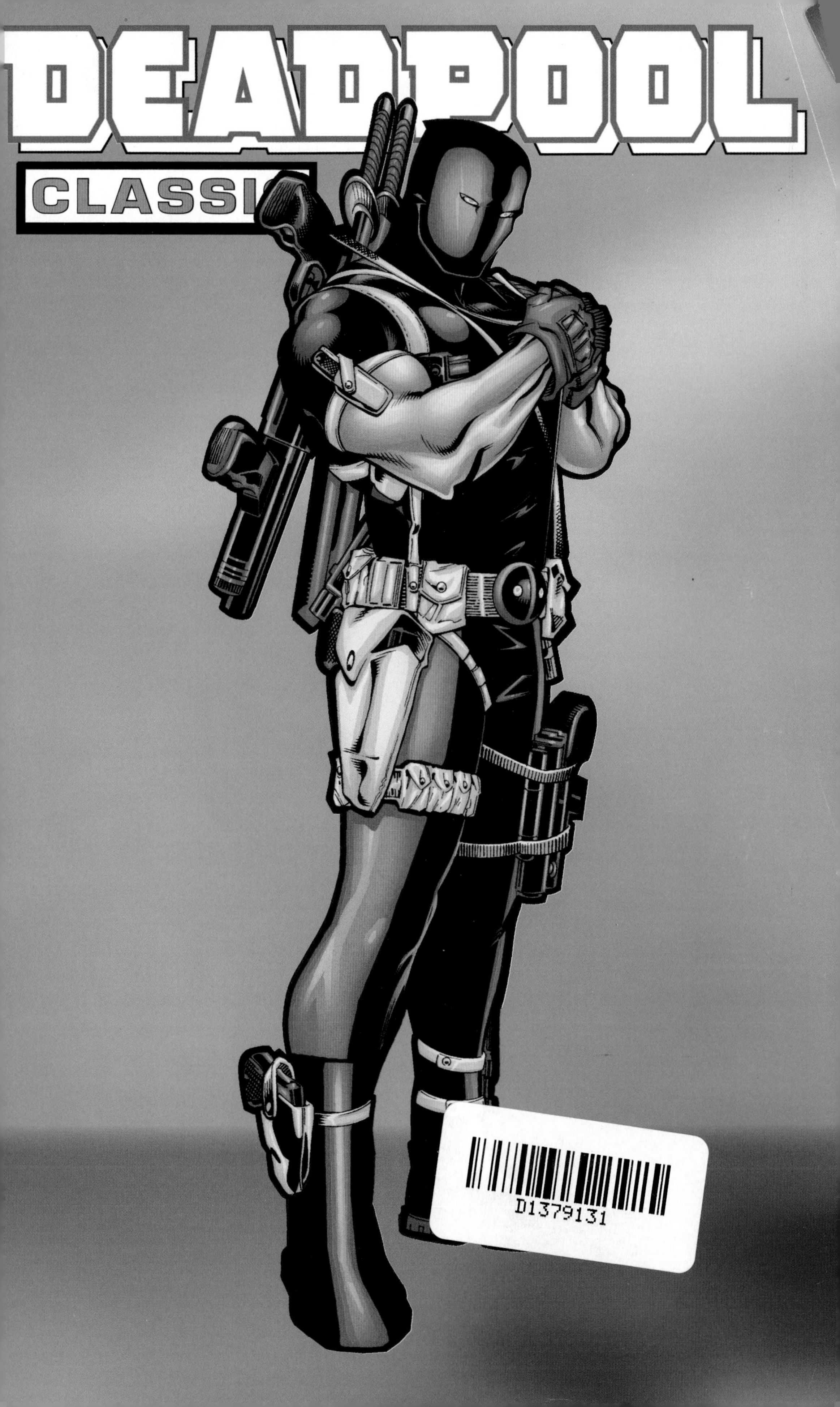

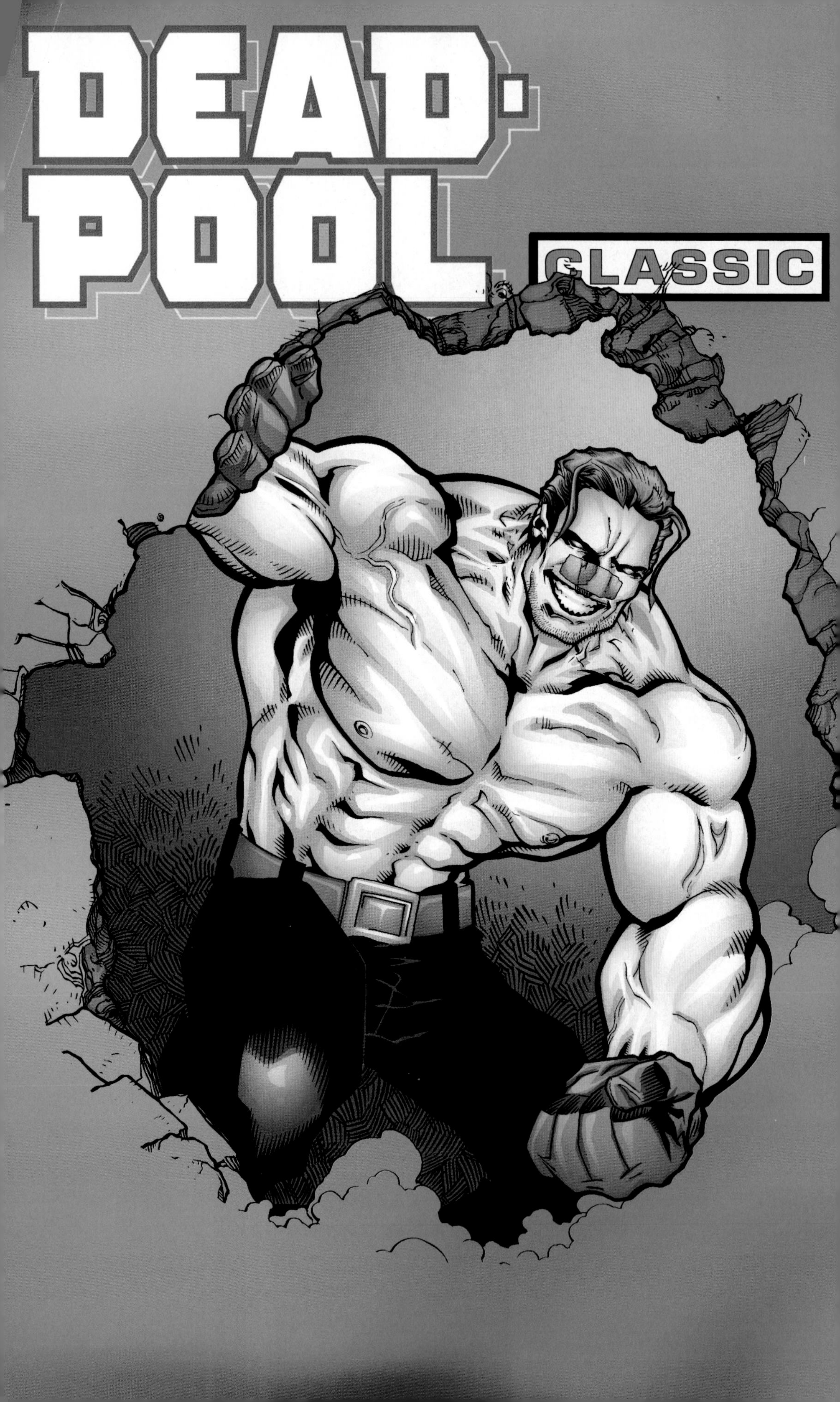
DEAD-
POOL
CLASSIC

WRITERS
Frank Tieri & Buddy Scalera

PENCILERS
Georges Jeanty & Jim Calafiore
INKERS
Jon Holdredge & Walden Wong with Dexter Vines, David Newbold & Mark McKenna
COLORIST
Tom Chu's Color Dojo
LETTERER
Sharpefont's Dave Sharpe

ASSISTANT EDITOR
Mike Raicht

EDITOR
Mike Marts

FRONT COVER ARTIST
Georges Jeanty

FRONT COVER COLORIST
ArtMonkey Studios

BACK COVER ARTIST
Udon Studios & Alvin Lee

BACK COVER COLORIST
Ramil Sunga

COLLECTION EDITOR: Nelson Ribeiro
ASSISTANT EDITOR: Alex Starbuck
EDITORS, SPECIAL PROJECTS: Mark D. Beazley & Jennifer Grünwald
SENIOR EDITOR, SPECIAL PROJECTS: Jeff Youngquist
SVP OF PRINT & DIGITAL PUBLISHING SALES: David Gabriel
RESEARCH & LAYOUT: Jeph York

EDITOR IN CHIEF: Axel Alonso
CHIEF CREATIVE OFFICER: Joe Quesada
PUBLISHER: Dan Buckley
EXECUTIVE PRODUCER: Alan Fine

Deadpool created by Rob Liefeld and Fabian Nicieza

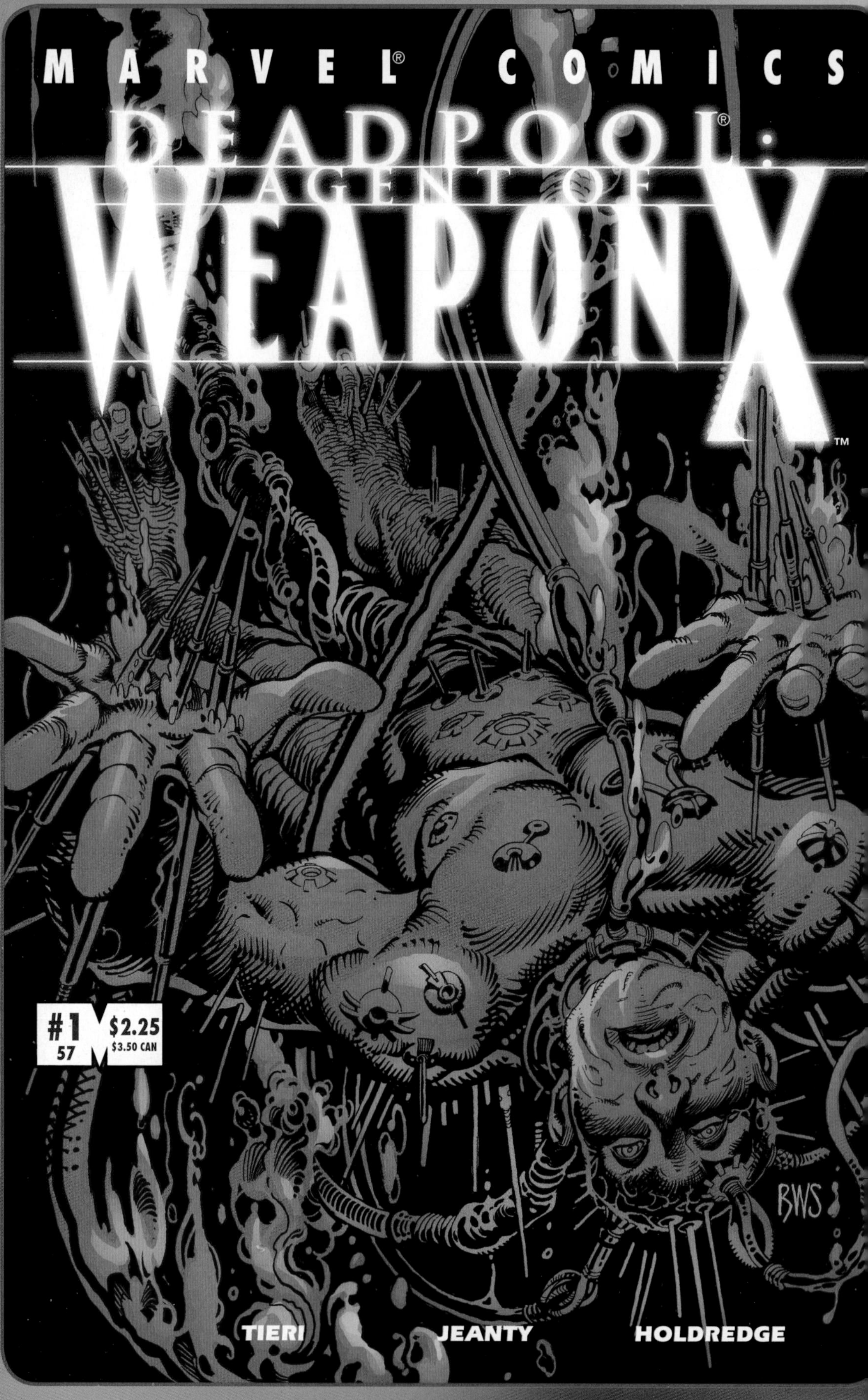

MARVEL® COMICS
DEADPOOL®:
AGENT OF
WEAPON X™
#1
57
$2.25
$3.50 CAN
BWS
TIERI
JEANTY
HOLDREDGE

AGENT OF WEAPON X
PT 1: FACELIFT

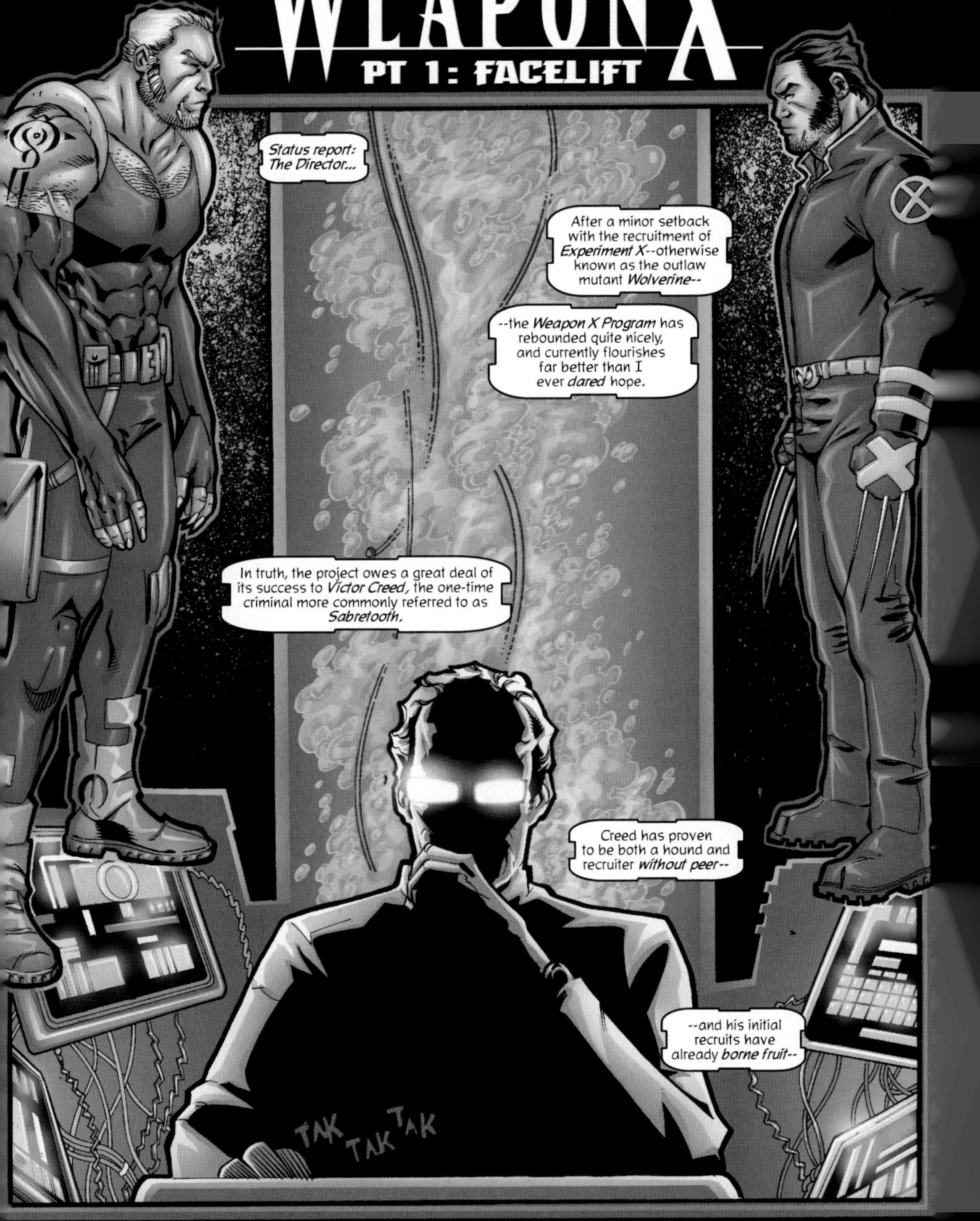
Status report: The Director...
After a minor setback with the recruitment of *Experiment X*--otherwise known as the outlaw mutant *Wolverine*--
--the *Weapon X Program* has rebounded quite nicely, and currently flourishes far better than I ever *dared* hope.
In truth, the project owes a great deal of its success to *Victor Creed*, the one-time criminal more commonly referred to as *Sabretooth*.
Creed has proven to be both a hound and recruiter *without peer*--
--and his initial recruits have already *borne fruit*--
TAK TAK TAK

FRANK TIERI : WRITER GEORGES JEANTY : PENCILER JON HOLDREDGE W/ VINES : INKER
BARRY WINDSOR-SMITH COVER TOM CHU : COLORIST SHARPEFONT'S DAVE : LETTERER
MIKE RAICHT : ASSISTANT EDITOR MIKE MARTS : EDITOR JOE QUESADA : CHIEF BILL JEMAS : PRESIDENT

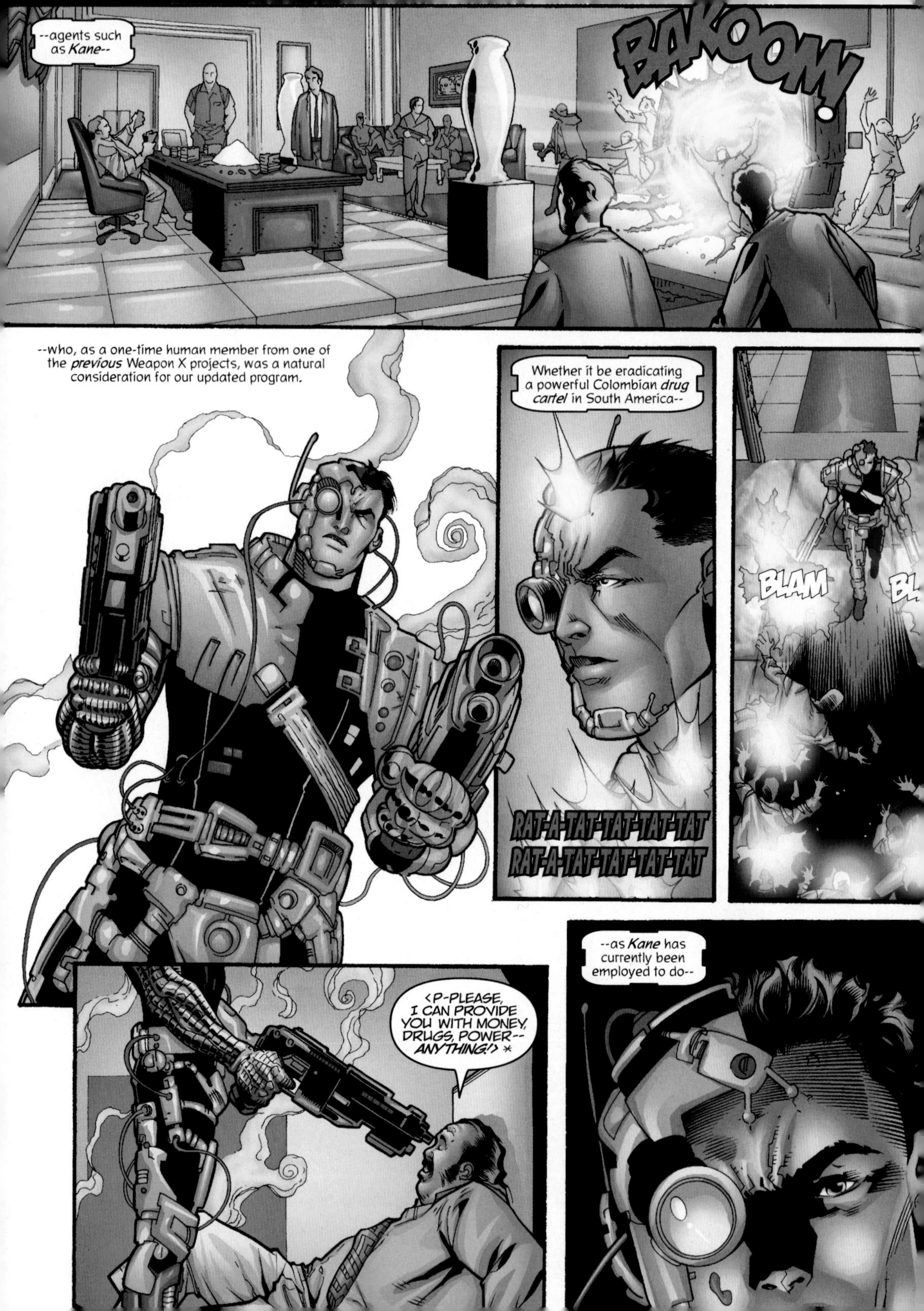
--agents such as Kane--
BAKOOM!
--who, as a one-time human member from one of the previous Weapon X projects, was a natural consideration for our updated program.
Whether it be eradicating a powerful Colombian drug cartel in South America--
RAT-A-TAT-TAT-TAT-TAT
RAT-A-TAT-TAT-TAT-TAT
BLAM
<P-PLEASE, I CAN PROVIDE YOU WITH MONEY, DRUGS, POWER-- ANYTHING!> *
--as Kane has currently been employed to do--

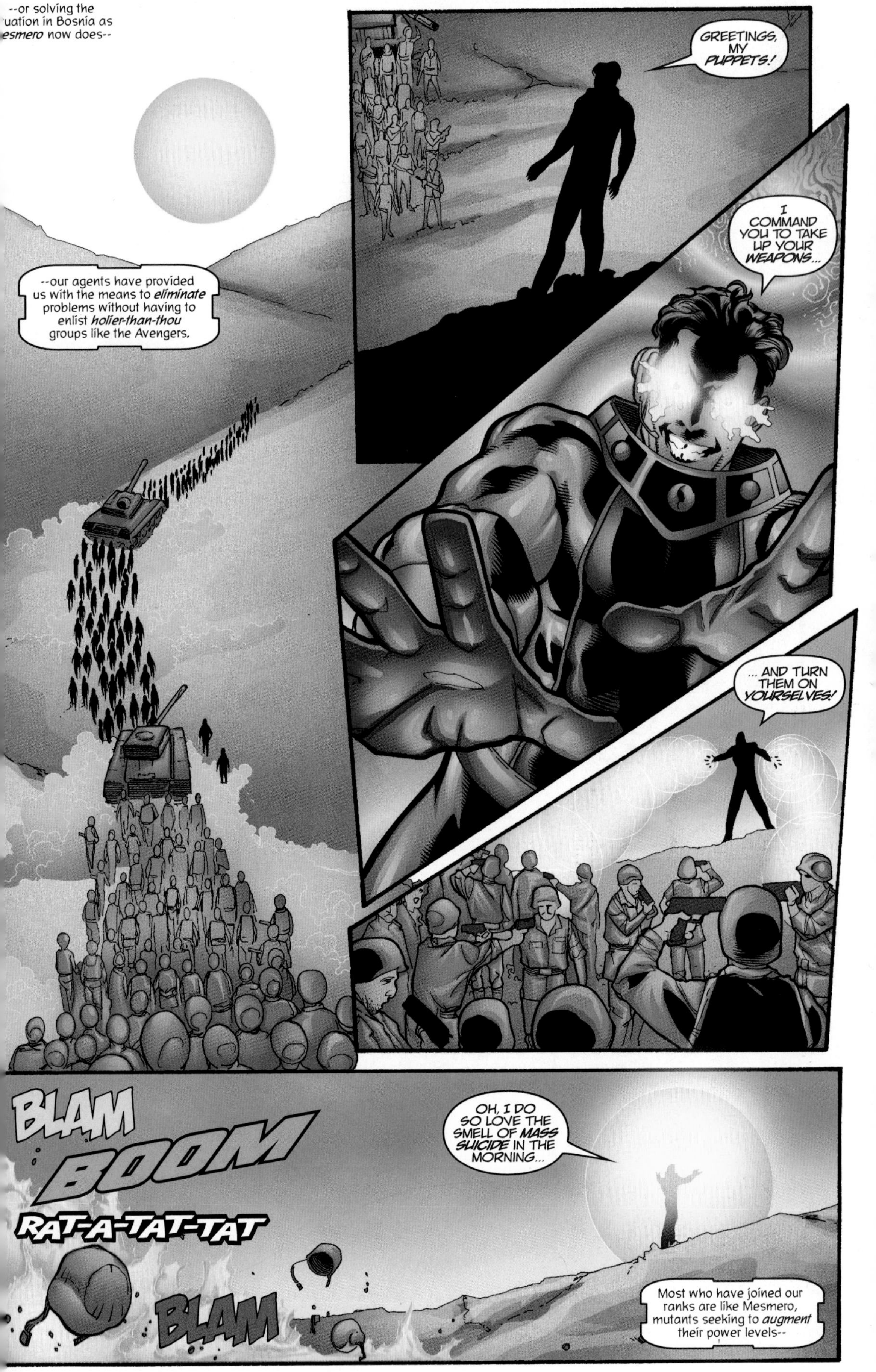
--or solving the
uation in Bosnia as
esmero now does--
GREETINGS, MY PUPPETS!
--our agents have provided us with the means to eliminate problems without having to enlist holier-than-thou groups like the Avengers.
I COMMAND YOU TO TAKE UP YOUR WEAPONS...
... AND TURN THEM ON YOURSELVES!
BLAM
BOOM
RAT-A-TAT-TAT
BLAM
OH, I DO SO LOVE THE SMELL OF MASS SUICIDE IN THE MORNING...
Most who have joined our ranks are like Mesmero, mutants seeking to augment their power levels--

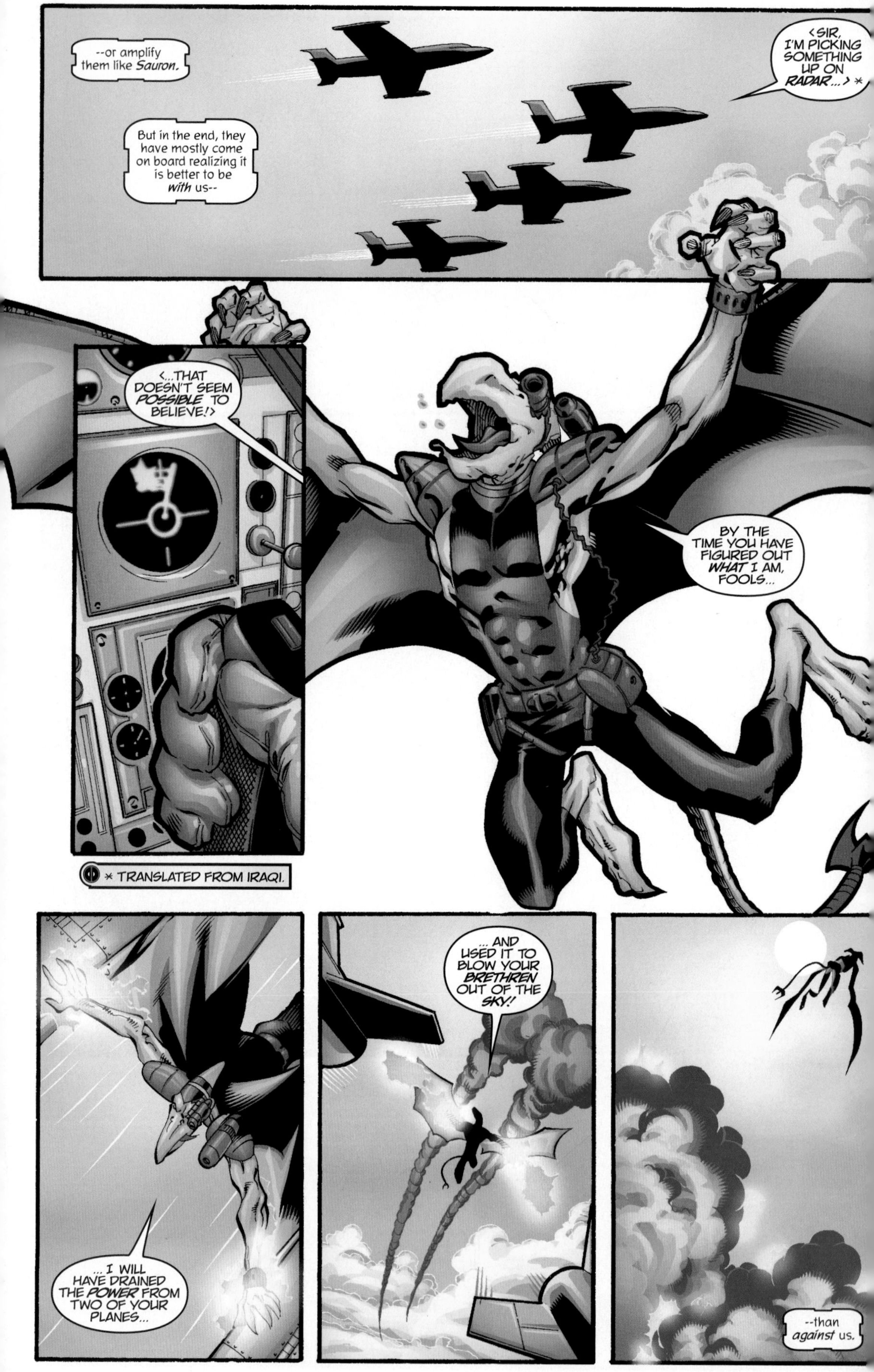
--or amplify them like *Sauron.*
But in the end, they have mostly come on board realizing it is better to be *with* us--
<SIR, I'M PICKING SOMETHING UP ON *RADAR...*> *
<...THAT DOESN'T SEEM *POSSIBLE* TO BELIEVE!>
BY THE TIME YOU HAVE FIGURED OUT *WHAT* I AM, FOOLS...
* TRANSLATED FROM IRAQI.
...I WILL HAVE DRAINED THE *POWER* FROM TWO OF YOUR PLANES...
...AND USED IT TO BLOW YOUR *BRETHREN* OUT OF THE *SKY!*
--than *against* us.

True, some of their fellow homo-superiors would consider the members of our organization as *"sell-outs"*--

LOOK, YOU CAN DENY IT ALL YOU *WANT*, BUT WE KNOW FOR A *FACT* THAT ONE OF YOU IS *LYING.*

WE KNOW THAT ONE OF YOU IS A--

--*SPY?*

Oh...Uh... YOU MUST BE THE *SPECIALIST* THEY SENT.

--but unlike *our* mutants, they are not afforded the knowledge that when the inevitable *war* between man and mutant arrives--

Um... JUST TO FILL YOU IN, WE'VE *NARROWED* THE SEARCH DOWN TO THESE *THREE*... WE JUST HAVEN'T FIGURED OUT *WHICH ONE...*

--they will be *assured* survival.

Snif Snif

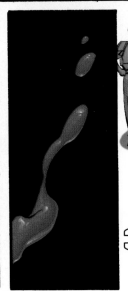

Yes, everything in *phase one* is proceeding according to *plan.*

I... GUESS *THAT'S OUR MAN.*

And yet, as well as Creed's first recruits like *Wild Child* have worked out--

--I am still having certain ... *reservations* about his newest prospect, a certain *loose cannon* by the name of--

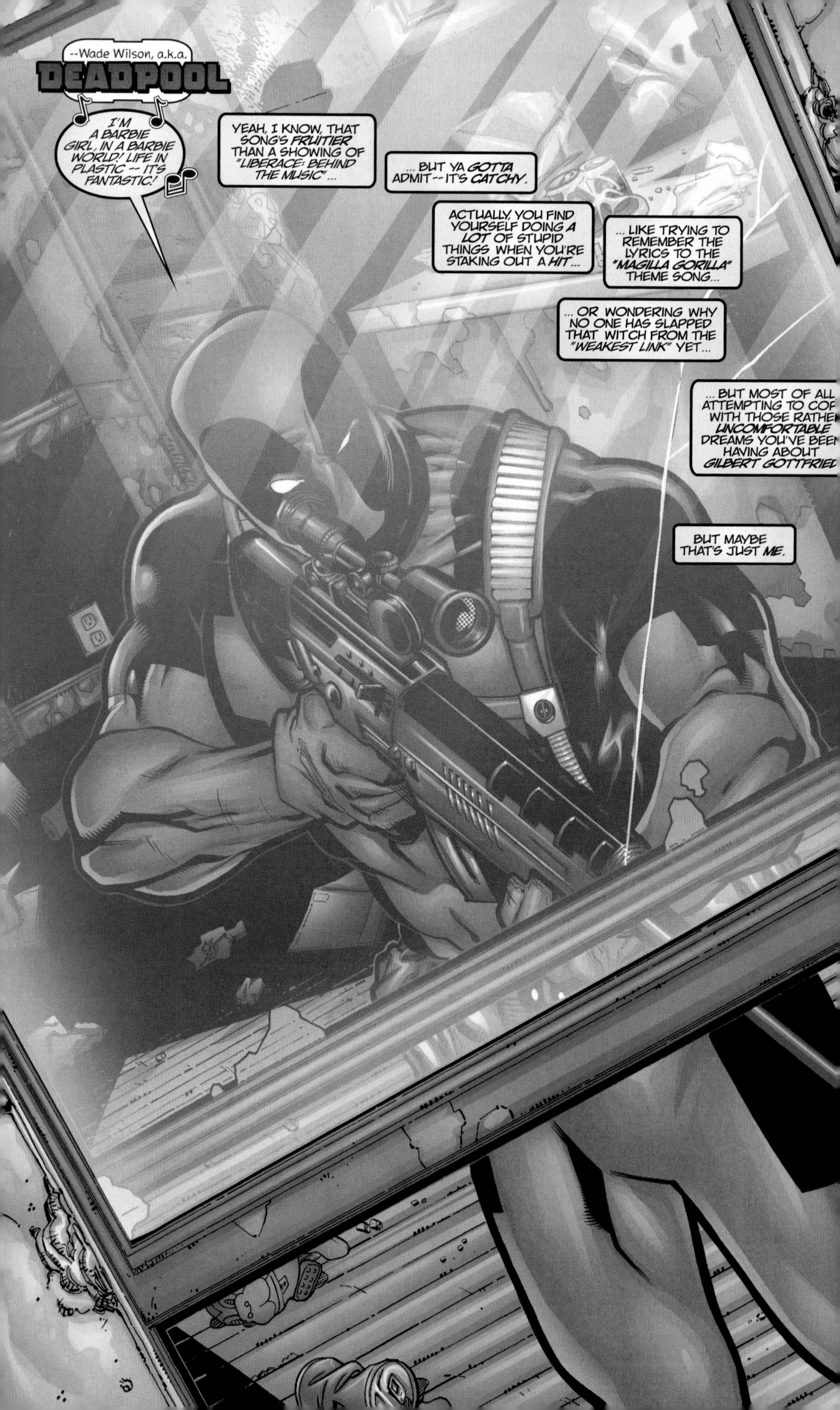
--Wade Wilson, a.k.a.
DEADPOOL
I'M A BARBIE GIRL, IN A BARBIE WORLD! LIFE IN PLASTIC -- IT'S FANTASTIC!
YEAH, I KNOW, THAT SONG'S FRUITIER THAN A SHOWING OF "LIBERACE: BEHIND THE MUSIC"...
... BUT YA GOTTA ADMIT-- IT'S CATCHY.
ACTUALLY, YOU FIND YOURSELF DOING A LOT OF STUPID THINGS WHEN YOU'RE STAKING OUT A HIT...
... LIKE TRYING TO REMEMBER THE LYRICS TO THE "MAGILLA GORILLA" THEME SONG...
... OR WONDERING WHY NO ONE HAS SLAPPED THAT WITCH FROM THE "WEAKEST LINK" YET...
... BUT MOST OF ALL ATTEMPTING TO COP WITH THOSE RATHE UNCOMFORTABLE DREAMS YOU'VE BEEN HAVING ABOUT GILBERT GOTTFRIE
BUT MAYBE THAT'S JUST ME.

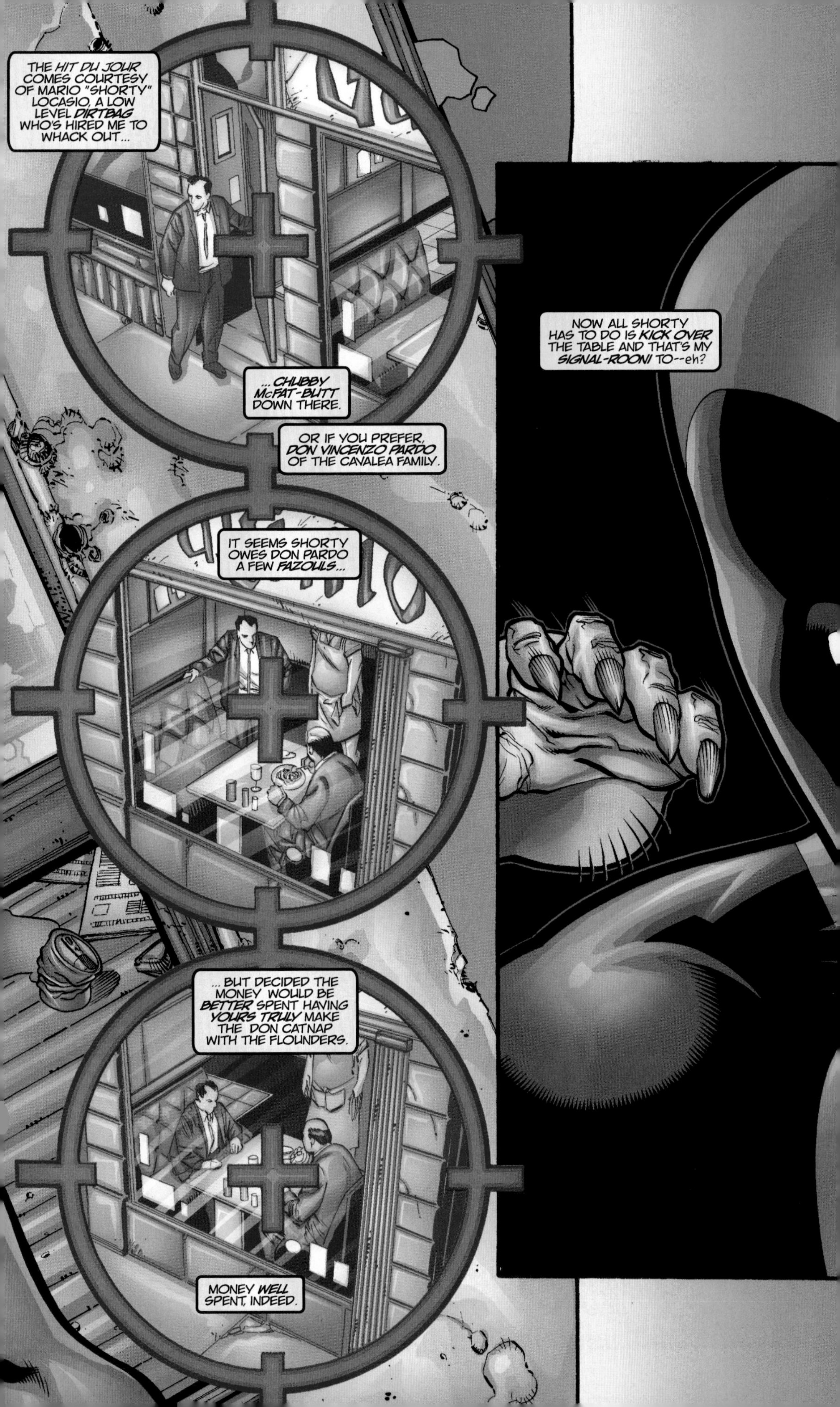
THE HIT DU JOUR COMES COURTESY OF MARIO "SHORTY" LOCASIO, A LOW LEVEL DIRTBAG WHO'S HIRED ME TO WHACK OUT...
...CHUBBY McFAT-BUTT DOWN THERE.
OR IF YOU PREFER, DON VINCENZO PARDO OF THE CAVALEA FAMILY.
IT SEEMS SHORTY OWES DON PARDO A FEW FAZOULS...
...BUT DECIDED THE MONEY WOULD BE BETTER SPENT HAVING YOURS TRULY MAKE THE DON CATNAP WITH THE FLOUNDERS.
MONEY WELL SPENT, INDEED.
NOW ALL SHORTY HAS TO DO IS KICK OVER THE TABLE AND THAT'S MY SIGNAL-ROONI TO--eh?

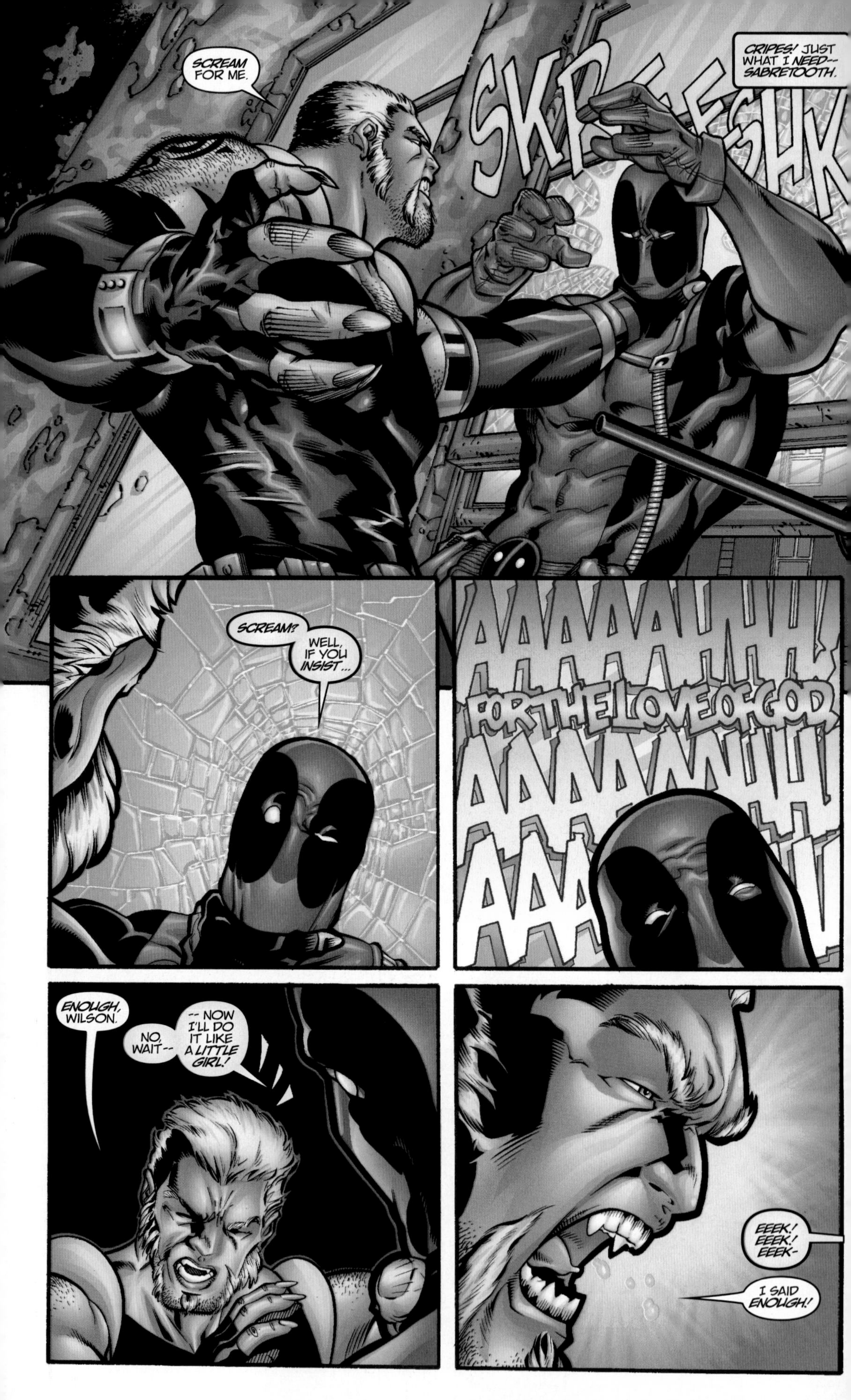
SCREAM FOR ME.
CRIPES! JUST WHAT I NEED-- SABRETOOTH.
SKRAASHK
SCREAM?
WELL, IF YOU INSIST...
AAAAAAUHH!
FOR THE LOVE OF GOD
AAAAAAUHH
ENOUGH, WILSON.
NO, WAIT--
-- NOW I'LL DO IT LIKE A LITTLE GIRL!
EEEK! EEEK! EEEK-
I SAID ENOUGH!

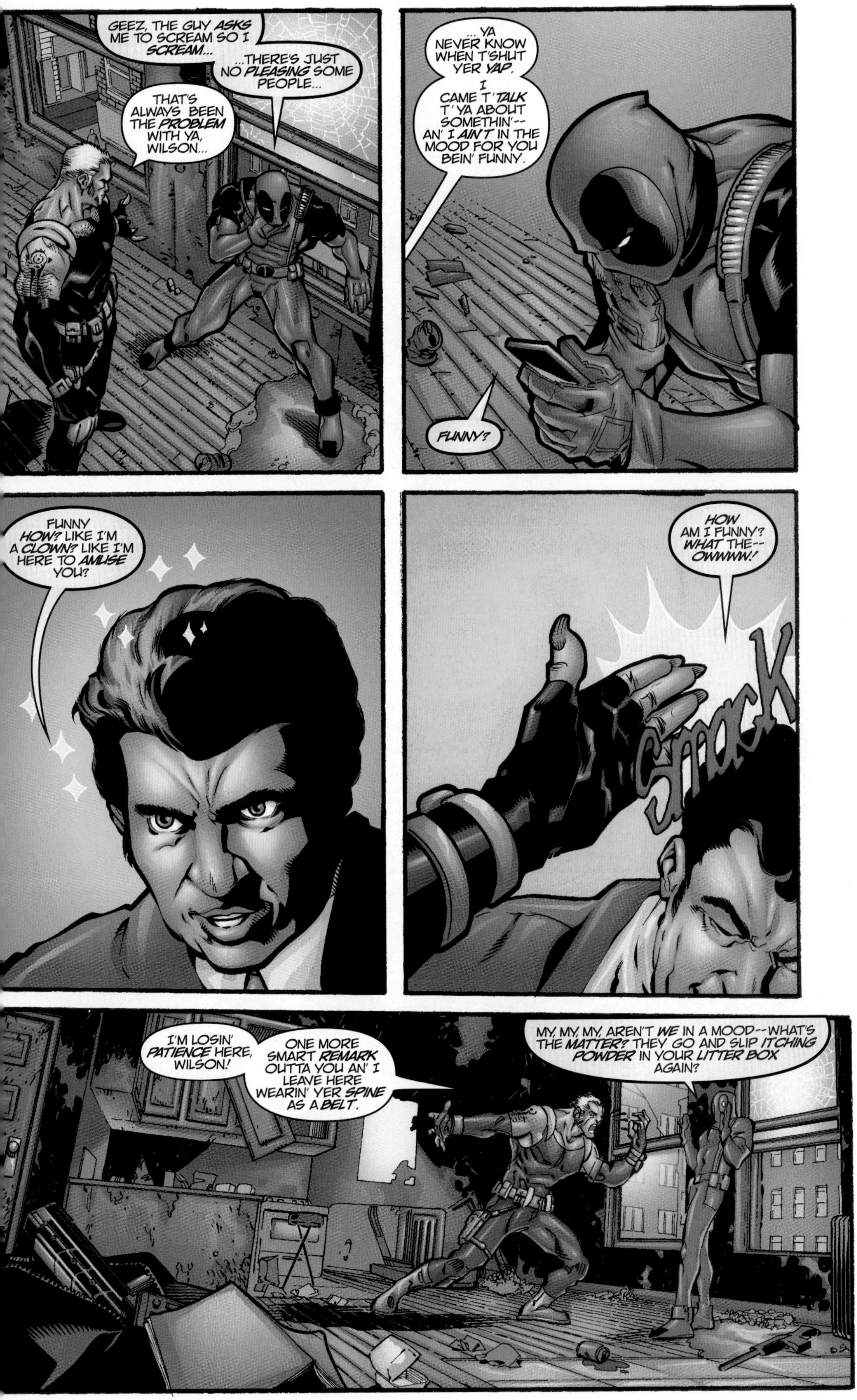
GEEZ, THE GUY ASKS ME TO SCREAM SO I SCREAM...
...THERE'S JUST NO PLEASING SOME PEOPLE...
THAT'S ALWAYS BEEN THE PROBLEM WITH YA, WILSON...
...YA NEVER KNOW WHEN T'SHUT YER YAP.
I CAME T'TALK T'YA ABOUT SOMETHIN'-- AN' I AIN'T IN THE MOOD FOR YOU BEIN' FUNNY.
FUNNY?
FUNNY HOW? LIKE I'M A CLOWN? LIKE I'M HERE TO AMUSE YOU?
HOW AM I FUNNY? WHAT THE-- OWWWW!
SMACK
I'M LOSIN' PATIENCE HERE, WILSON!
ONE MORE SMART REMARK OUTTA YOU AN' I LEAVE HERE WEARIN' YER SPINE AS A BELT.
MY, MY, MY, AREN'T WE IN A MOOD--WHAT'S THE MATTER? THEY GO AND SLIP ITCHING POWDER IN YOUR LITTER BOX AGAIN?

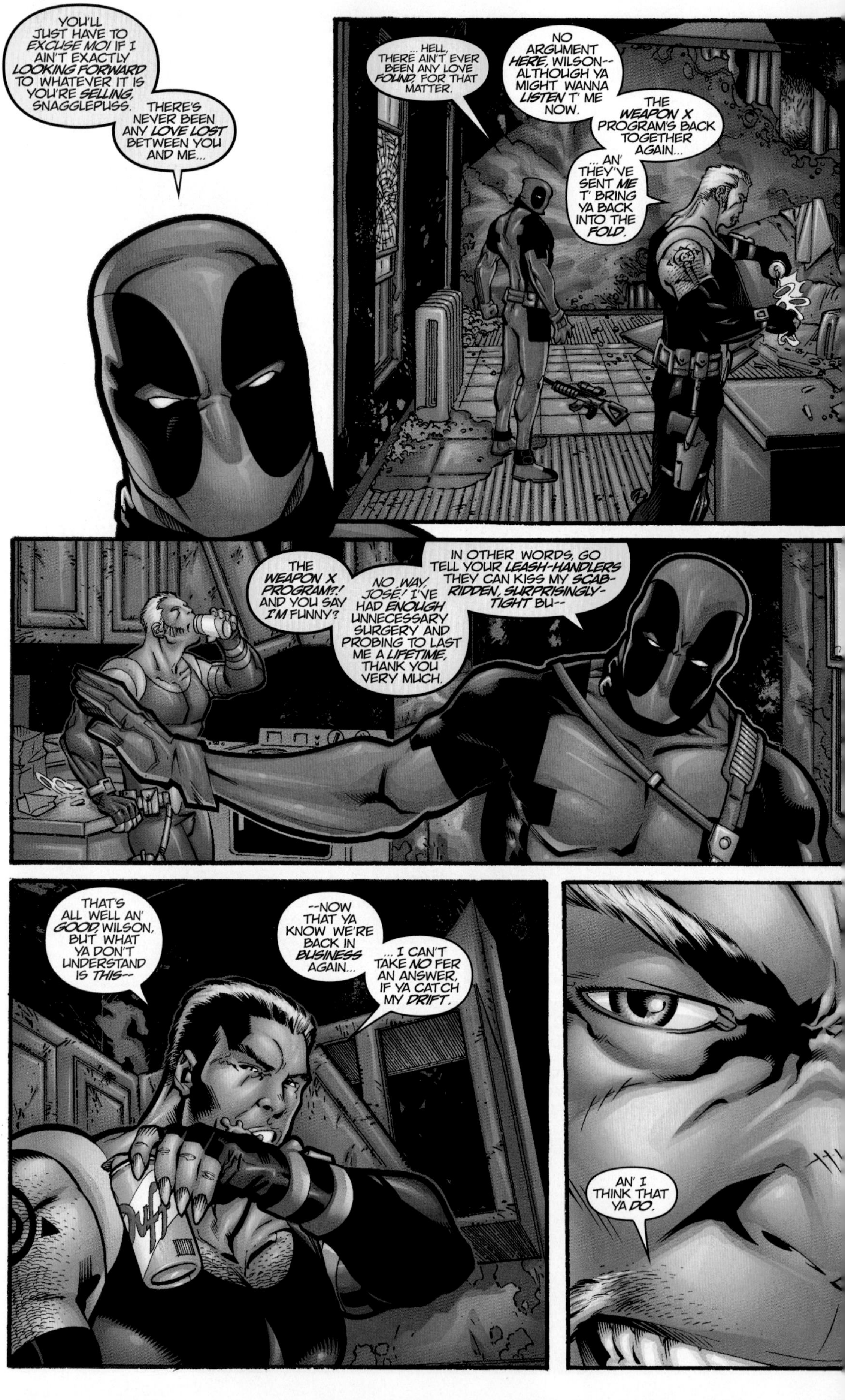
YOU'LL JUST HAVE TO EXCUSE MOI IF I AIN'T EXACTLY LOOKING FORWARD TO WHATEVER IT IS YOU'RE SELLING, SNAGGLEPUSS.
THERE'S NEVER BEEN ANY LOVE LOST BETWEEN YOU AND ME...
... HELL, THERE AIN'T EVER BEEN ANY LOVE FOUND, FOR THAT MATTER.
NO ARGUMENT HERE, WILSON-- ALTHOUGH YA MIGHT WANNA LISTEN T' ME NOW.
THE WEAPON X PROGRAM'S BACK TOGETHER AGAIN...
... AN' THEY'VE SENT ME T' BRING YA BACK INTO THE FOLD.
THE WEAPON X PROGRAM?! AND YOU SAY I'M FUNNY?
NO WAY, JOSÉ! I'VE HAD ENOUGH UNNECESSARY SURGERY AND PROBING TO LAST ME A LIFETIME, THANK YOU VERY MUCH.
IN OTHER WORDS, GO TELL YOUR LEASH-HANDLERS THEY CAN KISS MY SCAB-RIDDEN, SURPRISINGLY-TIGHT BU--
THAT'S ALL WELL AN' GOOD, WILSON, BUT WHAT YA DON'T UNDERSTAND IS THIS--
--NOW THAT YA KNOW WE'RE BACK IN BUSINESS AGAIN...
... I CAN'T TAKE NO FER AN ANSWER, IF YA CATCH MY DRIFT.
AN' I THINK THAT YA DO.

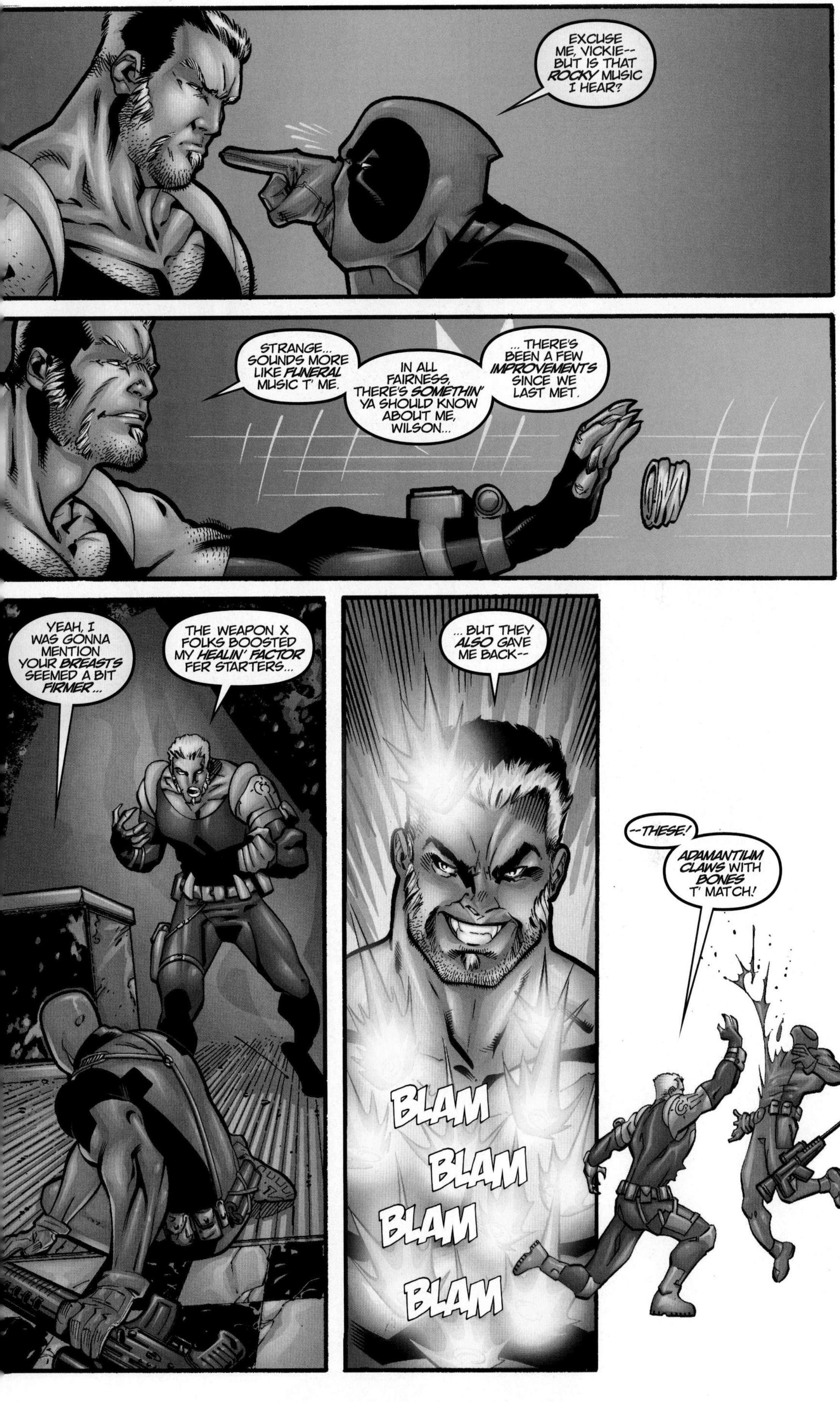
EXCUSE ME, VICKIE-- BUT IS THAT ROCKY MUSIC I HEAR?
STRANGE... SOUNDS MORE LIKE FUNERAL MUSIC T' ME.
IN ALL FAIRNESS, THERE'S SOMETHIN' YA SHOULD KNOW ABOUT ME, WILSON...
... THERE'S BEEN A FEW IMPROVEMENTS SINCE WE LAST MET.
YEAH, I WAS GONNA MENTION YOUR BREASTS SEEMED A BIT FIRMER...
THE WEAPON X FOLKS BOOSTED MY HEALIN' FACTOR FER STARTERS...
... BUT THEY ALSO GAVE ME BACK--
BLAM
BLAM
BLAM
BLAM
--THESE!
ADAMANTIUM CLAWS WITH BONES T' MATCH!

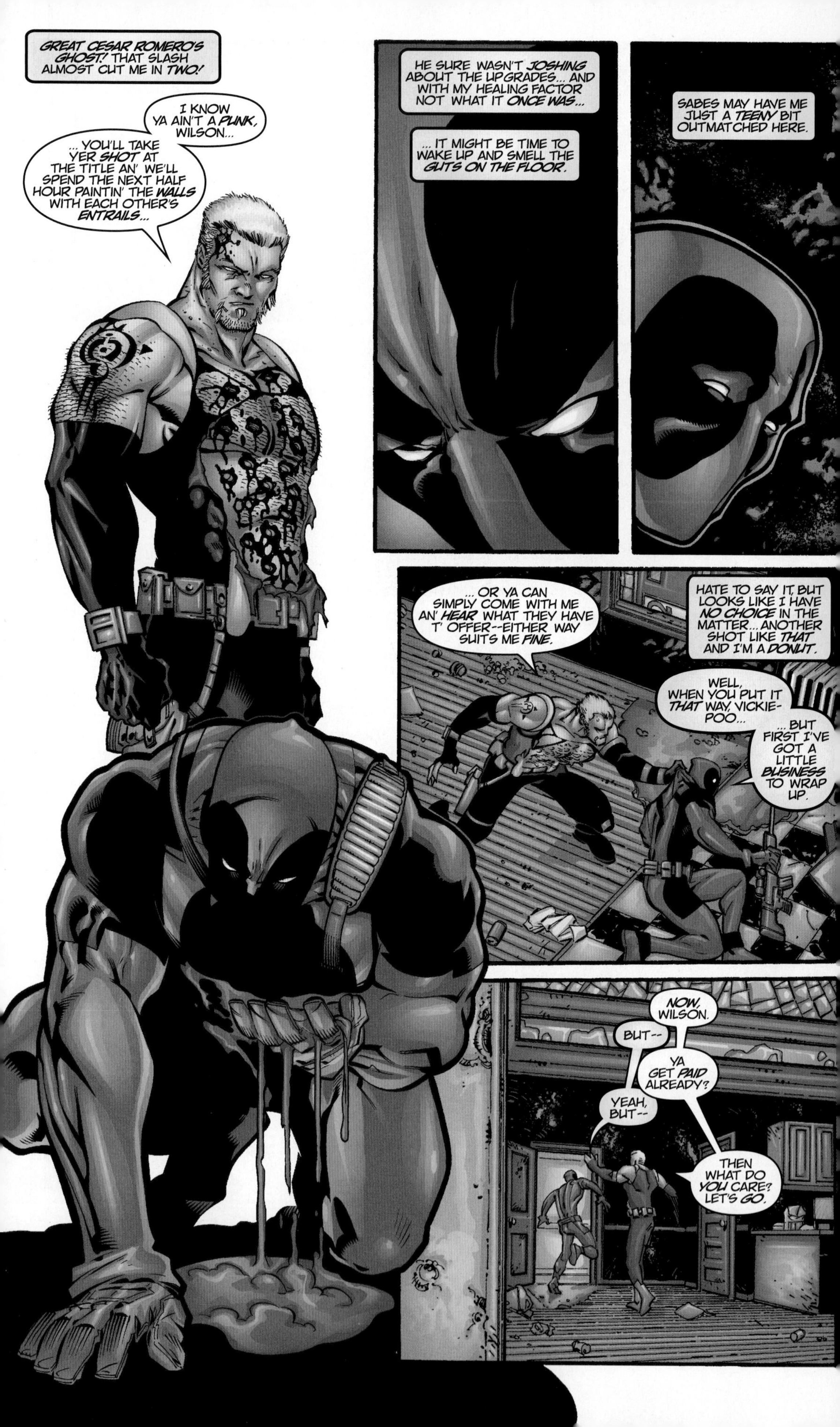
GREAT CESAR ROMERO'S GHOST! THAT SLASH ALMOST CUT ME IN TWO!
I KNOW YA AIN'T A PUNK, WILSON...
... YOU'LL TAKE YER SHOT AT THE TITLE AN' WE'LL SPEND THE NEXT HALF HOUR PAINTIN' THE WALLS WITH EACH OTHER'S ENTRAILS...
HE SURE WASN'T JOSHING ABOUT THE UPGRADES... AND WITH MY HEALING FACTOR NOT WHAT IT ONCE WAS...
... IT MIGHT BE TIME TO WAKE UP AND SMELL THE GUTS ON THE FLOOR.
SABES MAY HAVE ME JUST A TEENY BIT OUTMATCHED HERE.
... OR YA CAN SIMPLY COME WITH ME AN' HEAR WHAT THEY HAVE T' OFFER--EITHER WAY SUITS ME FINE.
HATE TO SAY IT, BUT LOOKS LIKE I HAVE NO CHOICE IN THE MATTER... ANOTHER SHOT LIKE THAT AND I'M A DONUT.
WELL, WHEN YOU PUT IT THAT WAY, VICKIE-POO...
... BUT FIRST I'VE GOT A LITTLE BUSINESS TO WRAP UP.
NOW, WILSON.
BUT--
YA GET PAID ALREADY?
YEAH, BUT--
THEN WHAT DO YOU CARE? LET'S GO.

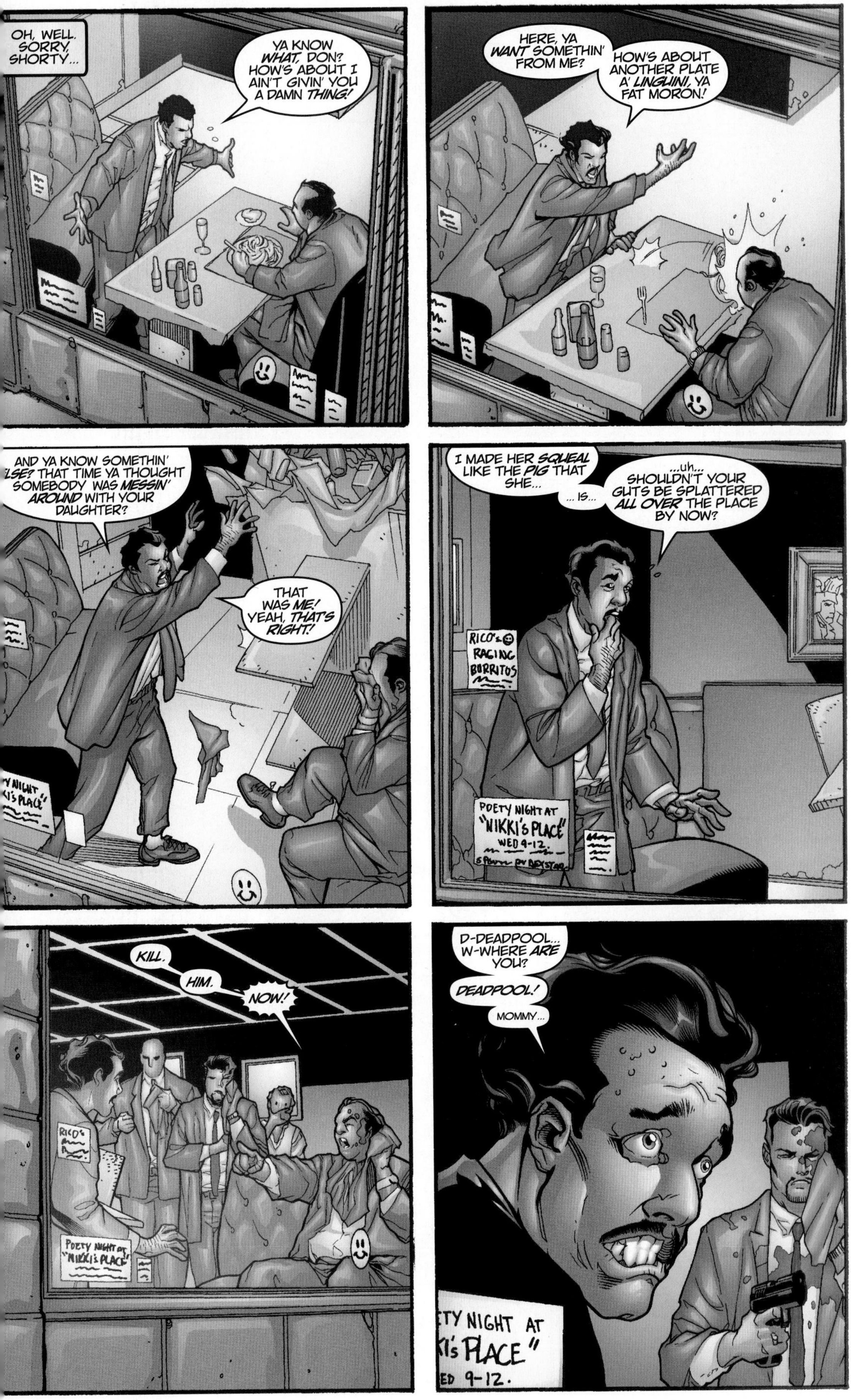
OH, WELL. SORRY, SHORTY...
YA KNOW WHAT, DON? HOW'S ABOUT I AIN'T GIVIN' YOU A DAMN THING!
HERE, YA WANT SOMETHIN' FROM ME?
HOW'S ABOUT ANOTHER PLATE A' LINGUINI, YA FAT MORON!
AND YA KNOW SOMETHIN' ELSE? THAT TIME YA THOUGHT SOMEBODY WAS MESSIN' AROUND WITH YOUR DAUGHTER?
THAT WAS ME! YEAH, THAT'S RIGHT!
I MADE HER SQUEAL LIKE THE PIG THAT SHE...
... IS...
...uh... SHOULDN'T YOUR GUTS BE SPLATTERED ALL OVER THE PLACE BY NOW?
RICO'S RAGING BURRITOS
POETY NIGHT AT "NIKKI'S PLACE" WED 9-12.
KILL.
HIM.
NOW!
D-DEADPOOL... W-WHERE ARE YOU?
DEADPOOL!
MOMMY...

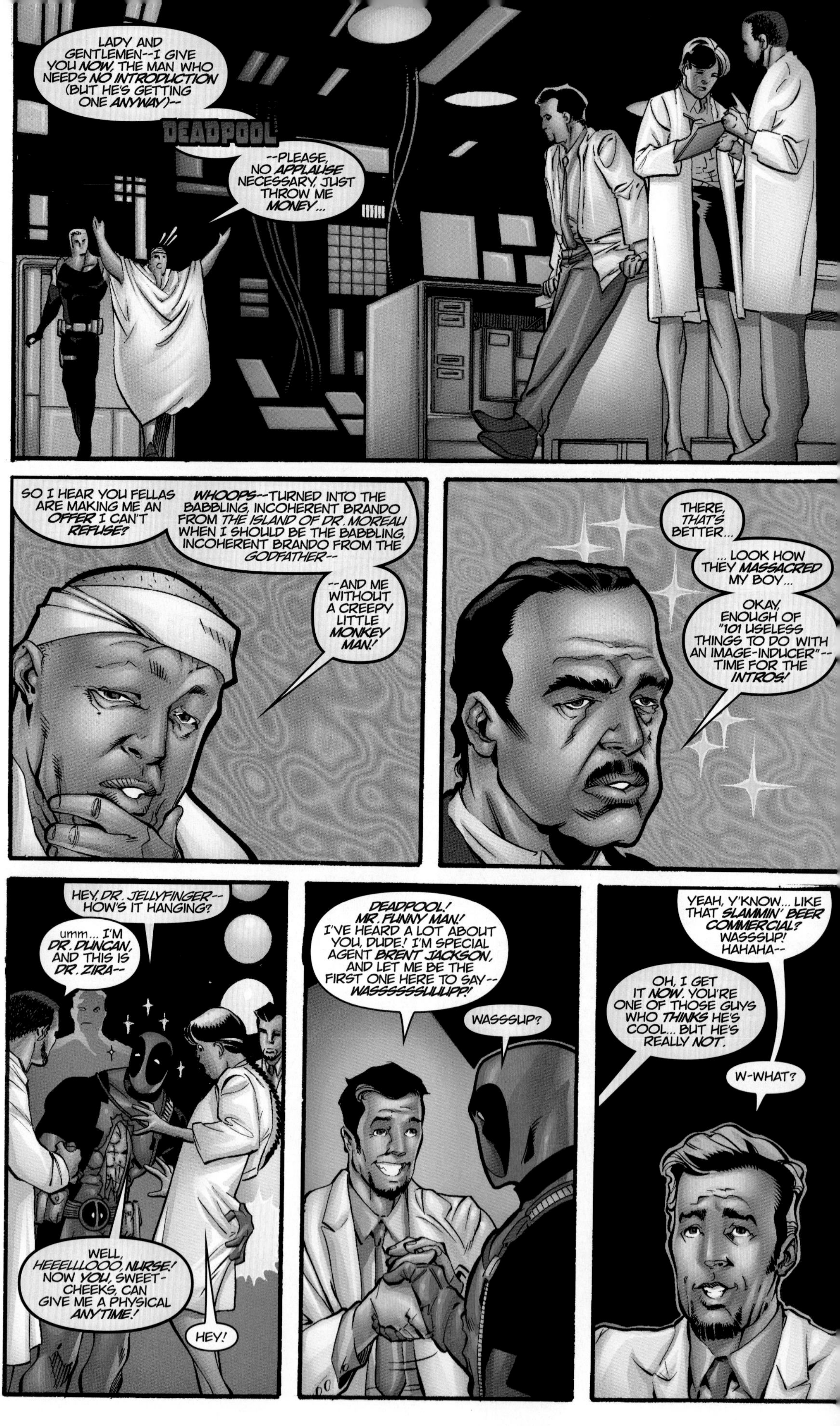

LADY AND GENTLEMEN--I GIVE YOU NOW, THE MAN WHO NEEDS NO INTRODUCTION (BUT HE'S GETTING ONE ANYWAY)--
DEADPOOL
--PLEASE, NO APPLAUSE NECESSARY, JUST THROW ME MONEY...
SO I HEAR YOU FELLAS ARE MAKING ME AN OFFER I CAN'T REFUSE?
WHOOPS--TURNED INTO THE BABBLING, INCOHERENT BRANDO FROM THE ISLAND OF DR. MOREAU WHEN I SHOULD BE THE BABBLING, INCOHERENT BRANDO FROM THE GODFATHER--
--AND ME WITHOUT A CREEPY LITTLE MONKEY MAN!
THERE, THAT'S BETTER...
...LOOK HOW THEY MASSACRED MY BOY...
OKAY, ENOUGH OF "101 USELESS THINGS TO DO WITH AN IMAGE-INDUCER"--TIME FOR THE INTROS!
HEY, DR. JELLYFINGER--HOW'S IT HANGING?
umm... I'M DR. DUNCAN, AND THIS IS DR. ZIRA--
WELL, HEEELLLOOO, NURSE! NOW YOU, SWEET-CHEEKS, CAN GIVE ME A PHYSICAL ANYTIME!
HEY!
DEADPOOL! MR. FUNNY MAN! I'VE HEARD A LOT ABOUT YOU, DUDE! I'M SPECIAL AGENT BRENT JACKSON, AND LET ME BE THE FIRST ONE HERE TO SAY--WASSSSSSUUUPP!
WASSSUP?
YEAH, Y'KNOW... LIKE THAT SLAMMIN' BEER COMMERCIAL? WASSSUP! HAHAHA--
OH, I GET IT NOW. YOU'RE ONE OF THOSE GUYS WHO THINKS HE'S COOL... BUT HE'S REALLY NOT.
W-WHAT?

YOU USE *OUTDATED* EXPRESSIONS, YOU'VE GOT THE *PLAYED-OUT* GOATEE MOTIF GOING...

... YOU'RE THE *WEAPON X* VERSION OF *POOCHIE!* BWAHAHAHAAAA... WHAT A *STOOGE.* I-I...

OKAY, DOWN TO *CASES,* KIDS--WHICH ONE OF YOU QUACKS IS IN *CHARGE* OF THIS LITTLE SHINDIG?

THAT WOULD BE *ME,* MR. WILSON.

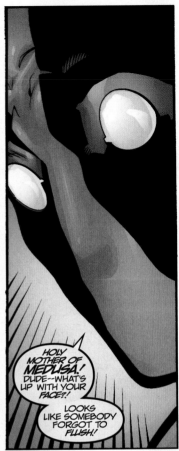

HOLY MOTHER OF *MEDUSA!* DUDE--WHAT'S UP WITH YOUR *FACE?!*

LOOKS LIKE SOMEBODY FORGOT TO *FLUSH!*

VERY *AMUSING,* MR. WILSON... I WAS PRE-WARNED ABOUT YOUR RATHER *OUTLANDISH* NATURE. AS FOR MY *APPEARANCE,* I HAVE YOUR FRIEND *WOLVERINE* TO THANK FOR *THAT.*

HE AIN'T NO *FRIEND* OF *MINE,* CHOP-MEAT FACE! THE ONLY THING WORSE THAN THAT GUY'S ATTITUDE IS HIS *BREATH--PEEE-EWWWWW!* HORSE MANURE CALLED, WOLVIE--IT WANTS ITS *SMELL* BACK!

BUT MAN, DID HE DO A *NUMBER* ON YOU! I HAVEN'T BEEN *THIS* REPULSED SINCE I SAW THOSE *NAKED* PICTURES OF *BEA ARTHUR* ON THE 'NET!

I BELIEVE THAT WILL *SUFFICE,* MR. WILSON--OR NEED I *REMIND* YOU OF THE GROTESQUENESS *YOU* SPORT UNDER THAT MASK, *AS WELL?*

TOUCHÉ, FUGLY... *TOUCHÉ.*

BUT BEFORE THIS SPILLS OVER INTO A *"YO' MAMA'S SO FAT"* RANK SESSION, HOW'S ABOUT WE CUT TO THE *CHASE* INSTEAD?

BUT JUST SO YOU KNOW IN *ADVANCE,* I'D RATHER PULL A *HAMLET* THAN SIGN UP WITH YOU *PUSBAGS* AGAIN...

... NOT TO MENTION HAVING THE *SABRETOOTH-FAIRY* BRING ME HERE *AGAINST* MY *WILL* CERTAINLY DIDN'T SCORE YOU ANY *POINTS.*

I'M AFRAID I MUST *APOLOGIZE* IF VICTOR WAS A BIT *OVERZEALOUS,* MR. WILSON--

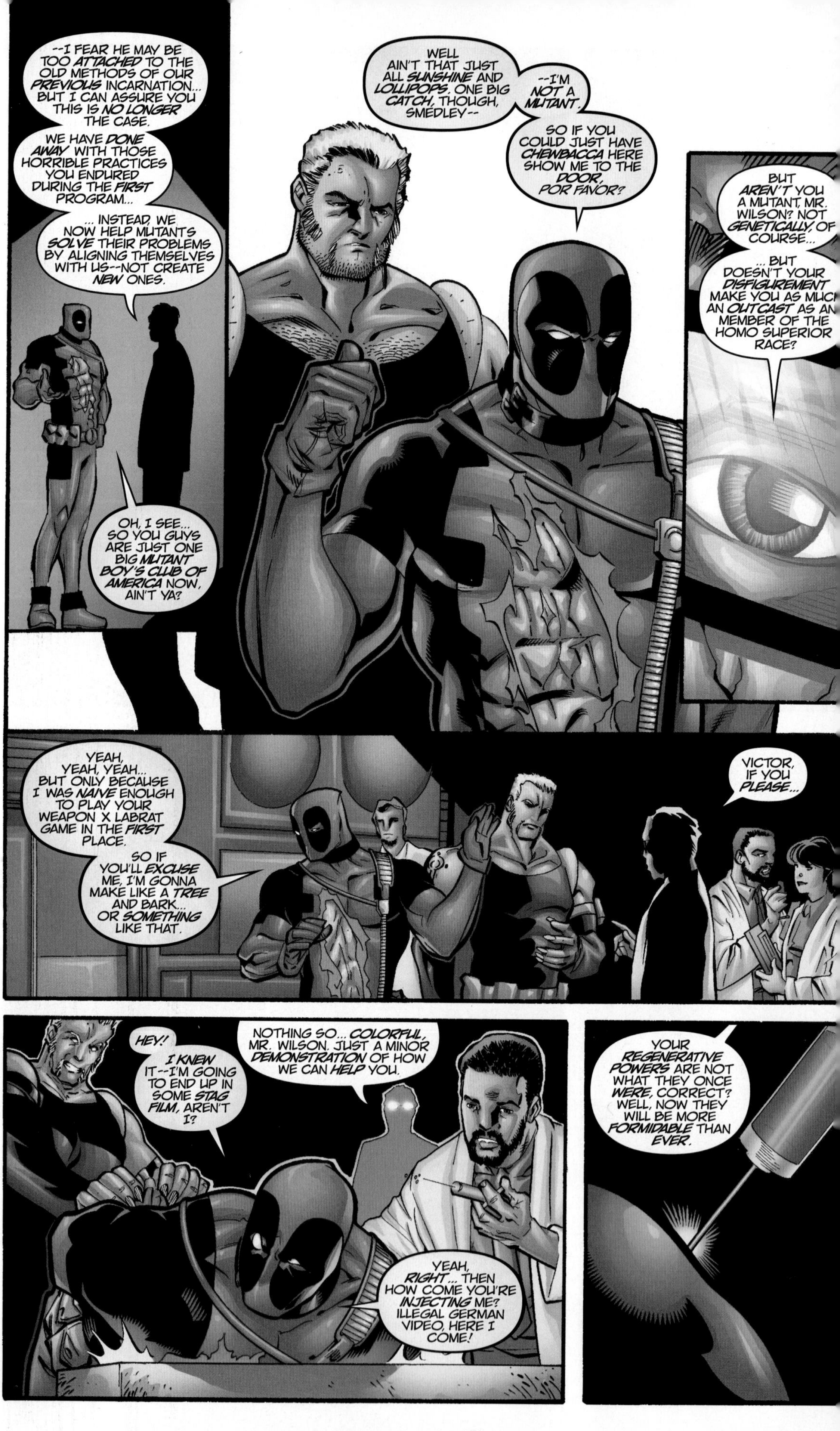
--I FEAR HE MAY BE TOO ATTACHED TO THE OLD METHODS OF OUR PREVIOUS INCARNATION... BUT I CAN ASSURE YOU THIS IS NO LONGER THE CASE.
WE HAVE DONE AWAY WITH THOSE HORRIBLE PRACTICES YOU ENDURED DURING THE FIRST PROGRAM...
... INSTEAD, WE NOW HELP MUTANTS SOLVE THEIR PROBLEMS BY ALIGNING THEMSELVES WITH US--NOT CREATE NEW ONES.
OH, I SEE... SO YOU GUYS ARE JUST ONE BIG MUTANT BOY'S CLUB OF AMERICA NOW, AIN'T YA?
WELL AIN'T THAT JUST ALL SUNSHINE AND LOLLIPOPS. ONE BIG CATCH, THOUGH, SMEDLEY--
--I'M NOT A MUTANT.
SO IF YOU COULD JUST HAVE CHEWBACCA HERE SHOW ME TO THE DOOR, POR FAVOR?
BUT AREN'T YOU A MUTANT, MR. WILSON? NOT GENETICALLY, OF COURSE...
... BUT DOESN'T YOUR DISFIGUREMENT MAKE YOU AS MUCH AN OUTCAST AS ANY MEMBER OF THE HOMO SUPERIOR RACE?
YEAH, YEAH, YEAH... BUT ONLY BECAUSE I WAS NAIVE ENOUGH TO PLAY YOUR WEAPON X LABRAT GAME IN THE FIRST PLACE.
SO IF YOU'LL EXCUSE ME, I'M GONNA MAKE LIKE A TREE AND BARK... OR SOMETHING LIKE THAT.
VICTOR, IF YOU PLEASE...
HEY!
I KNEW IT--I'M GOING TO END UP IN SOME STAG FILM, AREN'T I?
NOTHING SO... COLORFUL, MR. WILSON. JUST A MINOR DEMONSTRATION OF HOW WE CAN HELP YOU.
YEAH, RIGHT... THEN HOW COME YOU'RE INJECTING ME? ILLEGAL GERMAN VIDEO, HERE I COME!
YOUR REGENERATIVE POWERS ARE NOT WHAT THEY ONCE WERE, CORRECT? WELL, NOW THEY WILL BE MORE FORMIDABLE THAN EVER.

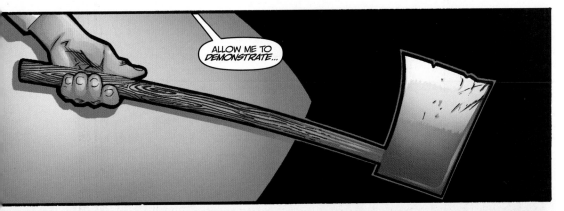

ALLOW ME TO DEMONSTRATE...

YEW-OUCH!

SHLUMPP!

HEY-- I WAS USING THAT!

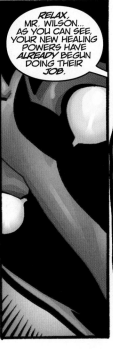

RELAX, MR. WILSON... AS YOU CAN SEE, YOUR NEW HEALING POWERS HAVE ALREADY BEGUN DOING THEIR JOB.

JIMINY JILIKERS! MY ARM--

--IT'S ALREADY GROWN BACK-- GOOD AS NEW!

AND MY ARM... IT'S NOT SCALY... IT'S LIKE IT WAS...

BETTER THAN NEW, IN FACT. YOUR HEALING PROWESS IS SUCH THAT YOU CAN NOW REGROW BODY PARTS AT WILL--BETTER AND STRONGER THAN BEFORE.

...THEN THAT MEANS...

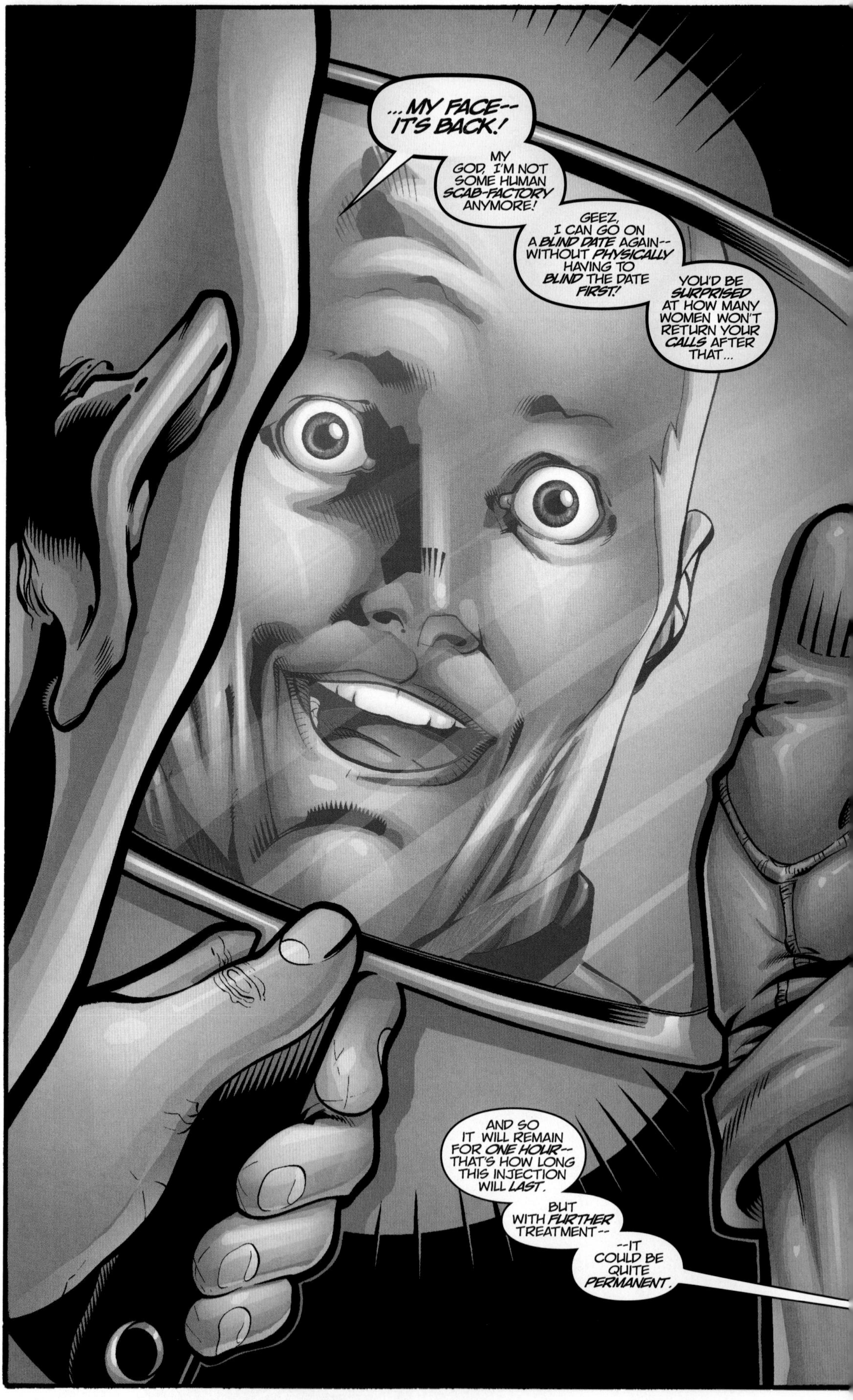
...MY FACE-- IT'S BACK!
MY GOD, I'M NOT SOME HUMAN SCAB-FACTORY ANYMORE!
GEEZ, I CAN GO ON A BLIND DATE AGAIN-- WITHOUT PHYSICALLY HAVING TO BLIND THE DATE FIRST!
YOU'D BE SURPRISED AT HOW MANY WOMEN WON'T RETURN YOUR CALLS AFTER THAT...
AND SO IT WILL REMAIN FOR ONE HOUR-- THAT'S HOW LONG THIS INJECTION WILL LAST.
BUT WITH FURTHER TREATMENT--
--IT COULD BE QUITE PERMANENT.

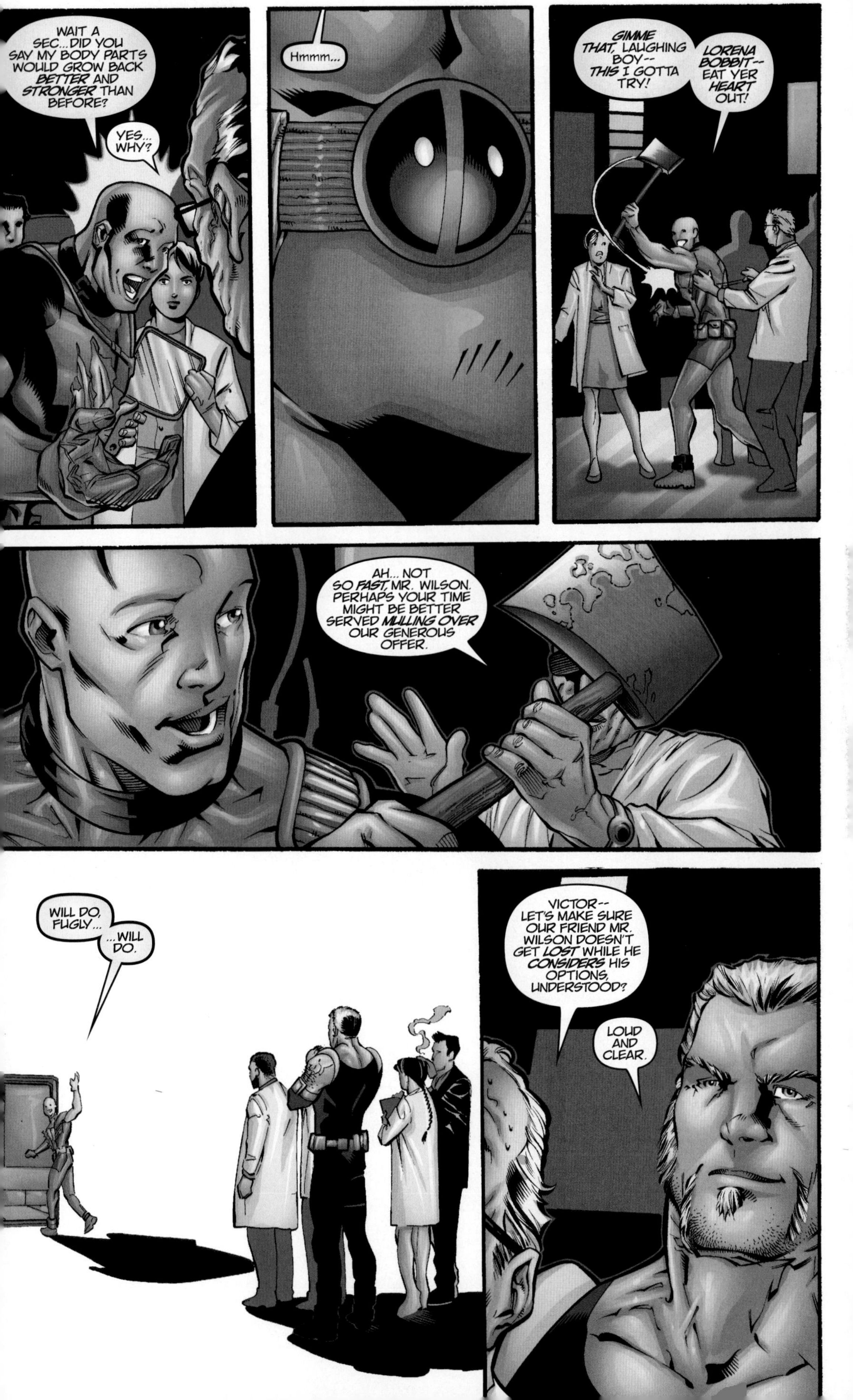
WAIT A SEC... DID YOU SAY MY BODY PARTS WOULD GROW BACK BETTER AND STRONGER THAN BEFORE?
YES... WHY?
Hmmm...
GIMME THAT, LAUGHING BOY-- THIS I GOTTA TRY!
LORENA BOBBIT-- EAT YER HEART OUT!
AH... NOT SO FAST, MR. WILSON. PERHAPS YOUR TIME MIGHT BE BETTER SERVED MULLING OVER OUR GENEROUS OFFER.
WILL DO, FUGLY...
...WILL DO.
VICTOR-- LET'S MAKE SURE OUR FRIEND MR. WILSON DOESN'T GET LOST WHILE HE CONSIDERS HIS OPTIONS, UNDERSTOOD?
LOUD AND CLEAR.

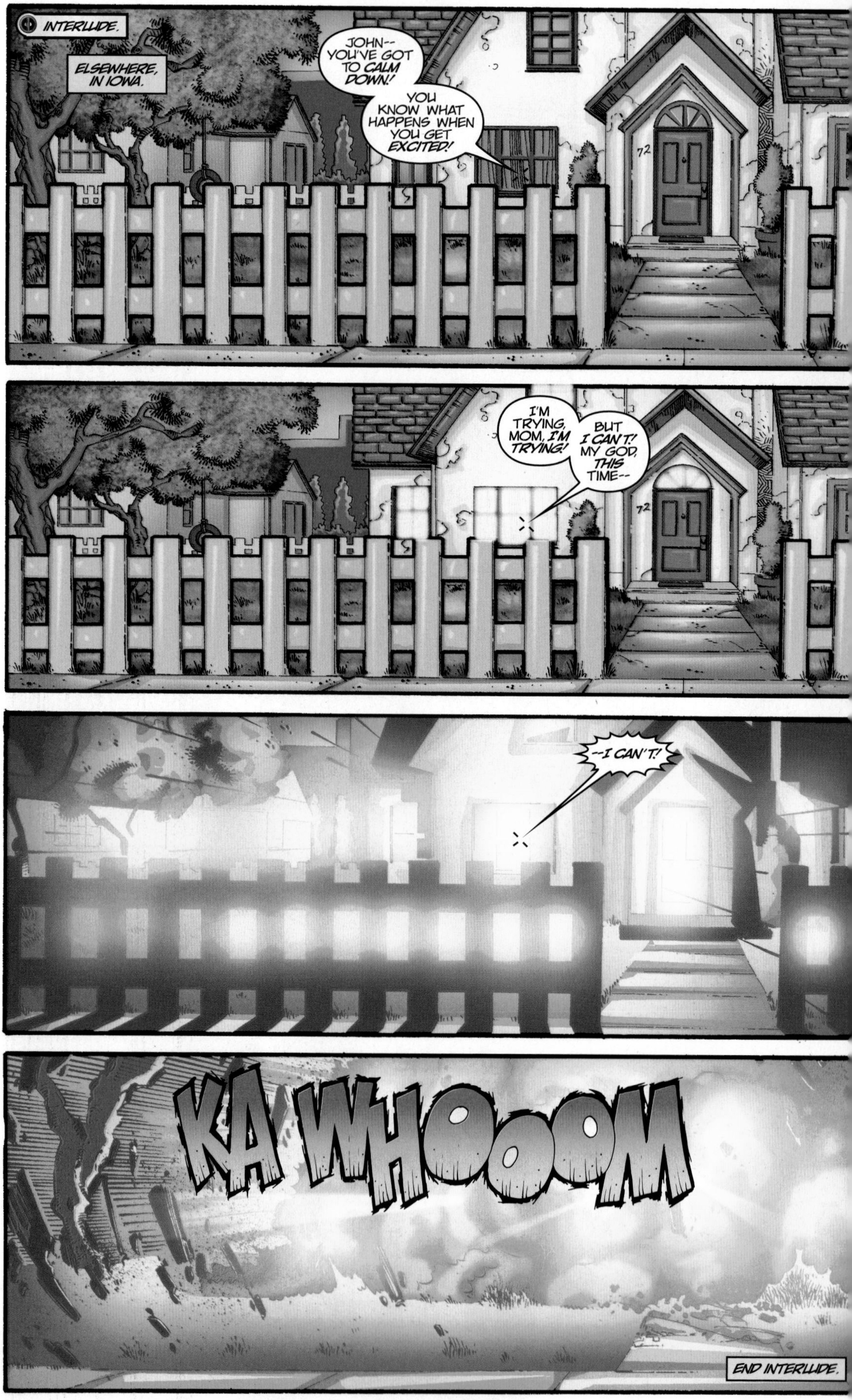
INTERLUDE.
ELSEWHERE, IN IOWA.
JOHN-- YOU'VE GOT TO CALM DOWN!
YOU KNOW WHAT HAPPENS WHEN YOU GET EXCITED!
I'M TRYING, MOM, I'M TRYING!
BUT I CAN'T! MY GOD, THIS TIME--
--I CAN'T!
KA WHOOOM
END INTERLUDE.

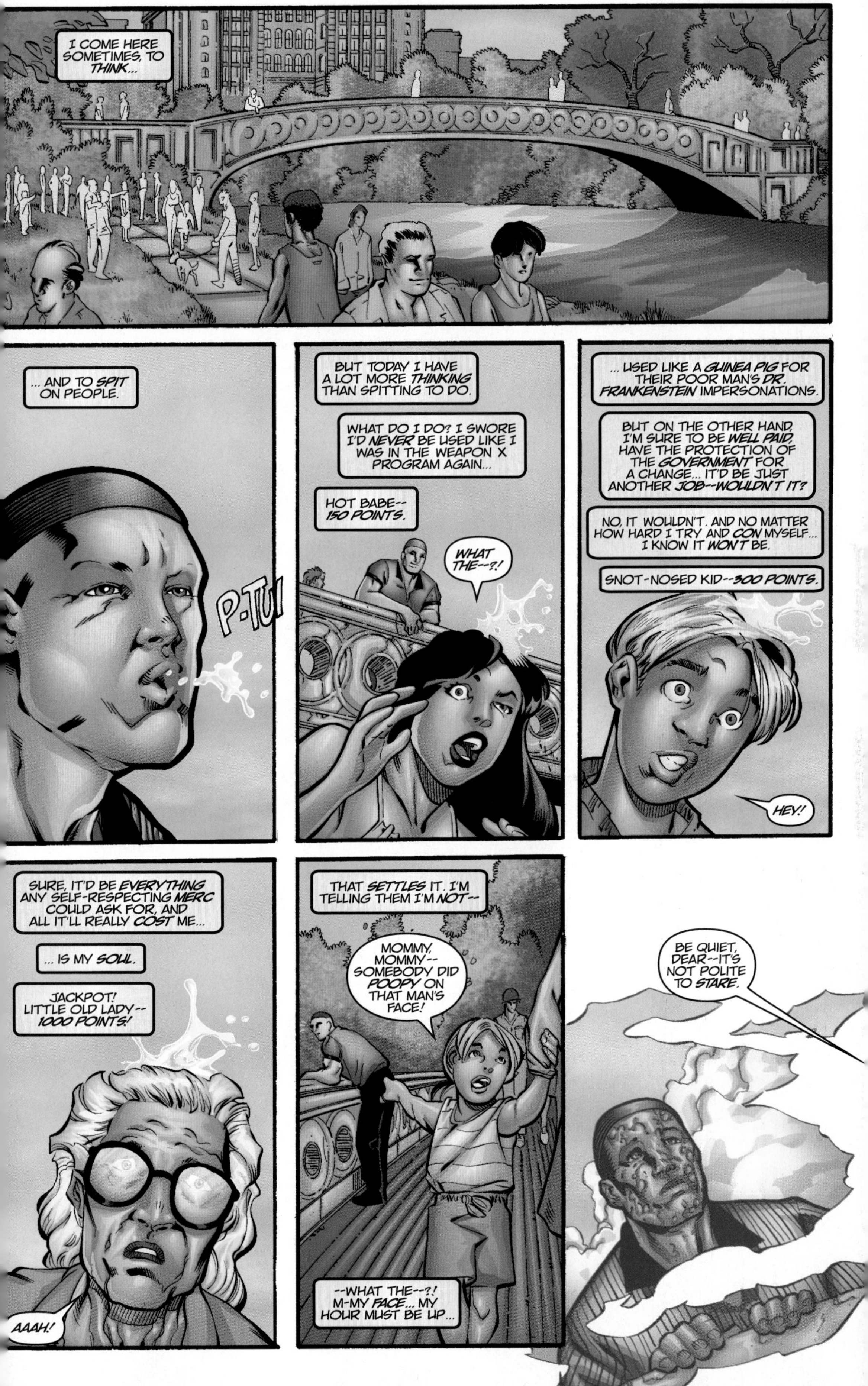
I COME HERE SOMETIMES, TO THINK...
...AND TO SPIT ON PEOPLE.
P-TUI
BUT TODAY I HAVE A LOT MORE THINKING THAN SPITTING TO DO.
WHAT DO I DO? I SWORE I'D NEVER BE USED LIKE I WAS IN THE WEAPON X PROGRAM AGAIN...
HOT BABE-- 150 POINTS.
WHAT THE--?!
...USED LIKE A GUINEA PIG FOR THEIR POOR MAN'S DR. FRANKENSTEIN IMPERSONATIONS.
BUT ON THE OTHER HAND, I'M SURE TO BE WELL PAID, HAVE THE PROTECTION OF THE GOVERNMENT FOR A CHANGE... IT'D BE JUST ANOTHER JOB--WOULDN'T IT?
NO, IT WOULDN'T. AND NO MATTER HOW HARD I TRY AND CON MYSELF... I KNOW IT WON'T BE.
SNOT-NOSED KID--300 POINTS.
HEY!
SURE, IT'D BE EVERYTHING ANY SELF-RESPECTING MERC COULD ASK FOR, AND ALL IT'LL REALLY COST ME...
...IS MY SOUL.
JACKPOT! LITTLE OLD LADY-- 1000 POINTS!
AAAH!
THAT SETTLES IT. I'M TELLING THEM I'M NOT--
MOMMY, MOMMY-- SOMEBODY DID POOPY ON THAT MAN'S FACE!
--WHAT THE--?! M-MY FACE... MY HOUR MUST BE UP...
BE QUIET, DEAR--IT'S NOT POLITE TO STARE.

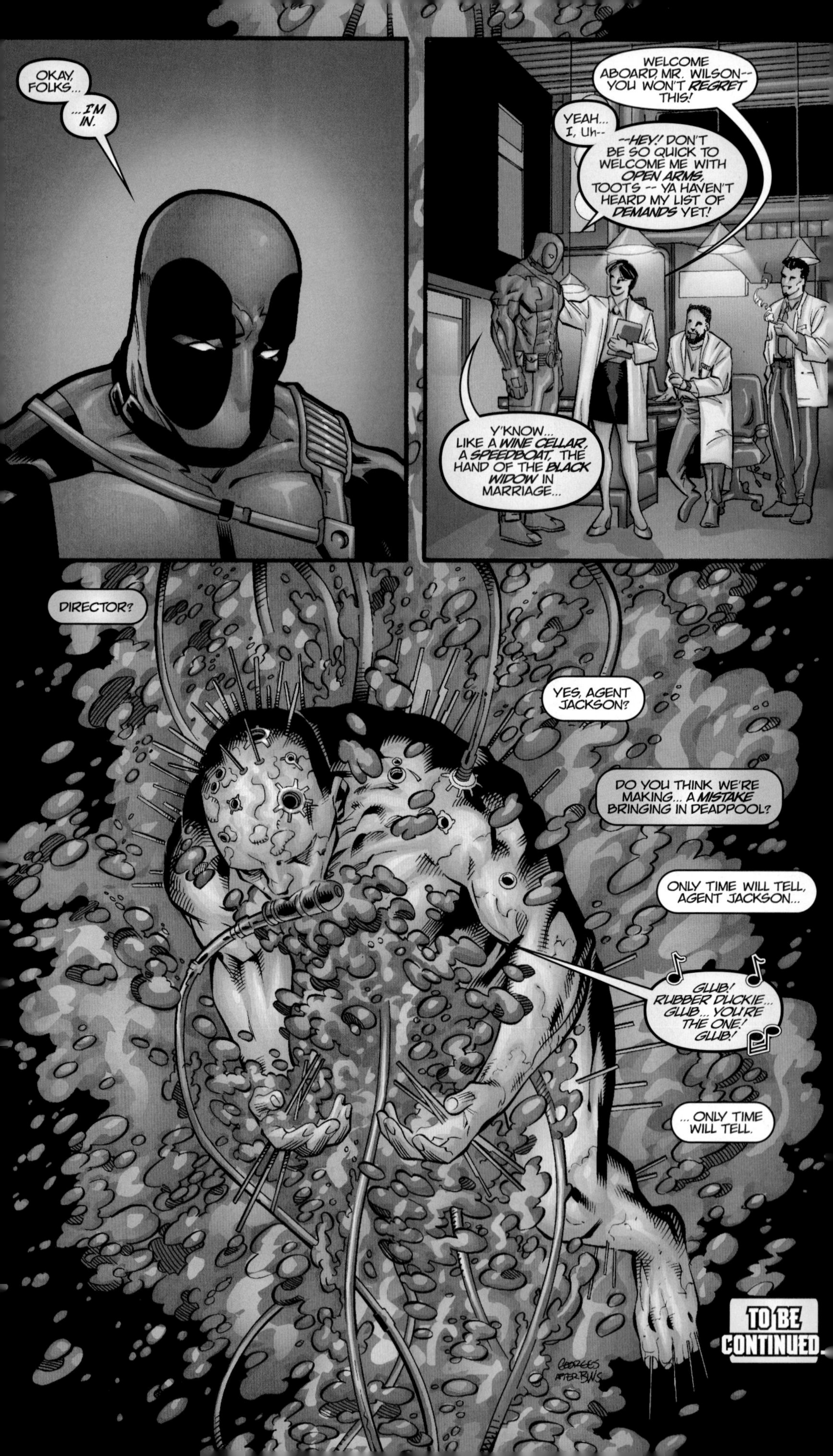
OKAY, FOLKS...
...I'M IN.
WELCOME ABOARD, MR. WILSON-- YOU WON'T REGRET THIS!
YEAH... I, Uh--
--HEY! DON'T BE SO QUICK TO WELCOME ME WITH OPEN ARMS, TOOTS -- YA HAVEN'T HEARD MY LIST OF DEMANDS YET!
Y'KNOW... LIKE A WINE CELLAR, A SPEEDBOAT, THE HAND OF THE BLACK WIDOW IN MARRIAGE...
DIRECTOR?
YES, AGENT JACKSON?
DO YOU THINK WE'RE MAKING... A MISTAKE BRINGING IN DEADPOOL?
ONLY TIME WILL TELL, AGENT JACKSON...
GLUB! RUBBER DUCKIE... GLUB... YOU'RE THE ONE! GLUB!
...ONLY TIME WILL TELL.
TO BE CONTINUED.

SABRETOOTH character design by Paul Tutrone

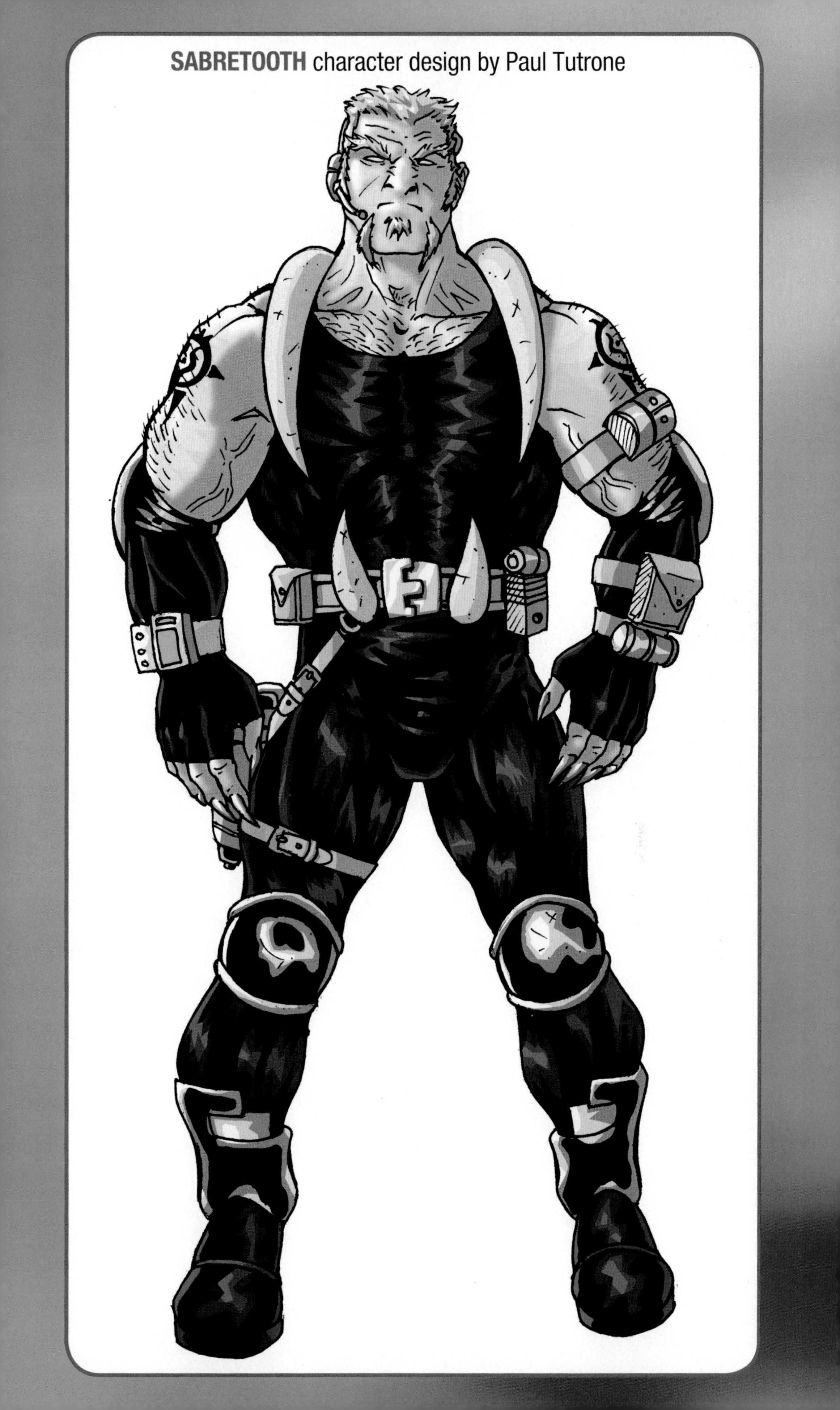

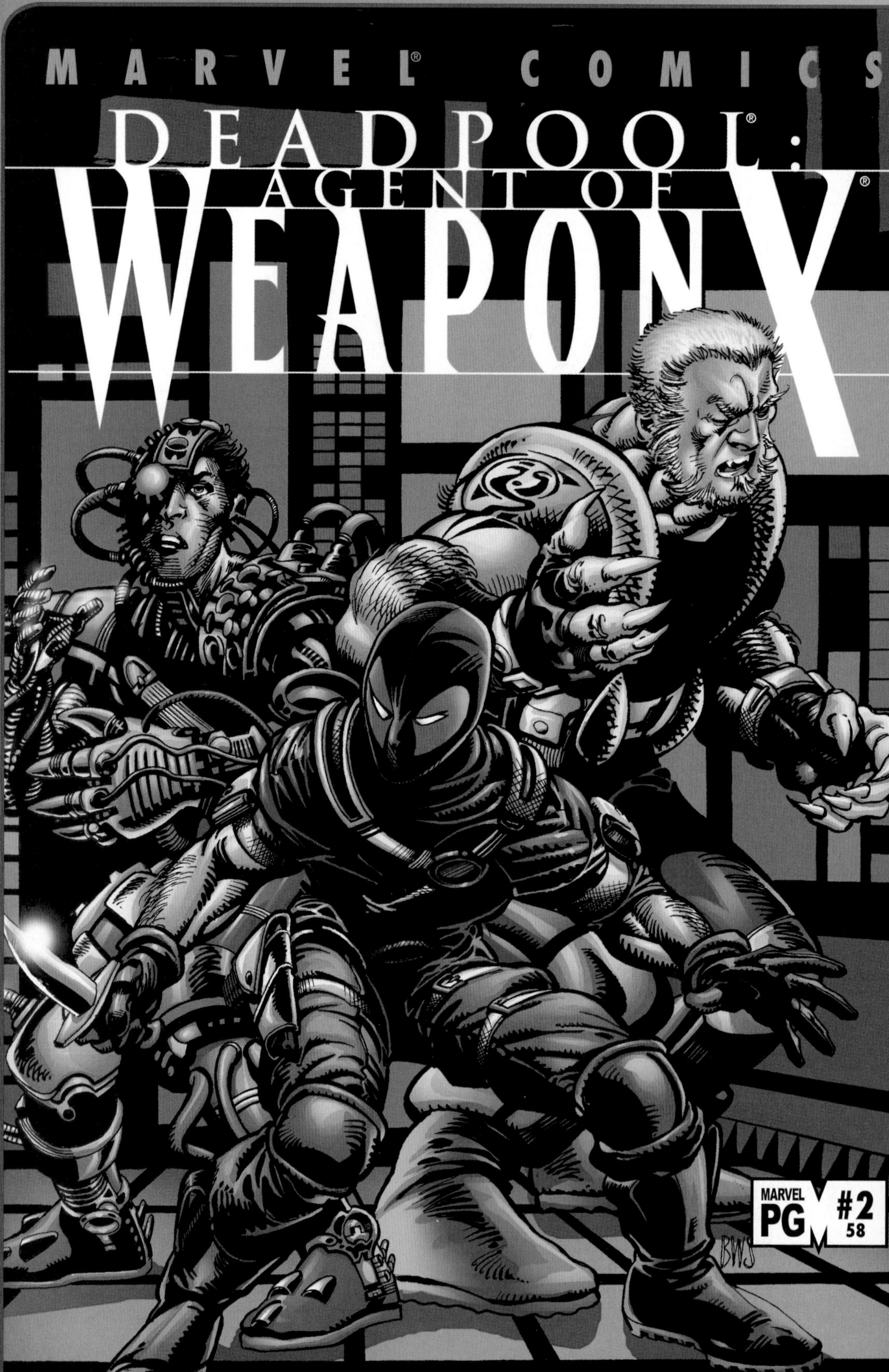
MARVEL® COMICS
DEADPOOL®:
AGENT OF
WEAPON X®
MARVEL PG
#2
58
BWS
TIERI JEANTY HOLDREDGE

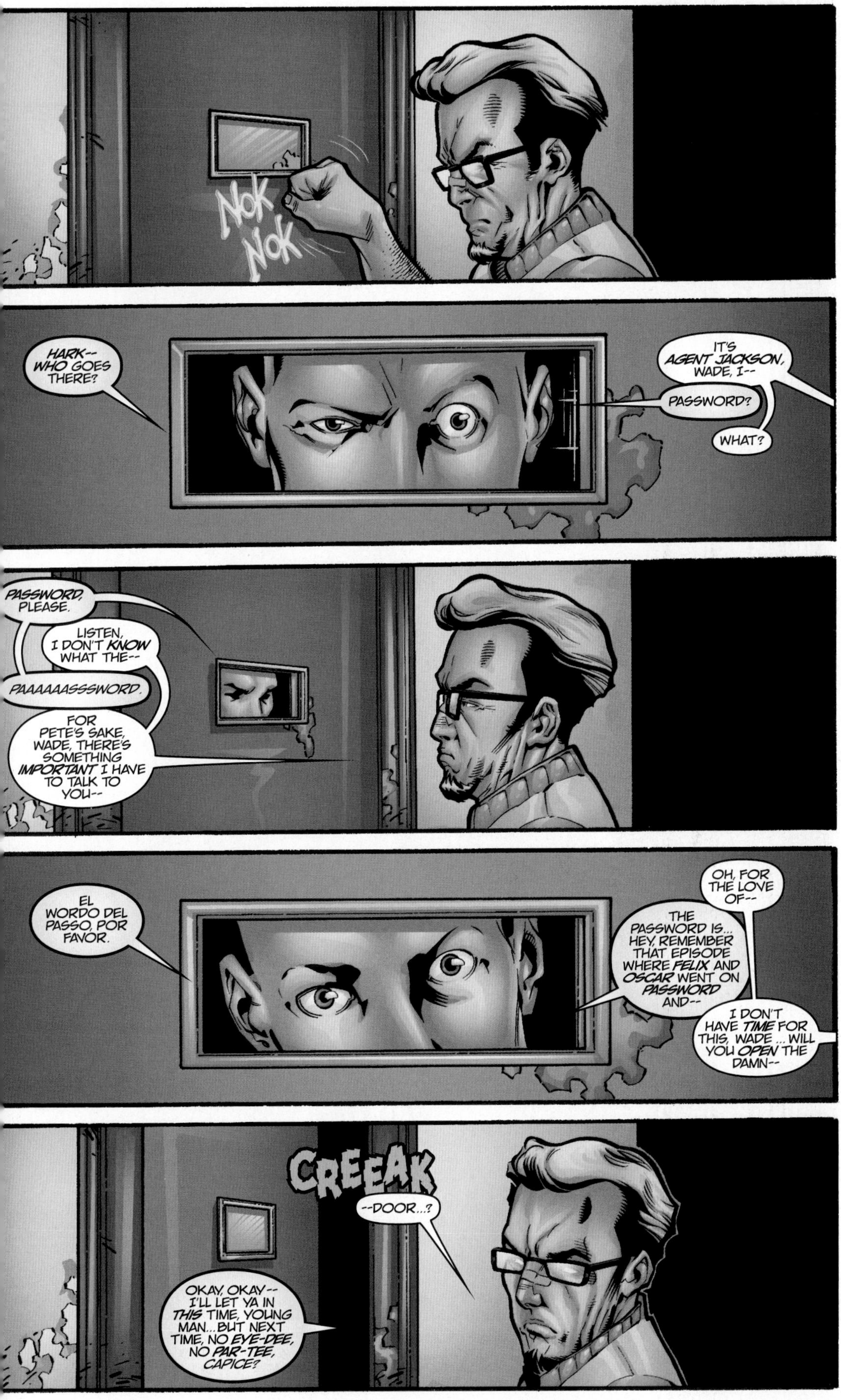
NOK NOK
HARK-- WHO GOES THERE?
IT'S AGENT JACKSON, WADE, I--
PASSWORD?
WHAT?
PASSWORD, PLEASE.
LISTEN, I DON'T KNOW WHAT THE--
PAAAAAASSSWORD.
FOR PETE'S SAKE, WADE, THERE'S SOMETHING IMPORTANT I HAVE TO TALK TO YOU--
EL WORDO DEL PASSO, POR FAVOR.
OH, FOR THE LOVE OF--
THE PASSWORD IS... HEY, REMEMBER THAT EPISODE WHERE FELIX AND OSCAR WENT ON PASSWORD AND--
I DON'T HAVE TIME FOR THIS, WADE ... WILL YOU OPEN THE DAMN--
CREEAK
--DOOR...?
OKAY, OKAY-- I'LL LET YA IN THIS TIME, YOUNG MAN... BUT NEXT TIME, NO EYE-DEE, NO PAR-TEE, CAPICE?

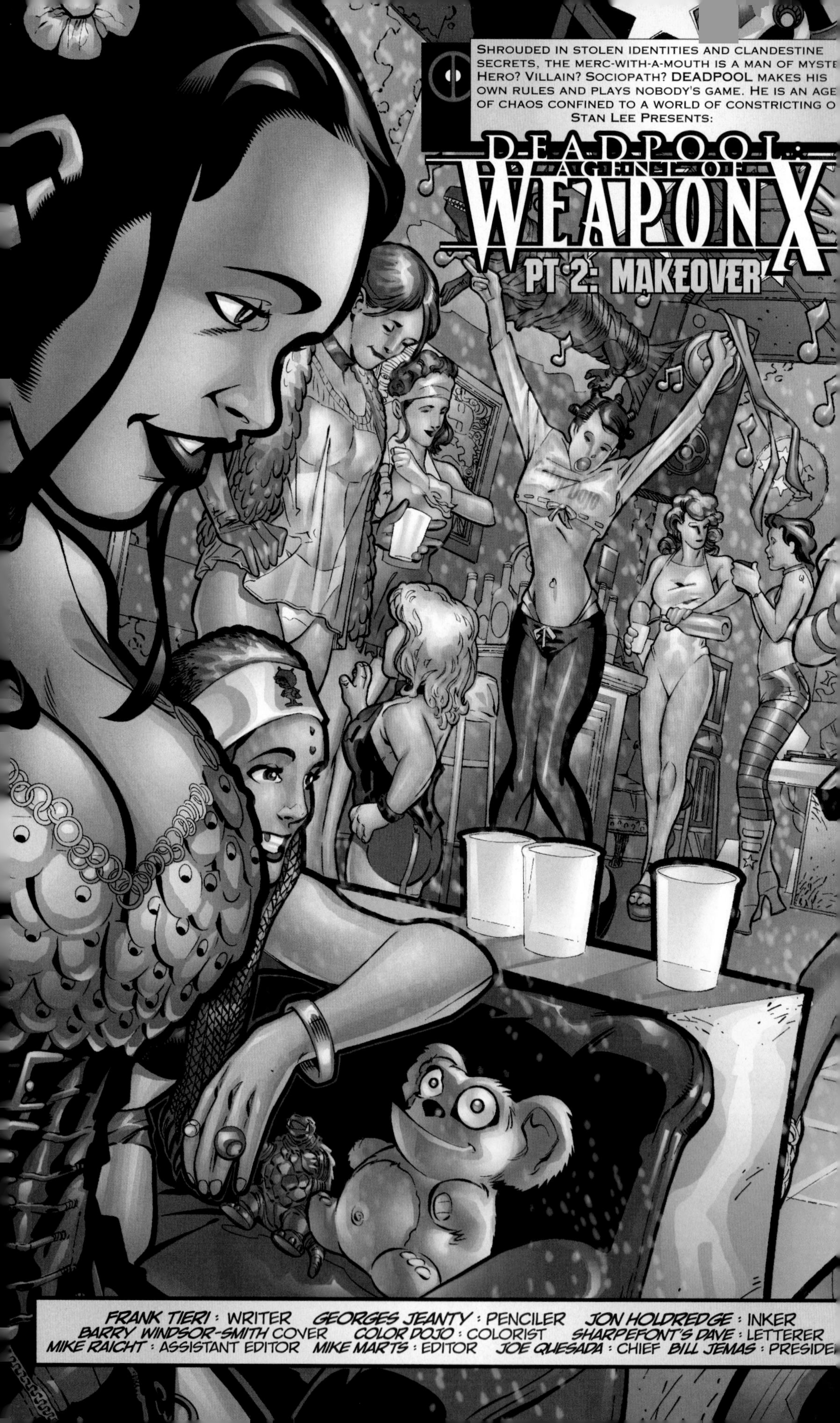
SHROUDED IN STOLEN IDENTITIES AND CLANDESTINE SECRETS, THE MERC-WITH-A-MOUTH IS A MAN OF MYSTE
HERO? VILLAIN? SOCIOPATH? DEADPOOL MAKES HIS OWN RULES AND PLAYS NOBODY'S GAME. HE IS AN AGE OF CHAOS CONFINED TO A WORLD OF CONSTRICTING O
STAN LEE PRESENTS:
DEADPOOL: AGENT OF WEAPON X
PT 2: MAKEOVER
FRANK TIERI : WRITER GEORGES JEANTY : PENCILER JON HOLDREDGE : INKER
BARRY WINDSOR-SMITH COVER COLOR DOJO : COLORIST SHARPEFONT'S DAVE : LETTERER
MIKE RAICHT : ASSISTANT EDITOR MIKE MARTS : EDITOR JOE QUESADA : CHIEF BILL JEMAS : PRESIDE

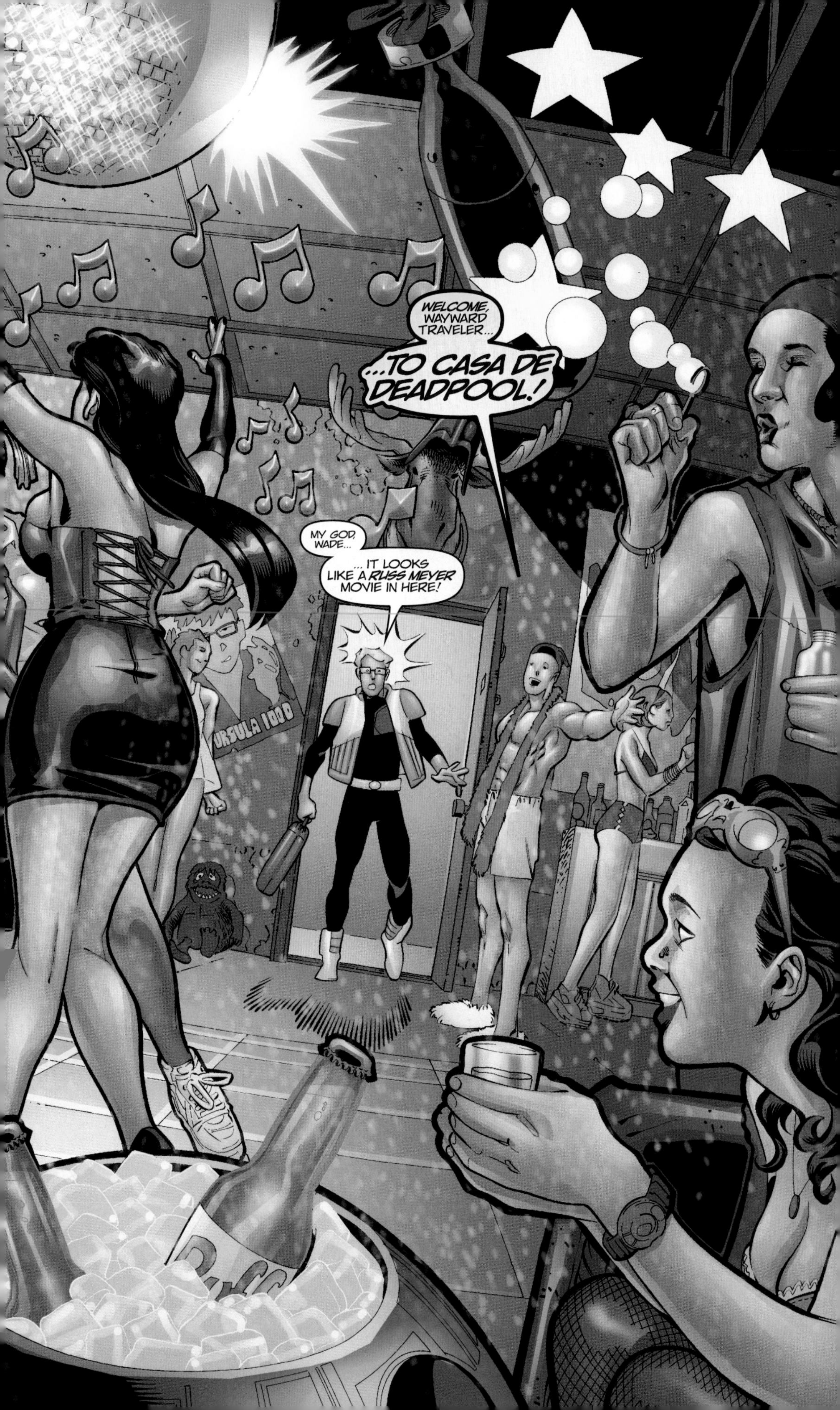
WELCOME, WAYWARD TRAVELER...
...TO CASA DE DEADPOOL!
MY GOD, WADE...
... IT LOOKS LIKE A RUSS MEYER MOVIE IN HERE!
URSULA 1000

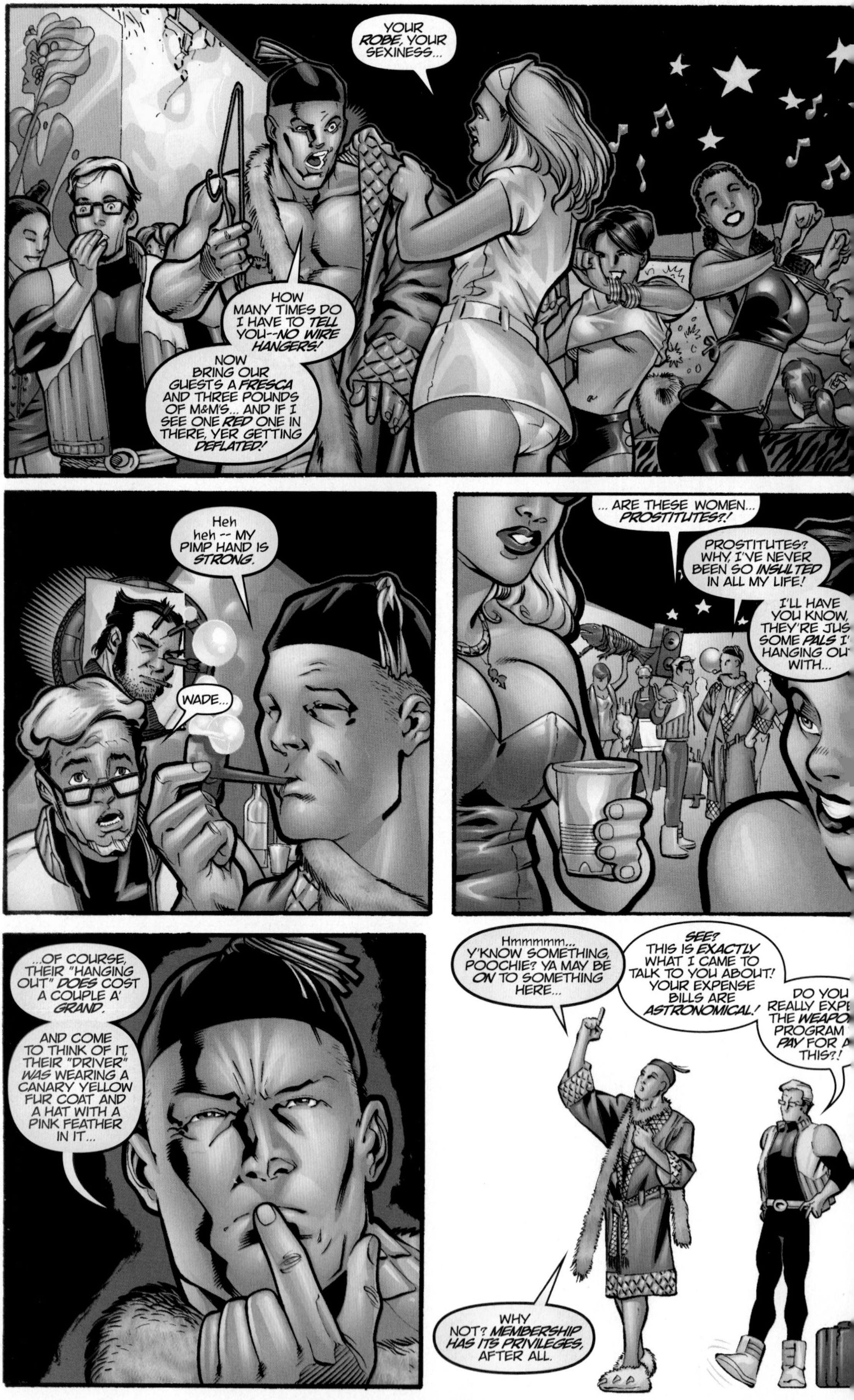
YOUR ROBE, YOUR SEXINESS...
HOW MANY TIMES DO I HAVE TO TELL YOU--NO WIRE HANGERS!
NOW BRING OUR GUESTS A FRESCA AND THREE POUNDS OF M&M'S... AND IF I SEE ONE RED ONE IN THERE, YER GETTING DEFLATED!
Heh heh -- MY PIMP HAND IS STRONG.
WADE...
... ARE THESE WOMEN... PROSTITUTES?!
PROSTITUTES? WHY, I'VE NEVER BEEN SO INSULTED IN ALL MY LIFE!
I'LL HAVE YOU KNOW, THEY'RE JUS SOME PALS I' HANGING OU WITH...
...OF COURSE, THEIR "HANGING OUT" DOES COST A COUPLE A' GRAND.
AND COME TO THINK OF IT, THEIR "DRIVER" WAS WEARING A CANARY YELLOW FUR COAT AND A HAT WITH A PINK FEATHER IN IT...
Hmmmmm... Y'KNOW SOMETHING, POOCHIE? YA MAY BE ON TO SOMETHING HERE...
SEE? THIS IS EXACTLY WHAT I CAME TO TALK TO YOU ABOUT! YOUR EXPENSE BILLS ARE ASTRONOMICAL!
DO YOU REALLY EXPE THE WEAPO PROGRAM PAY FOR A THIS?!
WHY NOT? MEMBERSHIP HAS ITS PRIVILEGES, AFTER ALL.

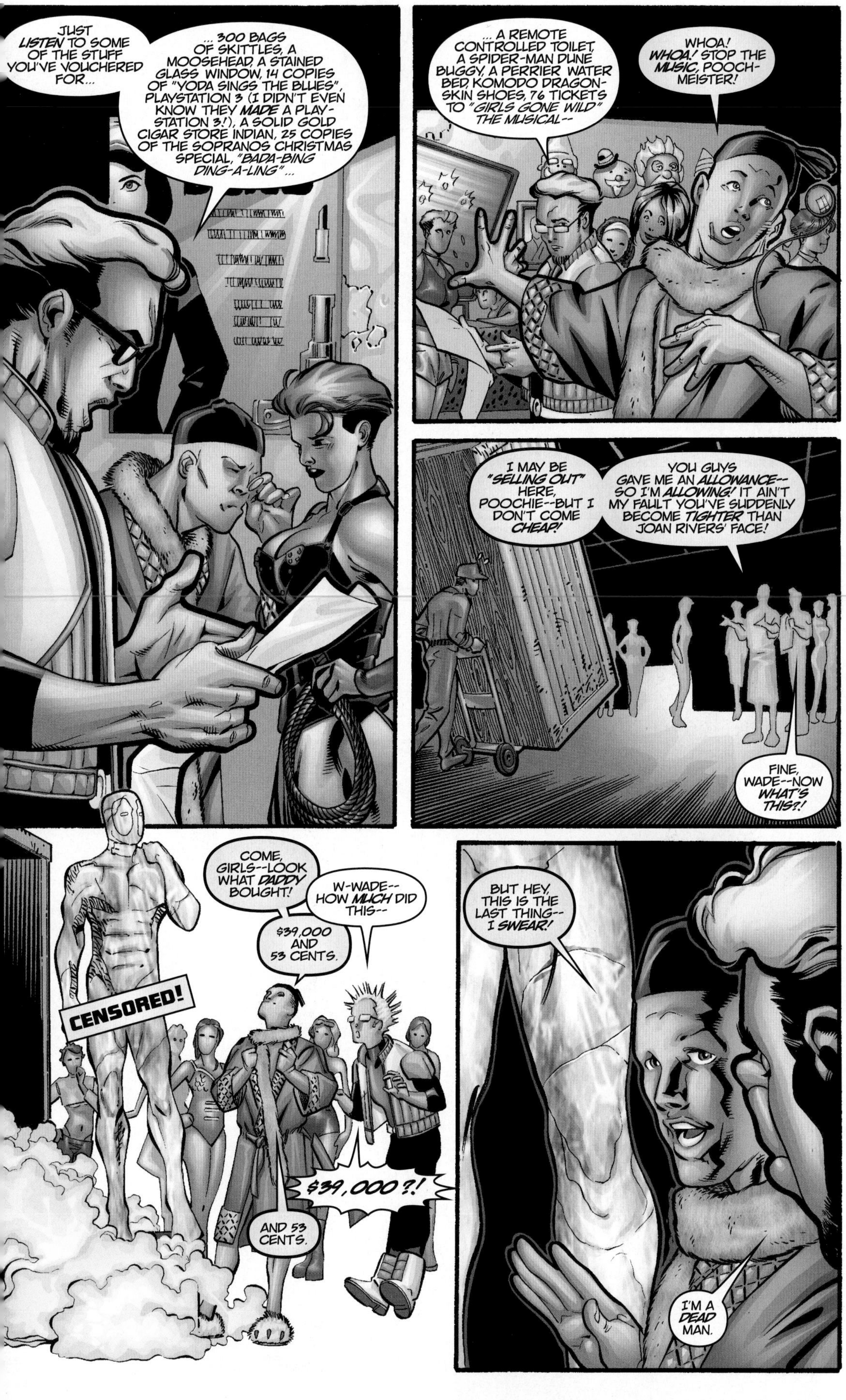
JUST LISTEN TO SOME OF THE STUFF YOU'VE VOUCHERED FOR...
... 300 BAGS OF SKITTLES, A MOOSEHEAD, A STAINED GLASS WINDOW, 14 COPIES OF "YODA SINGS THE BLUES", PLAYSTATION 3 (I DIDN'T EVEN KNOW THEY MADE A PLAY-STATION 3!), A SOLID GOLD CIGAR STORE INDIAN, 25 COPIES OF THE SOPRANOS CHRISTMAS SPECIAL, "BADA-BING DING-A-LING"...
... A REMOTE CONTROLLED TOILET, A SPIDER-MAN DUNE BUGGY, A PERRIER WATER BED, KOMODO DRAGON-SKIN SHOES, 76 TICKETS TO "GIRLS GONE WILD" THE MUSICAL--
WHOA! WHOA! STOP THE MUSIC, POOCH-MEISTER!
I MAY BE "SELLING OUT" HERE, POOCHIE--BUT I DON'T COME CHEAP!
YOU GUYS GAVE ME AN ALLOWANCE-- SO I'M ALLOWING! IT AIN'T MY FAULT YOU'VE SUDDENLY BECOME TIGHTER THAN JOAN RIVERS' FACE!
FINE, WADE--NOW WHAT'S THIS?!
CENSORED!
COME, GIRLS--LOOK WHAT DADDY BOUGHT!
W-WADE-- HOW MUCH DID THIS--
$39,000 AND 53 CENTS.
$39,000?!
AND 53 CENTS.
BUT HEY, THIS IS THE LAST THING-- I SWEAR!
I'M A DEAD MAN.

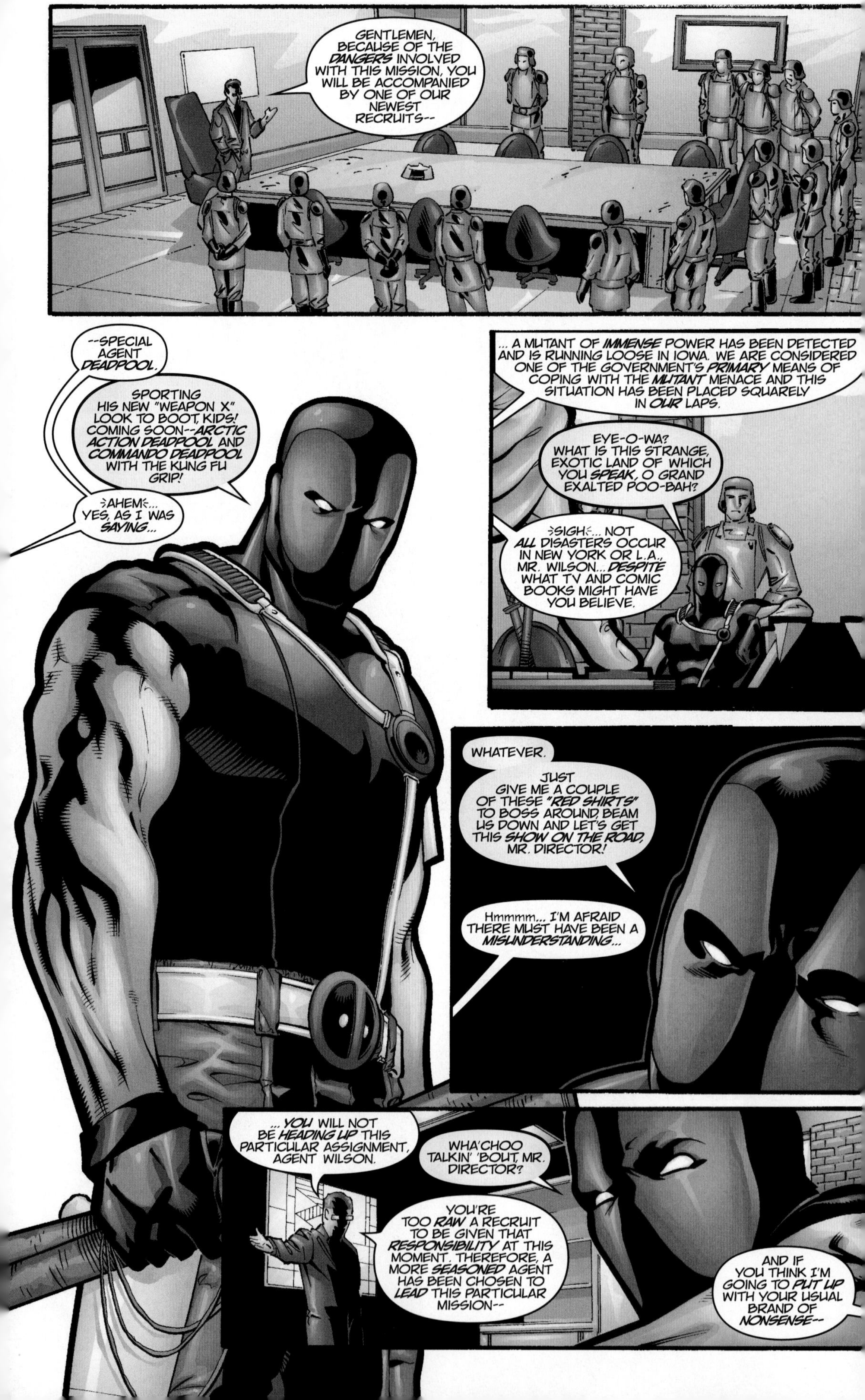
GENTLEMEN, BECAUSE OF THE DANGERS INVOLVED WITH THIS MISSION, YOU WILL BE ACCOMPANIED BY ONE OF OUR NEWEST RECRUITS--
--SPECIAL AGENT DEADPOOL.
SPORTING HIS NEW "WEAPON X" LOOK TO BOOT, KIDS! COMING SOON--ARCTIC ACTION DEADPOOL AND COMMANDO DEADPOOL WITH THE KUNG FU GRIP!
>AHEM<... YES, AS I WAS SAYING...
... A MUTANT OF IMMENSE POWER HAS BEEN DETECTED AND IS RUNNING LOOSE IN IOWA. WE ARE CONSIDERED ONE OF THE GOVERNMENT'S PRIMARY MEANS OF COPING WITH THE MUTANT MENACE AND THIS SITUATION HAS BEEN PLACED SQUARELY IN OUR LAPS.
EYE-O-WA? WHAT IS THIS STRANGE, EXOTIC LAND OF WHICH YOU SPEAK, O GRAND EXALTED POO-BAH?
>SIGH<... NOT ALL DISASTERS OCCUR IN NEW YORK OR L.A., MR. WILSON... DESPITE WHAT TV AND COMIC BOOKS MIGHT HAVE YOU BELIEVE.
WHATEVER.
JUST GIVE ME A COUPLE OF THESE "RED SHIRTS" TO BOSS AROUND, BEAM US DOWN AND LET'S GET THIS SHOW ON THE ROAD, MR. DIRECTOR!
Hmmmm... I'M AFRAID THERE MUST HAVE BEEN A MISUNDERSTANDING...
... YOU WILL NOT BE HEADING UP THIS PARTICULAR ASSIGNMENT, AGENT WILSON.
WHA'CHOO TALKIN' 'BOUT, MR. DIRECTOR?
YOU'RE TOO RAW A RECRUIT TO BE GIVEN THAT RESPONSIBILITY AT THIS MOMENT. THEREFORE, A MORE SEASONED AGENT HAS BEEN CHOSEN TO LEAD THIS PARTICULAR MISSION--
AND IF YOU THINK I'M GOING TO PUT UP WITH YOUR USUAL BRAND OF NONSENSE--

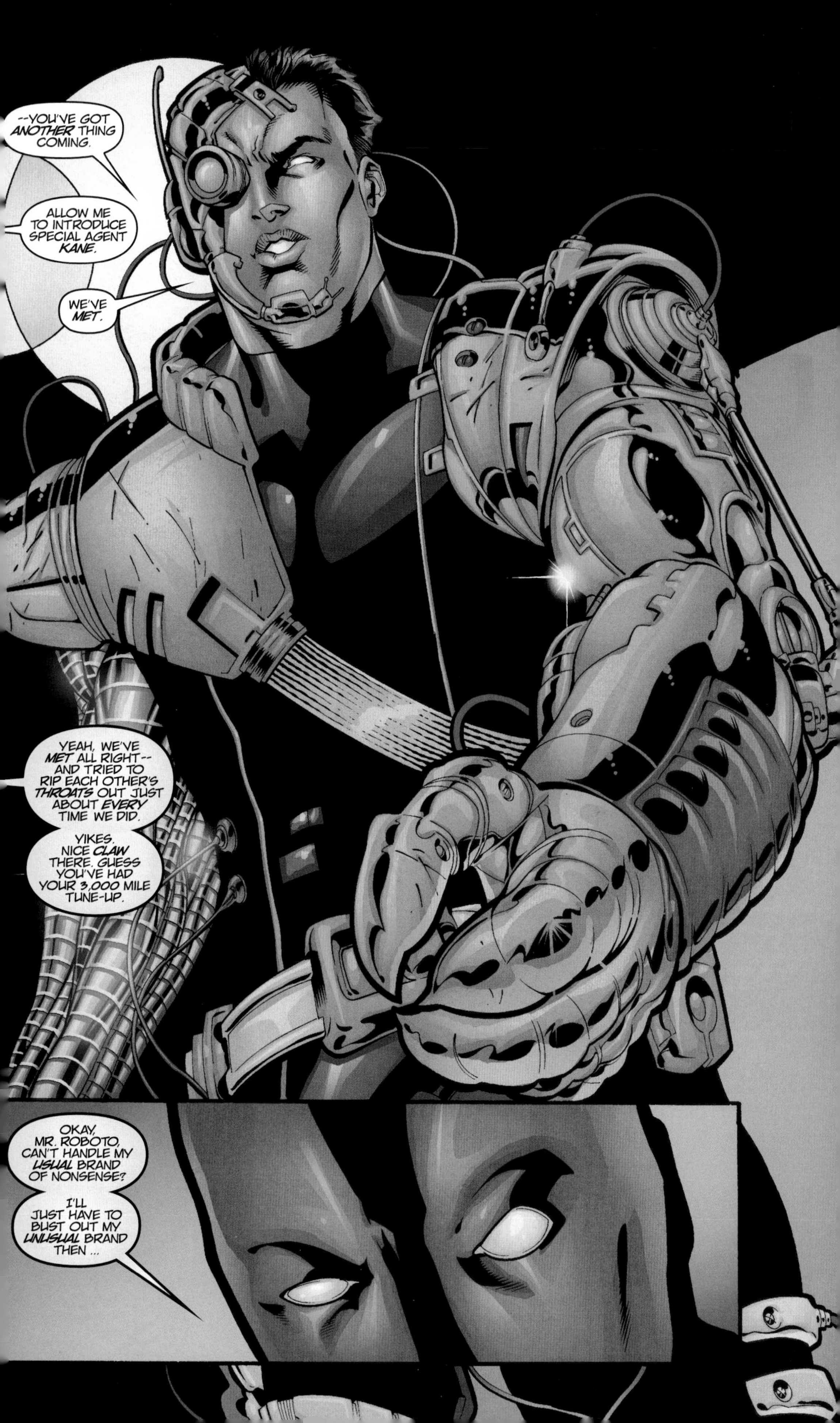
--YOU'VE GOT ANOTHER THING COMING.
ALLOW ME TO INTRODUCE SPECIAL AGENT KANE.
WE'VE MET.
YEAH, WE'VE MET ALL RIGHT-- AND TRIED TO RIP EACH OTHER'S THROATS OUT JUST ABOUT EVERY TIME WE DID.
YIKES. NICE CLAW THERE. GUESS YOU'VE HAD YOUR 3,000 MILE TUNE-UP.
OKAY, MR. ROBOTO, CAN'T HANDLE MY USUAL BRAND OF NONSENSE?
I'LL JUST HAVE TO BUST OUT MY UNUSUAL BRAND THEN ...

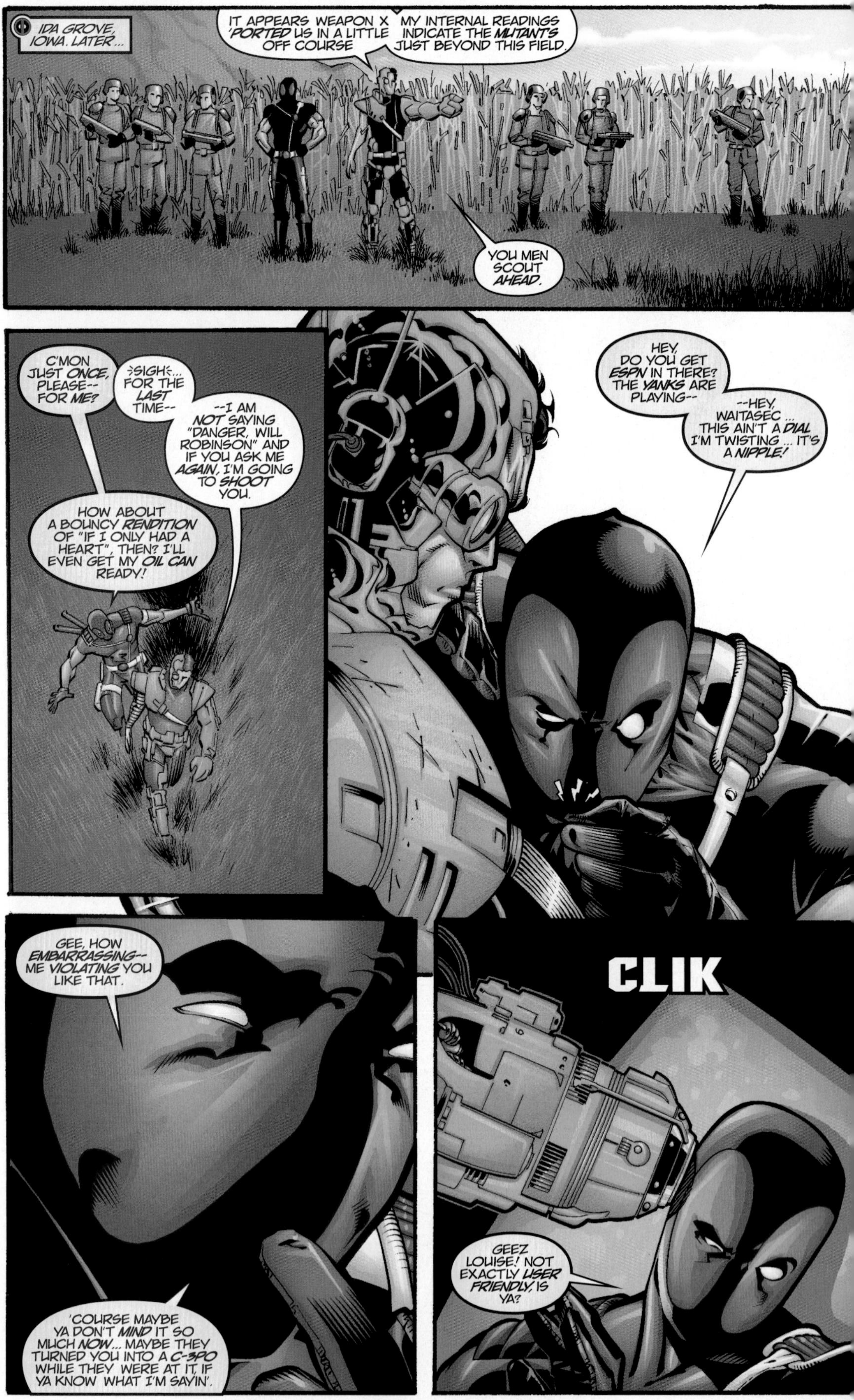
IDA GROVE, IOWA. LATER...
IT APPEARS WEAPON X 'PORTED US IN A LITTLE OFF COURSE
MY INTERNAL READINGS INDICATE THE MUTANT'S JUST BEYOND THIS FIELD.
YOU MEN SCOUT AHEAD.
C'MON JUST ONCE, PLEASE-- FOR ME?
SIGH... FOR THE LAST TIME--
--I AM NOT SAYING "DANGER, WILL ROBINSON" AND IF YOU ASK ME AGAIN, I'M GOING TO SHOOT YOU.
HOW ABOUT A BOUNCY RENDITION OF "IF I ONLY HAD A HEART", THEN? I'LL EVEN GET MY OIL CAN READY!
HEY, DO YOU GET ESPN IN THERE? THE YANKS ARE PLAYING--
--HEY, WAITASEC ... THIS AIN'T A DIAL I'M TWISTING ... IT'S A NIPPLE!
GEE, HOW EMBARRASSING-- ME VIOLATING YOU LIKE THAT.
'COURSE MAYBE YA DON'T MIND IT SO MUCH NOW... MAYBE THEY TURNED YOU INTO A C-3PO WHILE THEY WERE AT IT, IF YA KNOW WHAT I'M SAYIN'.
CLIK
GEEZ LOUISE! NOT EXACTLY USER FRIENDLY, IS YA?

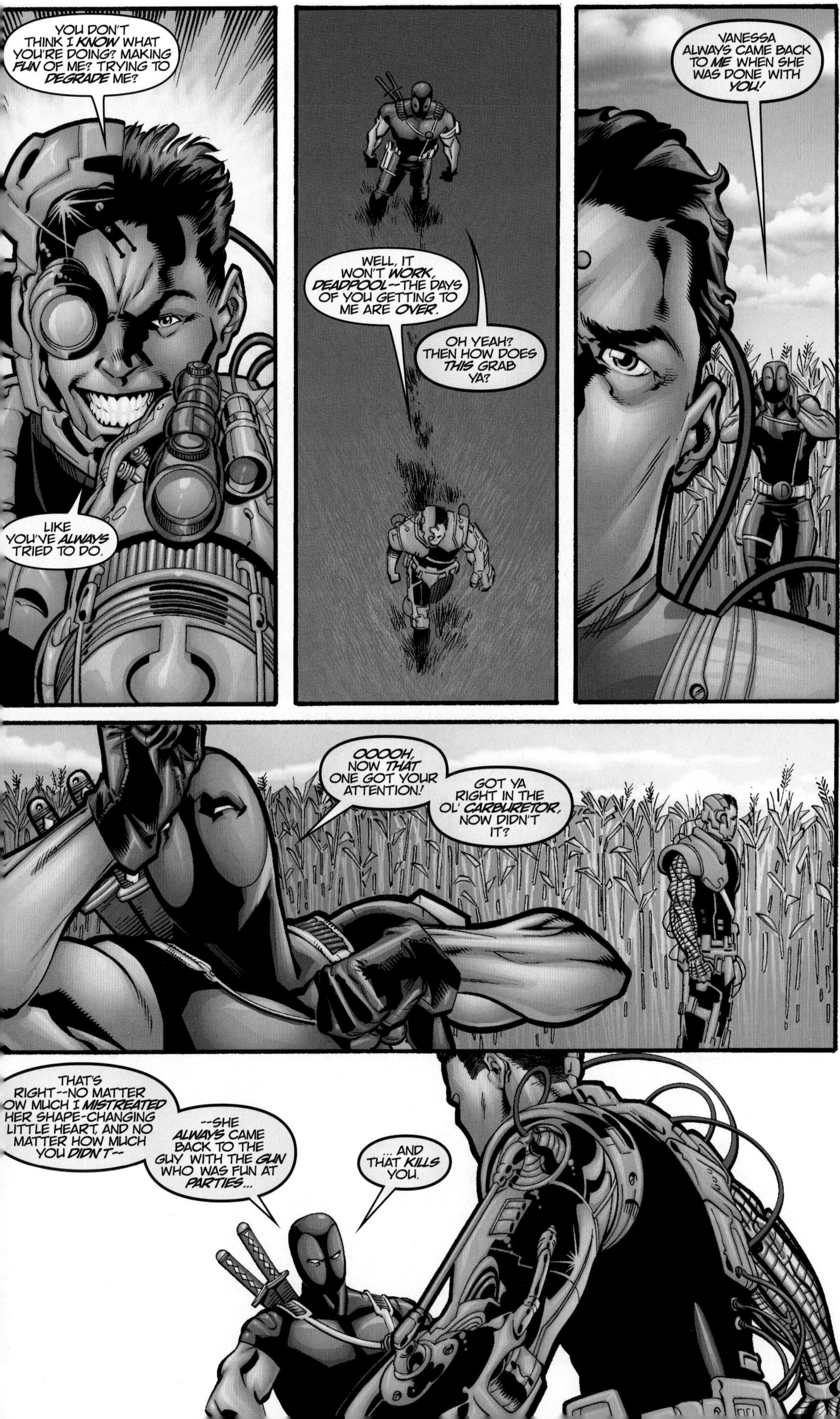

YOU DON'T THINK I KNOW WHAT YOU'RE DOING? MAKING FUN OF ME? TRYING TO DEGRADE ME?
LIKE YOU'VE ALWAYS TRIED TO DO.
WELL, IT WON'T WORK, DEADPOOL--THE DAYS OF YOU GETTING TO ME ARE OVER.
OH YEAH? THEN HOW DOES THIS GRAB YA?
VANESSA ALWAYS CAME BACK TO ME WHEN SHE WAS DONE WITH YOU!
OOOOH, NOW THAT ONE GOT YOUR ATTENTION!
GOT YA RIGHT IN THE OL' CARBURETOR, NOW DIDN'T IT?
THAT'S RIGHT--NO MATTER OW MUCH I MISTREATED HER SHAPE-CHANGING LITTLE HEART, AND NO MATTER HOW MUCH YOU DIDN'T--
--SHE ALWAYS CAME BACK TO THE GUY WITH THE GUN WHO WAS FUN AT PARTIES...
...AND THAT KILLS YOU.

IT *EATS* YOU UP INSIDE...*THAT* AND THE FACT THAT YOU'VE ALWAYS BEEN IN SOMEBODY ELSE'S *SHADOW* ALL YOUR ULTRA-PATHETIC *LIFE*... MINE, WOLVERINE'S, CABLE'S...

...HELL, YOU EVEN HAD *WEAPON X* TURN YOU INTO A K-MART VERSION OF OL' *GLOWING EYE!*

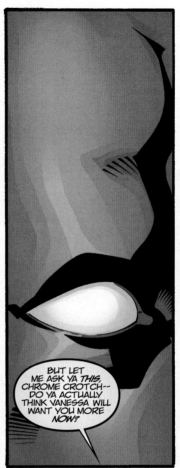

BUT LET ME ASK YA *THIS,* CHROME CROTCH-- DO YA ACTUALLY THINK VANESSA WILL WANT YOU MORE *NOW?*

EXCUSE ME WHILE I *LAUGH* UNCONTROLLABLY IN YOUR *FACE!*

Bwa hahaha haha haaa!

LAUGH *NOW,* WILSON--

--BUT I'D LOVE TO SEE THE EXPRESSION ON *YOUR* FACE WHEN YOU LEARN THE *TRUTH.*

THE *TRUTH?* WHAT'S THAT SUPPOSED TO--

S-SIRS--

--W-WE HAVE A *MAJOR* SITUATION HERE!

WHAT *IS* IT, *LASSIE?* DID *TIMMY* FALL IN THE WELL AGAIN?

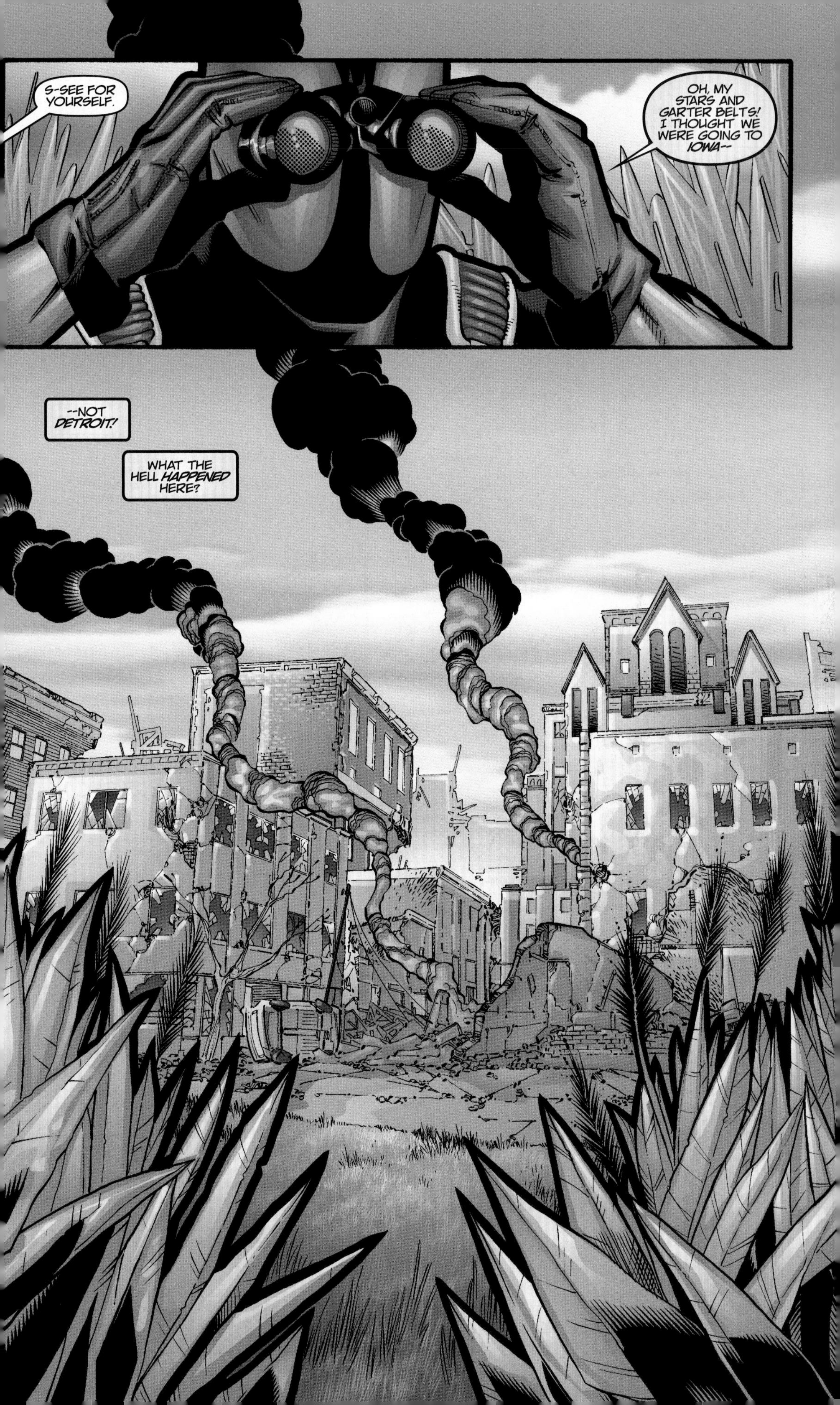
S-SEE FOR YOURSELF.
OH, MY STARS AND GARTER BELTS! I THOUGHT WE WERE GOING TO IOWA--
--NOT DETROIT!
WHAT THE HELL HAPPENED HERE?

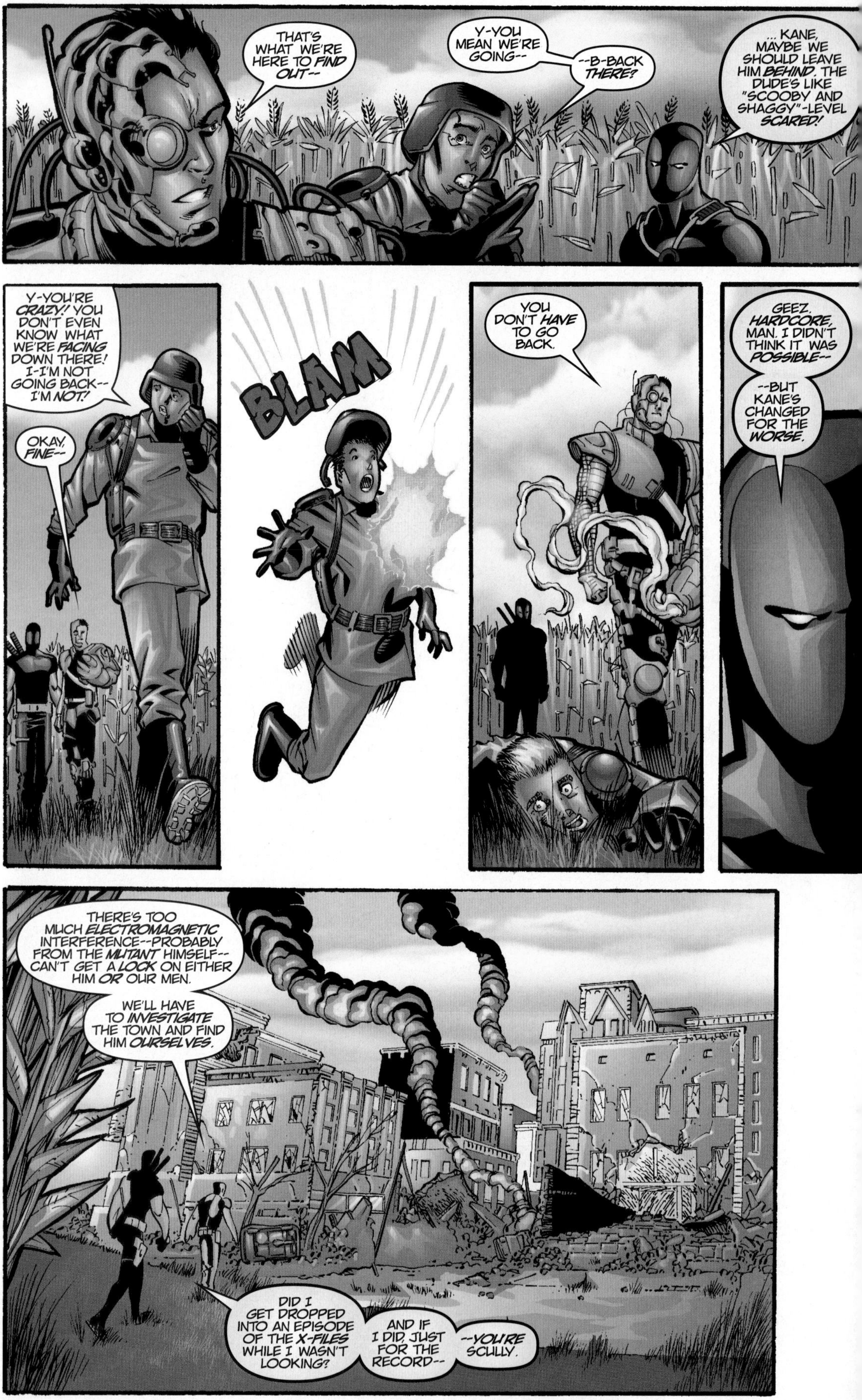
THAT'S WHAT WE'RE HERE TO FIND OUT--
Y-YOU MEAN WE'RE GOING--
--B-BACK THERE?
...KANE, MAYBE WE SHOULD LEAVE HIM BEHIND. THE DUDE'S LIKE "SCOOBY AND SHAGGY"-LEVEL SCARED!
Y-YOU'RE CRAZY! YOU DON'T EVEN KNOW WHAT WE'RE FACING DOWN THERE! I-I'M NOT GOING BACK-- I'M NOT!
OKAY, FINE--
BLAM
YOU DON'T HAVE TO GO BACK.
GEEZ. HARDCORE, MAN. I DIDN'T THINK IT WAS POSSIBLE--
--BUT KANE'S CHANGED FOR THE WORSE.
THERE'S TOO MUCH ELECTROMAGNETIC INTERFERENCE--PROBABLY FROM THE MUTANT HIMSELF-- CAN'T GET A LOCK ON EITHER HIM OR OUR MEN.
WE'LL HAVE TO INVESTIGATE THE TOWN AND FIND HIM OURSELVES.
DID I GET DROPPED INTO AN EPISODE OF THE X-FILES WHILE I WASN'T LOOKING?
AND IF I DID, JUST FOR THE RECORD--
--YOU'RE SCULLY.

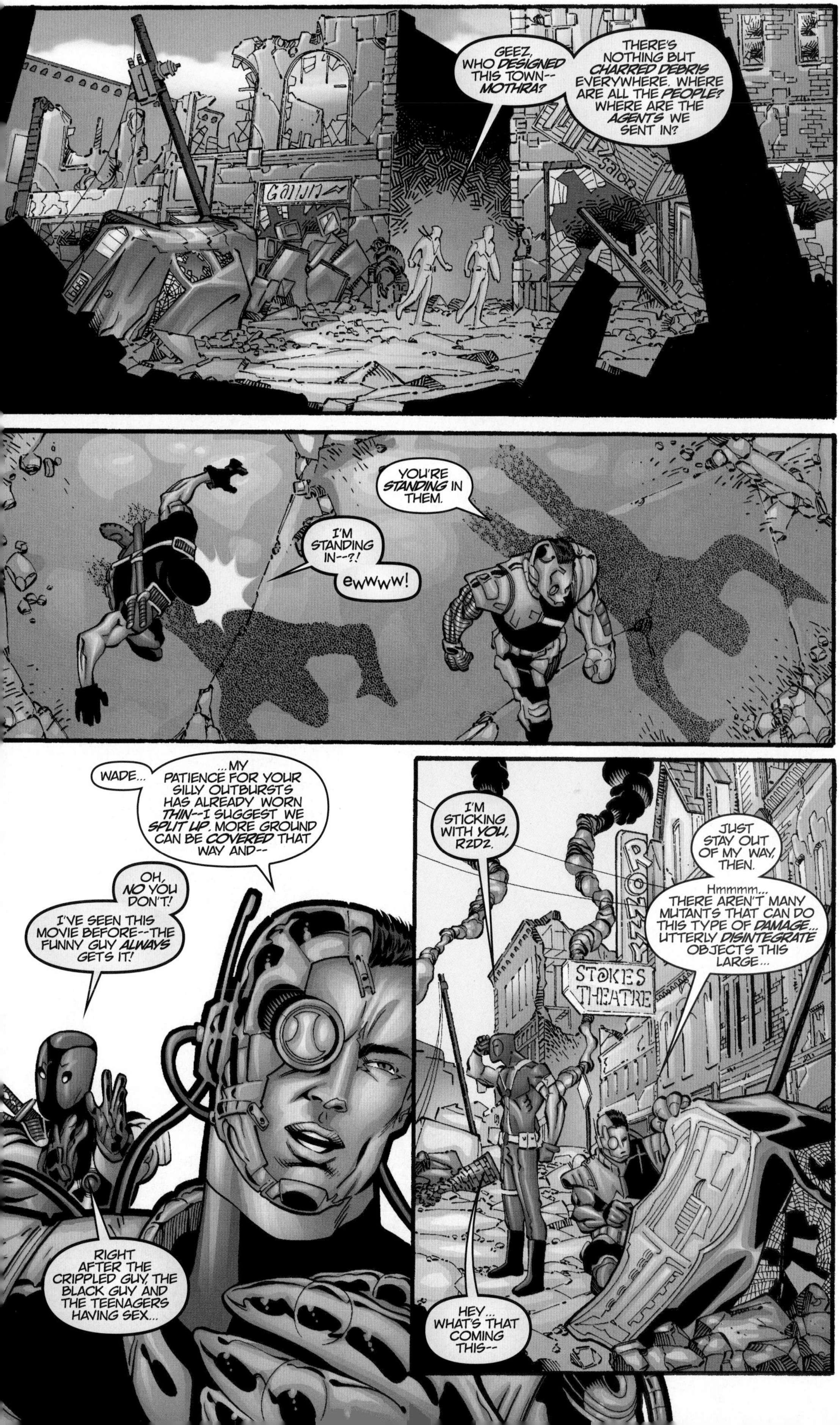
GEEZ, WHO DESIGNED THIS TOWN-- MOTHRA?
THERE'S NOTHING BUT CHARRED DEBRIS EVERYWHERE. WHERE ARE ALL THE PEOPLE? WHERE ARE THE AGENTS WE SENT IN?
YOU'RE STANDING IN THEM.
I'M STANDING IN--?!
eWWWW!
WADE...
...MY PATIENCE FOR YOUR SILLY OUTBURSTS HAS ALREADY WORN THIN--I SUGGEST WE SPLIT UP. MORE GROUND CAN BE COVERED THAT WAY AND--
OH, NO YOU DON'T!
I'VE SEEN THIS MOVIE BEFORE--THE FUNNY GUY ALWAYS GETS IT!
RIGHT AFTER THE CRIPPLED GUY, THE BLACK GUY AND THE TEENAGERS HAVING SEX...
I'M STICKING WITH YOU, R2D2.
JUST STAY OUT OF MY WAY, THEN.
Hmmmm... THERE AREN'T MANY MUTANTS THAT CAN DO THIS TYPE OF DAMAGE... UTTERLY DISINTEGRATE OBJECTS THIS LARGE...
STOKES THEATRE
HEY... WHAT'S THAT COMING THIS--

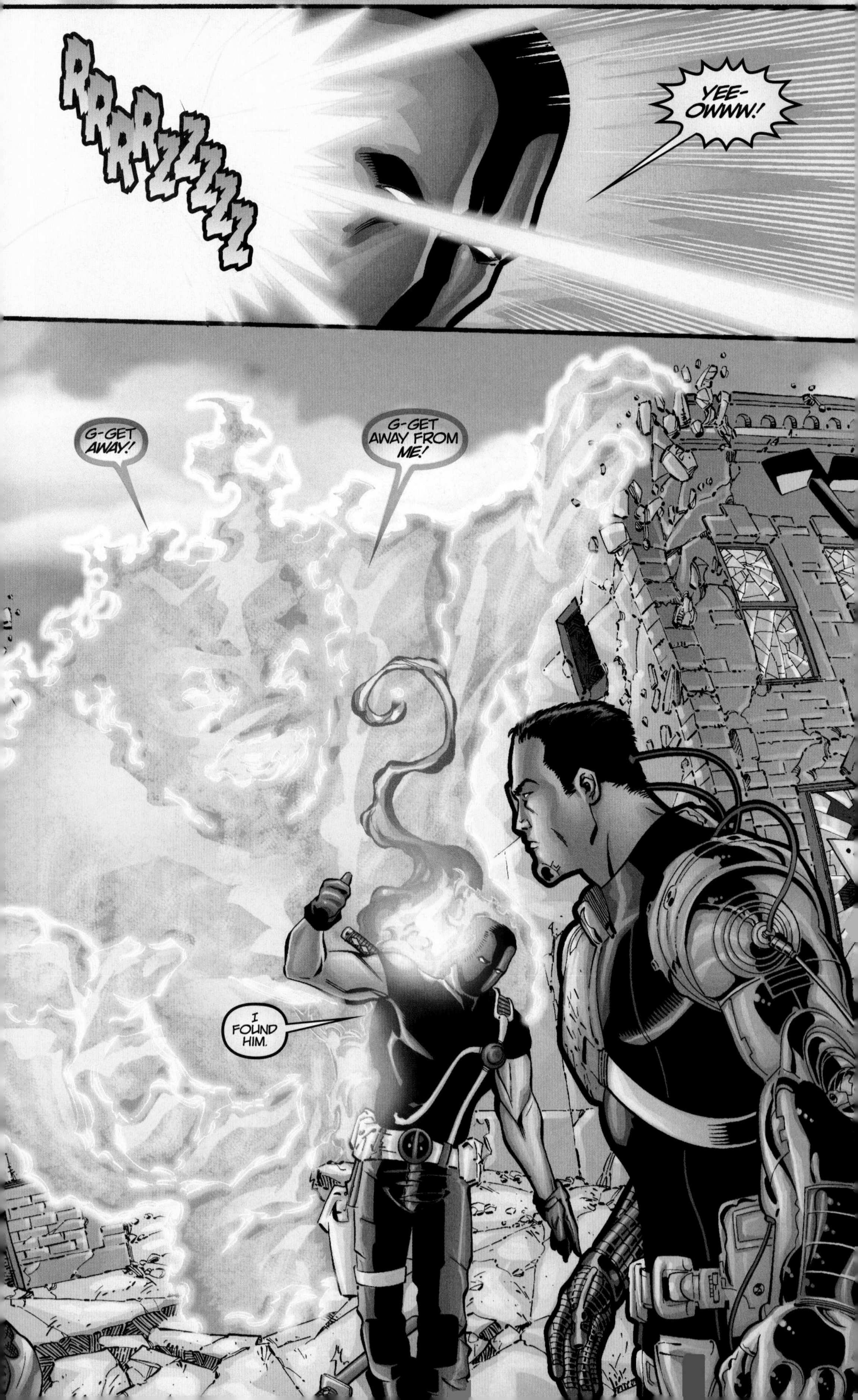
RRRRZZZZZZ
YEE-OWWW!
G-GET AWAY!
G-GET AWAY FROM ME!
I FOUND HIM.

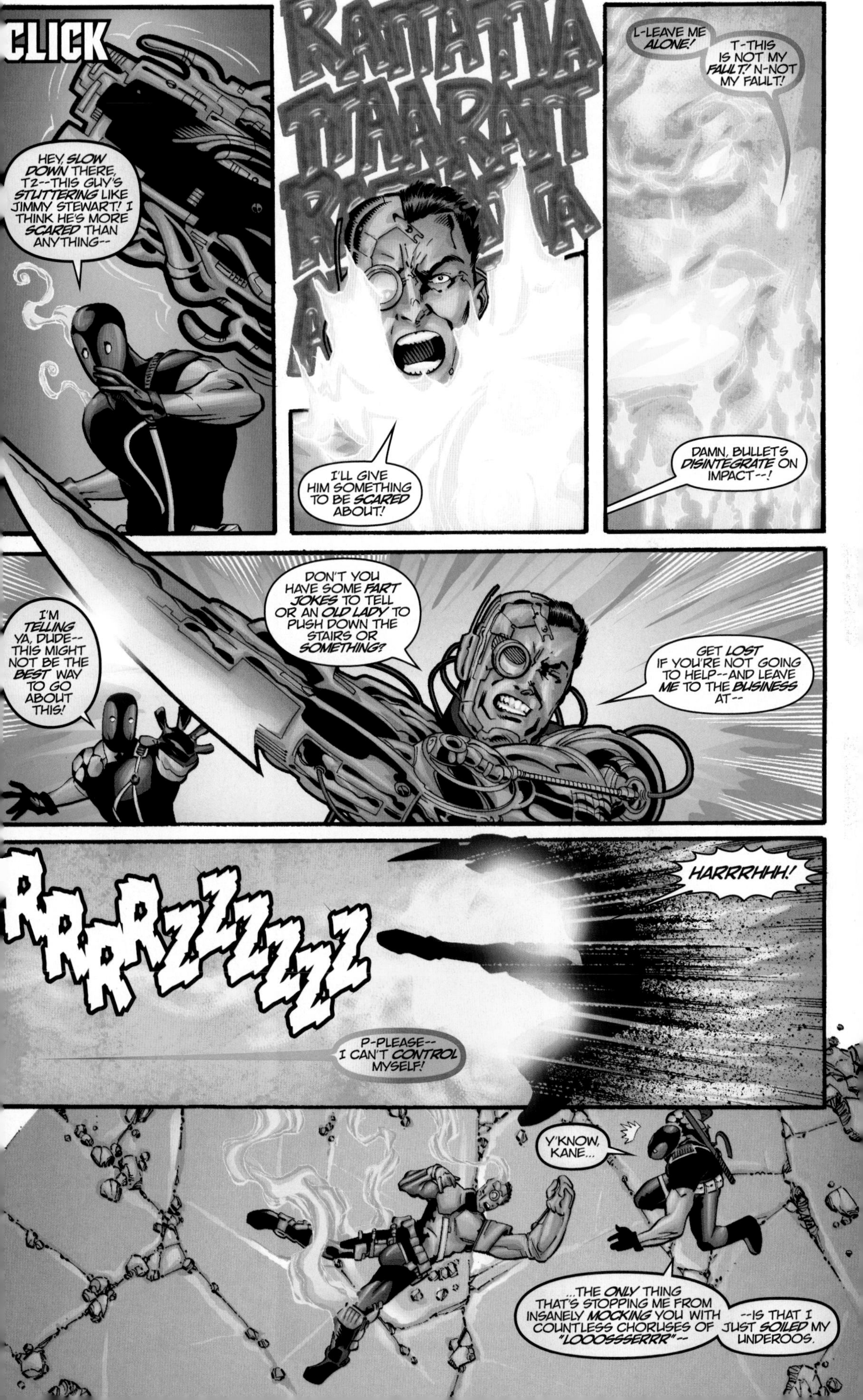
CLICK
HEY, SLOW DOWN THERE, T2--THIS GUY'S STUTTERING LIKE JIMMY STEWART! I THINK HE'S MORE SCARED THAN ANYTHING--
I'LL GIVE HIM SOMETHING TO BE SCARED ABOUT!
L-LEAVE ME ALONE!
T-THIS IS NOT MY FAULT! N-NOT MY FAULT!
DAMN, BULLETS DISINTEGRATE ON IMPACT--!
I'M TELLING YA, DUDE-- THIS MIGHT NOT BE THE BEST WAY TO GO ABOUT THIS!
DON'T YOU HAVE SOME FART JOKES TO TELL OR AN OLD LADY TO PUSH DOWN THE STAIRS OR SOMETHING?
GET LOST IF YOU'RE NOT GOING TO HELP--AND LEAVE ME TO THE BUSINESS AT--
RRRRZZZZZZZ
HARRRHHH!
P-PLEASE-- I CAN'T CONTROL MYSELF!
Y'KNOW, KANE...
...THE ONLY THING THAT'S STOPPING ME FROM INSANELY MOCKING YOU WITH COUNTLESS CHORUSES OF "LOOOSSSERRR"--
--IS THAT I JUST SOILED MY UNDEROOS.

OKAY, WADE--NOW *YOU'RE* UP TO THE PLATE. HEAT-MEISTER HERE DOESN'T SEEM *EVIL*, JUST REAL, REAL *NERVOUS*...

...SORT OF LIKE A HEAVILY CAFFEINATED *DON KNOTTS* WITH SUPER POWERS.

EASY THERE, BIG FELLA--I'M NOT HERE TO *HURT* YOU.

S-STAY AWAY--I'M *WARNING* YOU!

I THINK I CAN GET HIM UNDER CONTROL IF I JUST *CALM* HIM DOWN A TAD.

JUST *RELAX*, SPARKY--

I-I *CAN'T* RELAX!

HE'S GETTING MORE *JITTERY* AS I APPROACH. WELL, WHEN ALL ELSE FAILS...

LOOK, I JUST WANT TO *TALK*, Y'KNOW? HOW ABOUT I TELL YOU SOMETHING ABOUT *MYSELF* TO BREAK THE ICE--SOMETHING ABOUT MY *MAMA*?

W-WHAT?

MY MAMA'S SO FAT, SOMEBODY YELLED *"KOOL AID!"* AND SHE BROKE THROUGH A *WALL*!

SHE'S SO FAT, SHE WORE A *MALCOLM X* T-SHIRT AND A *HELICOPTER* LANDED ON HER!

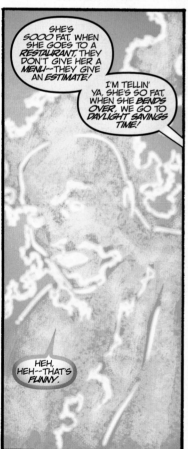

SHE'S *SOOO FAT*, WHEN SHE GOES TO A *RESTAURANT*, THEY DON'T GIVE HER A *MENU*--THEY GIVE AN *ESTIMATE*!

I'M TELLIN' YA, SHE'S SO FAT, WHEN SHE *BENDS OVER*, WE GO TO *DAYLIGHT SAVINGS TIME*!

HEH, HEH--THAT'S *FUNNY*.

IT'S *WORKING*. HE'S CALMING DOWN--AND OF THE UTMOST FREAKIN' IMPORTANCE... *POWERING* DOWN.

SEE? I CAN'T BE *THAT* BAD A GUY IF I'M WILLING TO ADMIT WHAT A *FAT SLOB* MY MOTHER WAS...

M-MY MOM'S *DEAD*.

AW, MAN--

--YOU'RE JUST A *KID*!

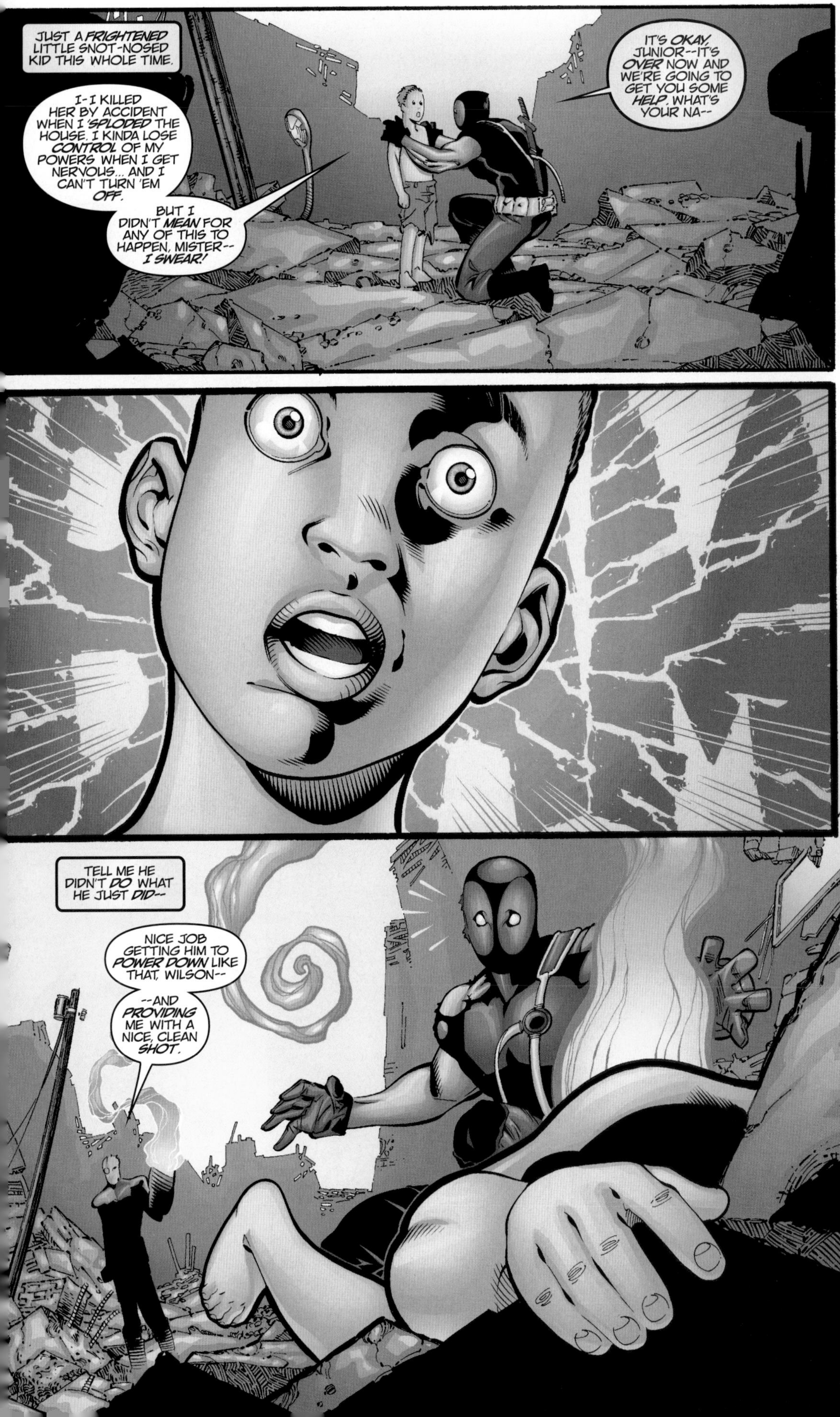
JUST A FRIGHTENED LITTLE SNOT-NOSED KID THIS WHOLE TIME.
IT'S OKAY, JUNIOR--IT'S OVER NOW AND WE'RE GOING TO GET YOU SOME HELP. WHAT'S YOUR NA--
I-I KILLED HER BY ACCIDENT WHEN I 'SPLODED THE HOUSE. I KINDA LOSE CONTROL OF MY POWERS WHEN I GET NERVOUS... AND I CAN'T TURN 'EM OFF.
BUT I DIDN'T MEAN FOR ANY OF THIS TO HAPPEN, MISTER-- I SWEAR!
TELL ME HE DIDN'T DO WHAT HE JUST DID--
NICE JOB GETTING HIM TO POWER DOWN LIKE THAT, WILSON--
--AND PROVIDING ME WITH A NICE, CLEAN SHOT.

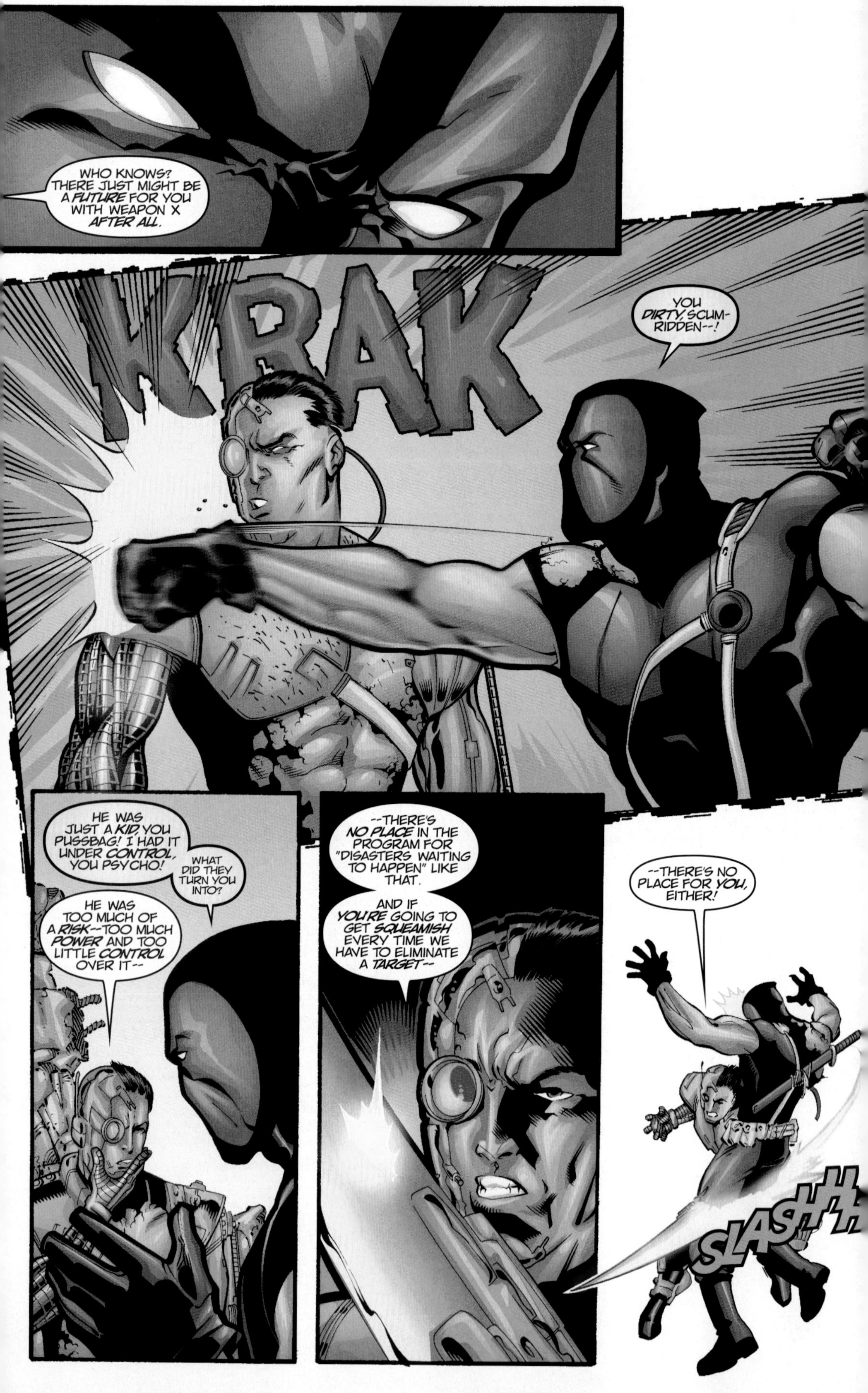
WHO KNOWS? THERE JUST MIGHT BE A FUTURE FOR YOU WITH WEAPON X AFTER ALL.
KRAK
YOU DIRTY, SCUM-RIDDEN--!
HE WAS JUST A KID, YOU PUSSBAG! I HAD IT UNDER CONTROL, YOU PSYCHO!
WHAT DID THEY TURN YOU INTO?
HE WAS TOO MUCH OF A RISK--TOO MUCH POWER AND TOO LITTLE CONTROL OVER IT--
--THERE'S NO PLACE IN THE PROGRAM FOR "DISASTERS WAITING TO HAPPEN" LIKE THAT.
AND IF YOU'RE GOING TO GET SQUEAMISH EVERY TIME WE HAVE TO ELIMINATE A TARGET--
--THERE'S NO PLACE FOR YOU, EITHER!
SLASHHH

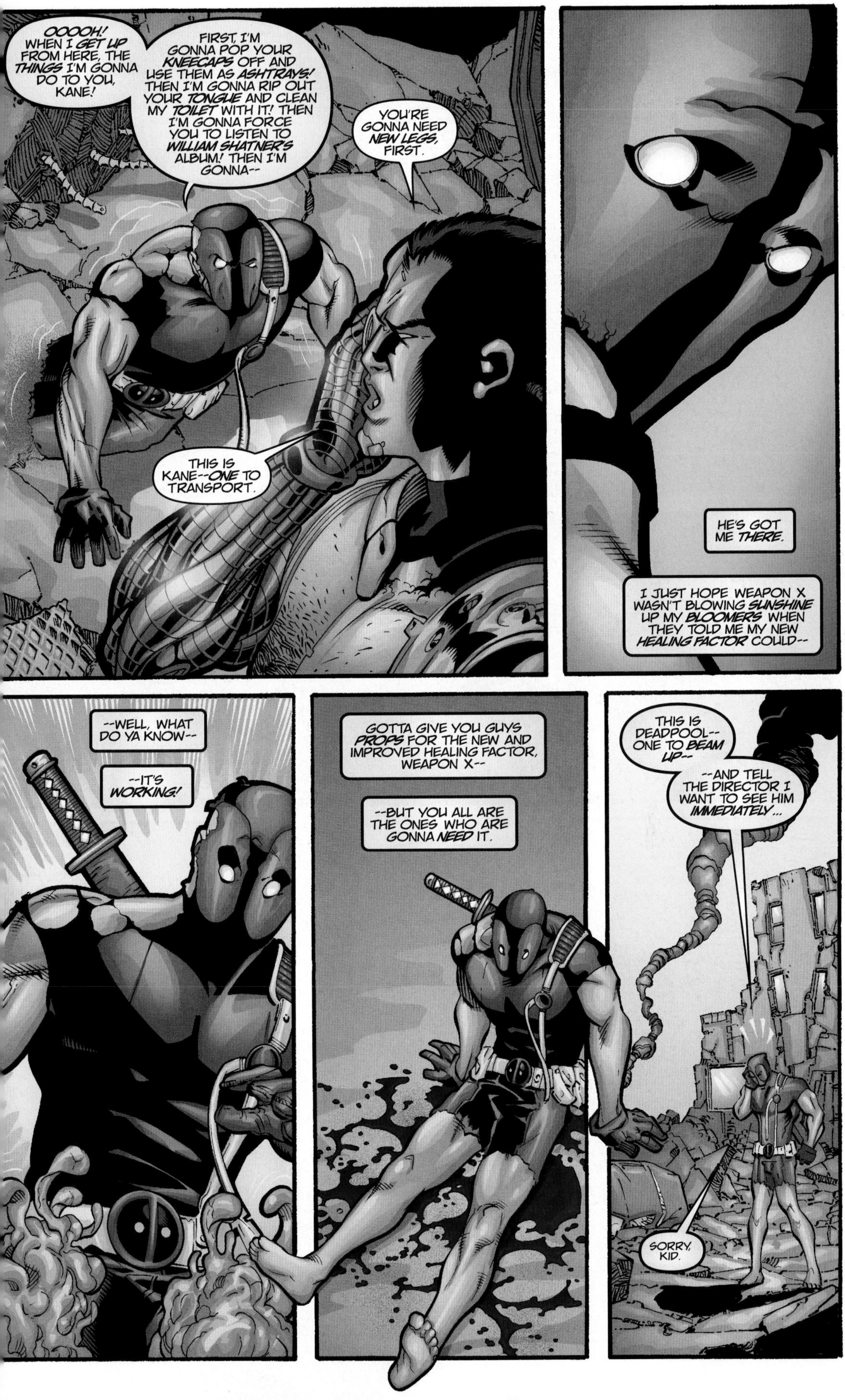

OOOOH! WHEN I GET UP FROM HERE, THE THINGS I'M GONNA DO TO YOU, KANE!
FIRST, I'M GONNA POP YOUR KNEECAPS OFF AND USE THEM AS ASHTRAYS! THEN I'M GONNA RIP OUT YOUR TONGUE AND CLEAN MY TOILET WITH IT! THEN I'M GONNA FORCE YOU TO LISTEN TO WILLIAM SHATNER'S ALBUM! THEN I'M GONNA--
YOU'RE GONNA NEED NEW LEGS, FIRST.
THIS IS KANE--ONE TO TRANSPORT.
HE'S GOT ME THERE.
I JUST HOPE WEAPON X WASN'T BLOWING SUNSHINE UP MY BLOOMERS WHEN THEY TOLD ME MY NEW HEALING FACTOR COULD--
--WELL, WHAT DO YA KNOW--
--IT'S WORKING!
GOTTA GIVE YOU GUYS PROPS FOR THE NEW AND IMPROVED HEALING FACTOR, WEAPON X--
--BUT YOU ALL ARE THE ONES WHO ARE GONNA NEED IT.
THIS IS DEADPOOL--ONE TO BEAM UP--
--AND TELL THE DIRECTOR I WANT TO SEE HIM IMMEDIATELY...
SORRY, KID.

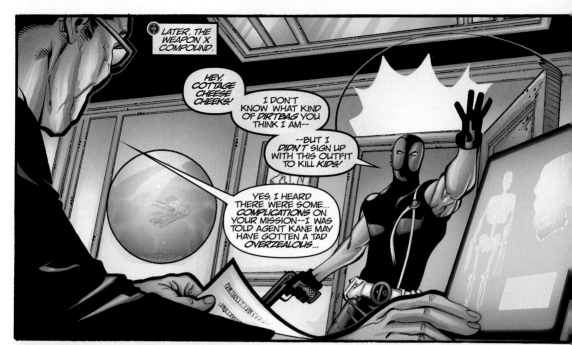

LATER, THE WEAPON X COMPOUND.

HEY, COTTAGE CHEESE CHEEKS!

I DON'T KNOW WHAT KIND OF *DIRTBAG* YOU THINK I AM--

--BUT I *DIDN'T* SIGN UP WITH THIS OUTFIT TO KILL *KIDS!*

YES, I HEARD THERE WERE SOME... *COMPLICATIONS* ON YOUR MISSION--I WAS TOLD AGENT KANE MAY HAVE GOTTEN A TAD *OVERZEALOUS...*

A *TAD* OVERZEALOUS? SPLATTERING A KID'S *BRAINS* ALL OVER HIS REEBOKS AIN'T A *TAD* OVERZEALOUS--IT'S DOWNRIGHT *HITLER-ESQUE!*

AND SPEAKING OF *BRAIN SPLATTERING...* UH...WHY ISN'T YOUR HEAD A *CANOE* RIGHT NOW?

OH, *THAT.* YOU *CAN'T* HURT ME, AGENT DEADPOOL--

--EACH OF OUR AGENTS IS *EQUIPPED* WITH A DEVICE TO MENTALLY *INHIBIT* THEM FROM HARMING US.

I HAVE A *DEVICE* IN MY HEAD? I WAS NEVER *TOLD* ABOUT *THAT!* ALL THAT *GUFF* ABOUT YOU GUYS *CHANGING* YOUR WAYS...

REMOVE IT...≳UNK≲... I'VE HAD IT...≳UNK≲... WITH THIS CHICKEN OUTFIT.

IT'S *STANDARD* PROCEDURE, WILSON. IT'S FOR YOUR OWN *GOOD.* THINGS GET A LOT LESS... *COMPLICATED* THIS WAY.

I WANT *OUT.*

SO I CAN KILL YOU.

YOU *DO?* AND HERE I WAS ABOUT TO SEND YOU ON *ANOTHER* MISSION...

YOU'RE *NUTTIER* THAN MR. SINISTER IF YA THINK I'M GOING *ANYWHERE* FOR YOU MOOKS. I'M *OUTTA* HERE.

ALL RIGHT, IF THAT'S THE WAY YOU *WANT* IT. BUT I THOUGHT YOU'D BE INTERESTED IN *THIS* ONE--WHAT WITH THE *PERSONAL* NATURE OF IT...

PERSONAL?

YES, YOU SEE, SABRETOOTH WASN'T THE *FIRST* AGENT SENT TO RECRUIT YOU...

...THERE WAS A *GIRL* WHO WAS *ORIGINALLY* ENLISTED--BROUGHT INTO THE PROGRAM AT THE *SAME TIME* AS KANE, I SEEM TO RECALL...

...SHE WAS THE *PERFECT* CHOICE, YOU UNDERSTAND, FOR AMONG *OTHER* THINGS SHE WAS A--

SHAPESHIFTER...

YES-- YES, SHE *WAS* AT THAT.

HOWEVER, UNLIKE KANE, WHO MERELY WANTED HIS POWERS *AMPLIFIED*, THIS GIRL'S POWERS HAD GROWN *UNSTABLE*.

NATURALLY, WE WERE ABLE TO HELP HER--IN FACT, AFTER SOME *TREATMENT*, SHE HAD *GREATER* USAGE OF HER POWERS THAN *EVER* BEFORE.

BUT SOMETHING WENT *WRONG*--BEING ABLE TO CHANGE *IDENTITIES* SO READILY LEFT THE GIRL QUITE... *CONFUSED*, I'M AFRAID.

SOON, SHE DIDN'T EVEN KNOW WHO SHE *WAS* ANYMORE.

AND NEITHER DID *WE*--WE EVENTUALLY LOST *TRACK* OF HER.

SHAME, REALLY--SUCH A *LOVELY* GIRL. AS A MATTER OF FACT-- I HAVE A *PICTURE* OF HER RIGHT HERE.

YOU DON'T EVEN *NEED* TO SHOW IT TO ME, LOWLIFE--

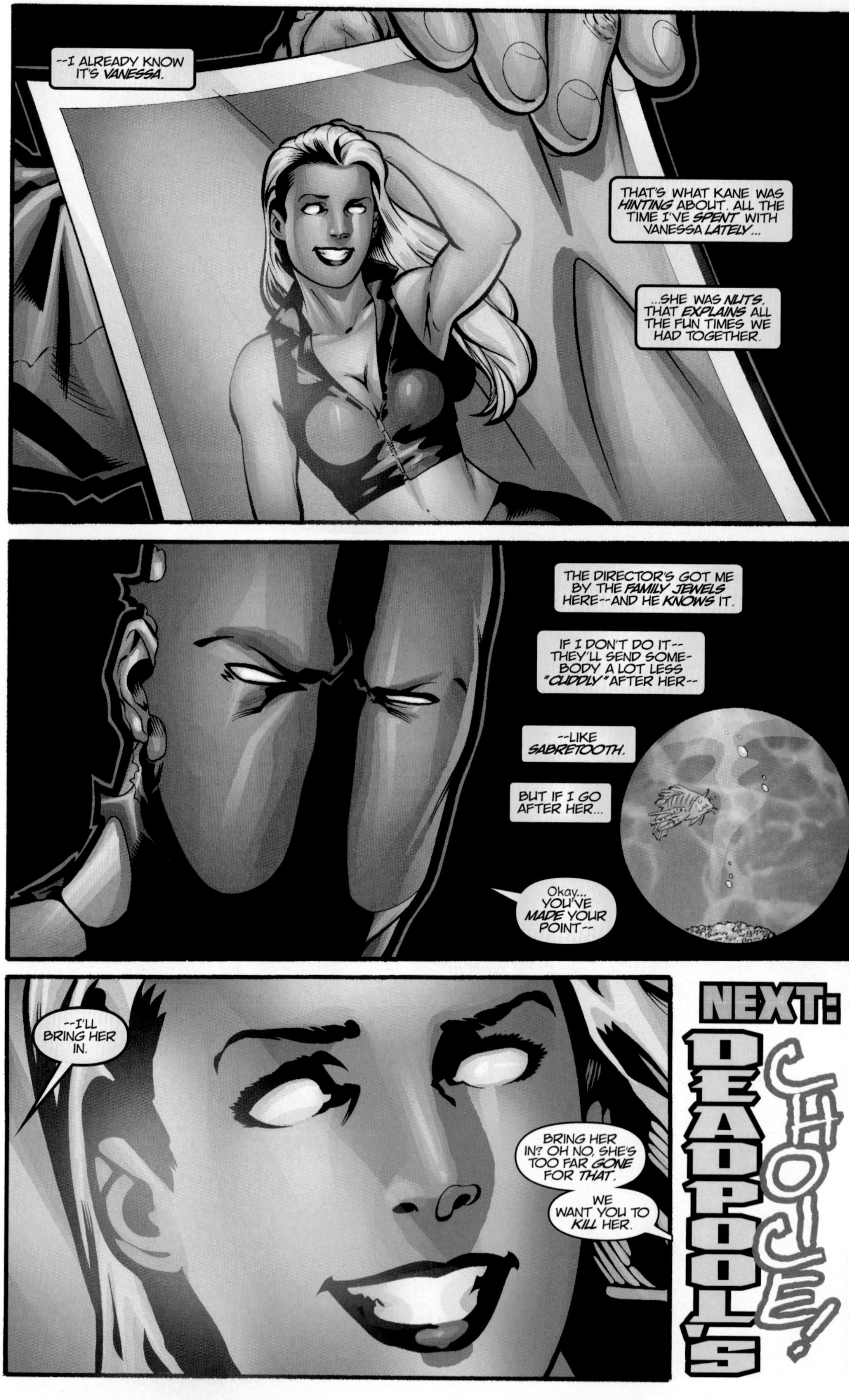
--I ALREADY KNOW IT'S VANESSA.
THAT'S WHAT KANE WAS HINTING ABOUT. ALL THE TIME I'VE SPENT WITH VANESSA LATELY...
...SHE WAS NUTS. THAT EXPLAINS ALL THE FUN TIMES WE HAD TOGETHER.
THE DIRECTOR'S GOT ME BY THE FAMILY JEWELS HERE--AND HE KNOWS IT.
IF I DON'T DO IT--THEY'LL SEND SOME-BODY A LOT LESS "CUDDLY" AFTER HER--
--LIKE SABRETOOTH.
BUT IF I GO AFTER HER...
Okay... YOU'VE MADE YOUR POINT--
--I'LL BRING HER IN.
BRING HER IN? OH NO, SHE'S TOO FAR GONE FOR THAT.
WE WANT YOU TO KILL HER.
NEXT:
DEADPOOL'S CHOICE!

DEADPOOL character design by Paul Tutrone

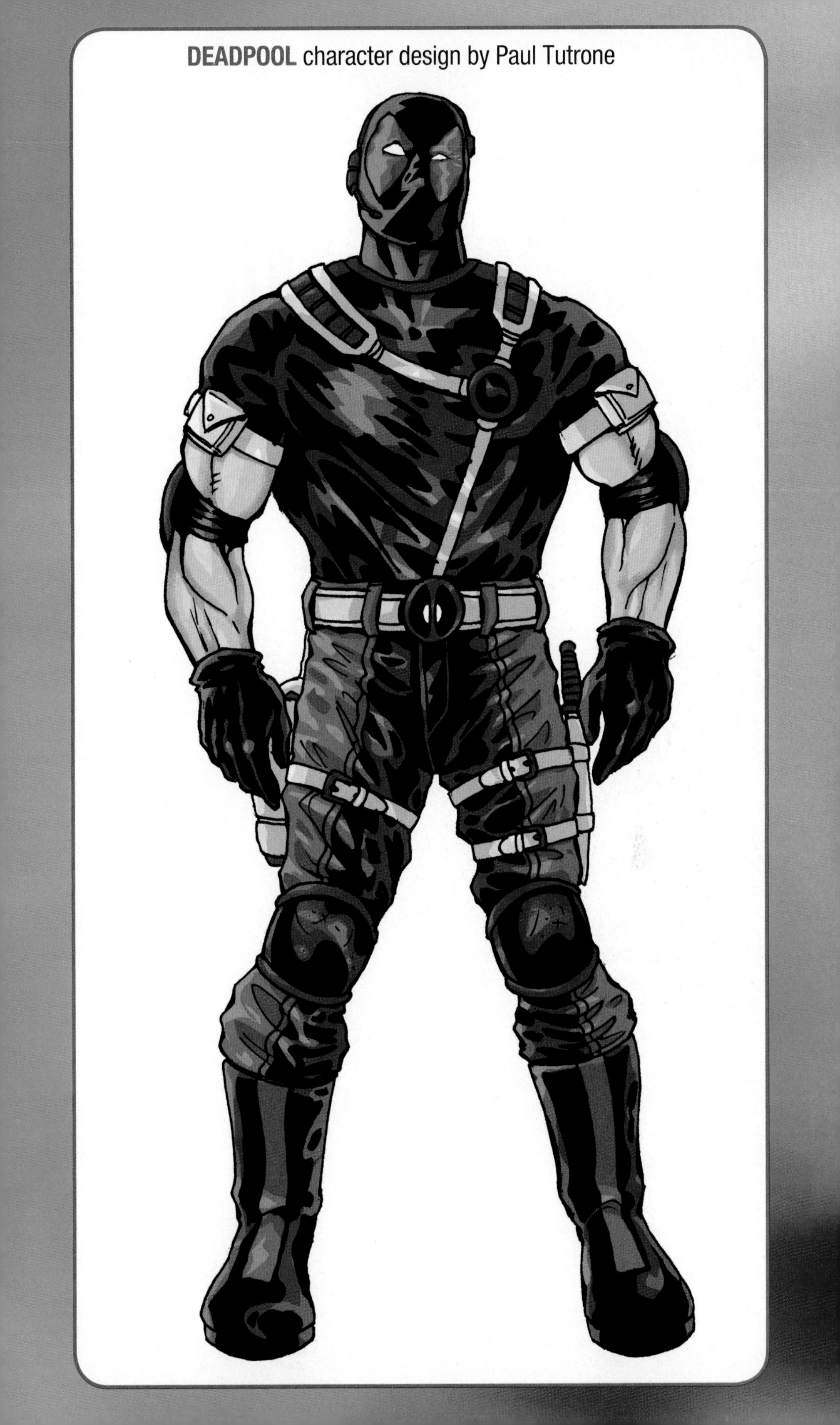

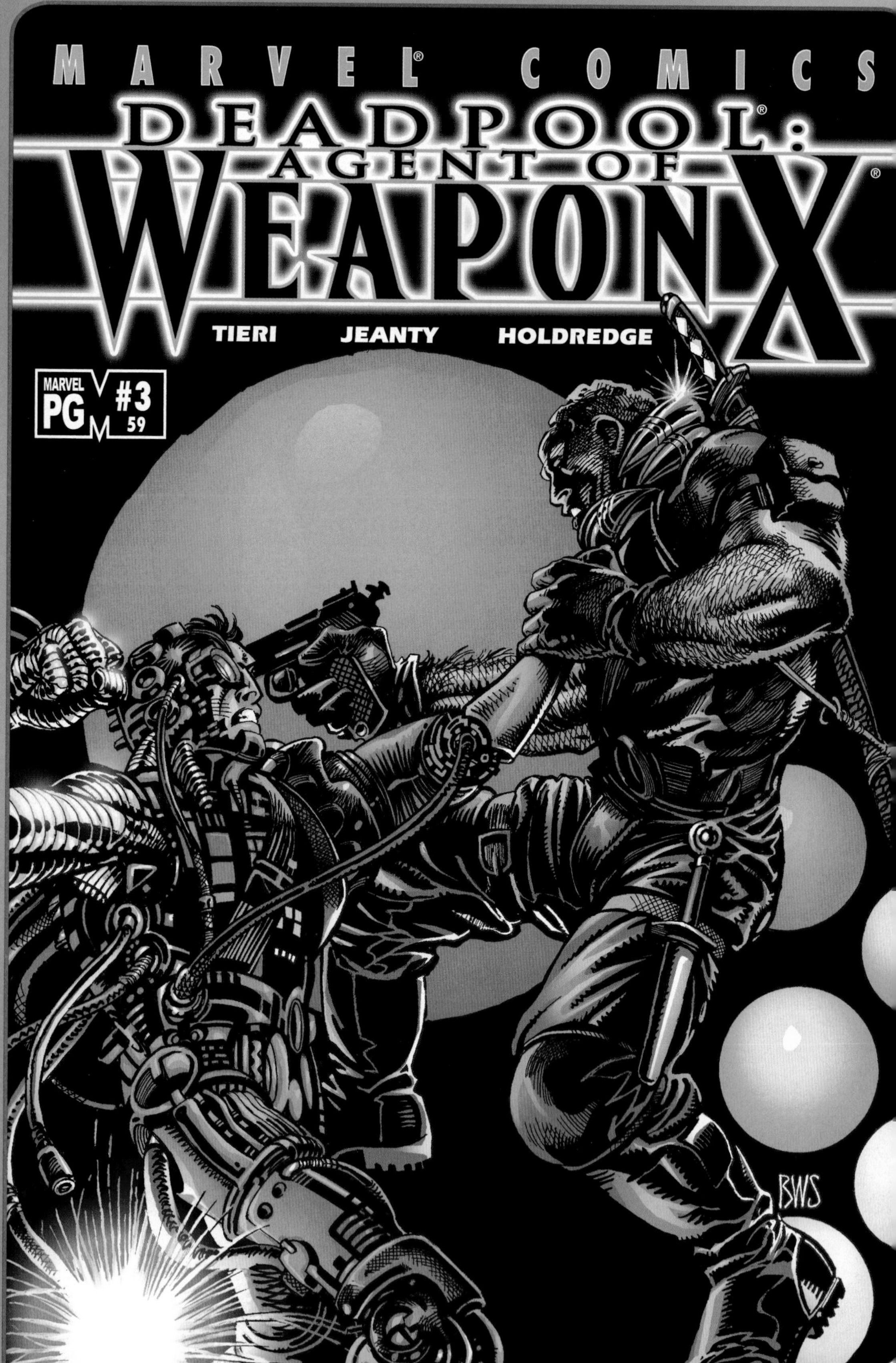
MARVEL® COMICS
DEADPOOL®: AGENT OF WEAPON X®
TIERI JEANTY HOLDREDGE
MARVEL PG
#3
59
BWS

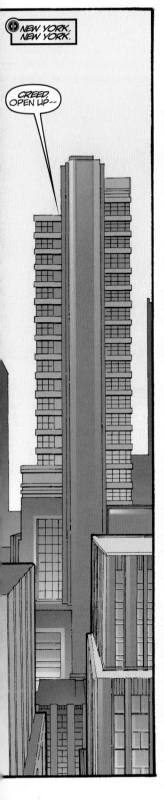

CREED, OPEN UP--

--IT'S *JACKSON.* WE HAVE TO *TALK.*

NoK NoK

GEEZ, WHAT IS IT *NOW?* I'M SORTA *BUSY,* Y'KNOW?

YEAH, WELL...WE MAY HAVE A *PROBLEM. DEADPOOL'S* BEEN ASSIGNED TO ELIMINATE OUR LITTLE *A.W.O.L., COPYCAT--*

YEAH-- *SO?*

SO... WHILE IT LOOKS LIKE HE'S *ACCEPTED* THE ASSIGNMENT--

HE *ACCEPTED?* THEN WHAT'S THE BLASTED *PROBLEM?*

CAN YOU LET ME *FINISH,* PLEASE?

THANK YOU. THE THING IS, THE *DIRECTOR* THINKS WILSON MIGHT *NOT* ENTIRELY BE ON THE UP AND UP.

AND SURE, WE'VE ALREADY TAKEN SOME *PRECAUTIONS...* BUT HE WANTS *YOU* ON STAND-BY, JUST IN CASE--

AHHHHHH!

CREED, WHAT ON EARTH IS *GOING ON* IN THERE?

WILL YOU *OPEN UP,* ALREADY? I'D RATHER NOT *DISCUSS* THIS THROUGH THE--

--DOOR...

CREAK

COME ON *IN,* JACKIE-BOY...

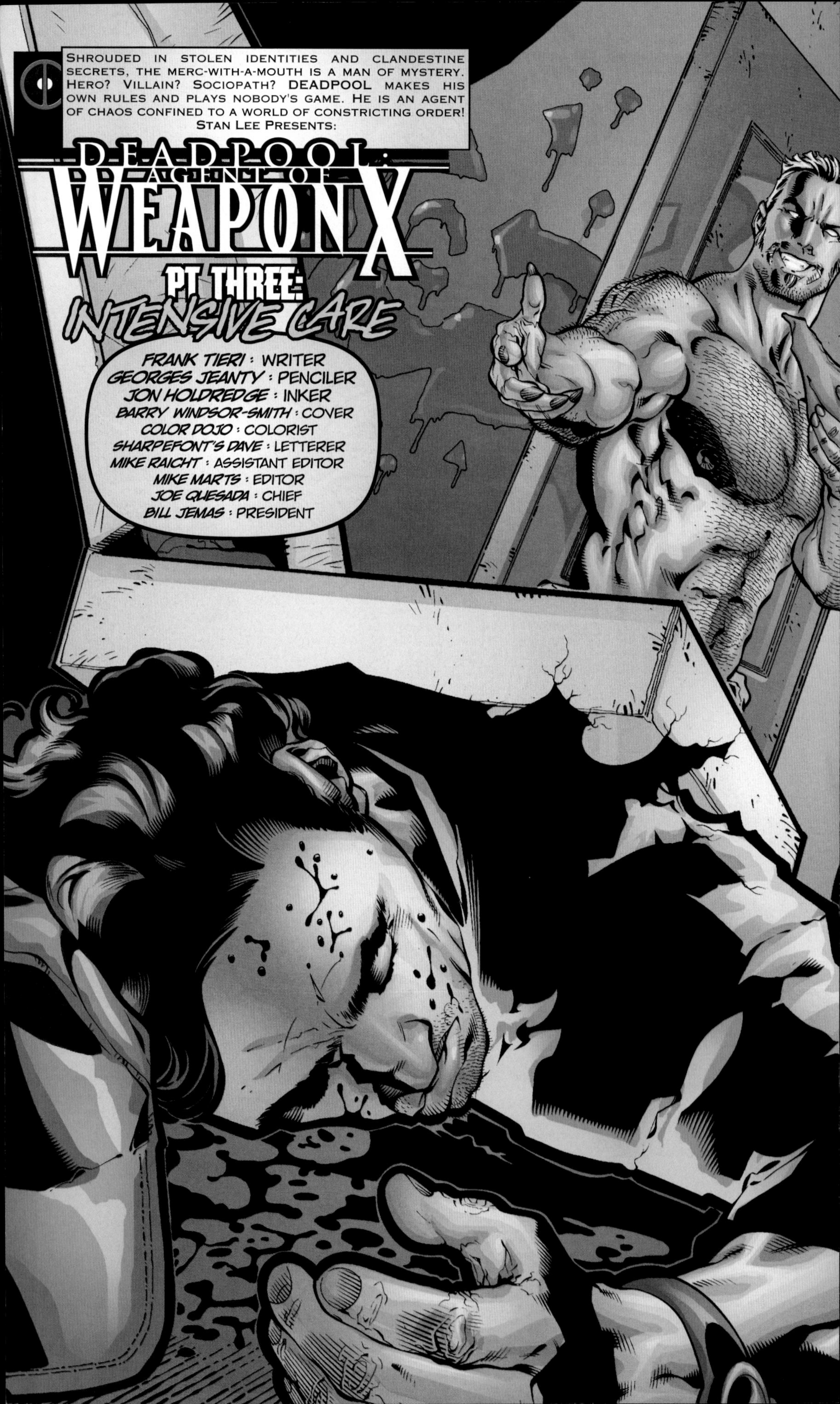
SHROUDED IN STOLEN IDENTITIES AND CLANDESTINE SECRETS, THE MERC-WITH-A-MOUTH IS A MAN OF MYSTERY. HERO? VILLAIN? SOCIOPATH? DEADPOOL MAKES HIS OWN RULES AND PLAYS NOBODY'S GAME. HE IS AN AGENT OF CHAOS CONFINED TO A WORLD OF CONSTRICTING ORDER!
STAN LEE PRESENTS:
DEADPOOL: AGENT OF WEAPON X
PT THREE:
INTENSIVE CARE
FRANK TIERI : WRITER
GEORGES JEANTY : PENCILER
JON HOLDREDGE : INKER
BARRY WINDSOR-SMITH : COVER
COLOR DOJO : COLORIST
SHARPEFONT'S DAVE : LETTERER
MIKE RAICHT : ASSISTANT EDITOR
MIKE MARTS : EDITOR
JOE QUESADA : CHIEF
BILL JEMAS : PRESIDENT

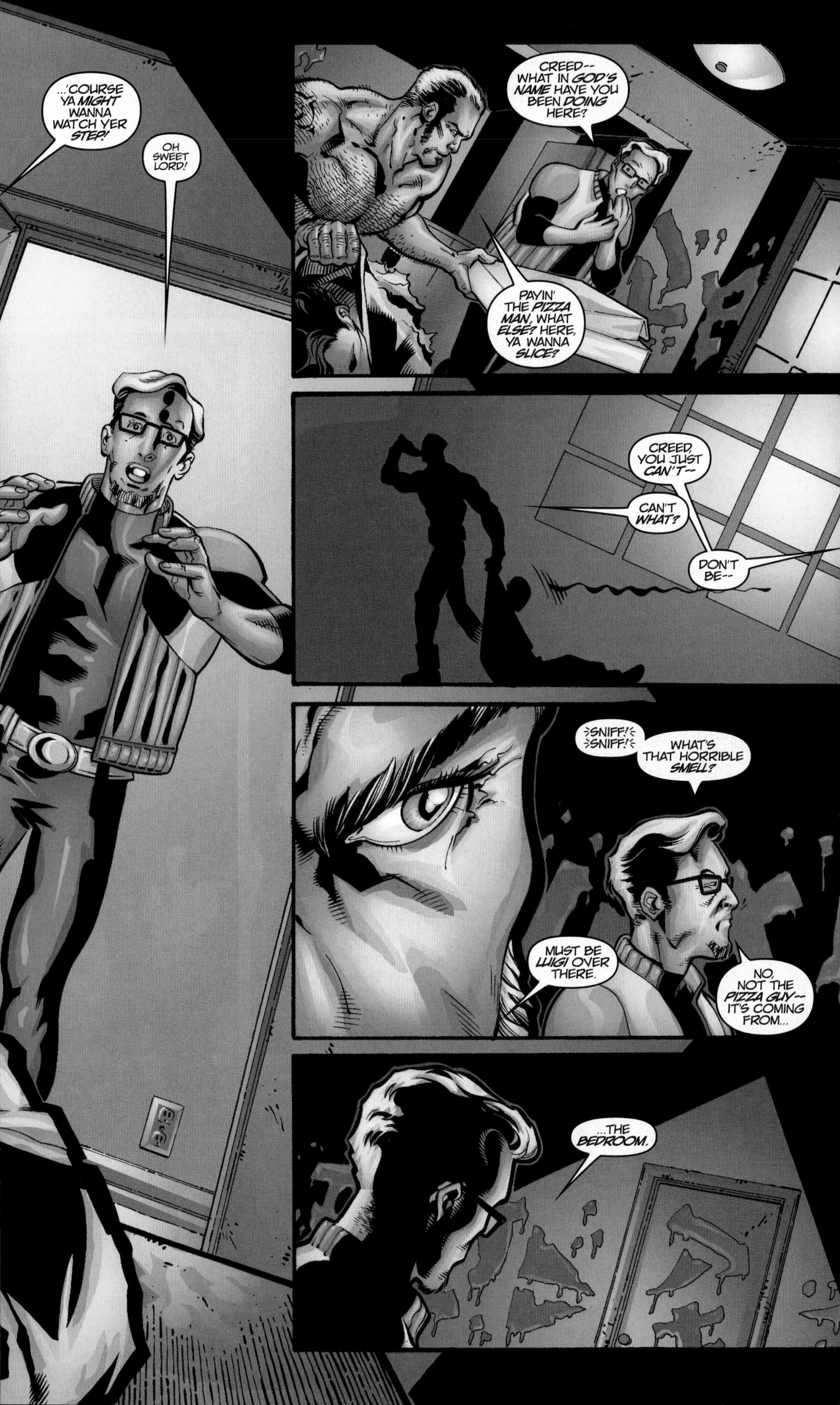

...'COURSE YA *MIGHT* WANNA WATCH YER *STEP!*
OH SWEET LORD!
CREED-- WHAT IN *GOD'S NAME* HAVE YOU BEEN *DOING* HERE?
PAYIN' THE *PIZZA MAN*, WHAT *ELSE?* HERE, YA WANNA *SLICE?*
CREED, YOU JUST *CAN'T*--
CAN'T *WHAT?*
DON'T BE--
SNIFF! *SNIFF!*
WHAT'S THAT HORRIBLE *SMELL?*
MUST BE *LUIGI* OVER THERE.
NO, NOT THE *PIZZA GUY*-- IT'S COMING FROM...
...THE *BEDROOM.*

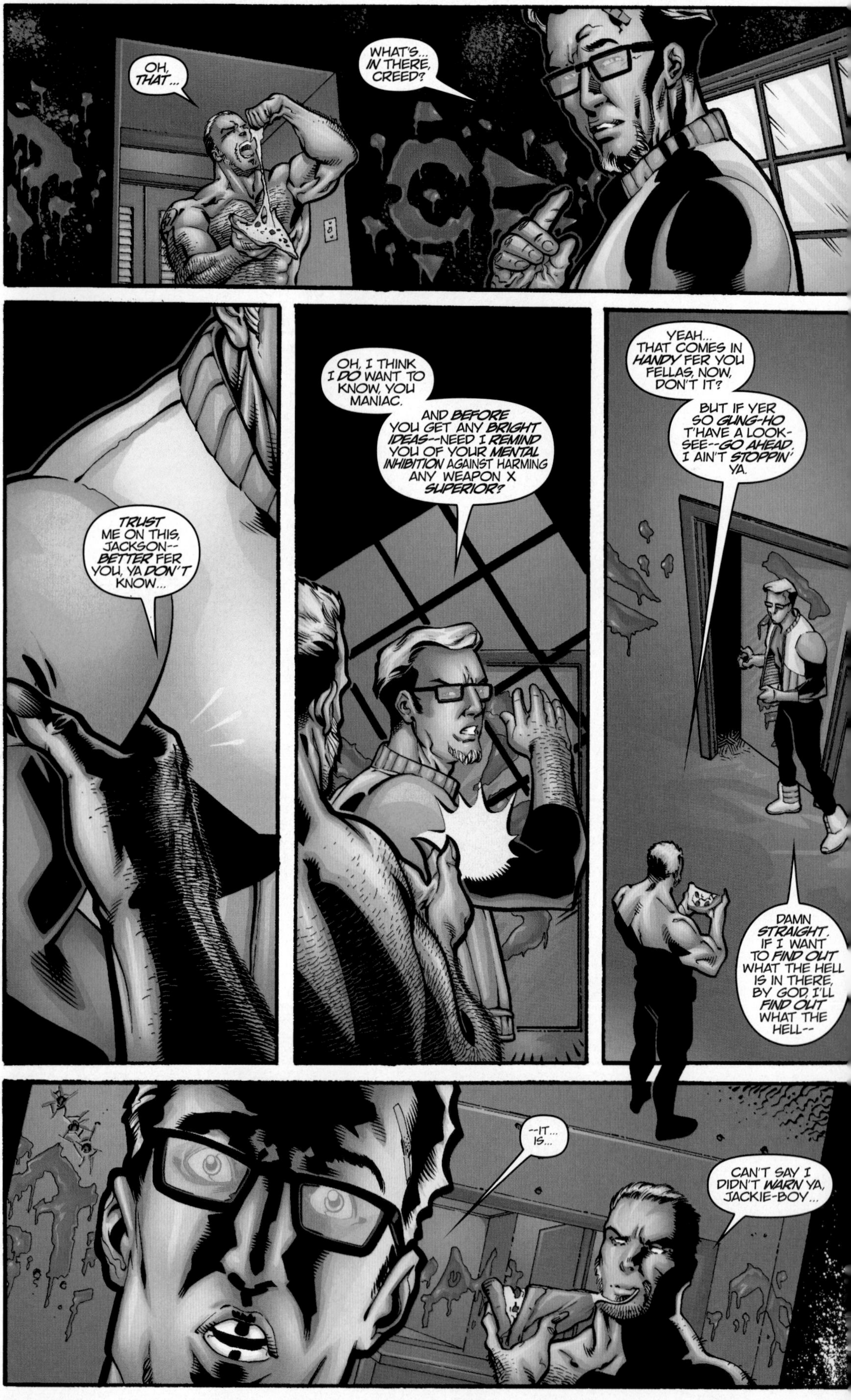
WHAT'S... IN THERE, CREED?
OH, THAT...
TRUST ME ON THIS, JACKSON-- BETTER FER YOU, YA DON'T KNOW...
OH, I THINK I DO WANT TO KNOW, YOU MANIAC.
AND BEFORE YOU GET ANY BRIGHT IDEAS--NEED I REMIND YOU OF YOUR MENTAL INHIBITION AGAINST HARMING ANY WEAPON X SUPERIOR?
YEAH... THAT COMES IN HANDY FER YOU FELLAS, NOW, DON'T IT?
BUT IF YER SO GUNG-HO T'HAVE A LOOK-SEE--GO AHEAD. I AIN'T STOPPIN' YA.
DAMN STRAIGHT. IF I WANT TO FIND OUT WHAT THE HELL IS IN THERE, BY GOD, I'LL FIND OUT WHAT THE HELL--
--IT... IS...
CAN'T SAY I DIDN'T WARN YA, JACKIE-BOY...

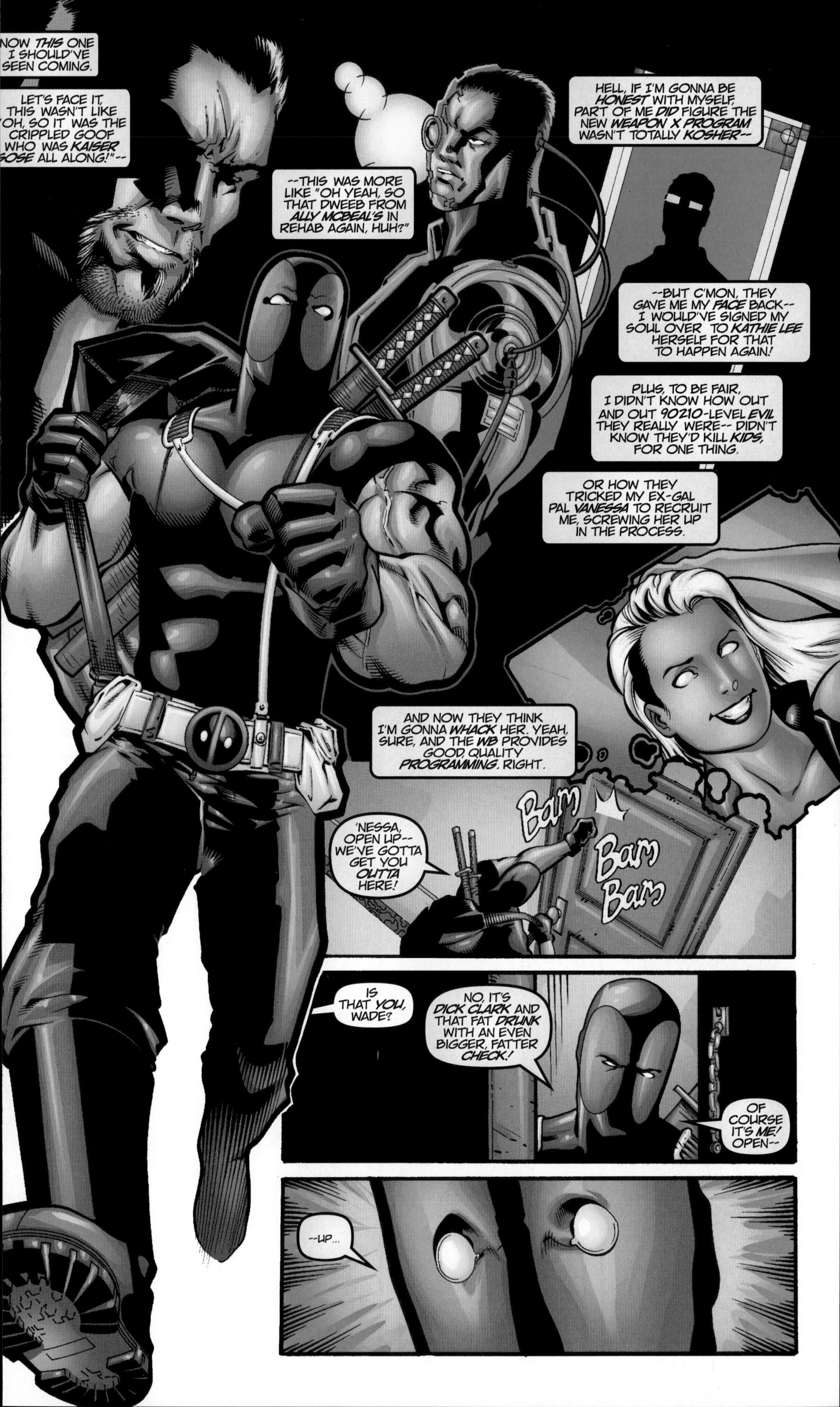

NOW THIS ONE I SHOULD'VE SEEN COMING.
LET'S FACE IT, THIS WASN'T LIKE "OH, SO IT WAS THE CRIPPLED GOOF WHO WAS KAISER SOSE ALL ALONG!"--
--THIS WAS MORE LIKE "OH YEAH, SO THAT DWEEB FROM ALLY MCBEAL'S IN REHAB AGAIN, HUH?"
HELL, IF I'M GONNA BE HONEST WITH MYSELF, PART OF ME DID FIGURE THE NEW WEAPON X PROGRAM WASN'T TOTALLY KOSHER--
--BUT C'MON, THEY GAVE ME MY FACE BACK-- I WOULD'VE SIGNED MY SOUL OVER TO KATHIE LEE HERSELF FOR THAT TO HAPPEN AGAIN!
PLUS, TO BE FAIR, I DIDN'T KNOW HOW OUT AND OUT 90210-LEVEL EVIL THEY REALLY WERE-- DIDN'T KNOW THEY'D KILL KIDS, FOR ONE THING.
OR HOW THEY TRICKED MY EX-GAL PAL VANESSA TO RECRUIT ME, SCREWING HER UP IN THE PROCESS.
AND NOW THEY THINK I'M GONNA WHACK HER. YEAH, SURE, AND THE WB PROVIDES GOOD, QUALITY PROGRAMMING. RIGHT.
Bam
'NESSA, OPEN UP-- WE'VE GOTTA GET YOU OUTTA HERE!
Bam Bam
IS THAT YOU, WADE?
NO, IT'S DICK CLARK AND THAT FAT DRUNK WITH AN EVEN BIGGER, FATTER CHECK!
OF COURSE IT'S ME! OPEN--
--UP...

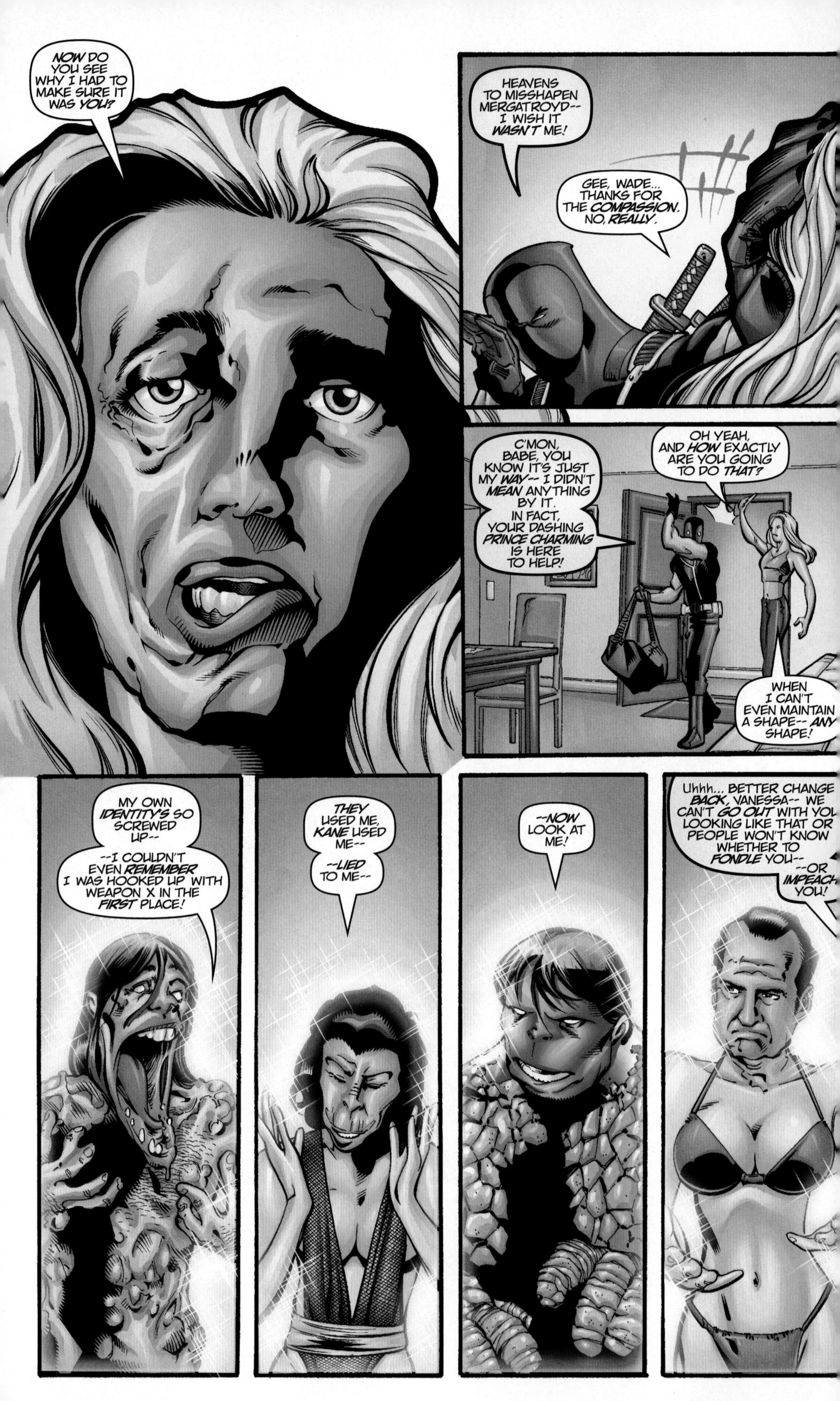
NOW DO YOU SEE WHY I HAD TO MAKE SURE IT WAS YOU?
HEAVENS TO MISSHAPEN MERGATROYD-- I WISH IT WASN'T ME!
GEE, WADE... THANKS FOR THE COMPASSION. NO, REALLY.
C'MON, BABE, YOU KNOW IT'S JUST MY WAY-- I DIDN'T MEAN ANYTHING BY IT. IN FACT, YOUR DASHING PRINCE CHARMING IS HERE TO HELP!
OH YEAH, AND HOW EXACTLY ARE YOU GOING TO DO THAT?
WHEN I CAN'T EVEN MAINTAIN A SHAPE-- ANY SHAPE!
MY OWN IDENTITY'S SO SCREWED UP--
--I COULDN'T EVEN REMEMBER I WAS HOOKED UP WITH WEAPON X IN THE FIRST PLACE!
THEY USED ME, KANE USED ME--
--LIED TO ME--
--NOW LOOK AT ME!
Uhhh... BETTER CHANGE BACK, VANESSA-- WE CAN'T GO OUT WITH YOU LOOKING LIKE THAT OR PEOPLE WON'T KNOW WHETHER TO FONDLE YOU--
--OR IMPEACH YOU!

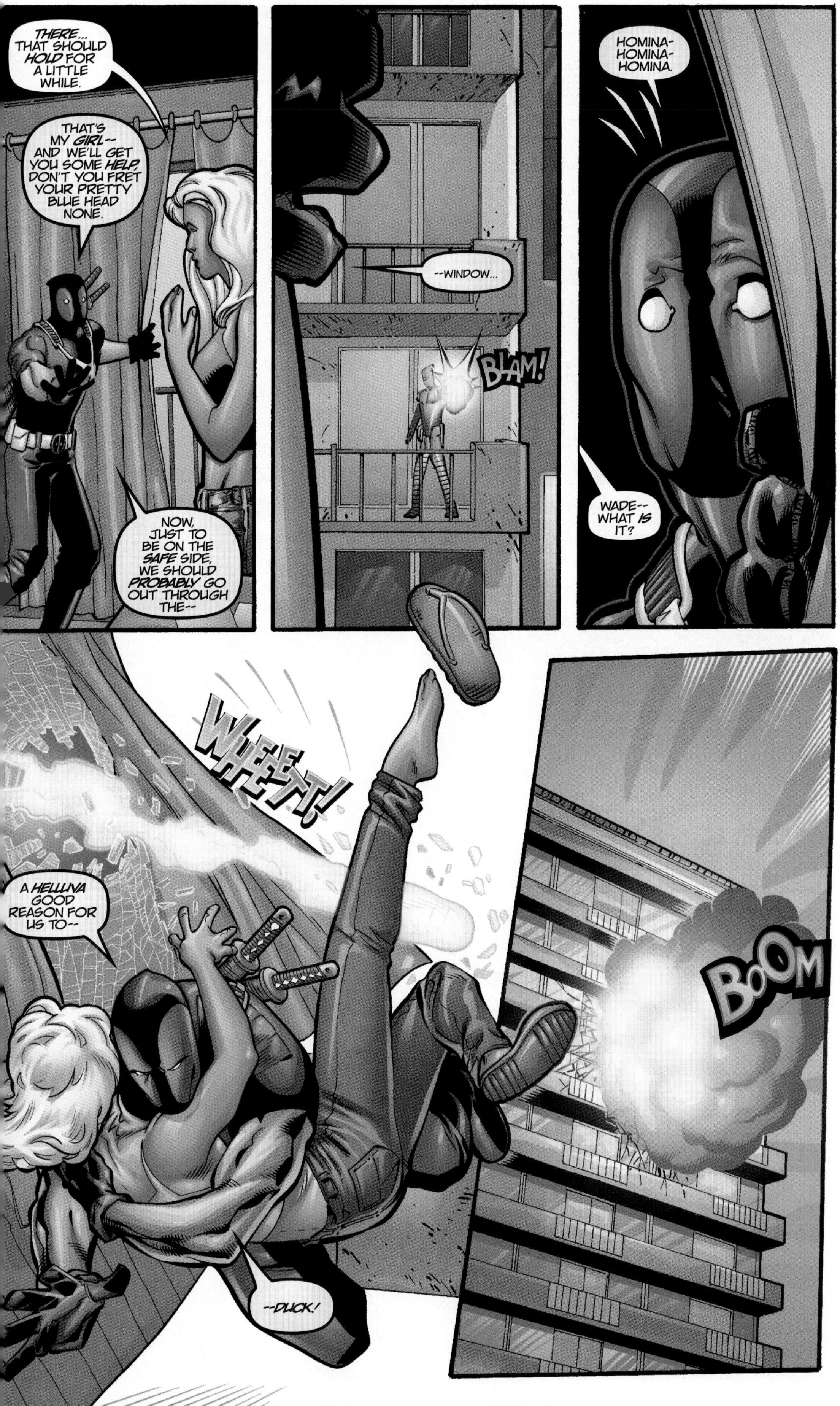
THERE... THAT SHOULD HOLD FOR A LITTLE WHILE.
THAT'S MY GIRL-- AND WE'LL GET YOU SOME HELP. DON'T YOU FRET YOUR PRETTY BLUE HEAD NONE.
NOW, JUST TO BE ON THE SAFE SIDE, WE SHOULD PROBABLY GO OUT THROUGH THE--
--WINDOW...
BLAM!
HOMINA-HOMINA-HOMINA.
WADE-- WHAT IS IT?
WHEEETT!
A HELLUVA GOOD REASON FOR US TO--
BOOM
--DUCK!

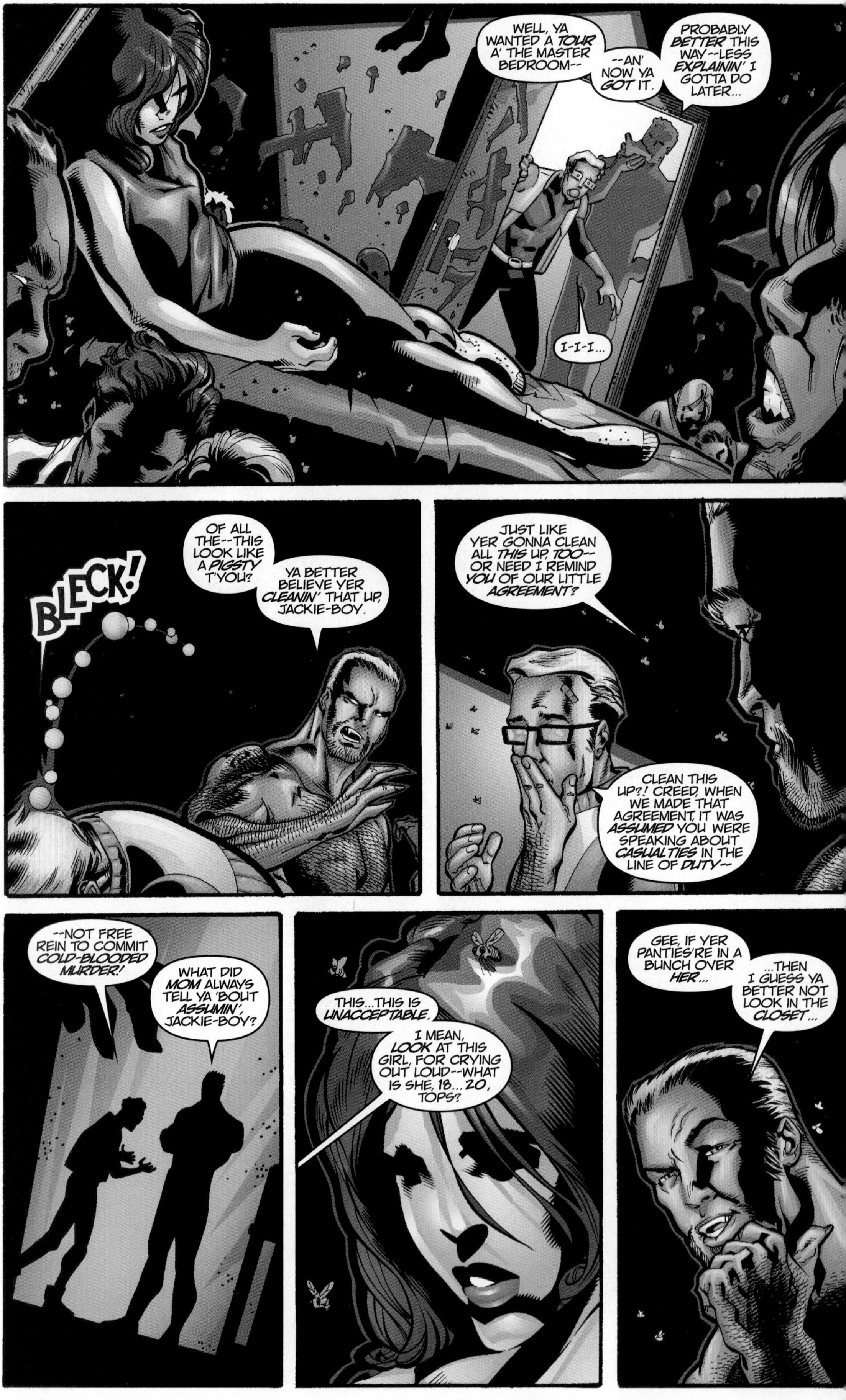

WELL, YA WANTED A TOUR A' THE MASTER BEDROOM--
--AN' NOW YA GOT IT.
PROBABLY BETTER THIS WAY--LESS EXPLAININ' I GOTTA DO LATER...
I-I-I...
BLECK!
OF ALL THE--THIS LOOK LIKE A PIGSTY T'YOU?
YA BETTER BELIEVE YER CLEANIN' THAT UP, JACKIE-BOY.
JUST LIKE YER GONNA CLEAN ALL THIS UP, TOO--OR NEED I REMIND YOU OF OUR LITTLE AGREEMENT?
CLEAN THIS UP?! CREED, WHEN WE MADE THAT AGREEMENT, IT WAS ASSUMED YOU WERE SPEAKING ABOUT CASUALTIES IN THE LINE OF DUTY--
--NOT FREE REIN TO COMMIT COLD-BLOODED MURDER!
WHAT DID MOM ALWAYS TELL YA 'BOUT ASSUMIN', JACKIE-BOY?
THIS...THIS IS UNACCEPTABLE.
I MEAN, LOOK AT THIS GIRL, FOR CRYING OUT LOUD--WHAT IS SHE, 18...20, TOPS?
GEE, IF YER PANTIES'RE IN A BUNCH OVER HER...
...THEN I GUESS YA BETTER NOT LOOK IN THE CLOSET...

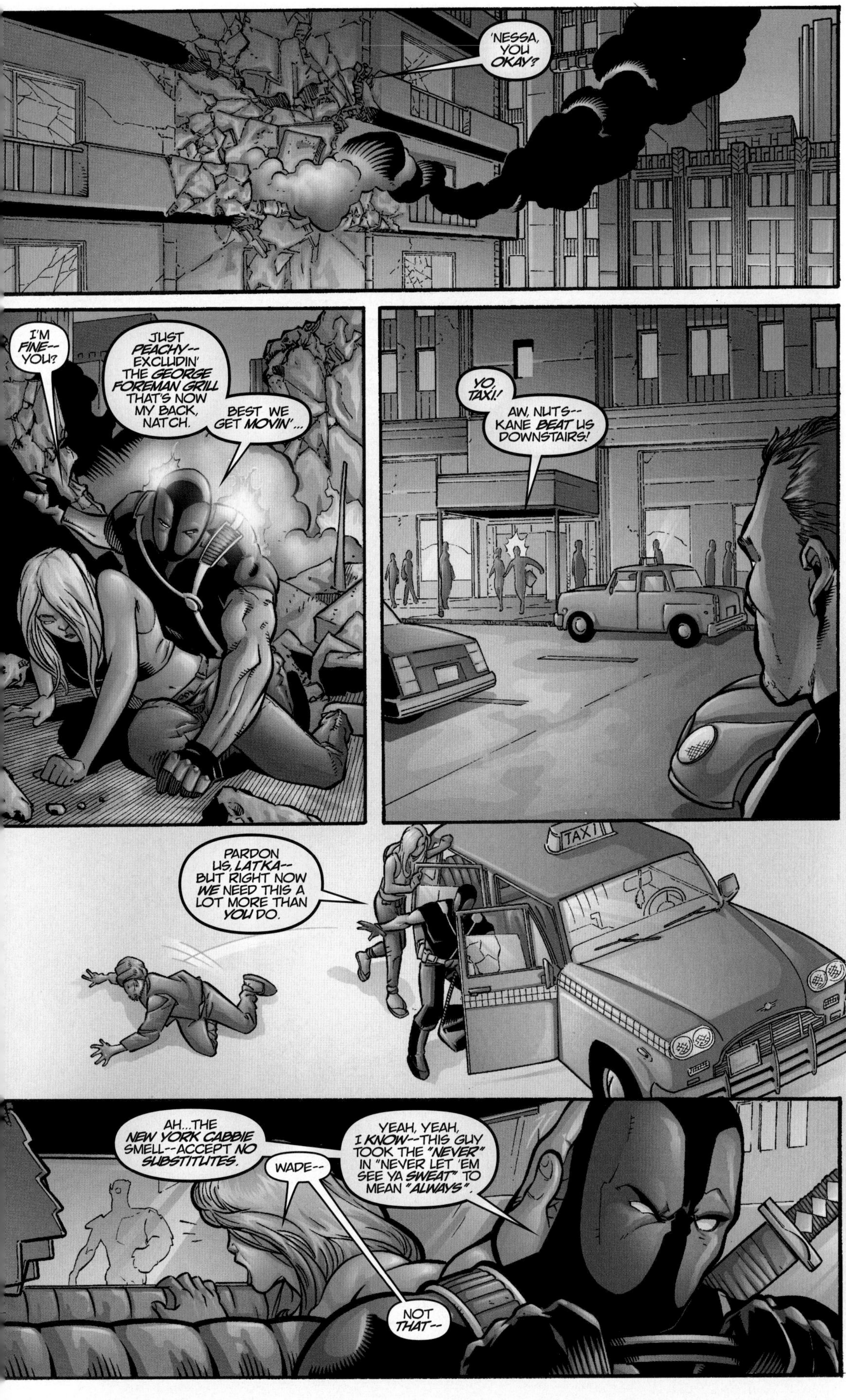
'NESSA, YOU OKAY?
I'M FINE-- YOU?
JUST PEACHY-- EXCLUDIN' THE GEORGE FOREMAN GRILL THAT'S NOW MY BACK, NATCH.
BEST WE GET MOVIN'...
YO, TAXI!
AW, NUTS-- KANE BEAT US DOWNSTAIRS!
TAXI
PARDON US, LATKA-- BUT RIGHT NOW WE NEED THIS A LOT MORE THAN YOU DO.
AH...THE NEW YORK CABBIE SMELL--ACCEPT NO SUBSTITUTES.
WADE--
YEAH, YEAH, I KNOW--THIS GUY TOOK THE "NEVER" IN "NEVER LET 'EM SEE YA SWEAT" TO MEAN "ALWAYS".
NOT THAT--

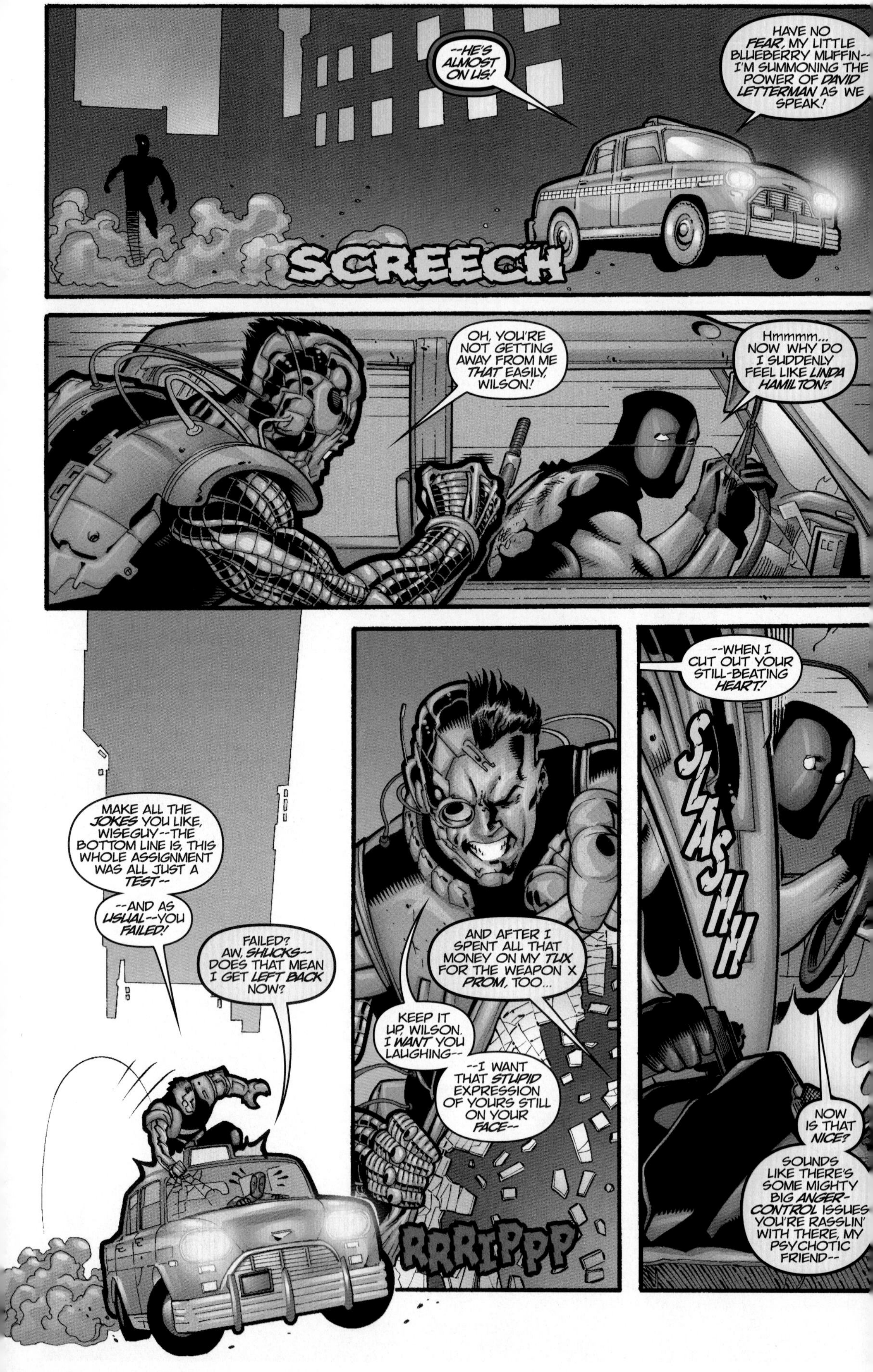
--HE'S ALMOST ON US!
HAVE NO FEAR, MY LITTLE BLUEBERRY MUFFIN--I'M SUMMONING THE POWER OF DAVID LETTERMAN AS WE SPEAK!
SCREECH
OH, YOU'RE NOT GETTING AWAY FROM ME THAT EASILY, WILSON!
Hmmmm... NOW WHY DO I SUDDENLY FEEL LIKE LINDA HAMILTON?
MAKE ALL THE JOKES YOU LIKE, WISEGUY--THE BOTTOM LINE IS, THIS WHOLE ASSIGNMENT WAS ALL JUST A TEST--
--AND AS USUAL--YOU FAILED!
FAILED? AW, SHUCKS--DOES THAT MEAN I GET LEFT BACK NOW?
AND AFTER I SPENT ALL THAT MONEY ON MY TUX FOR THE WEAPON X PROM, TOO...
KEEP IT UP, WILSON. I WANT YOU LAUGHING--
--I WANT THAT STUPID EXPRESSION OF YOURS STILL ON YOUR FACE--
RRRIPPP
--WHEN I CUT OUT YOUR STILL-BEATING HEART!
SLASHH
NOW IS THAT NICE?
SOUNDS LIKE THERE'S SOME MIGHTY BIG ANGER-CONTROL ISSUES YOU'RE RASSLIN' WITH THERE, MY PSYCHOTIC FRIEND--

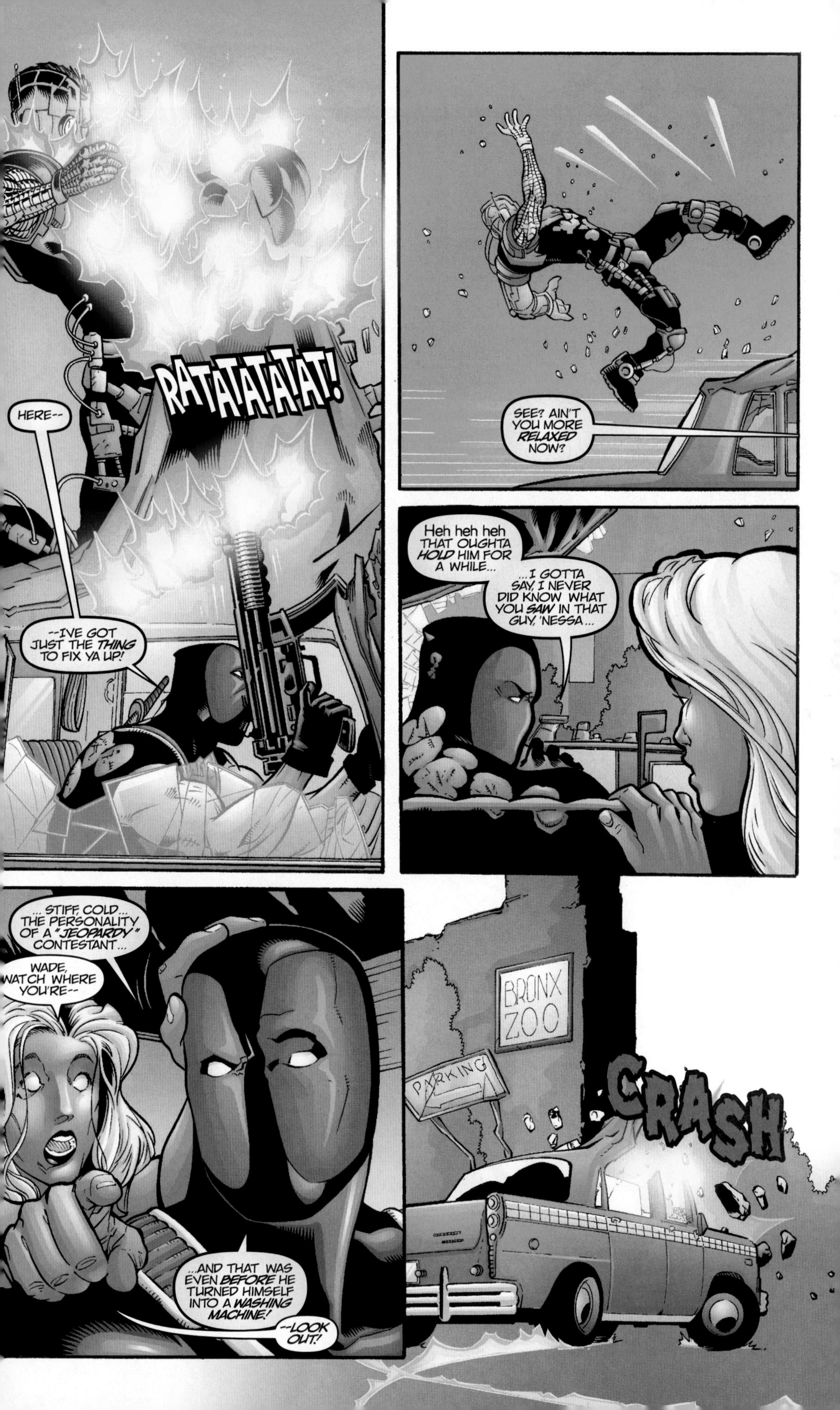

RATATATATAT!
HERE--
--I'VE GOT JUST THE THING TO FIX YA UP!
SEE? AIN'T YOU MORE RELAXED NOW?
Heh heh heh THAT OUGHTA HOLD HIM FOR A WHILE...
...I GOTTA SAY, I NEVER DID KNOW WHAT YOU SAW IN THAT GUY, 'NESSA...
...STIFF, COLD... THE PERSONALITY OF A "JEOPARDY" CONTESTANT...
WADE, WATCH WHERE YOU'RE--
...AND THAT WAS EVEN BEFORE HE TURNED HIMSELF INTO A WASHING MACHINE!
--LOOK OUT!
BRONX ZOO
PARKING
CRASH

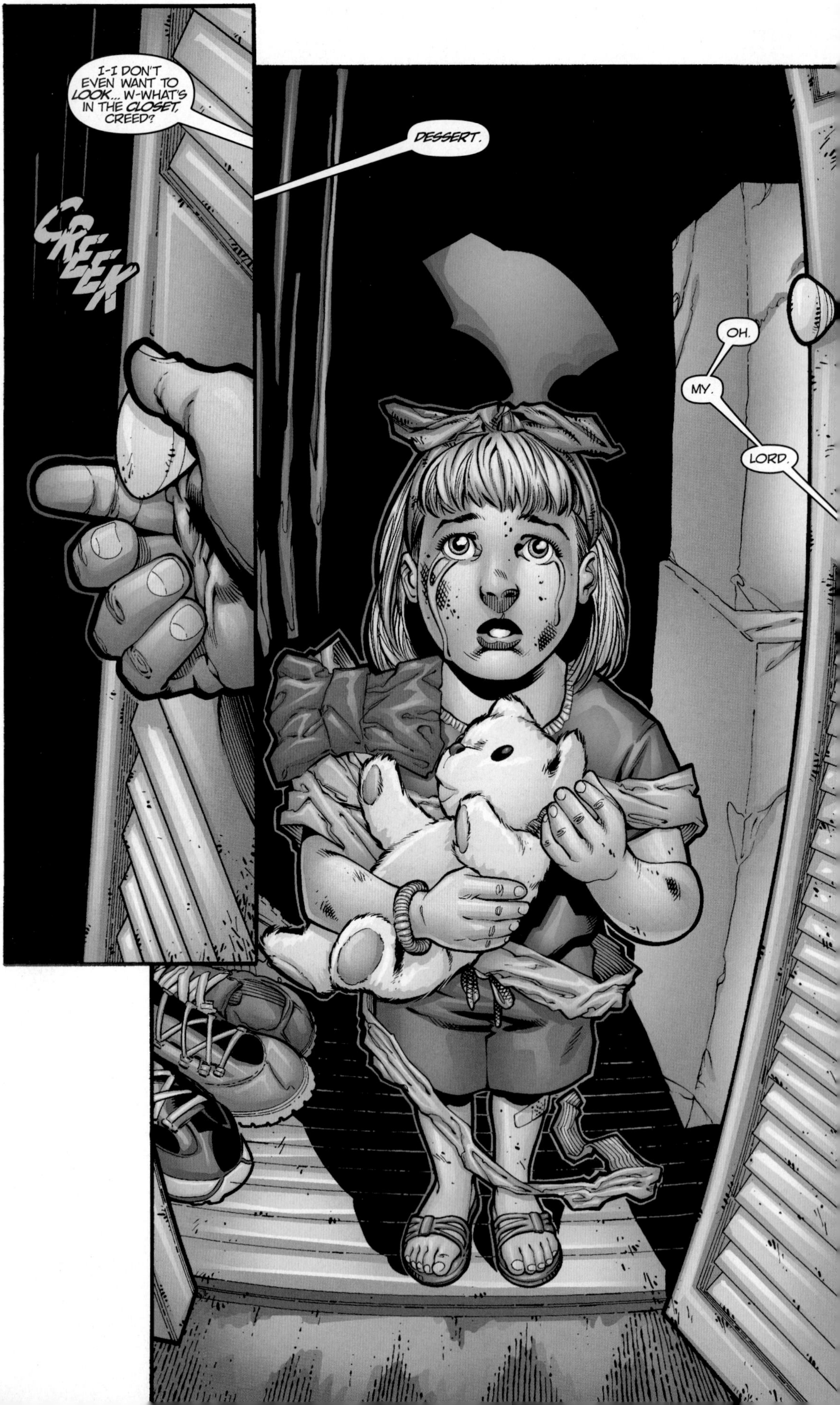

I-I DON'T EVEN WANT TO *LOOK*... W-WHAT'S IN THE *CLOSET*, CREED?
DESSERT.
CREEK
OH.
MY.
LORD.

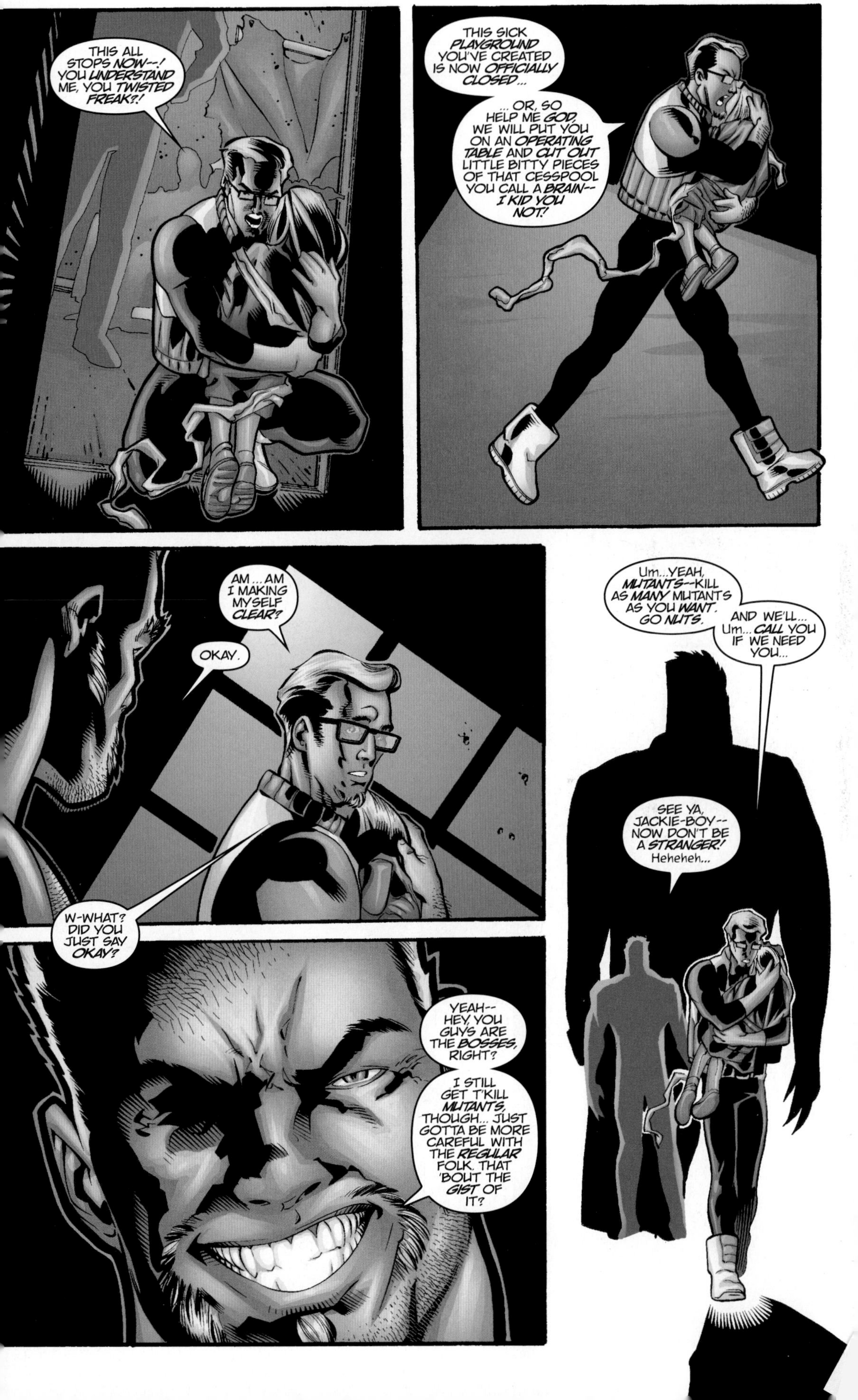
THIS ALL STOPS NOW--! YOU UNDERSTAND ME, YOU TWISTED FREAK?!
THIS SICK PLAYGROUND YOU'VE CREATED IS NOW OFFICIALLY CLOSED...
...OR, SO HELP ME GOD, WE WILL PUT YOU ON AN OPERATING TABLE AND CUT OUT LITTLE BITTY PIECES OF THAT CESSPOOL YOU CALL A BRAIN-- I KID YOU NOT!
AM...AM I MAKING MYSELF CLEAR?
OKAY.
W-WHAT? DID YOU JUST SAY OKAY?
YEAH-- HEY, YOU GUYS ARE THE BOSSES, RIGHT?
I STILL GET T'KILL MUTANTS, THOUGH... JUST GOTTA BE MORE CAREFUL WITH THE REGULAR FOLK. THAT 'BOUT THE GIST OF IT?
Um...YEAH, MUTANTS--KILL AS MANY MUTANTS AS YOU WANT. GO NUTS.
AND WE'LL... Um...CALL YOU IF WE NEED YOU...
SEE YA, JACKIE-BOY-- NOW DON'T BE A STRANGER! Heheheh...

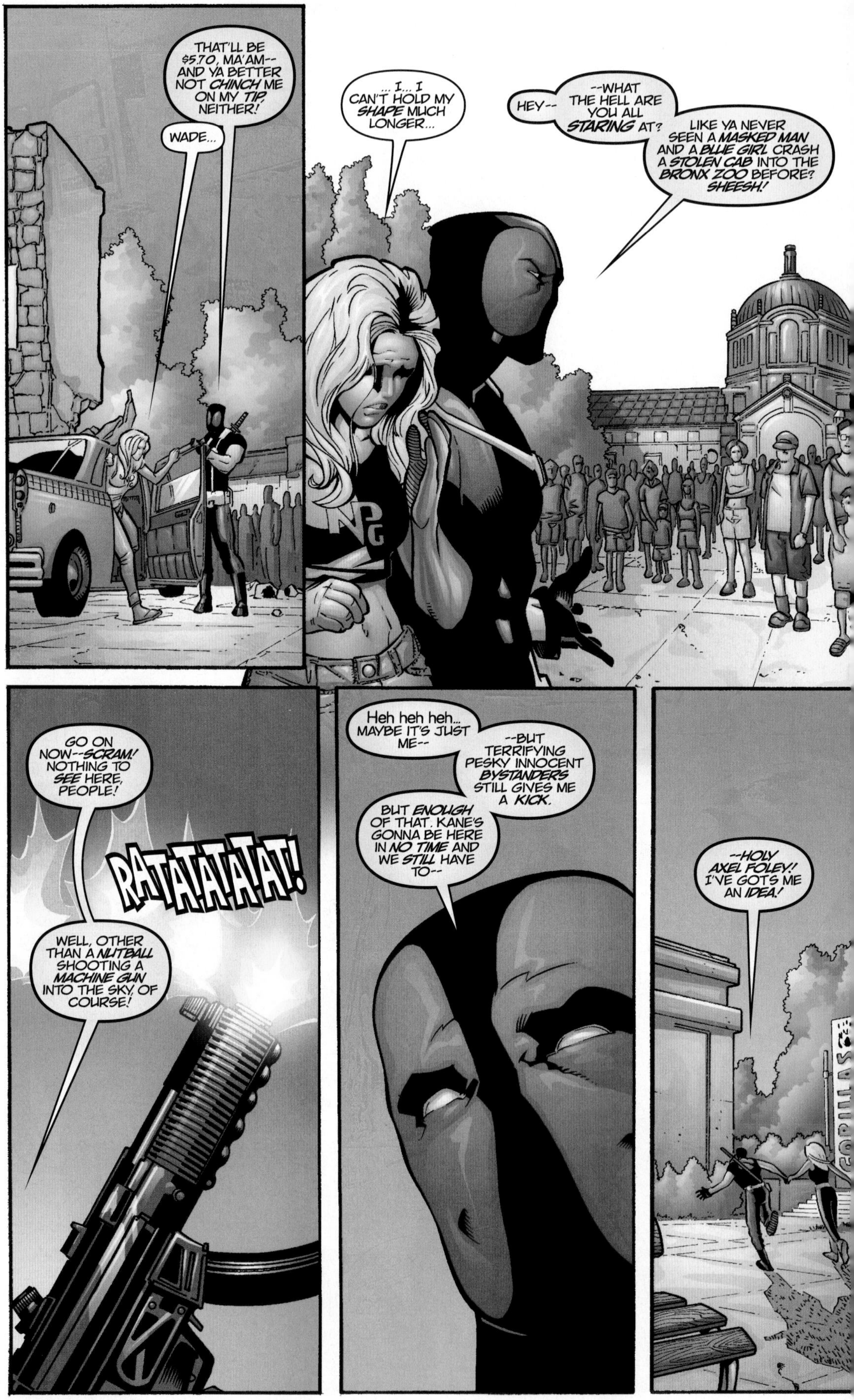
THAT'LL BE $5.70, MA'AM-- AND YA BETTER NOT CHINCH ME ON MY TIP NEITHER!
WADE...
... I... I CAN'T HOLD MY SHAPE MUCH LONGER...
HEY--
--WHAT THE HELL ARE YOU ALL STARING AT?
LIKE YA NEVER SEEN A MASKED MAN AND A BLUE GIRL CRASH A STOLEN CAB INTO THE BRONX ZOO BEFORE? SHEESH!
GO ON NOW--SCRAM! NOTHING TO SEE HERE, PEOPLE!
RATATATATAT!
WELL, OTHER THAN A NUTBALL SHOOTING A MACHINE GUN INTO THE SKY, OF COURSE!
Heh heh heh... MAYBE IT'S JUST ME--
--BUT TERRIFYING PESKY INNOCENT BYSTANDERS STILL GIVES ME A KICK.
BUT ENOUGH OF THAT. KANE'S GONNA BE HERE IN NO TIME AND WE STILL HAVE TO--
--HOLY AXEL FOLEY! I'VE GOTS ME AN IDEA!
GORILLAS

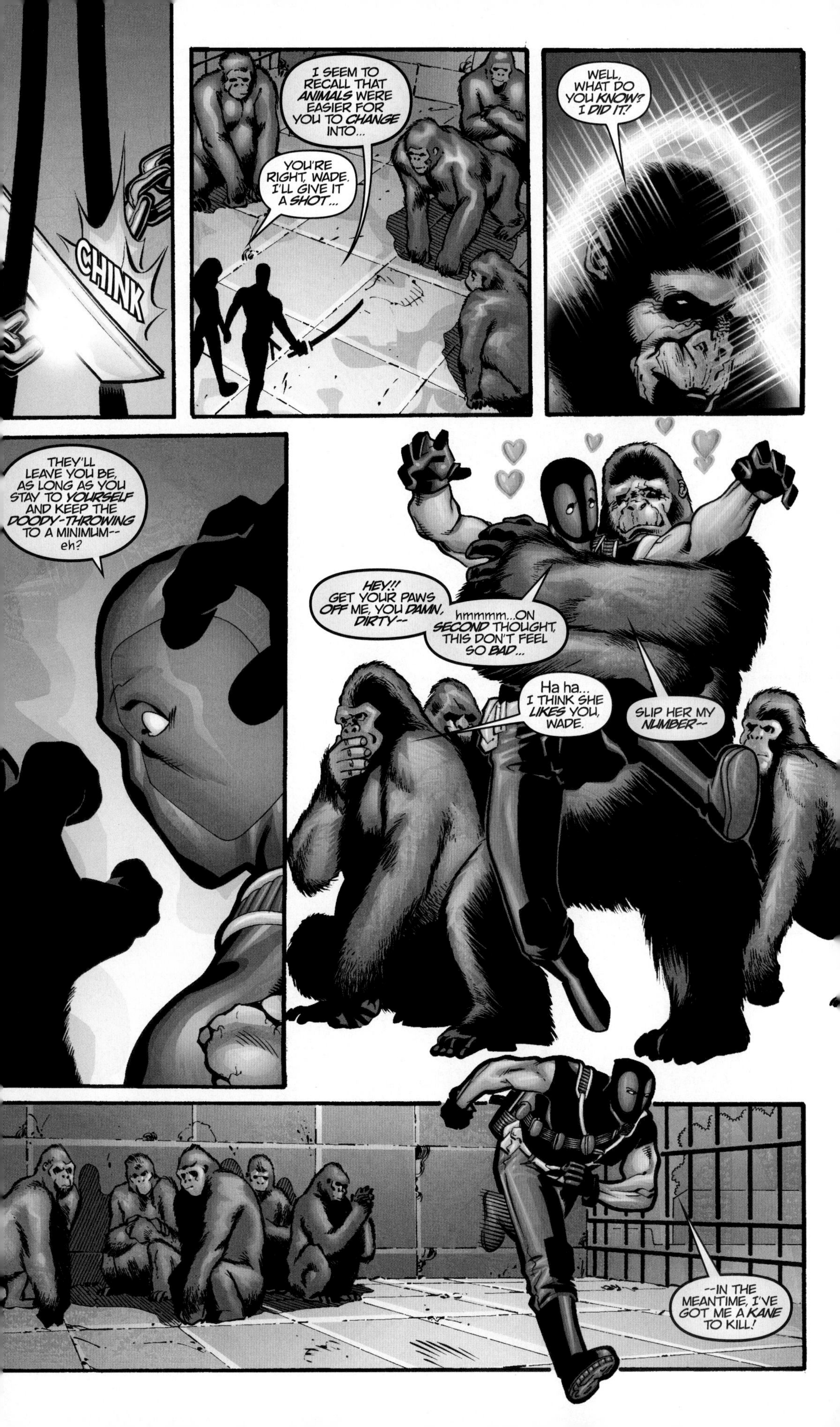
CHINK
I SEEM TO RECALL THAT ANIMALS WERE EASIER FOR YOU TO CHANGE INTO...
YOU'RE RIGHT, WADE. I'LL GIVE IT A SHOT...
WELL, WHAT DO YOU KNOW? I DID IT!
THEY'LL LEAVE YOU BE, AS LONG AS YOU STAY TO YOURSELF AND KEEP THE DOODY-THROWING TO A MINIMUM-- eh?
HEY!! GET YOUR PAWS OFF ME, YOU DAMN, DIRTY--
hmmmm...ON SECOND THOUGHT, THIS DON'T FEEL SO BAD...
Ha ha... I THINK SHE LIKES YOU, WADE.
SLIP HER MY NUMBER--
--IN THE MEANTIME, I'VE GOT ME A KANE TO KILL!

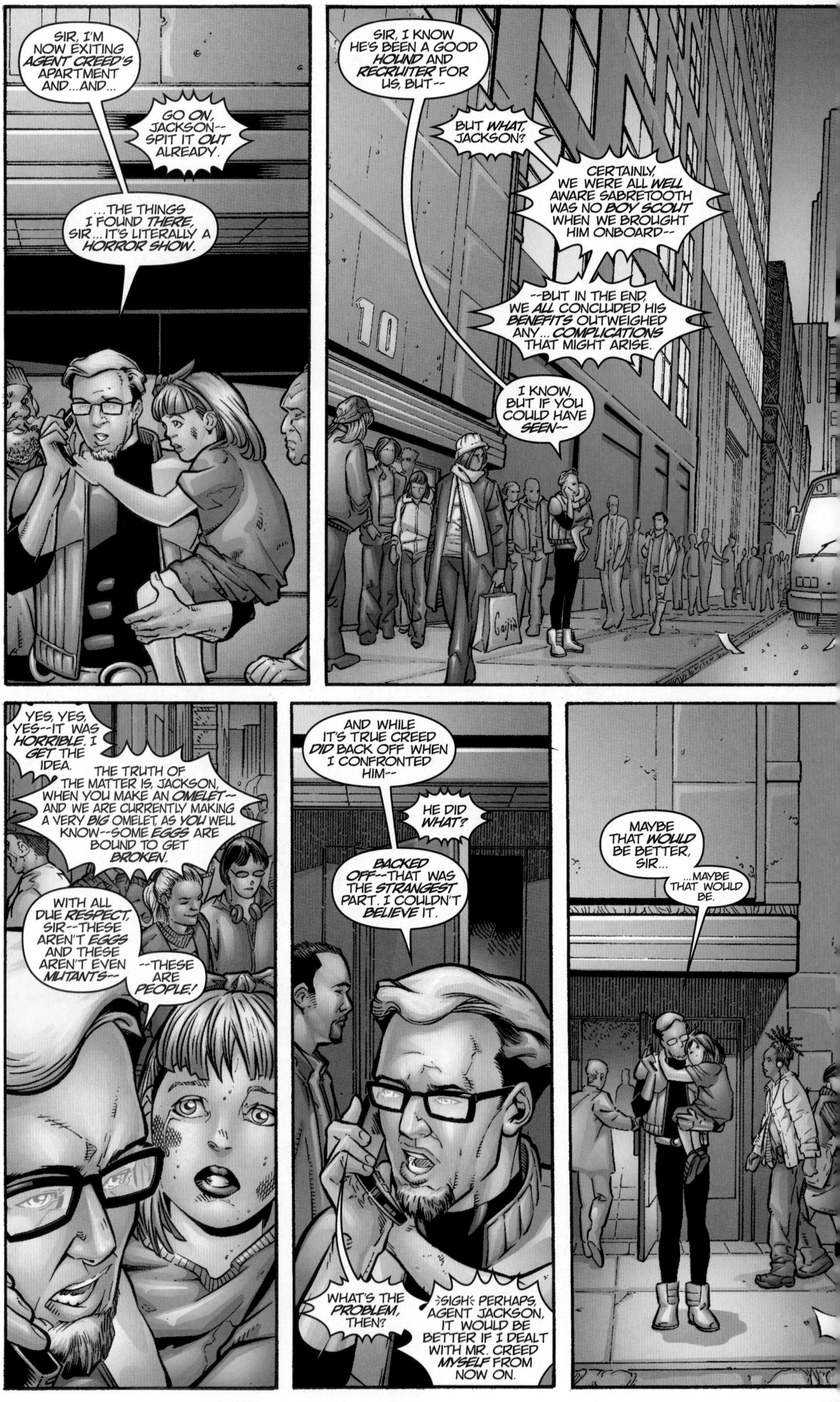
SIR, I'M NOW EXITING AGENT CREED'S APARTMENT AND...AND...
GO ON, JACKSON-- SPIT IT OUT ALREADY.
...THE THINGS I FOUND THERE, SIR...IT'S LITERALLY A HORROR SHOW.
SIR, I KNOW HE'S BEEN A GOOD HOUND AND RECRUITER FOR US, BUT--
BUT WHAT, JACKSON?
CERTAINLY, WE WERE ALL WELL AWARE SABRETOOTH WAS NO BOY SCOUT WHEN WE BROUGHT HIM ONBOARD--
--BUT IN THE END, WE ALL CONCLUDED HIS BENEFITS OUTWEIGHED ANY...COMPLICATIONS THAT MIGHT ARISE.
I KNOW, BUT IF YOU COULD HAVE SEEN--
10
Gaijin
YES, YES, YES--IT WAS HORRIBLE. I GET THE IDEA.
THE TRUTH OF THE MATTER IS, JACKSON, WHEN YOU MAKE AN OMELET--AND WE ARE CURRENTLY MAKING A VERY BIG OMELET, AS YOU WELL KNOW--SOME EGGS ARE BOUND TO GET BROKEN.
WITH ALL DUE RESPECT, SIR--THESE AREN'T EGGS AND THESE AREN'T EVEN MUTANTS--
--THESE ARE PEOPLE!
AND WHILE IT'S TRUE CREED DID BACK OFF WHEN I CONFRONTED HIM--
HE DID WHAT?
BACKED OFF--THAT WAS THE STRANGEST PART. I COULDN'T BELIEVE IT.
WHAT'S THE PROBLEM, THEN?
SIGH PERHAPS, AGENT JACKSON, IT WOULD BE BETTER IF I DEALT WITH MR. CREED MYSELF FROM NOW ON.
MAYBE THAT WOULD BE BETTER, SIR...
...MAYBE THAT WOULD BE.

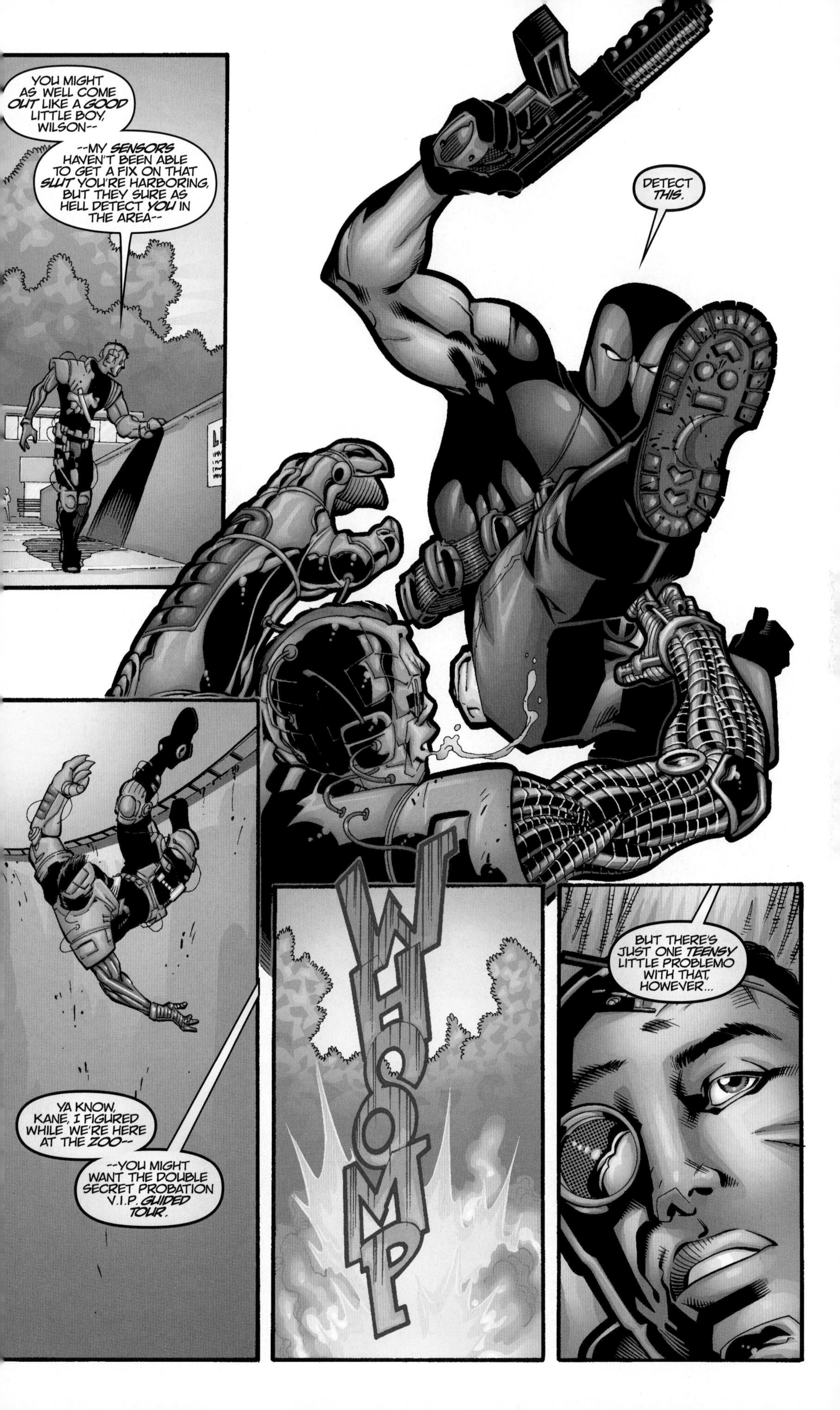

YOU MIGHT AS WELL COME OUT LIKE A GOOD LITTLE BOY, WILSON--
--MY SENSORS HAVEN'T BEEN ABLE TO GET A FIX ON THAT SLUT YOU'RE HARBORING, BUT THEY SURE AS HELL DETECT YOU IN THE AREA--
DETECT THIS.
YA KNOW, KANE, I FIGURED WHILE WE'RE HERE AT THE ZOO--
--YOU MIGHT WANT THE DOUBLE SECRET PROBATION V.I.P. GUIDED TOUR.
WHOMP
BUT THERE'S JUST ONE TEENSY LITTLE PROBLEMO WITH THAT, HOWEVER...

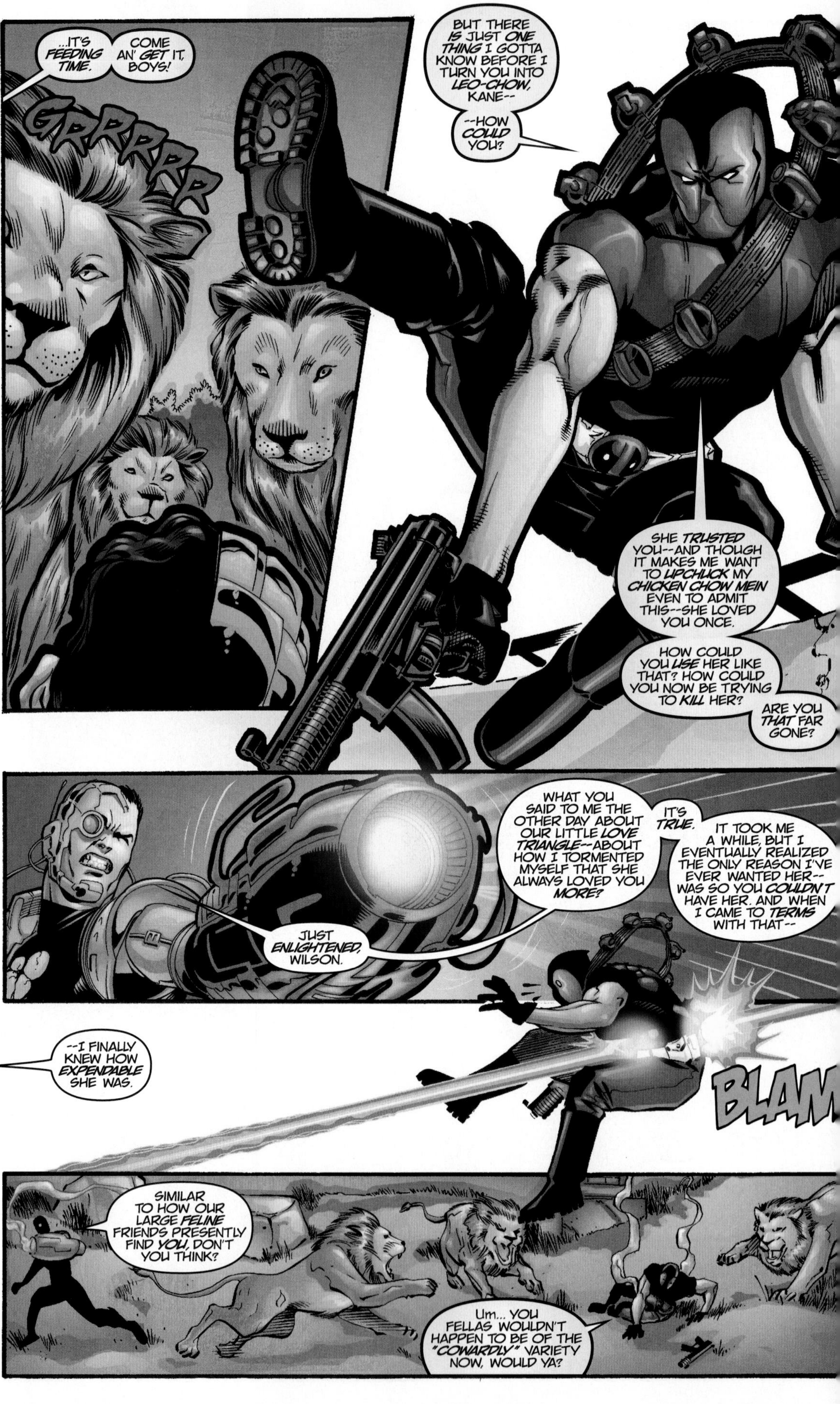

...IT'S FEEDING TIME.
COME AN' GET IT, BOYS!
GRRRRRR
BUT THERE IS JUST ONE THING I GOTTA KNOW BEFORE I TURN YOU INTO LEO-CHOW, KANE--
--HOW COULD YOU?
SHE TRUSTED YOU--AND THOUGH IT MAKES ME WANT TO UPCHUCK MY CHICKEN CHOW MEIN EVEN TO ADMIT THIS--SHE LOVED YOU ONCE.
HOW COULD YOU USE HER LIKE THAT? HOW COULD YOU NOW BE TRYING TO KILL HER?
ARE YOU THAT FAR GONE?
JUST ENLIGHTENED, WILSON.
WHAT YOU SAID TO ME THE OTHER DAY ABOUT OUR LITTLE LOVE TRIANGLE--ABOUT HOW I TORMENTED MYSELF THAT SHE ALWAYS LOVED YOU MORE?
IT'S TRUE.
IT TOOK ME A WHILE, BUT I EVENTUALLY REALIZED THE ONLY REASON I'VE EVER WANTED HER--WAS SO YOU COULDN'T HAVE HER. AND WHEN I CAME TO TERMS WITH THAT--
--I FINALLY KNEW HOW EXPENDABLE SHE WAS.
BLAM
SIMILAR TO HOW OUR LARGE FELINE FRIENDS PRESENTLY FIND YOU, DON'T YOU THINK?
Um... YOU FELLAS WOULDN'T HAPPEN TO BE OF THE "COWARDLY" VARIETY NOW, WOULD YA?

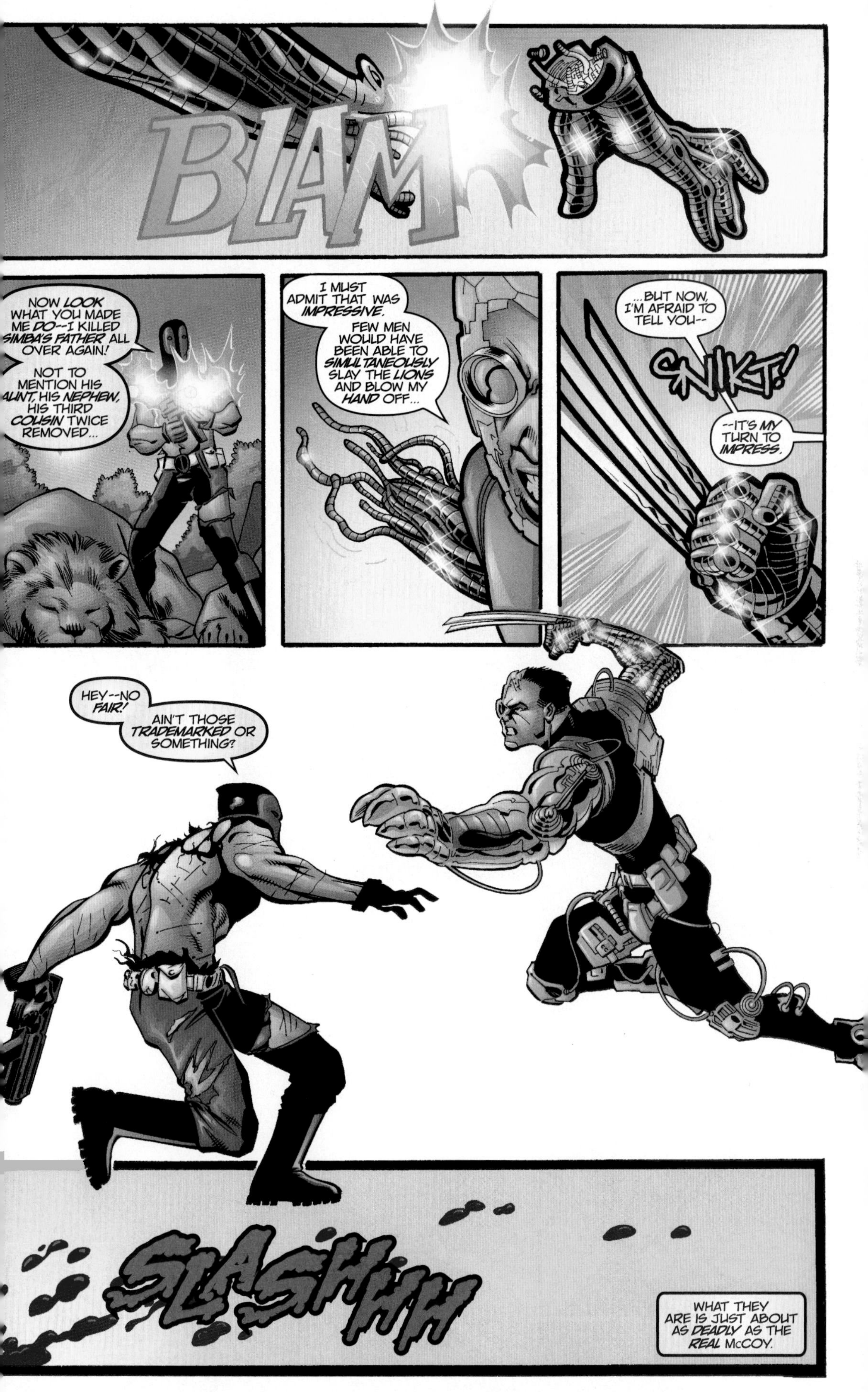
BLAM
NOW LOOK WHAT YOU MADE ME DO--I KILLED SIMBA'S FATHER ALL OVER AGAIN!
NOT TO MENTION HIS AUNT, HIS NEPHEW, HIS THIRD COUSIN TWICE REMOVED...
I MUST ADMIT THAT WAS IMPRESSIVE.
FEW MEN WOULD HAVE BEEN ABLE TO SIMULTANEOUSLY SLAY THE LIONS AND BLOW MY HAND OFF...
...BUT NOW, I'M AFRAID TO TELL YOU--
SNIKT!
--IT'S MY TURN TO IMPRESS.
HEY--NO FAIR!
AIN'T THOSE TRADEMARKED OR SOMETHING?
SLASHHH
WHAT THEY ARE IS JUST ABOUT AS DEADLY AS THE REAL McCOY.

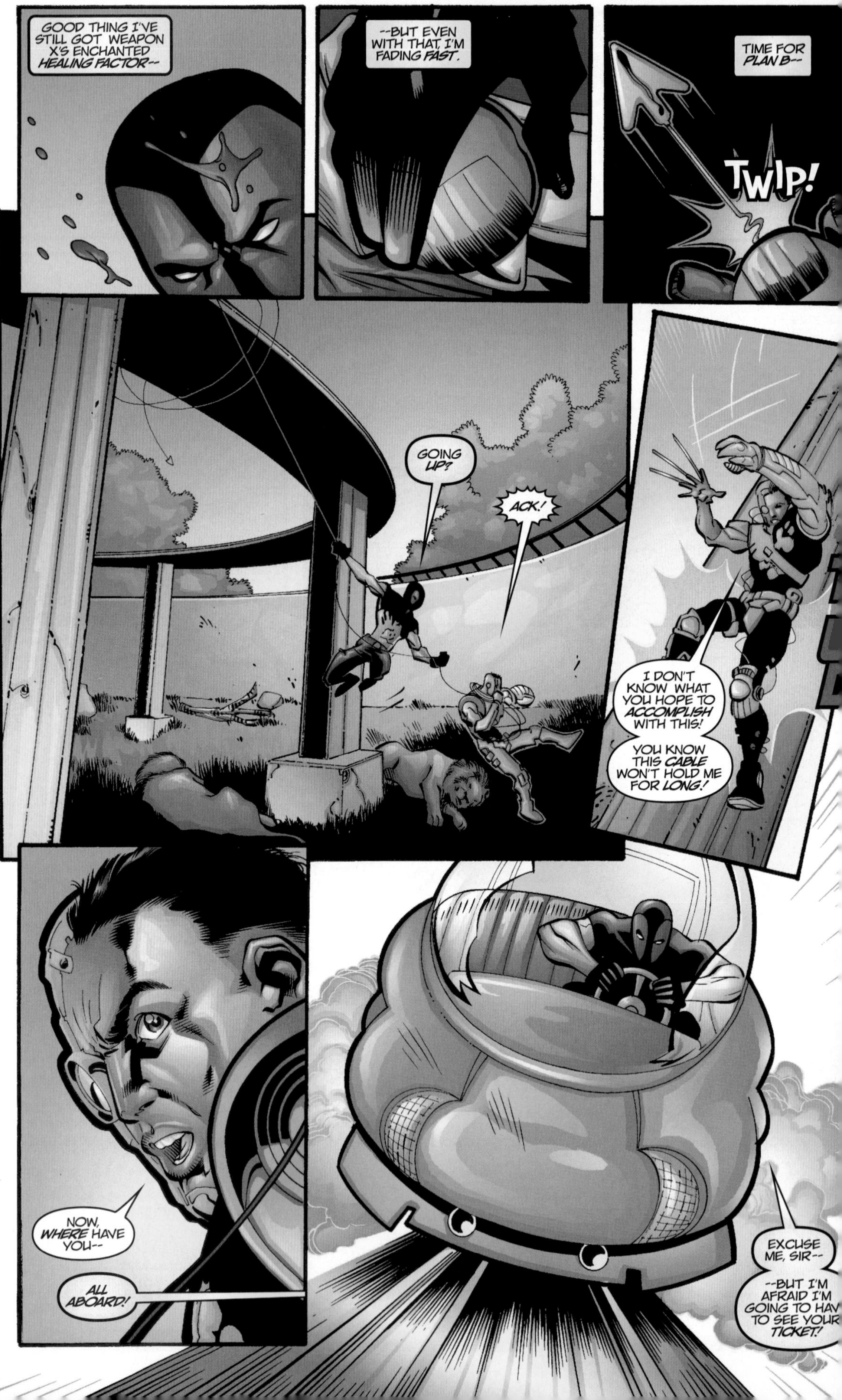

GOOD THING I'VE STILL GOT WEAPON X'S ENCHANTED *HEALING FACTOR*--
--BUT EVEN WITH THAT, I'M FADING *FAST*.
TIME FOR *PLAN B*--
TWIP!
GOING *UP*?
ACK!
I DON'T KNOW WHAT YOU HOPE TO *ACCOMPLISH* WITH THIS!
YOU KNOW THIS *CABLE* WON'T HOLD ME FOR *LONG*!
NOW, *WHERE* HAVE YOU--
ALL ABOARD!
EXCUSE ME, SIR--
--BUT I'M AFRAID I'M GOING TO HAV TO SEE YOUR *TICKET*!

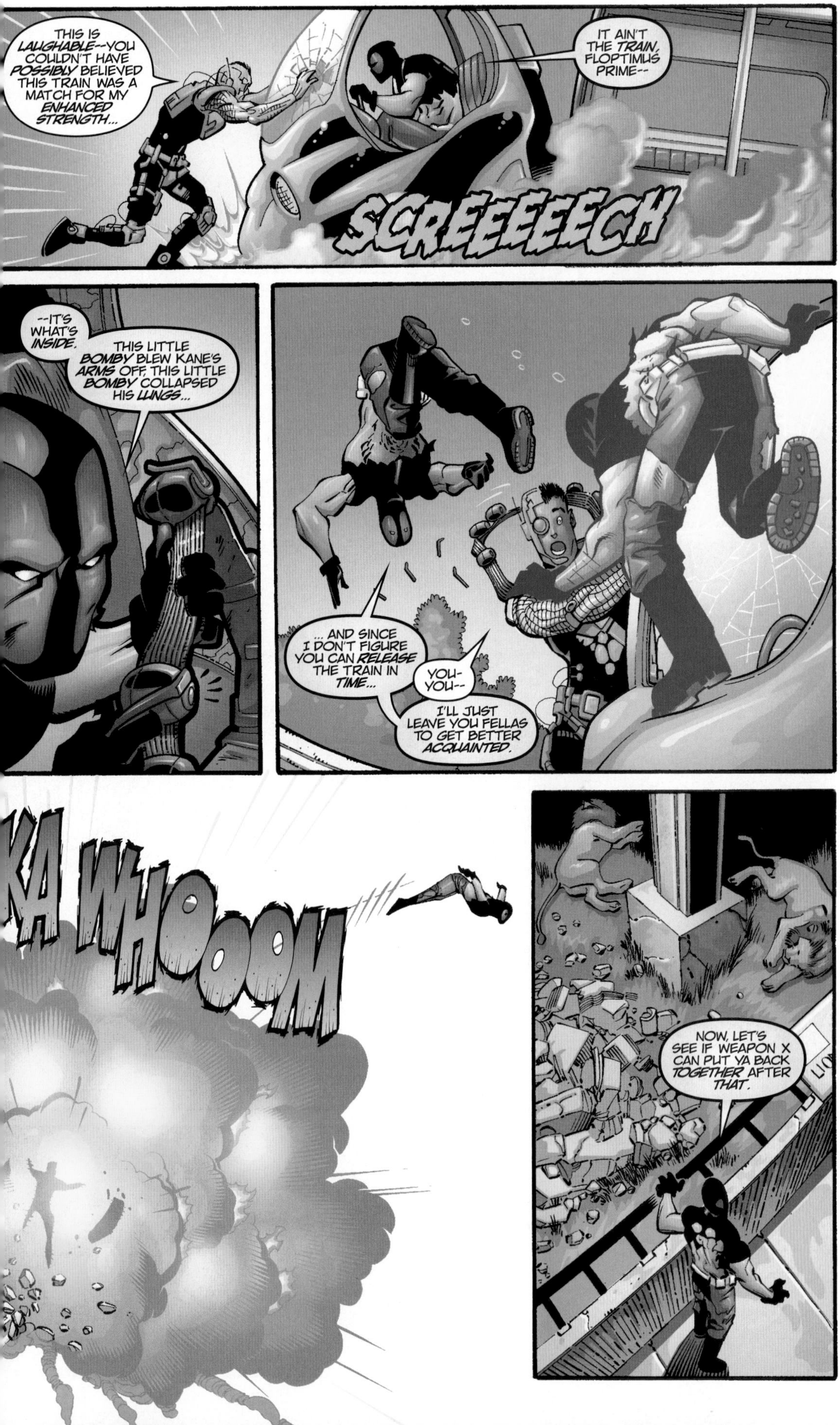
THIS IS LAUGHABLE--YOU COULDN'T HAVE POSSIBLY BELIEVED THIS TRAIN WAS A MATCH FOR MY ENHANCED STRENGTH...
IT AIN'T THE TRAIN, FLOPTIMUS PRIME--
SCREEEEEECH
--IT'S WHAT'S INSIDE.
THIS LITTLE BOMBY BLEW KANE'S ARMS OFF, THIS LITTLE BOMBY COLLAPSED HIS LUNGS...
... AND SINCE I DON'T FIGURE YOU CAN RELEASE THE TRAIN IN TIME...
YOU-YOU--
I'LL JUST LEAVE YOU FELLAS TO GET BETTER ACQUAINTED.
KA WHOOOM
NOW, LET'S SEE IF WEAPON X CAN PUT YA BACK TOGETHER AFTER THAT.

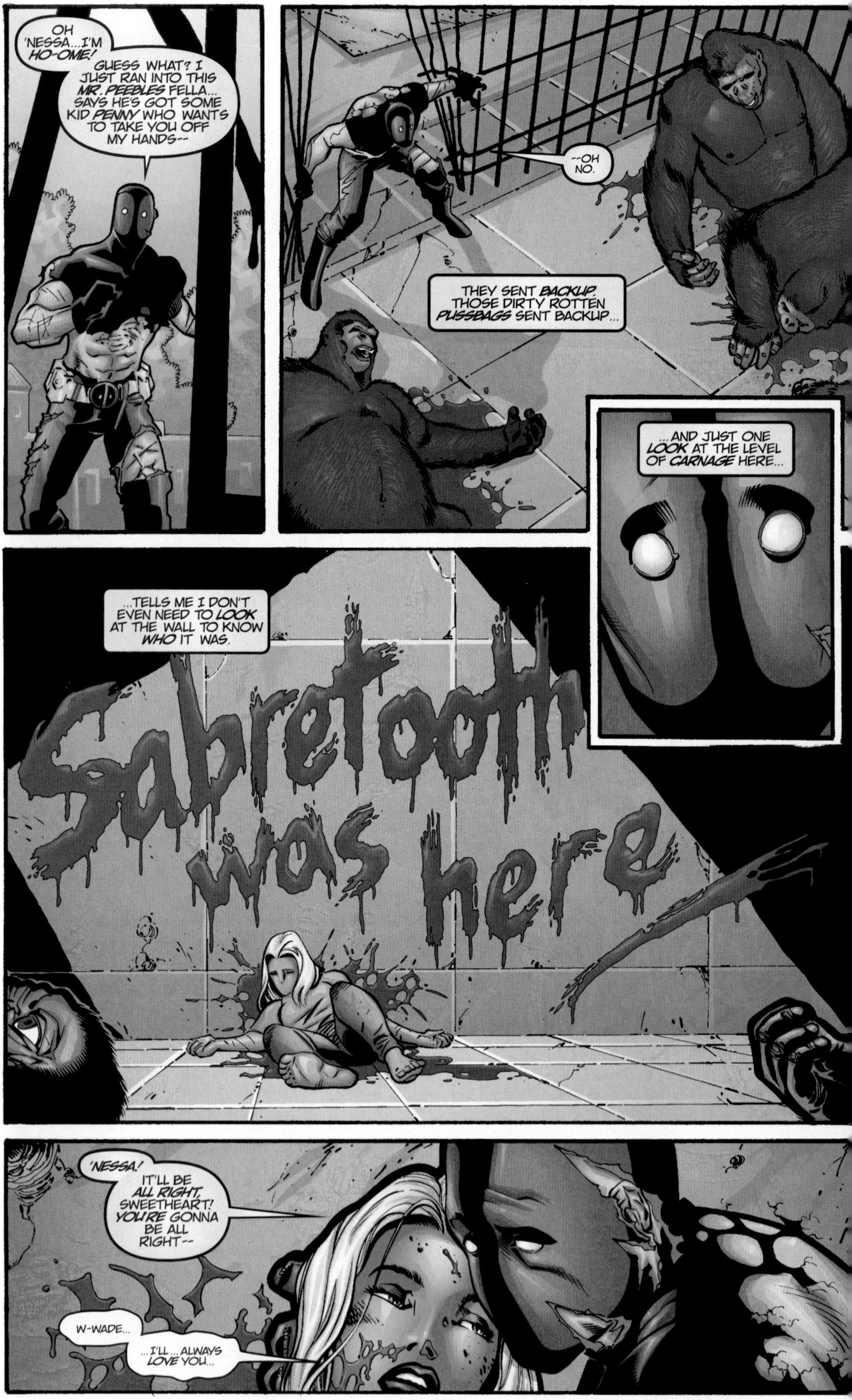
OH 'NESSA...I'M HO-OME!
GUESS WHAT? I JUST RAN INTO THIS MR. PEEBLES FELLA... SAYS HE'S GOT SOME KID PENNY WHO WANTS TO TAKE YOU OFF MY HANDS--
--OH NO.
THEY SENT BACKUP. THOSE DIRTY ROTTEN PUSSBAGS SENT BACKUP...
...AND JUST ONE LOOK AT THE LEVEL OF CARNAGE HERE...
...TELLS ME I DON'T EVEN NEED TO LOOK AT THE WALL TO KNOW WHO IT WAS.
Sabretooth was here
'NESSA!
IT'LL BE ALL RIGHT, SWEETHEART! YOU'RE GONNA BE ALL RIGHT--
W-WADE...
...I'LL... ALWAYS LOVE YOU...

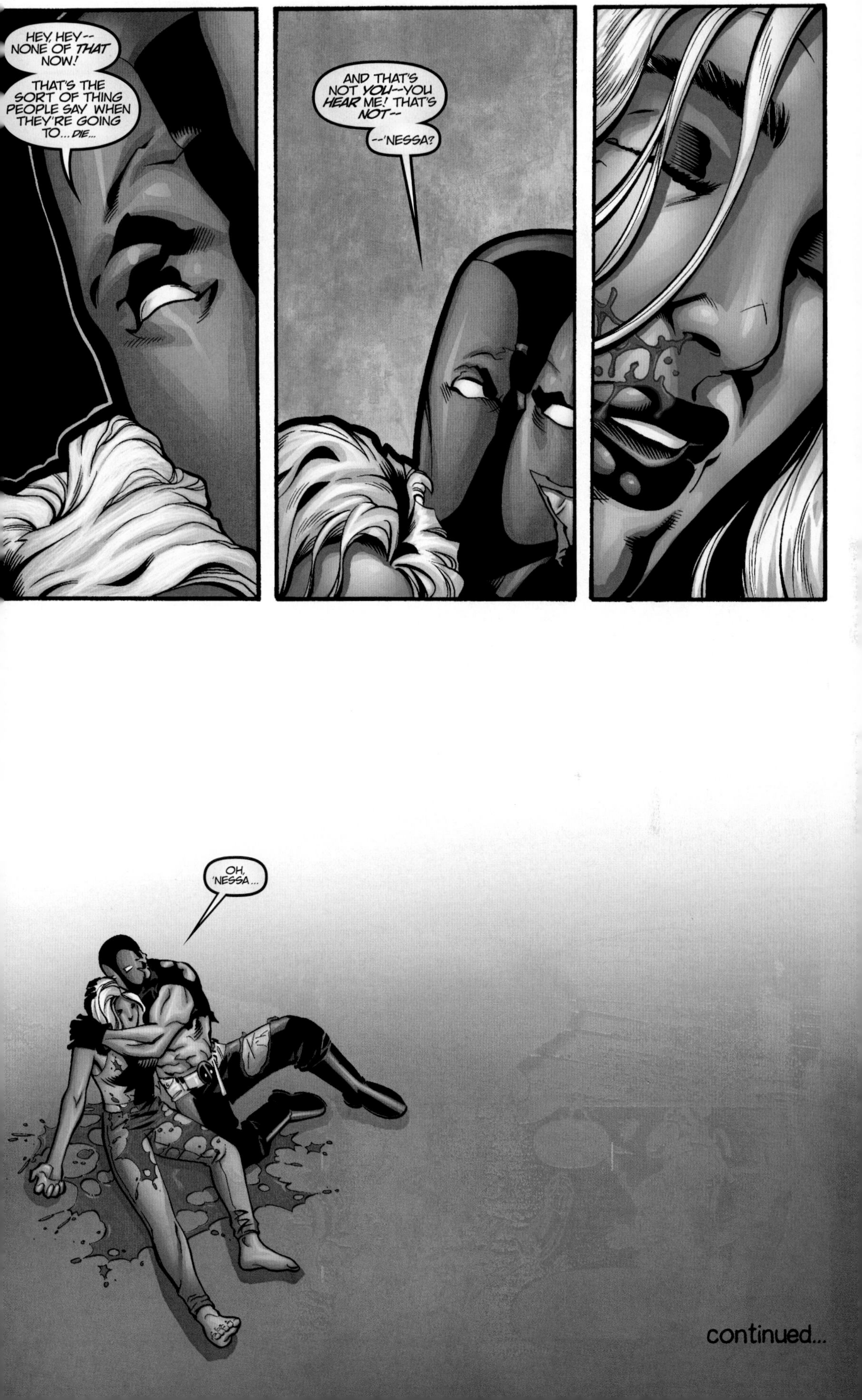
HEY, HEY-- NONE OF THAT NOW!
THAT'S THE SORT OF THING PEOPLE SAY WHEN THEY'RE GOING TO... DIE...
AND THAT'S NOT YOU--YOU HEAR ME! THAT'S NOT--
--'NESSA?
OH, 'NESSA...
continued...

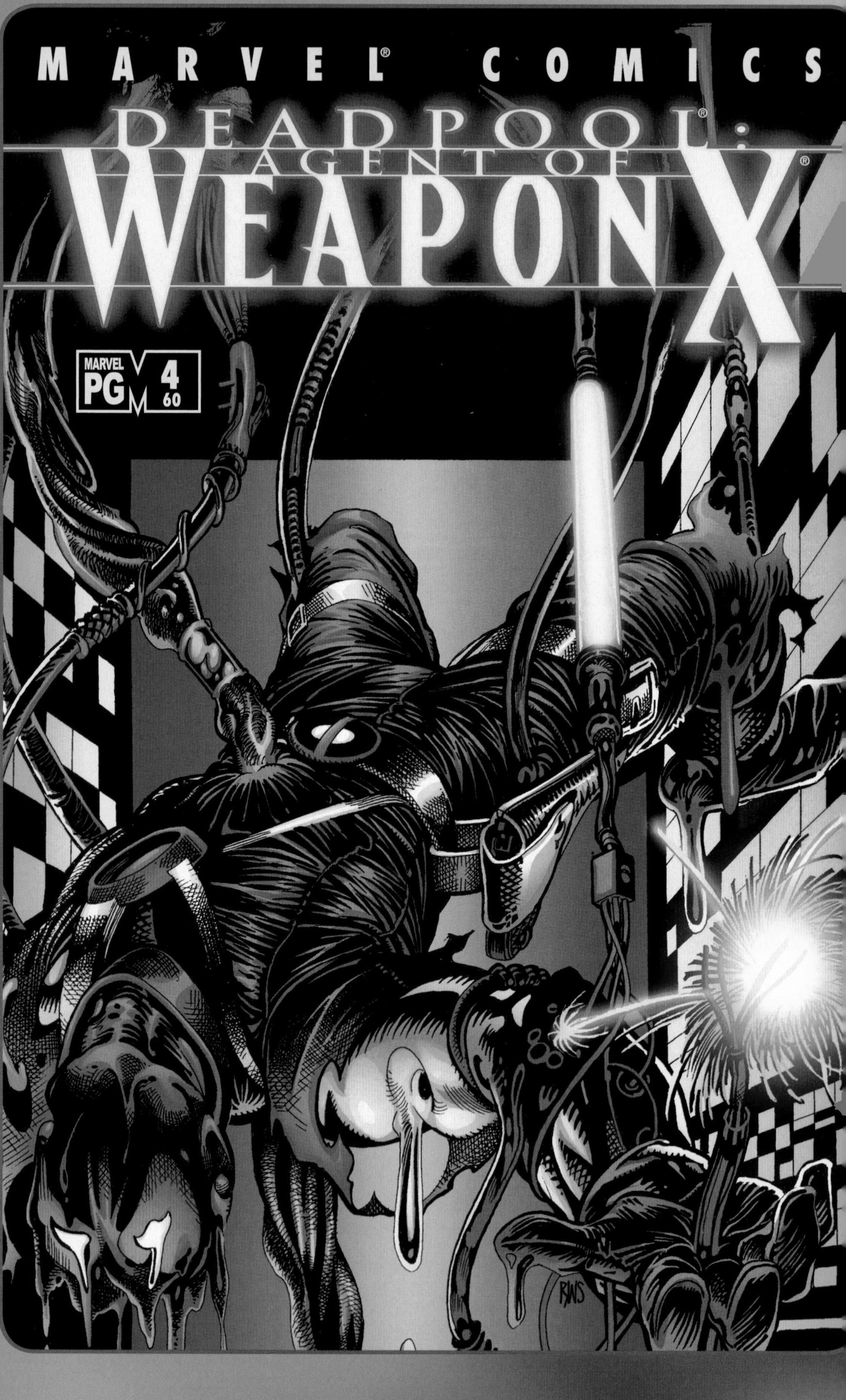
MARVEL® COMICS
DEADPOOL®: AGENT OF WEAPON X®
MARVEL PG
4
60
RWS

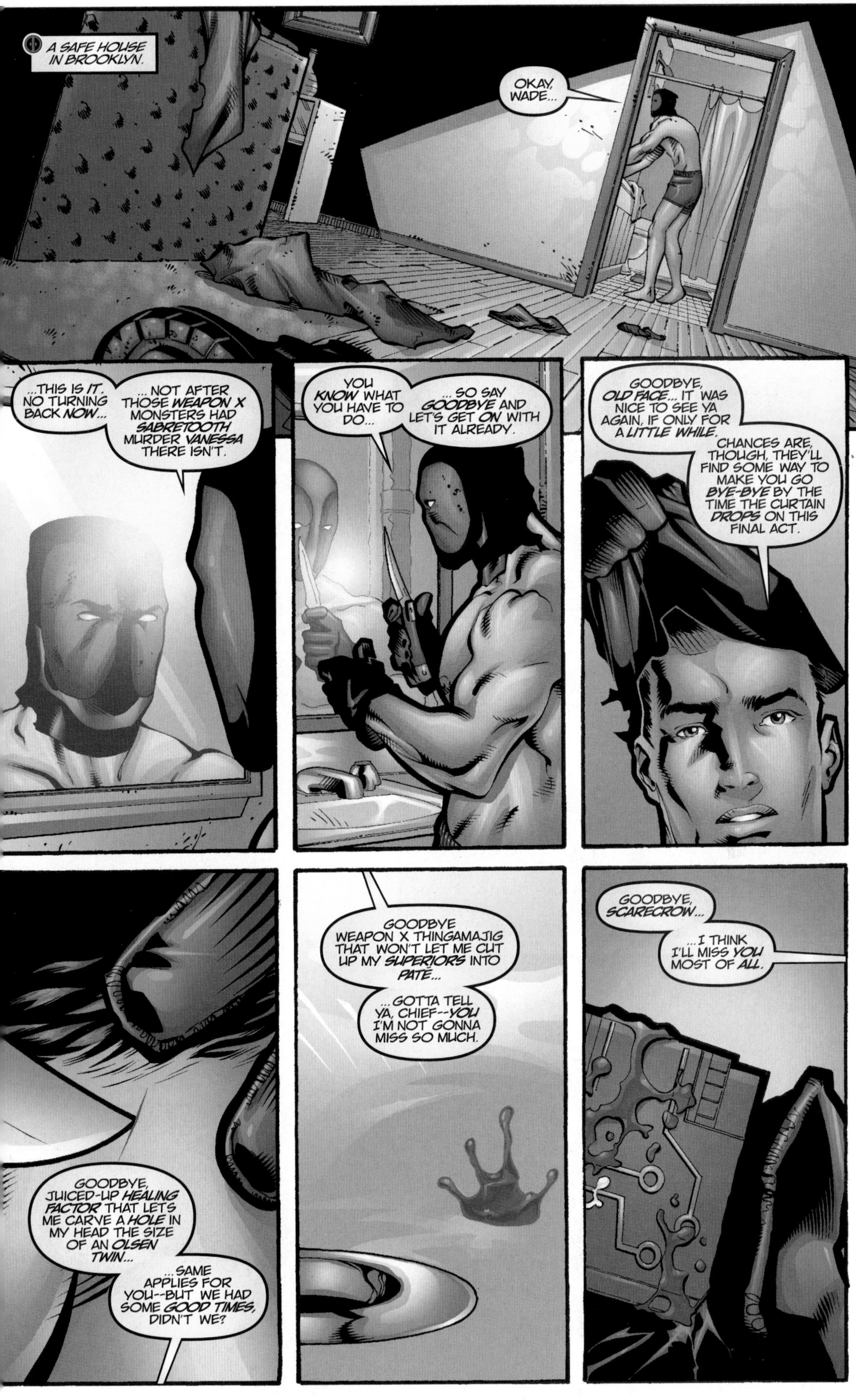
A SAFE HOUSE IN BROOKLYN.
OKAY, WADE...
...THIS IS IT. NO TURNING BACK NOW...
...NOT AFTER THOSE WEAPON X MONSTERS HAD SABRETOOTH MURDER VANESSA THERE ISN'T.
YOU KNOW WHAT YOU HAVE TO DO...
...SO SAY GOODBYE AND LET'S GET ON WITH IT ALREADY.
GOODBYE, OLD FACE... IT WAS NICE TO SEE YA AGAIN, IF ONLY FOR A LITTLE WHILE.
CHANCES ARE, THOUGH, THEY'LL FIND SOME WAY TO MAKE YOU GO BYE-BYE BY THE TIME THE CURTAIN DROPS ON THIS FINAL ACT.
GOODBYE, JUICED-UP HEALING FACTOR THAT LETS ME CARVE A HOLE IN MY HEAD THE SIZE OF AN OLSEN TWIN...
...SAME APPLIES FOR YOU--BUT WE HAD SOME GOOD TIMES, DIDN'T WE?
GOODBYE WEAPON X THINGAMAJIG THAT WON'T LET ME CUT UP MY SUPERIORS INTO PATÉ...
...GOTTA TELL YA, CHIEF--YOU I'M NOT GONNA MISS SO MUCH.
GOODBYE, SCARECROW...
...I THINK I'LL MISS YOU MOST OF ALL.

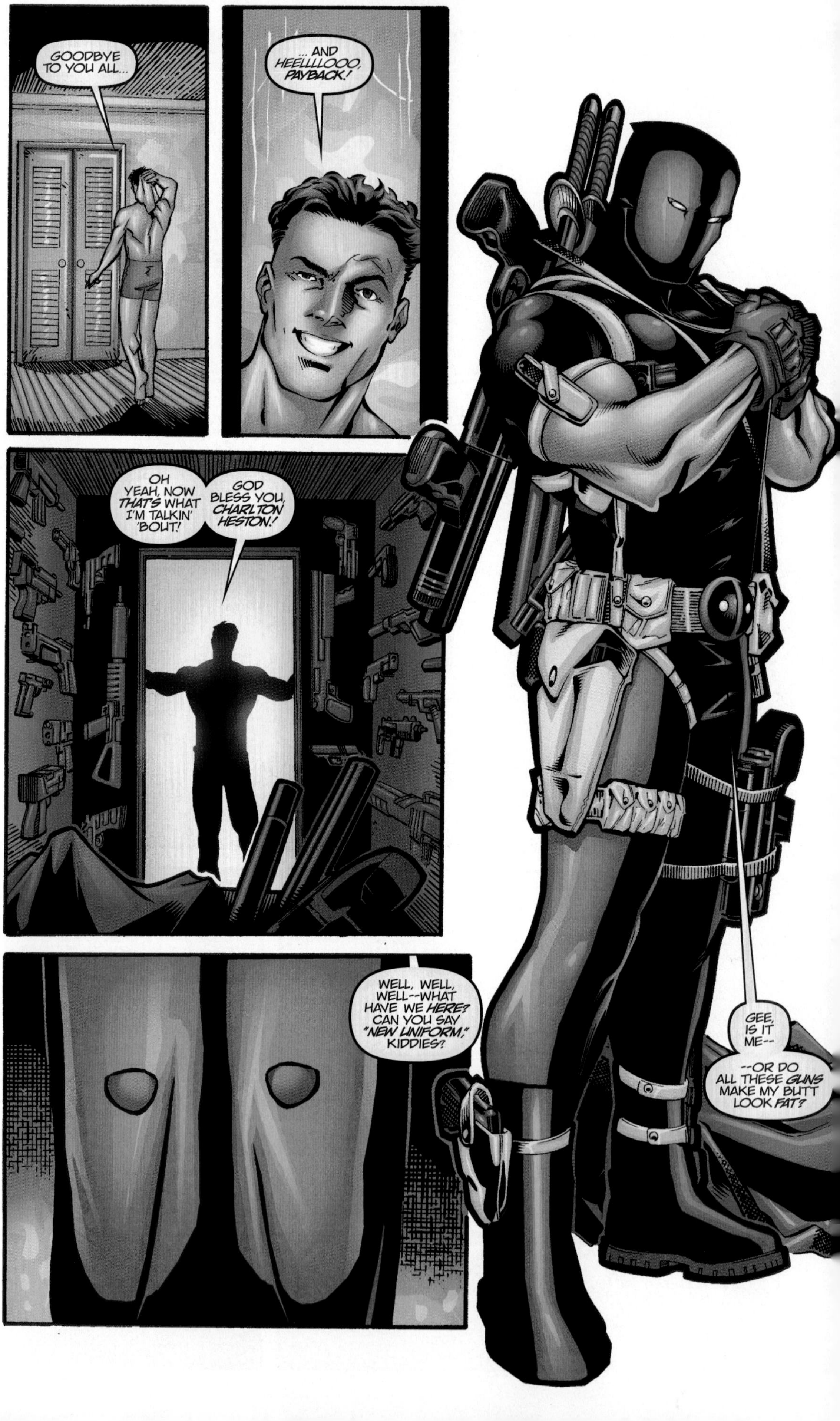
GOODBYE TO YOU ALL...
... AND HEELLLLOOO, PAYBACK!
OH YEAH, NOW THAT'S WHAT I'M TALKIN' 'BOUT!
GOD BLESS YOU, CHARLTON HESTON!
WELL, WELL, WELL--WHAT HAVE WE HERE? CAN YOU SAY "NEW UNIFORM," KIDDIES?
GEE, IS IT ME--
--OR DO ALL THESE GUNS MAKE MY BUTT LOOK FAT?

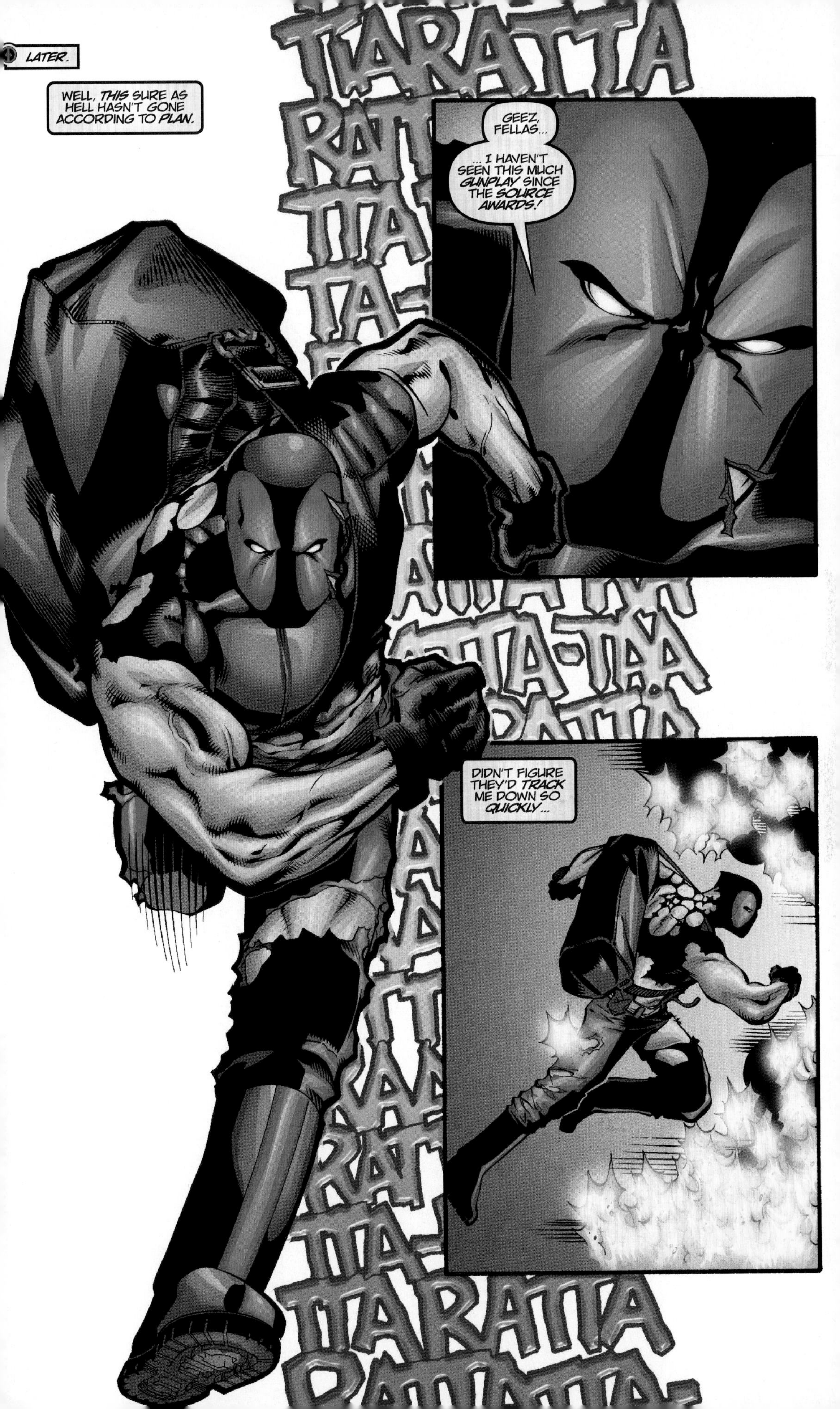
LATER.
WELL, THIS SURE AS HELL HASN'T GONE ACCORDING TO PLAN.
TTARATTA RATTA TTA-TA-
GEEZ, FELLAS...
... I HAVEN'T SEEN THIS MUCH GUNPLAY SINCE THE SOURCE AWARDS!
DIDN'T FIGURE THEY'D TRACK ME DOWN SO QUICKLY...
TTARATTA

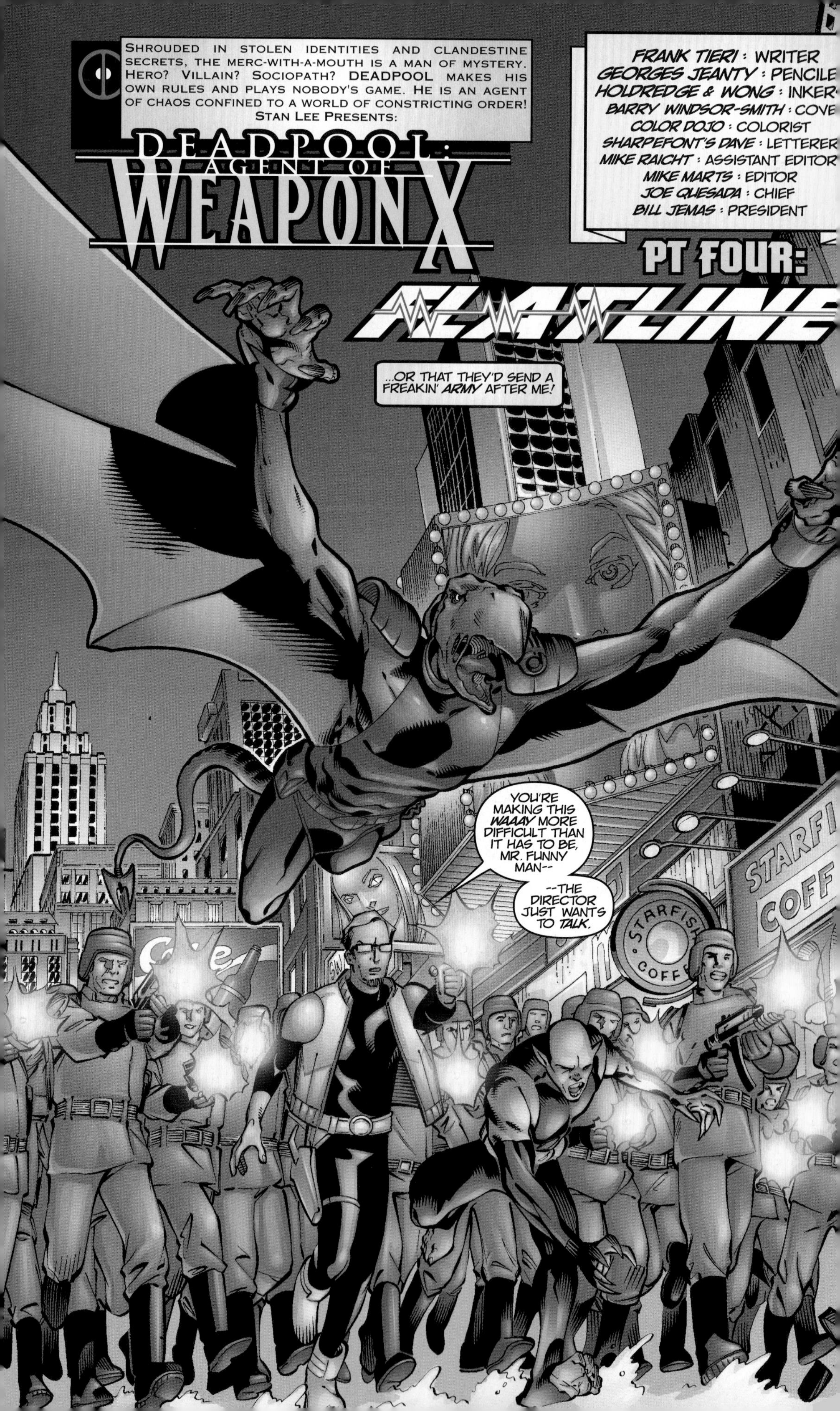

SHROUDED IN STOLEN IDENTITIES AND CLANDESTINE SECRETS, THE MERC-WITH-A-MOUTH IS A MAN OF MYSTERY. HERO? VILLAIN? SOCIOPATH? DEADPOOL MAKES HIS OWN RULES AND PLAYS NOBODY'S GAME. HE IS AN AGENT OF CHAOS CONFINED TO A WORLD OF CONSTRICTING ORDER!
STAN LEE PRESENTS:
DEADPOOL: AGENT OF WEAPON X
FRANK TIERI : WRITER
GEORGES JEANTY : PENCILE
HOLDREDGE & WONG : INKER
BARRY WINDSOR-SMITH : COVE
COLOR DOJO : COLORIST
SHARPEFONT'S DAVE : LETTERER
MIKE RAICHT : ASSISTANT EDITOR
MIKE MARTS : EDITOR
JOE QUESADA : CHIEF
BILL JEMAS : PRESIDENT
PT FOUR:
...OR THAT THEY'D SEND A FREAKIN' ARMY AFTER ME!
YOU'RE MAKING THIS WAAAY MORE DIFFICULT THAN IT HAS TO BE, MR. FUNNY MAN--
--THE DIRECTOR JUST WANTS TO TALK.
STARFISH COFF

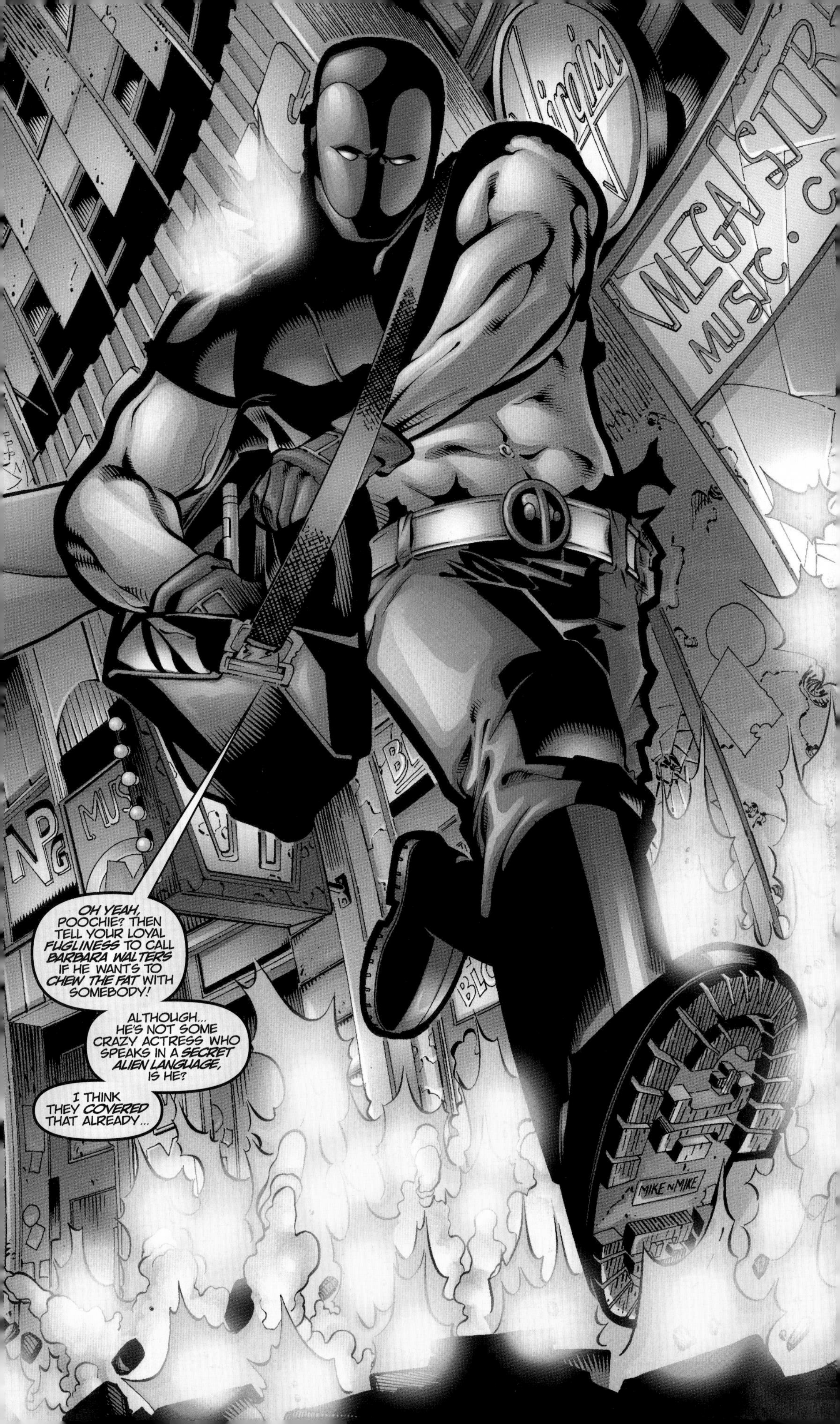
Virgin
MEGASTOR
MUSIC.
OH YEAH, POOCHIE? THEN TELL YOUR LOYAL FUGLINESS TO CALL BARBARA WALTERS IF HE WANTS TO CHEW THE FAT WITH SOMEBODY!
ALTHOUGH... HE'S NOT SOME CRAZY ACTRESS WHO SPEAKS IN A SECRET ALIEN LANGUAGE, IS HE?
I THINK THEY COVERED THAT ALREADY...
MIKE N MIKE

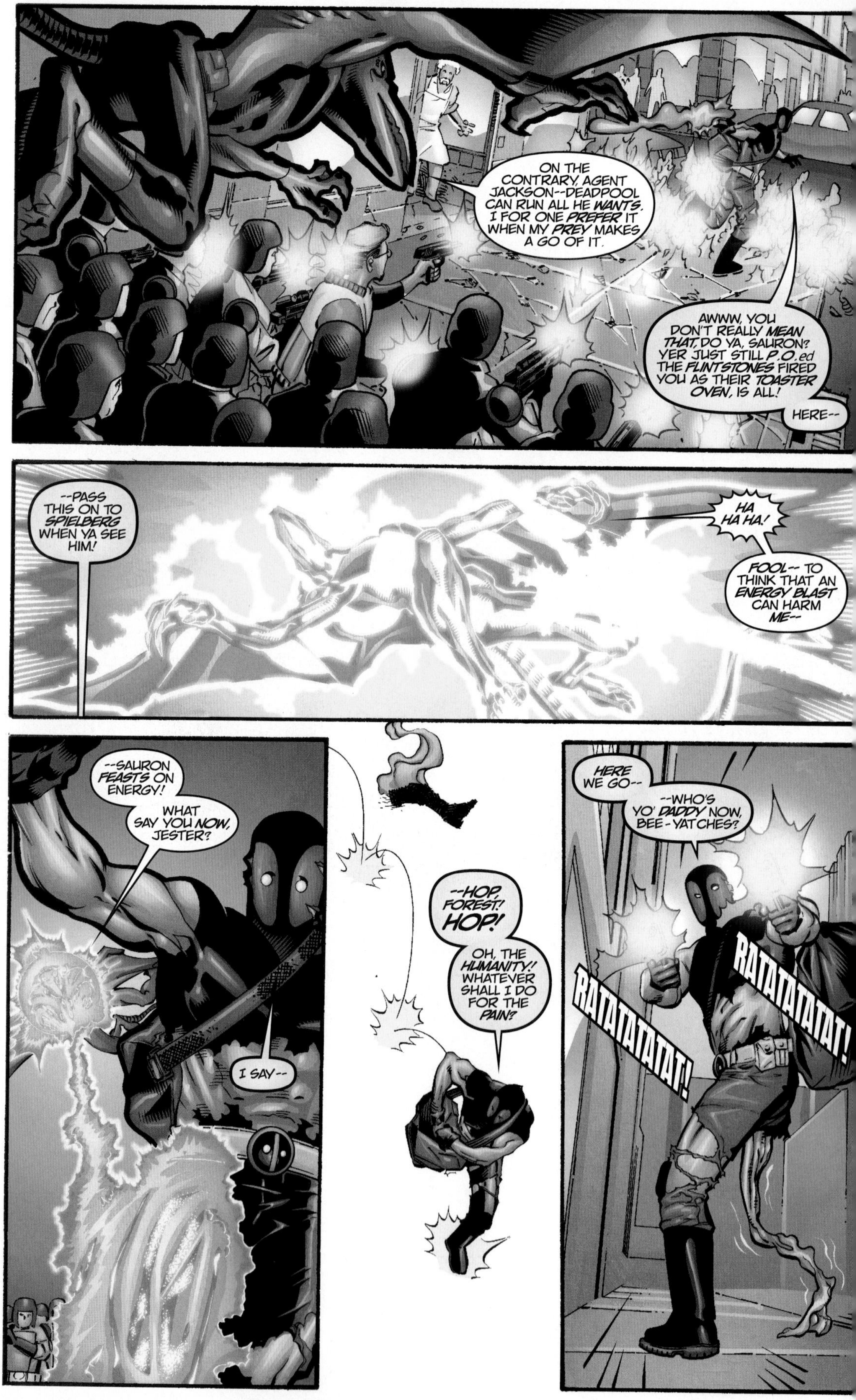
ON THE CONTRARY, AGENT JACKSON--DEADPOOL CAN RUN ALL HE WANTS. I FOR ONE PREFER IT WHEN MY PREY MAKES A GO OF IT.
AWWW, YOU DON'T REALLY MEAN THAT, DO YA, SAURON? YER JUST STILL P.O.ed THE FLINTSTONES FIRED YOU AS THEIR TOASTER OVEN, IS ALL!
HERE--
--PASS THIS ON TO SPIELBERG WHEN YA SEE HIM!
HA HA HA!
FOOL-- TO THINK THAT AN ENERGY BLAST CAN HARM ME--
--SAURON FEASTS ON ENERGY!
WHAT SAY YOU NOW, JESTER?
I SAY--
--HOP, FOREST! HOP!
OH, THE HUMANITY! WHATEVER SHALL I DO FOR THE PAIN?
HERE WE GO--
--WHO'S YO' DADDY NOW, BEE-YATCHES?
RATATATATAT!
RATATATATAT!

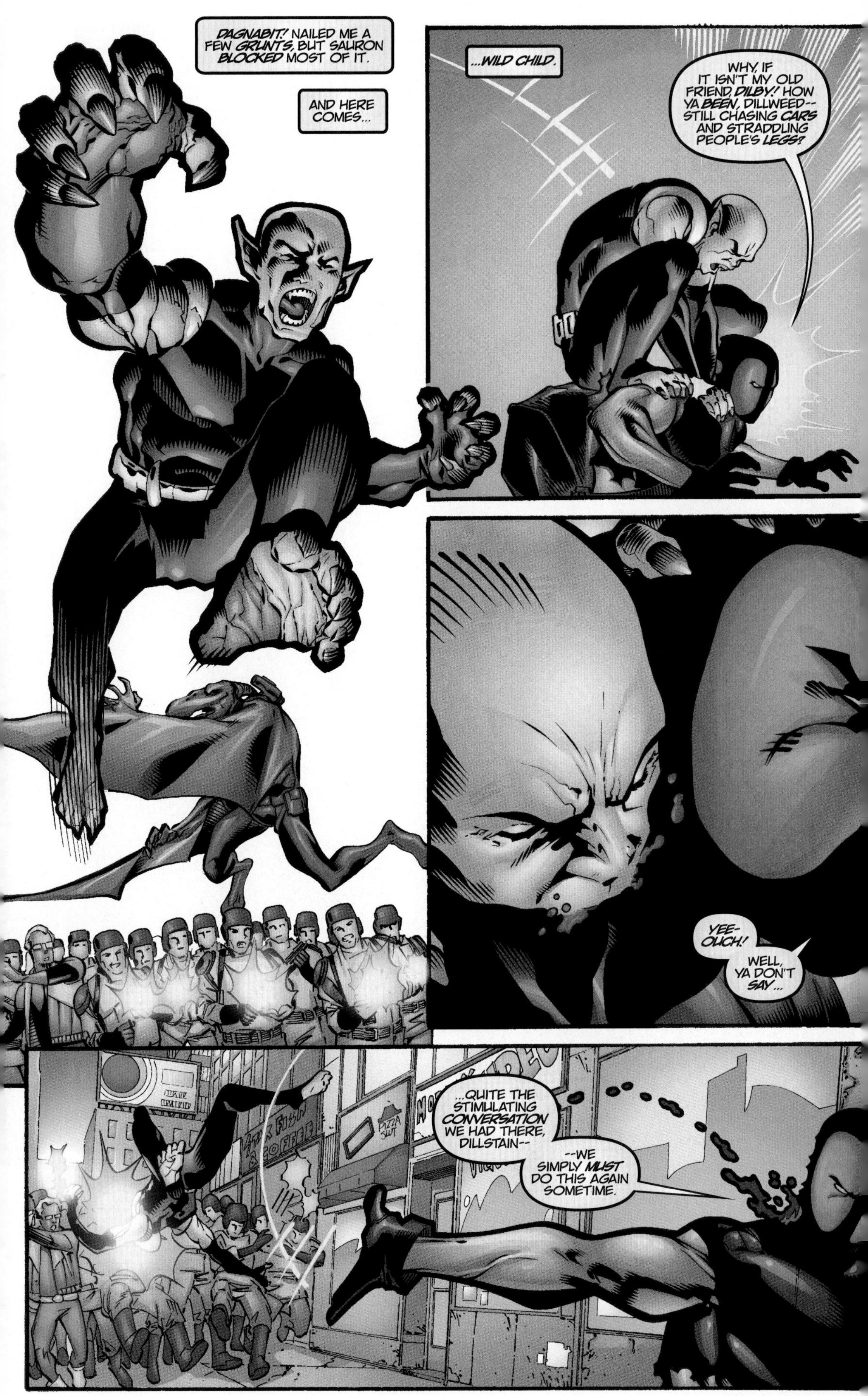
DAGNABIT! NAILED ME A FEW GRUNTS, BUT SAURON BLOCKED MOST OF IT.
AND HERE COMES...
...WILD CHILD.
WHY, IF IT ISN'T MY OLD FRIEND DILBY! HOW YA BEEN, DILLWEED-- STILL CHASING CARS AND STRADDLING PEOPLE'S LEGS?
YEE-OUCH!
WELL, YA DON'T SAY...
...QUITE THE STIMULATING CONVERSATION WE HAD THERE, DILLSTAIN--
--WE SIMPLY MUST DO THIS AGAIN SOMETIME.
PIZZA SLUT
COFFEE

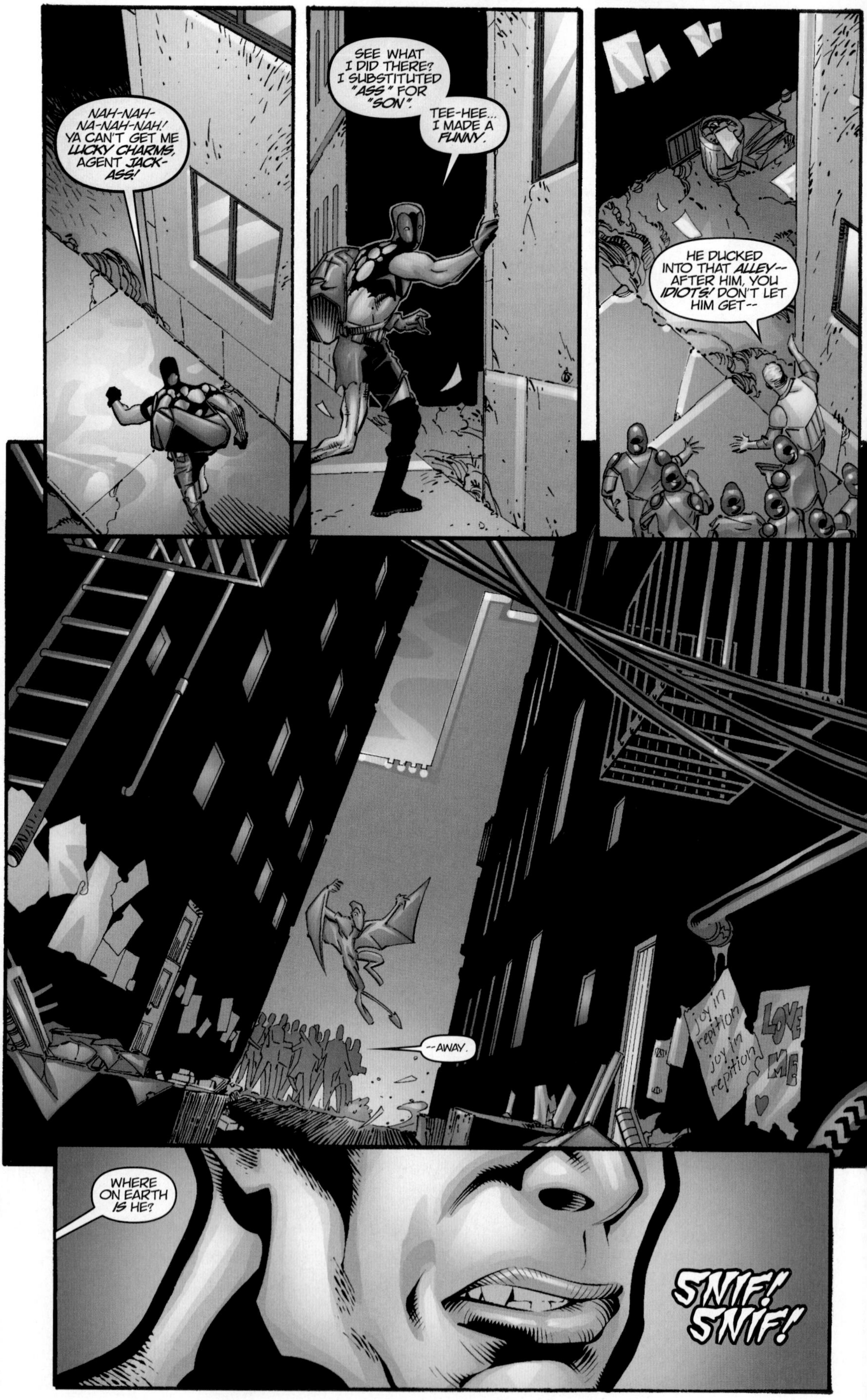
NAH-NAH-NA-NAH-NAH! YA CAN'T GET ME LUCKY CHARMS, AGENT JACK-ASS!
SEE WHAT I DID THERE? I SUBSTITUTED "ASS" FOR "SON".
TEE-HEE... I MADE A FUNNY.
HE DUCKED INTO THAT ALLEY-- AFTER HIM, YOU IDIOTS! DON'T LET HIM GET--
--AWAY.
joy in repition joy in repition
LOVE ME
WHERE ON EARTH IS HE?
SNIF! SNIF!

Hmm... NOWHERE TO BE FOUND... BUT WILD CHILD'S SNOOT SHOULD TELL US OTHERWISE...

SIR! I THINK WILD CHILD'S PICKED UP HIS SCENT!

EXCELLENT... SO IS THAT...?

SNIF! SNIF!

YEP... MY BVD'S. THAT IS THE SCENT ROVER'S PICKING UP...

...PARDON MOI IF THEY'RE A LITTLE RIPE, BUT I JUST HAD MEXICAN AND, WELL, YA KNOW...

...ACCIDENTS WILL HAPPEN.

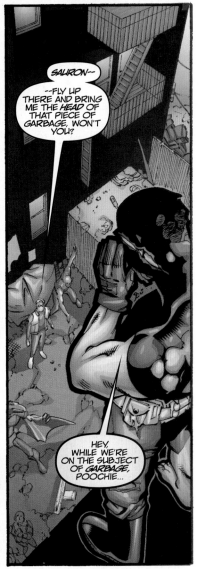

SAURON--

--FLY UP THERE AND BRING ME THE HEAD OF THAT PIECE OF GARBAGE, WON'T YOU?

HEY, WHILE WE'RE ON THE SUBJECT OF GARBAGE, POOCHIE...

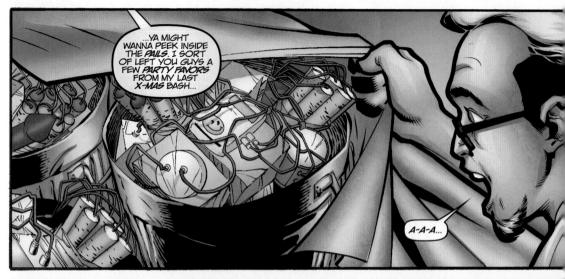

...YA MIGHT WANNA PEEK INSIDE THE *PAILS.* I SORT OF LEFT YOU GUYS A FEW *PARTY FAVORS* FROM MY LAST *X-MAS BASH...*

A-A-A...

I BELIEVE THE WORD YOU'RE LOOKING FOR IS...

CLICK

AAAAAHHHH!

KA WHOOOM

Heh heh... THE WORD YOU'RE LOOKING FOR IS *"AAAHHH"...*

...SOMETIMES I JUST *KILL* MYSELF

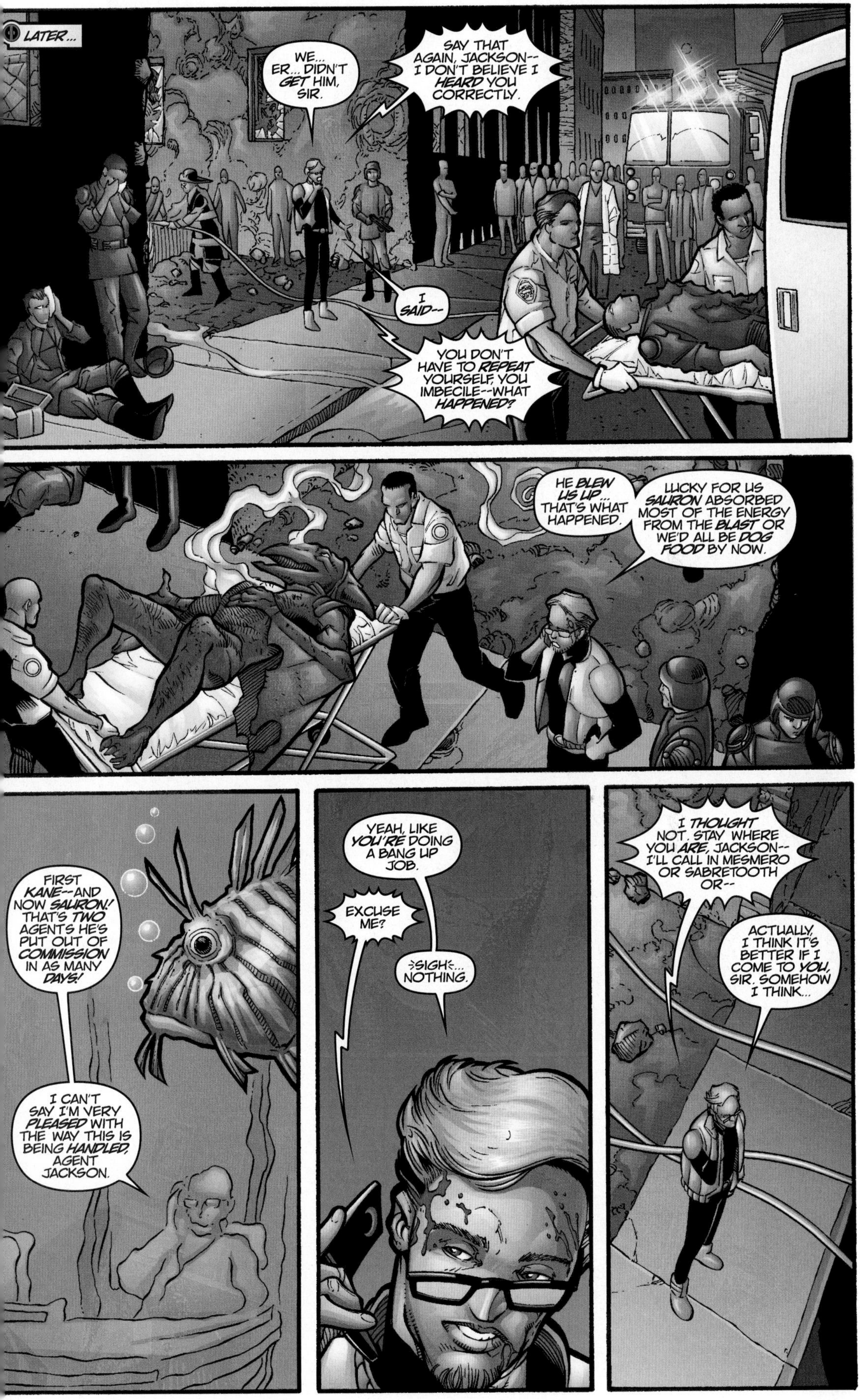
LATER...
WE... ER... DIDN'T GET HIM, SIR.
SAY THAT AGAIN, JACKSON-- I DON'T BELIEVE I HEARD YOU CORRECTLY.
I SAID--
YOU DON'T HAVE TO REPEAT YOURSELF, YOU IMBECILE--WHAT HAPPENED?
HE BLEW US UP... THAT'S WHAT HAPPENED.
LUCKY FOR US SAURON ABSORBED MOST OF THE ENERGY FROM THE BLAST OR WE'D ALL BE DOG FOOD BY NOW.
FIRST KANE--AND NOW SAURON! THAT'S TWO AGENTS HE'S PUT OUT OF COMMISSION IN AS MANY DAYS!
I CAN'T SAY I'M VERY PLEASED WITH THE WAY THIS IS BEING HANDLED, AGENT JACKSON.
YEAH, LIKE YOU'RE DOING A BANG UP JOB.
EXCUSE ME?
SIGH... NOTHING.
I THOUGHT NOT. STAY WHERE YOU ARE, JACKSON-- I'LL CALL IN MESMERO OR SABRETOOTH OR--
ACTUALLY, I THINK IT'S BETTER IF I COME TO YOU, SIR. SOMEHOW I THINK...

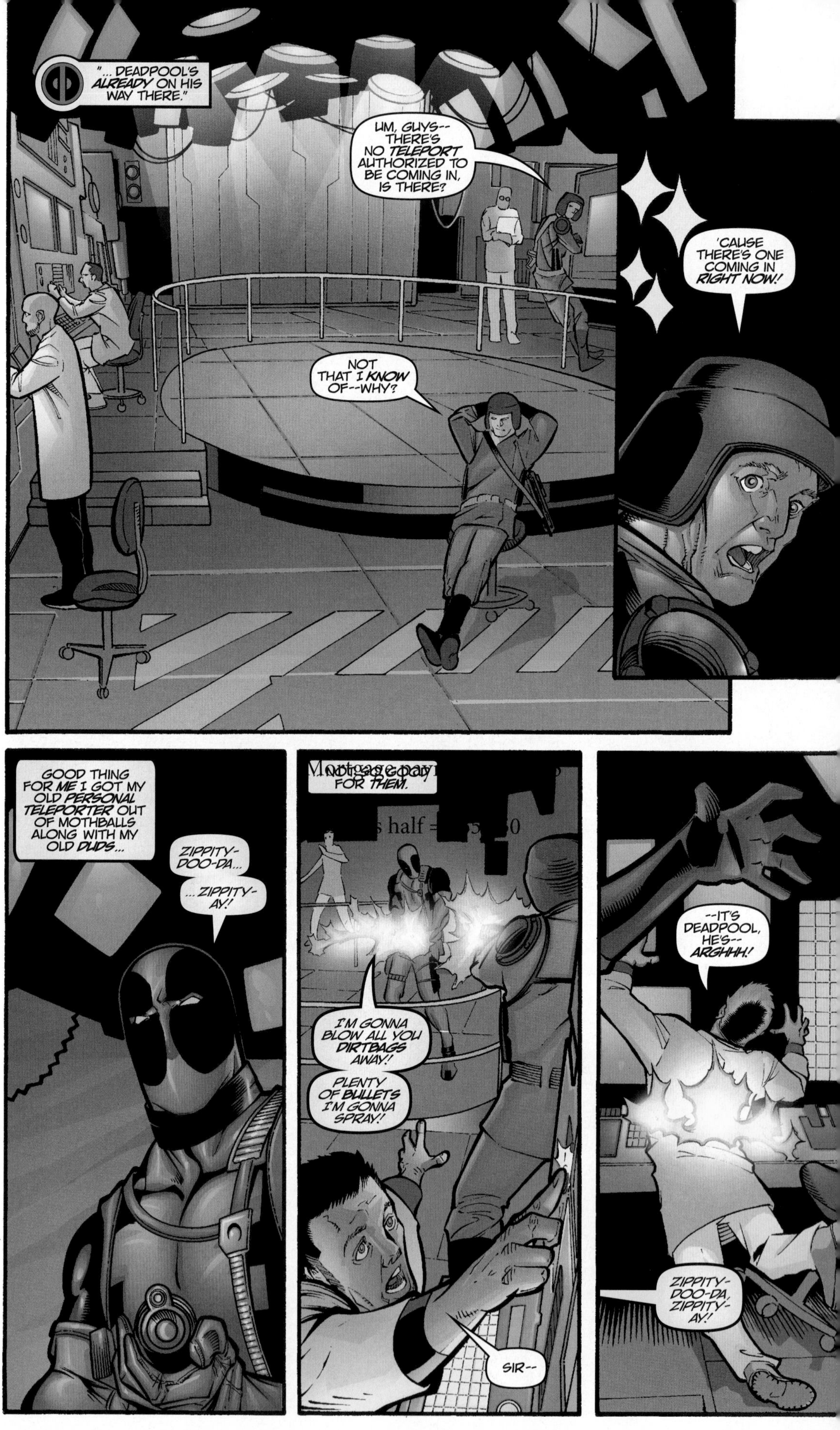
"... DEADPOOL'S ALREADY ON HIS WAY THERE."
UM, GUYS-- THERE'S NO TELEPORT AUTHORIZED TO BE COMING IN, IS THERE?
NOT THAT I KNOW OF--WHY?
'CAUSE THERE'S ONE COMING IN RIGHT NOW!
GOOD THING FOR ME I GOT MY OLD PERSONAL TELEPORTER OUT OF MOTHBALLS ALONG WITH MY OLD DUDS...
ZIPPITY-DOO-DA...
... ZIPPITY-AY!
FOR THEM.
Mortgage pay[redacted]
[redacted]s half = [redacted]
I'M GONNA BLOW ALL YOU DIRTBAGS AWAY!
PLENTY OF BULLETS I'M GONNA SPRAY!
SIR--
--IT'S DEADPOOL, HE'S-- ARGHHH!
ZIPPITY-DOO-DA, ZIPPITY-AY!

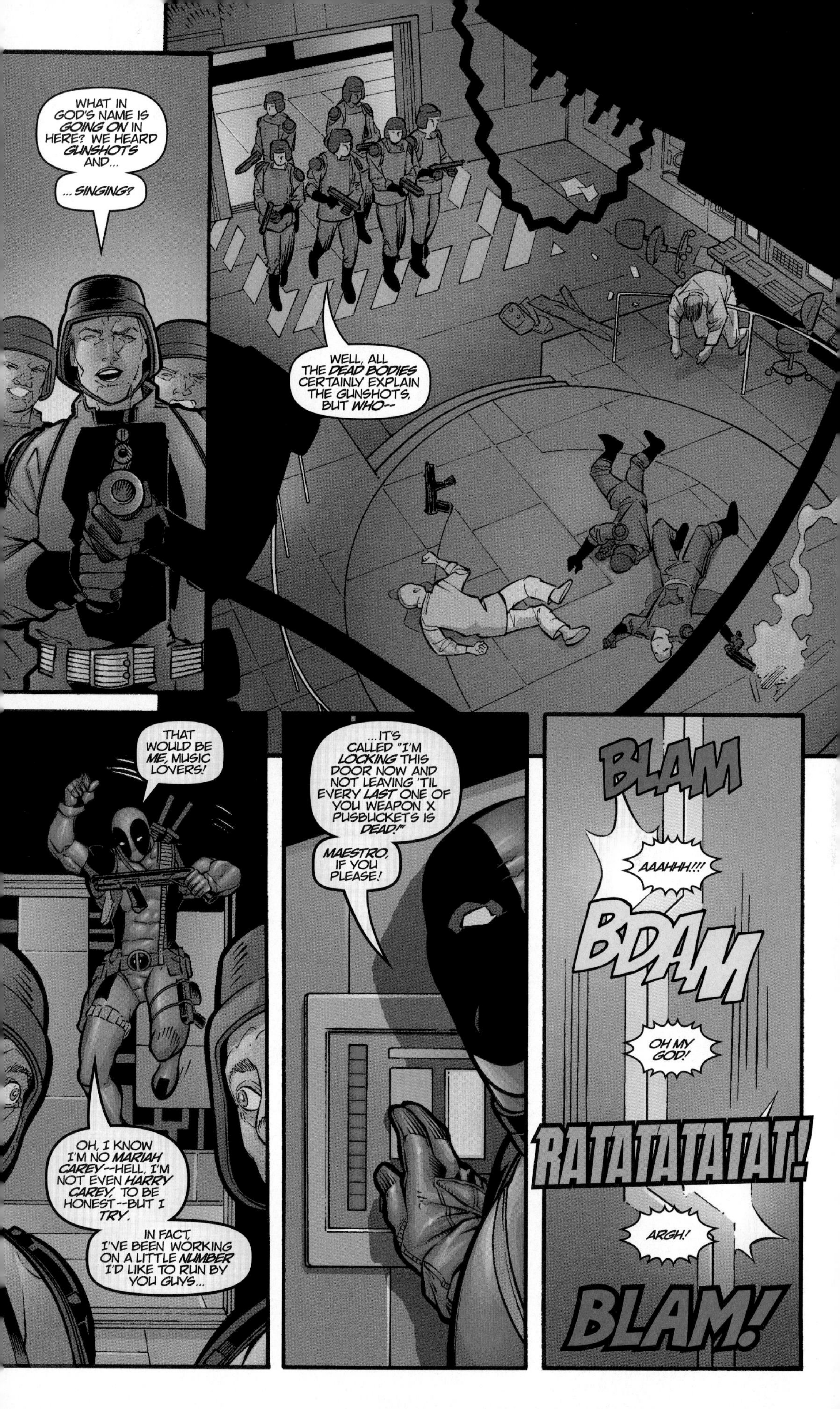
WHAT IN GOD'S NAME IS GOING ON IN HERE? WE HEARD GUNSHOTS AND...
...SINGING?
WELL, ALL THE DEAD BODIES CERTAINLY EXPLAIN THE GUNSHOTS, BUT WHO--
THAT WOULD BE ME, MUSIC LOVERS!
OH, I KNOW I'M NO MARIAH CAREY--HELL, I'M NOT EVEN HARRY CAREY, TO BE HONEST--BUT I TRY.
IN FACT, I'VE BEEN WORKING ON A LITTLE NUMBER I'D LIKE TO RUN BY YOU GUYS...
...IT'S CALLED "I'M LOCKING THIS DOOR NOW AND NOT LEAVING 'TIL EVERY LAST ONE OF YOU WEAPON X PUSBUCKETS IS DEAD!"
MAESTRO, IF YOU PLEASE!
BLAM
AAAHHH!!!
BDAM
OH MY GOD!
RATATATATAT!
ARGH!
BLAM!

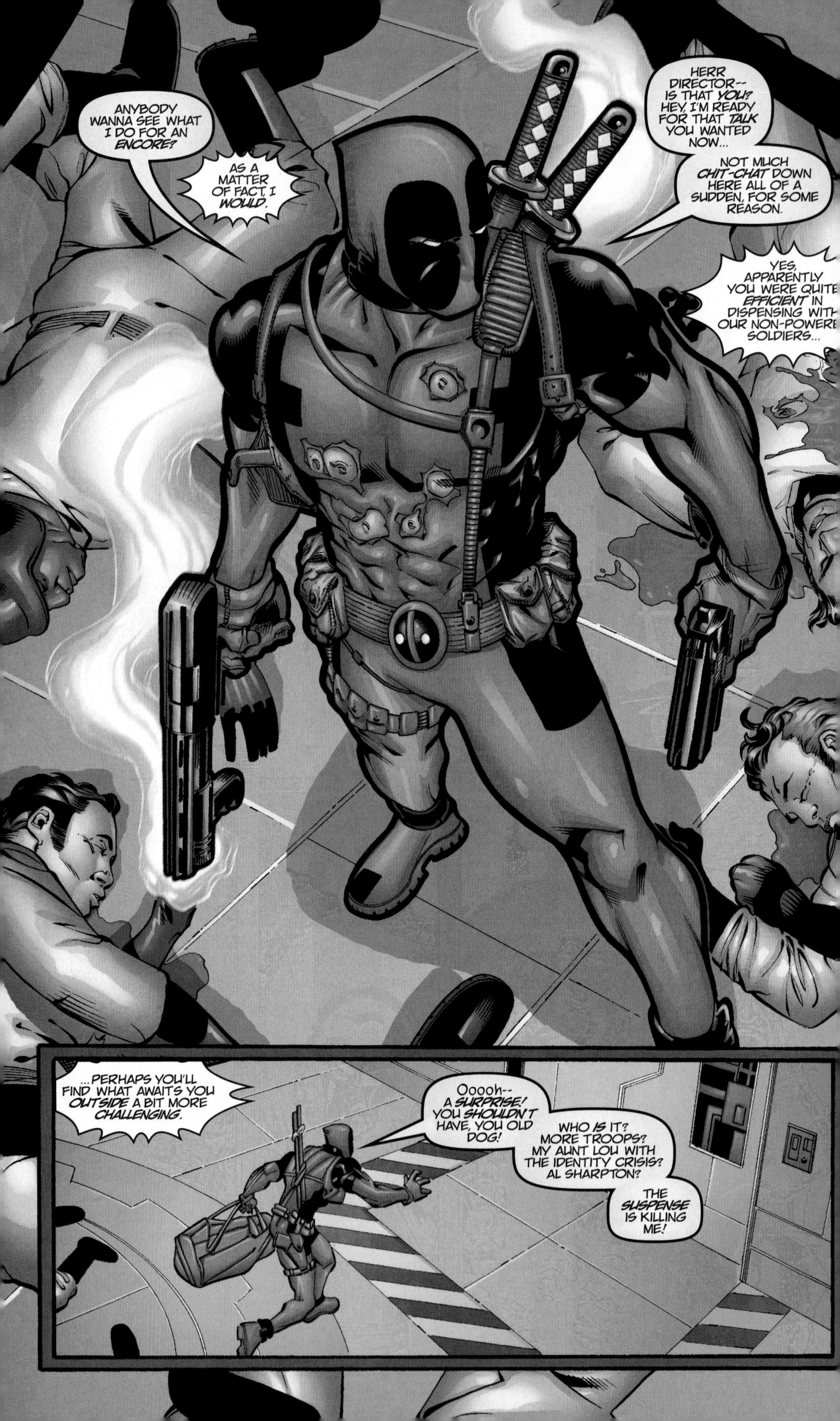
ANYBODY WANNA SEE WHAT I DO FOR AN ENCORE?
AS A MATTER OF FACT, I WOULD.
HERR DIRECTOR-- IS THAT YOU? HEY, I'M READY FOR THAT TALK YOU WANTED NOW...
NOT MUCH CHIT-CHAT DOWN HERE ALL OF A SUDDEN, FOR SOME REASON.
YES, APPARENTLY YOU WERE QUITE EFFICIENT IN DISPENSING WITH OUR NON-POWERE SOLDIERS...
...PERHAPS YOU'LL FIND WHAT AWAITS YOU OUTSIDE A BIT MORE CHALLENGING.
Ooooh-- A SURPRISE! YOU SHOULDN'T HAVE, YOU OLD DOG!
WHO IS IT? MORE TROOPS? MY AUNT LOU WITH THE IDENTITY CRISIS? AL SHARPTON?
THE SUSPENSE IS KILLING ME!

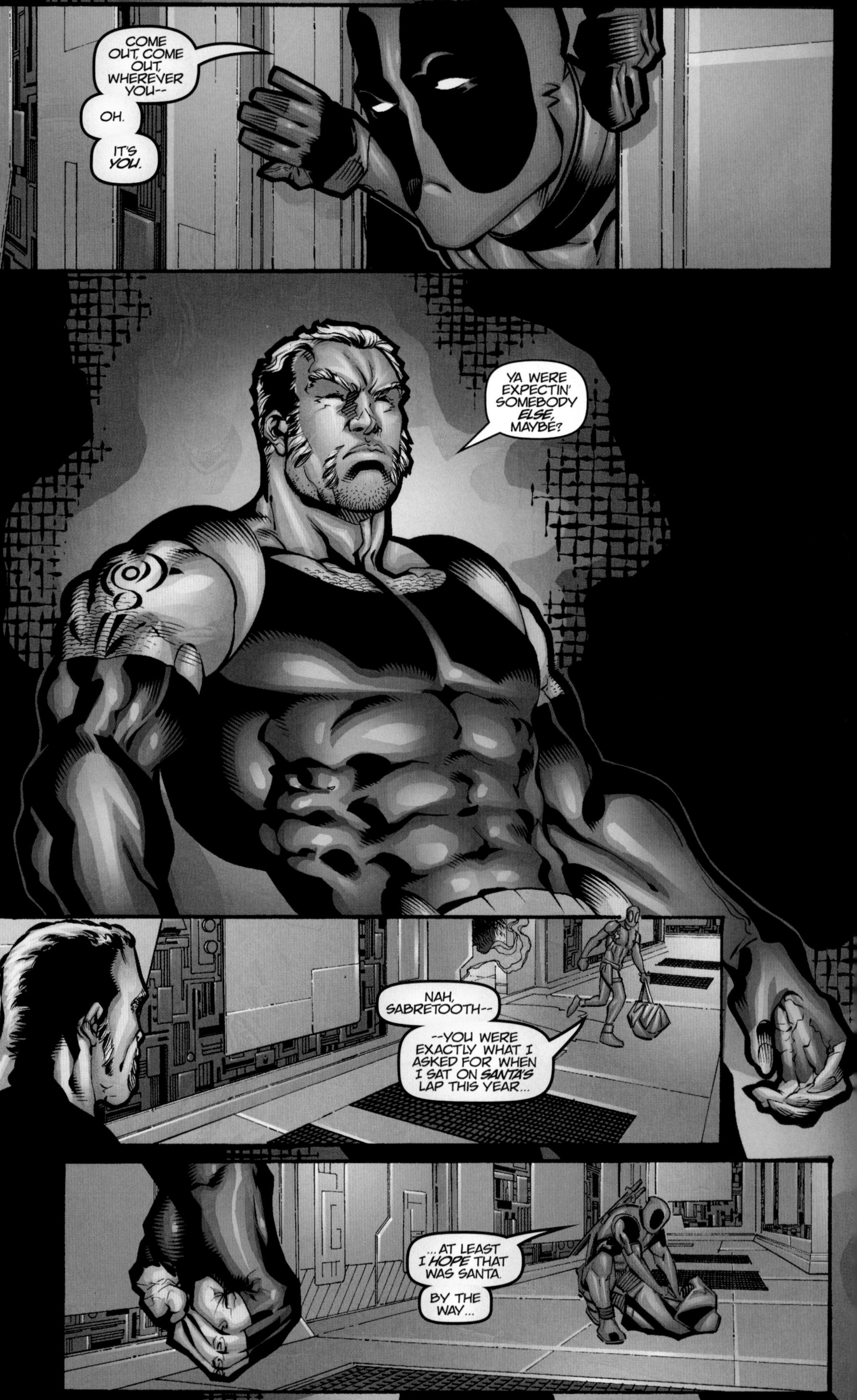
COME OUT, COME OUT, WHEREVER YOU--
OH.
IT'S YOU.
YA WERE EXPECTIN' SOMEBODY ELSE, MAYBE?
NAH, SABRETOOTH--
--YOU WERE EXACTLY WHAT I ASKED FOR WHEN I SAT ON SANTA'S LAP THIS YEAR...
...AT LEAST I HOPE THAT WAS SANTA.
BY THE WAY...

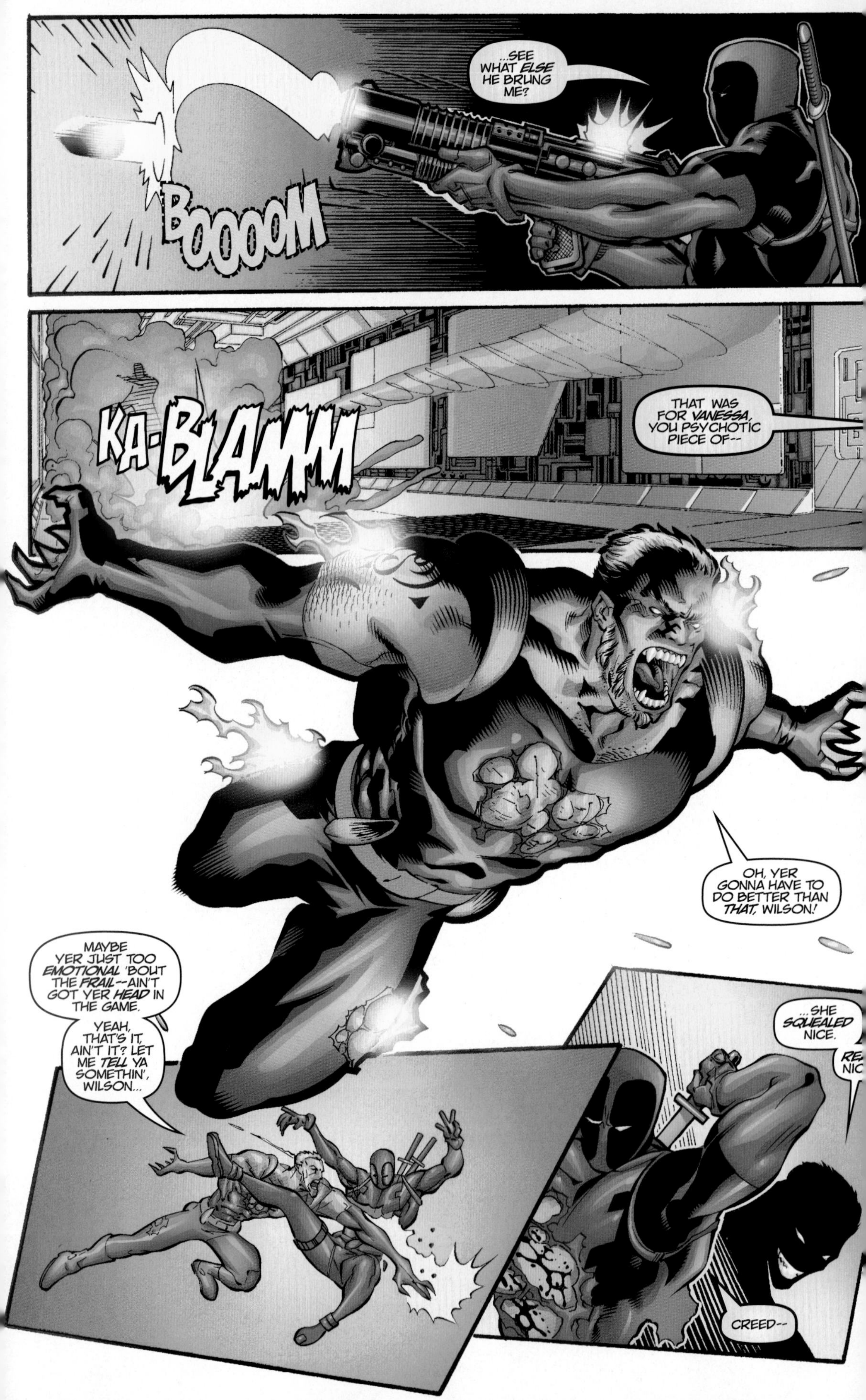
...SEE WHAT ELSE HE BRUNG ME?
BOOOOM
KA-BLAMM
THAT WAS FOR VANESSA, YOU PSYCHOTIC PIECE OF--
OH, YER GONNA HAVE TO DO BETTER THAN THAT, WILSON!
MAYBE YER JUST TOO EMOTIONAL 'BOUT THE FRAIL--AIN'T GOT YER HEAD IN THE GAME.
YEAH, THAT'S IT, AIN'T IT? LET ME TELL YA SOMETHIN', WILSON...
...SHE SQUEALED NICE.
CREED--

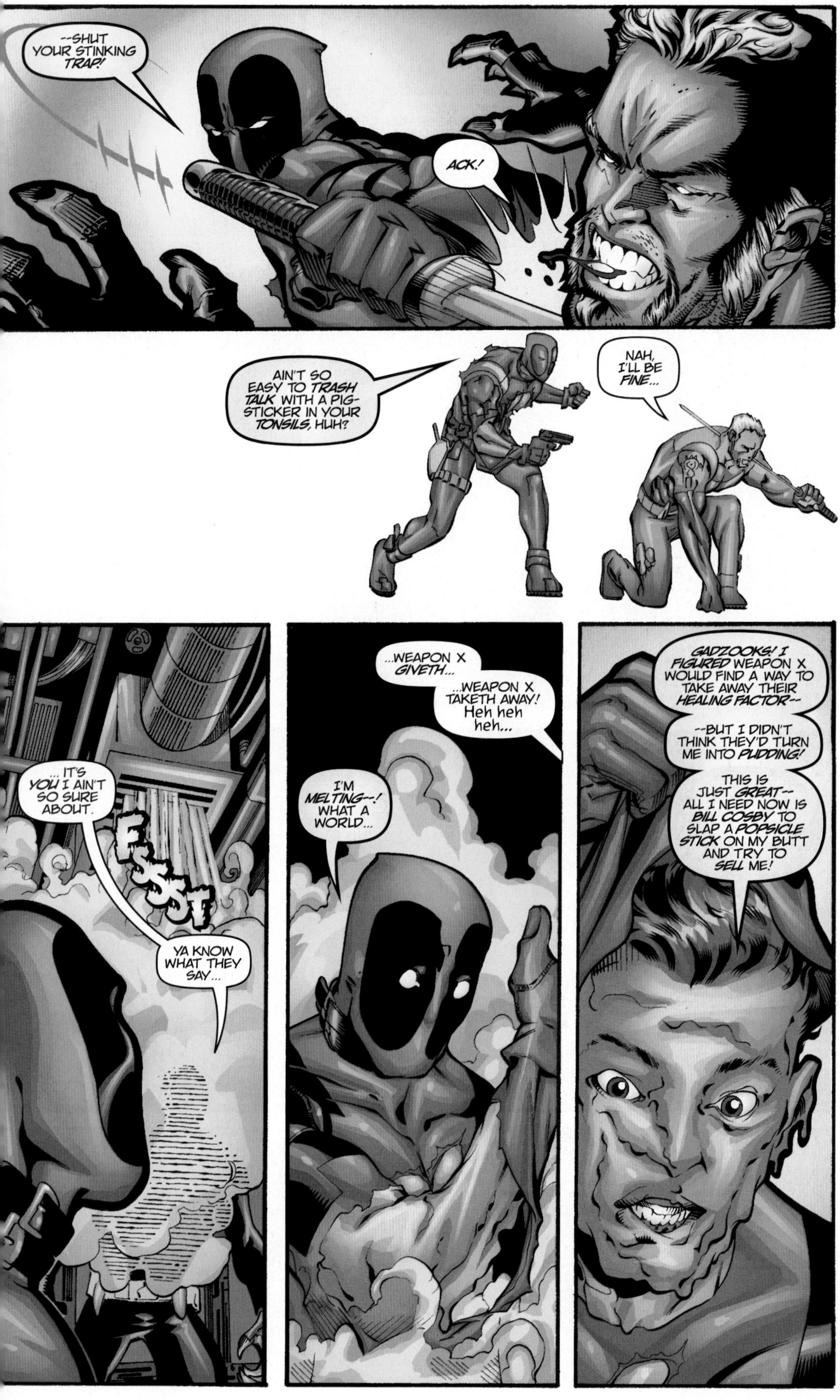
--SHUT YOUR STINKING TRAP!
ACK!
AIN'T SO EASY TO TRASH TALK WITH A PIG-STICKER IN YOUR TONSILS, HUH?
NAH, I'LL BE FINE...
... IT'S YOU I AIN'T SO SURE ABOUT.
FSSST
YA KNOW WHAT THEY SAY...
...WEAPON X GIVETH...
...WEAPON X TAKETH AWAY! Heh heh heh...
I'M MELTING--! WHAT A WORLD...
GADZOOKS! I FIGURED WEAPON X WOULD FIND A WAY TO TAKE AWAY THEIR HEALING FACTOR--
--BUT I DIDN'T THINK THEY'D TURN ME INTO PUDDING!
THIS IS JUST GREAT-- ALL I NEED NOW IS BILL COSBY TO SLAP A POPSICLE STICK ON MY BUTT AND TRY TO SELL ME!

Heh heh heh... LOOK AT YA--YA CAN *BARELY* HOLD YERSELF *TOGETHER.*

FACE IT, WILSON--YOU WERE *USED.*

BY WEAPON X, FER STARTERS. BUT *MOST OF ALL*--

--BY *ME!*

YA DIDN'T THINK I *KNEW* YA'D *SCREW UP* WHEN I BRUNG YA ONBOARD, WILSON?

HELL-- I *COUNTED* ON IT! WEAPON X THINKS THEY GOT ME ON A NICE TIGHT *LEASH*--AN' THAT'S WHAT I *LET* 'EM THINK.

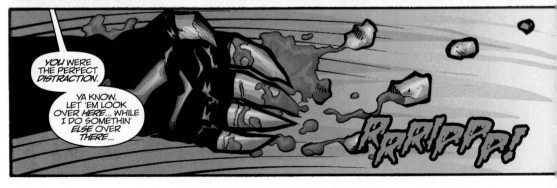

YOU WERE THE PERFECT *DISTRACTION.*

YA KNOW, LET 'EM LOOK OVER *HERE*... WHILE I DO SOMETHIN' ELSE OVER *THERE*...

RRRIPPP!

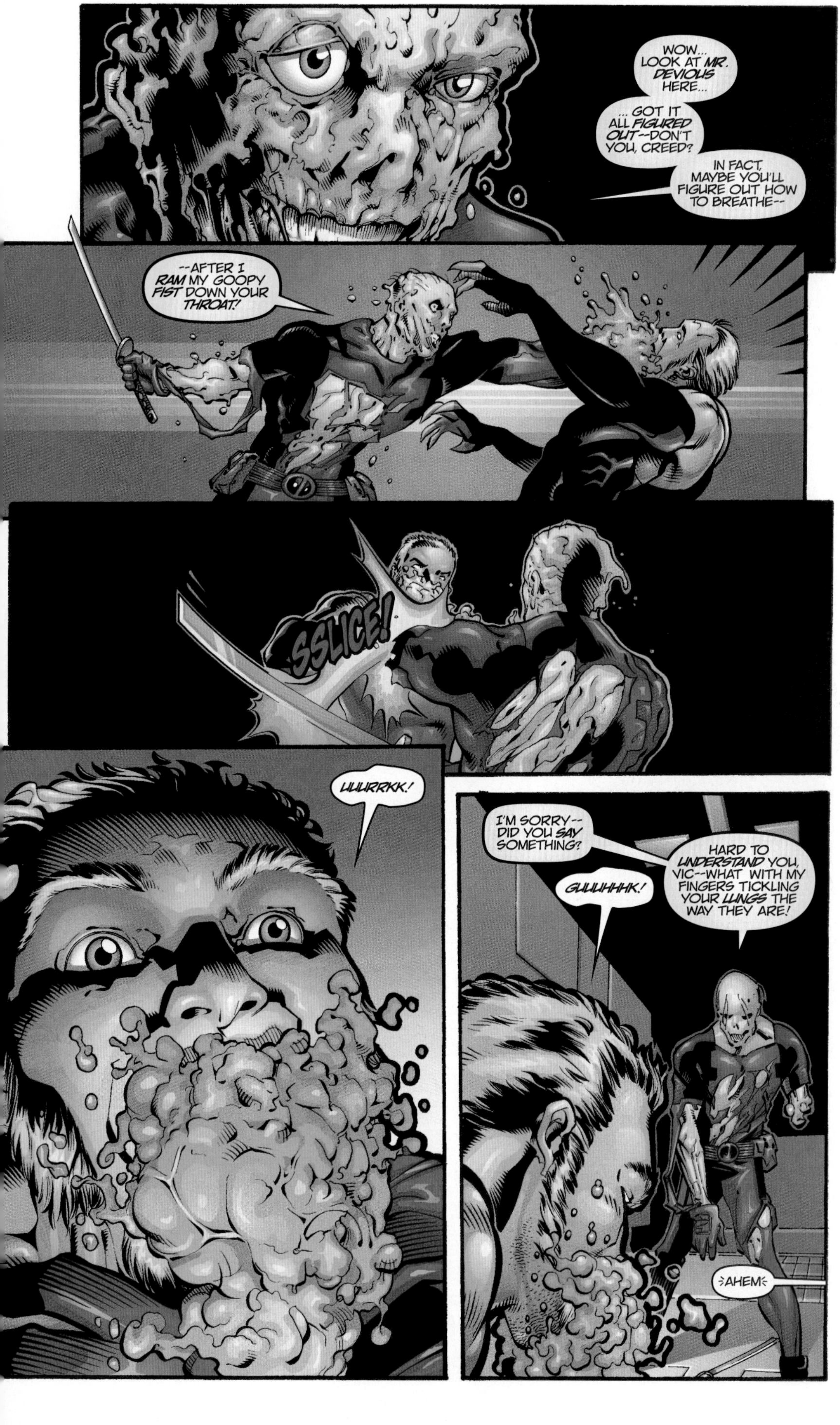
WOW... LOOK AT MR. DEVIOUS HERE...
... GOT IT ALL FIGURED OUT--DON'T YOU, CREED?
IN FACT, MAYBE YOU'LL FIGURE OUT HOW TO BREATHE--
--AFTER I RAM MY GOOPY FIST DOWN YOUR THROAT!
SSLICE!
UUURRKK!
I'M SORRY--DID YOU SAY SOMETHING?
GUUUHHHK!
HARD TO UNDERSTAND YOU, VIC--WHAT WITH MY FINGERS TICKLING YOUR LUNGS THE WAY THEY ARE!
AHEM

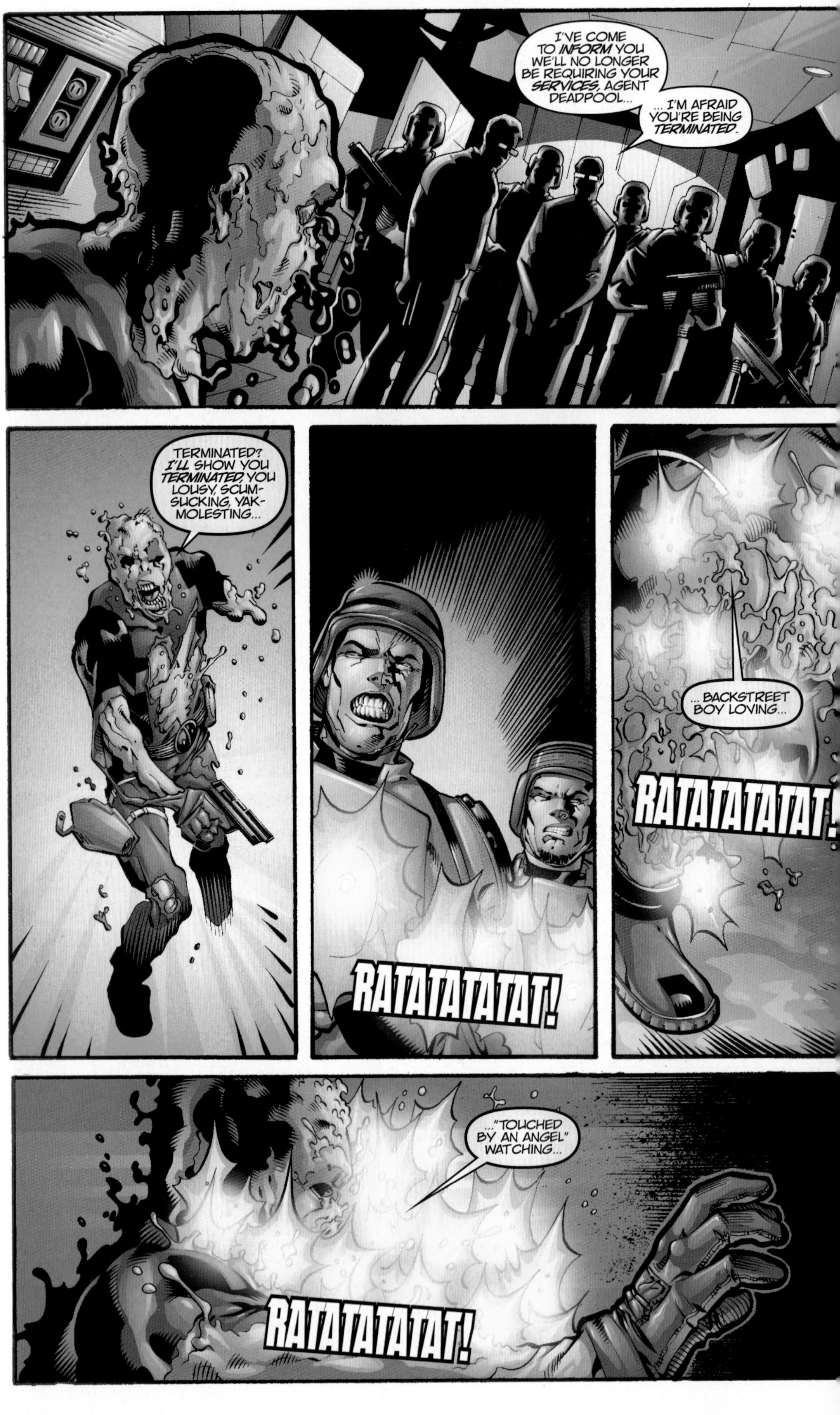
I'VE COME TO INFORM YOU WE'LL NO LONGER BE REQUIRING YOUR SERVICES, AGENT DEADPOOL...
... I'M AFRAID YOU'RE BEING TERMINATED.
TERMINATED? I'LL SHOW YOU TERMINATED, YOU LOUSY, SCUM-SUCKING, YAK-MOLESTING...
RATATATATAT!
... BACKSTREET BOY LOVING...
RATATATATAT!
..."TOUCHED BY AN ANGEL" WATCHING...
RATATATATAT!

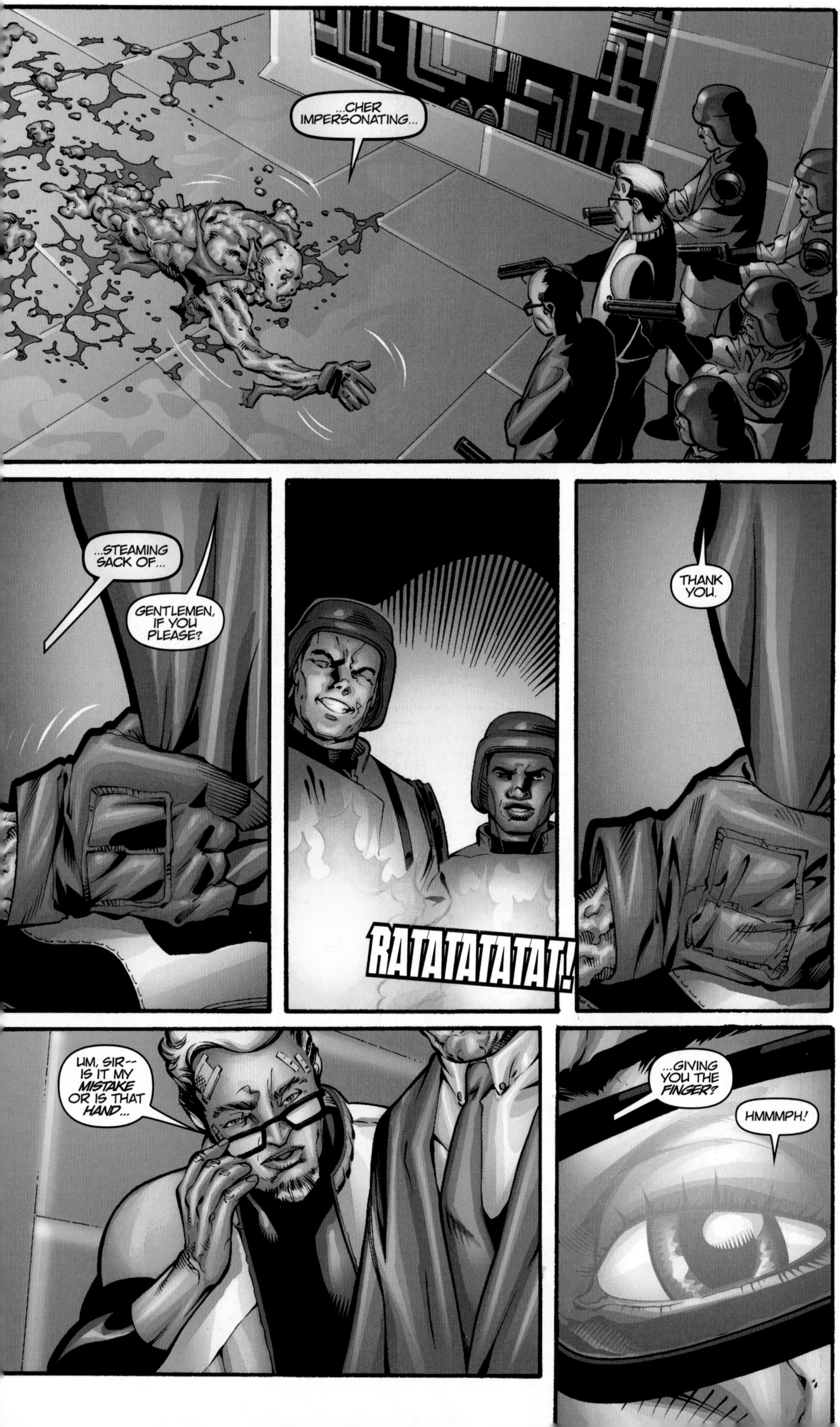
...CHER IMPERSONATING...
...STEAMING SACK OF...
GENTLEMEN, IF YOU PLEASE?
RATATATATAT!
THANK YOU.
UM, SIR-- IS IT MY *MISTAKE* OR IS THAT *HAND*...
...GIVING YOU THE *FINGER*?
HMMMPH!

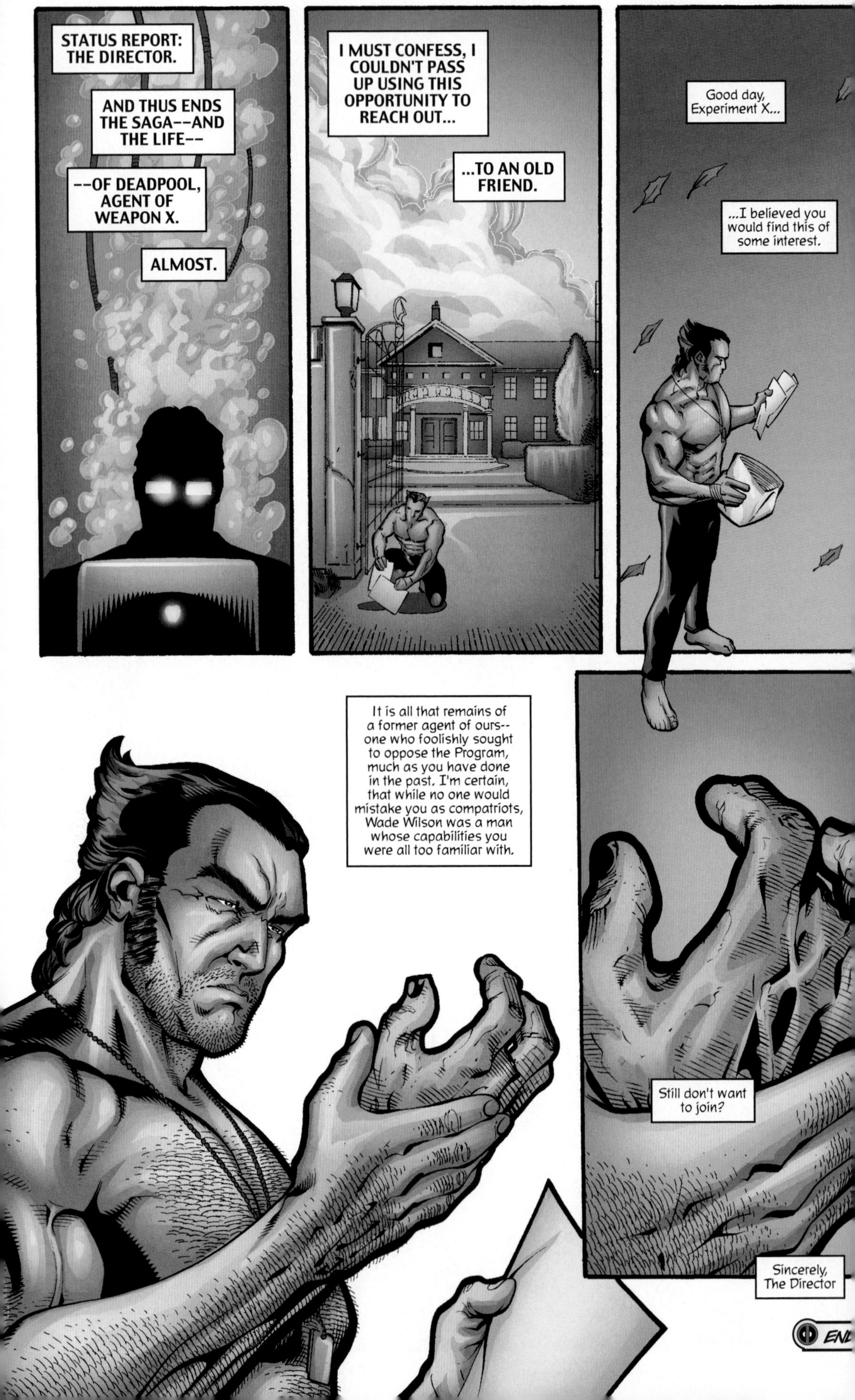
STATUS REPORT: THE DIRECTOR.
AND THUS ENDS THE SAGA--AND THE LIFE--
--OF DEADPOOL, AGENT OF WEAPON X.
ALMOST.
I MUST CONFESS, I COULDN'T PASS UP USING THIS OPPORTUNITY TO REACH OUT...
...TO AN OLD FRIEND.
Good day, Experiment X...
...I believed you would find this of some interest.
It is all that remains of a former agent of ours-- one who foolishly sought to oppose the Program, much as you have done in the past. I'm certain, that while no one would mistake you as compatriots, Wade Wilson was a man whose capabilities you were all too familiar with.
Still don't want to join?
Sincerely, The Director

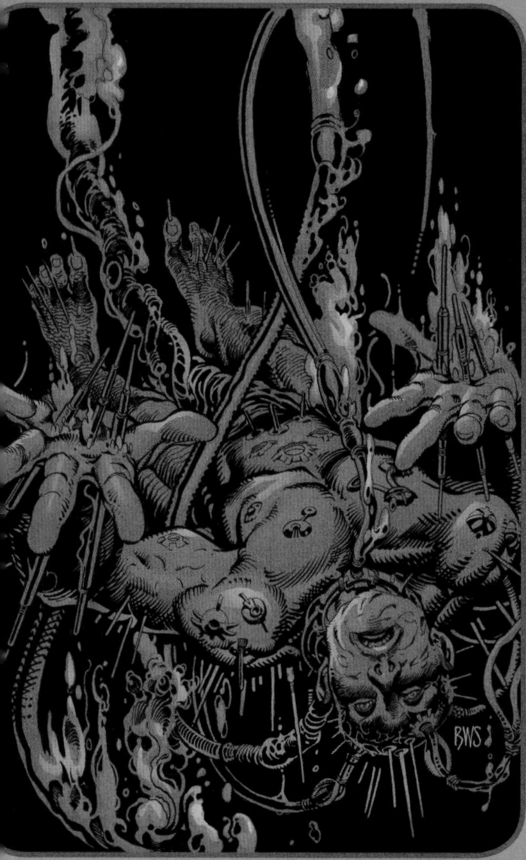
BWS

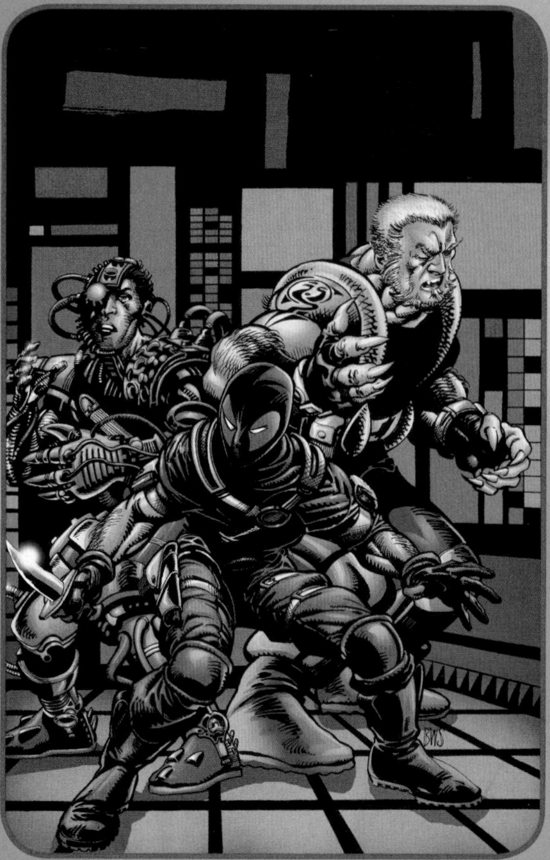
BWS

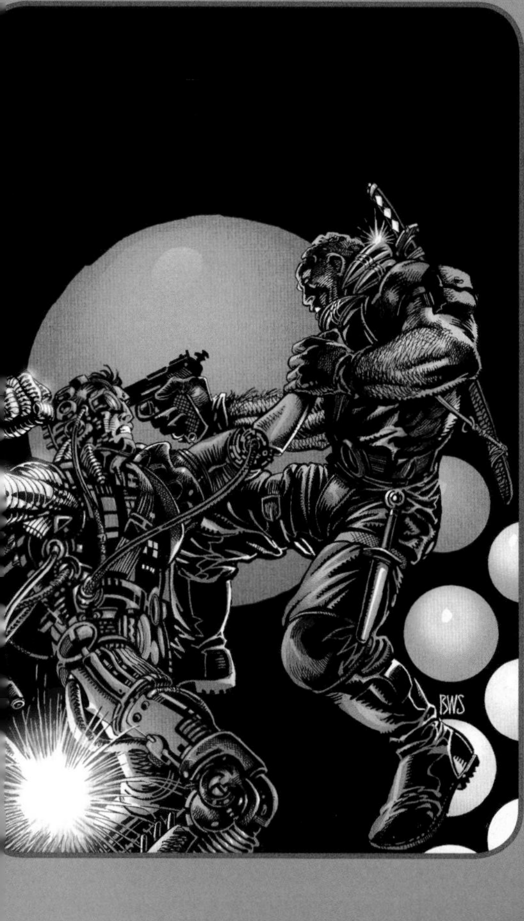
BWS

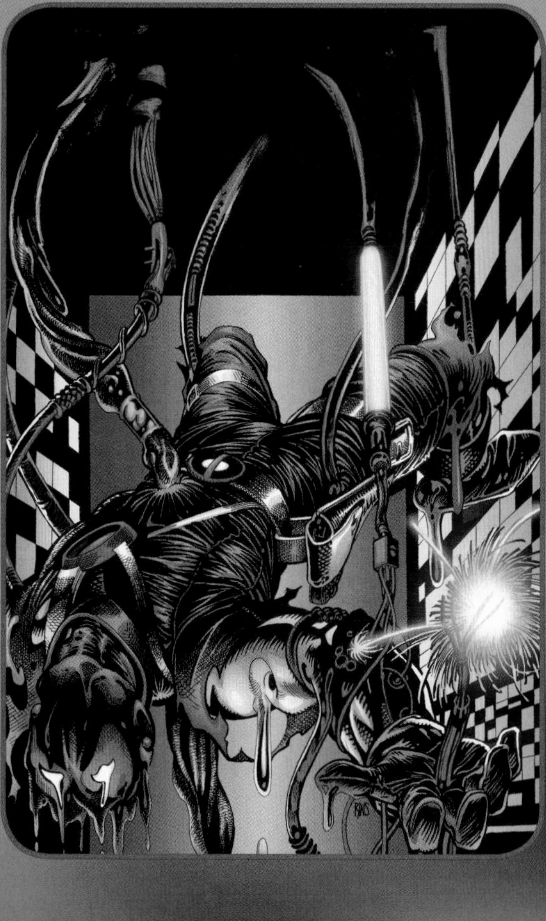
BWS

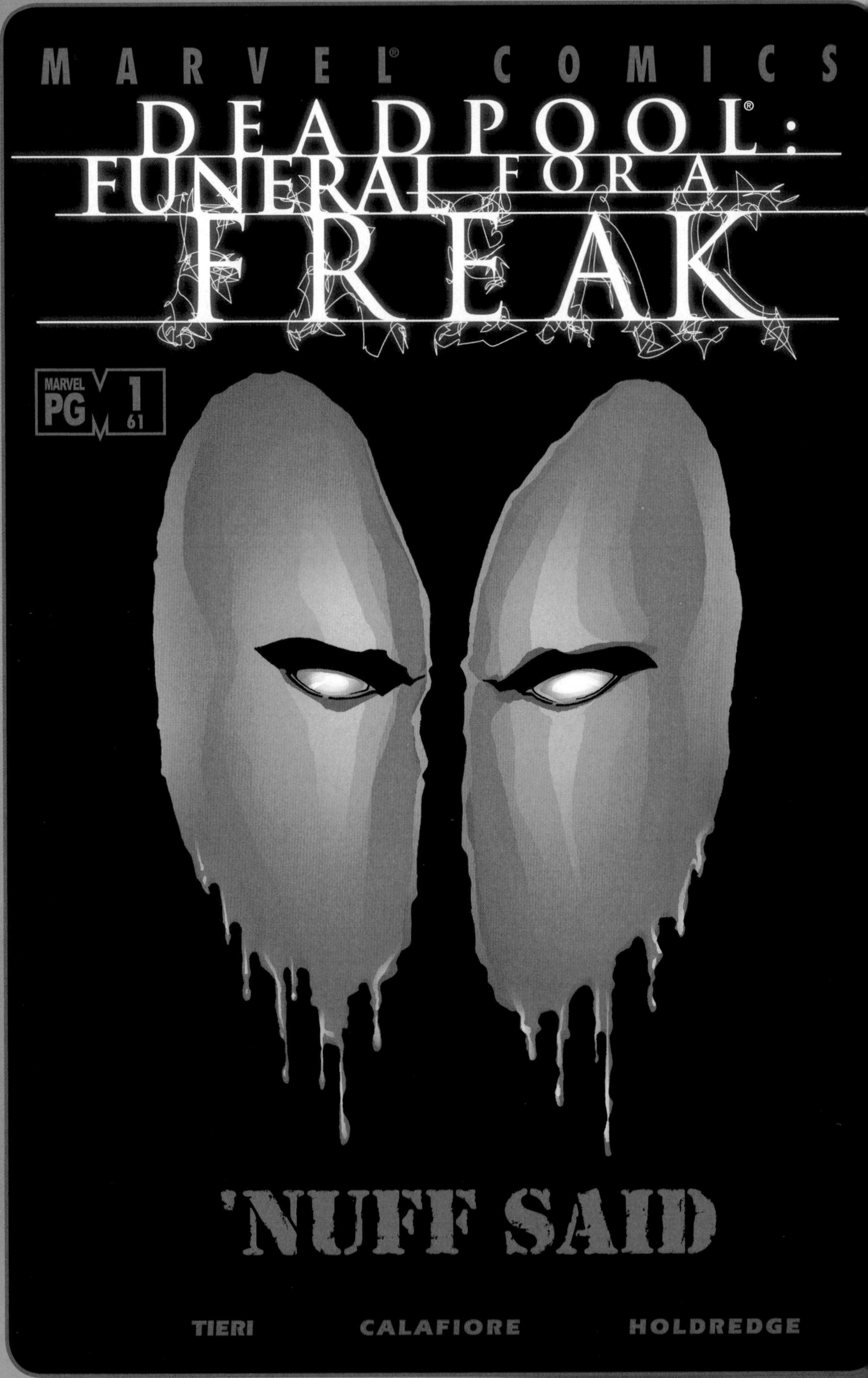
MARVEL® COMICS
DEADPOOL®: FUNERAL FOR A FREAK
MARVEL PG
1
61
'NUFF SAID
TIERI
CALAFIORE
HOLDREDGE

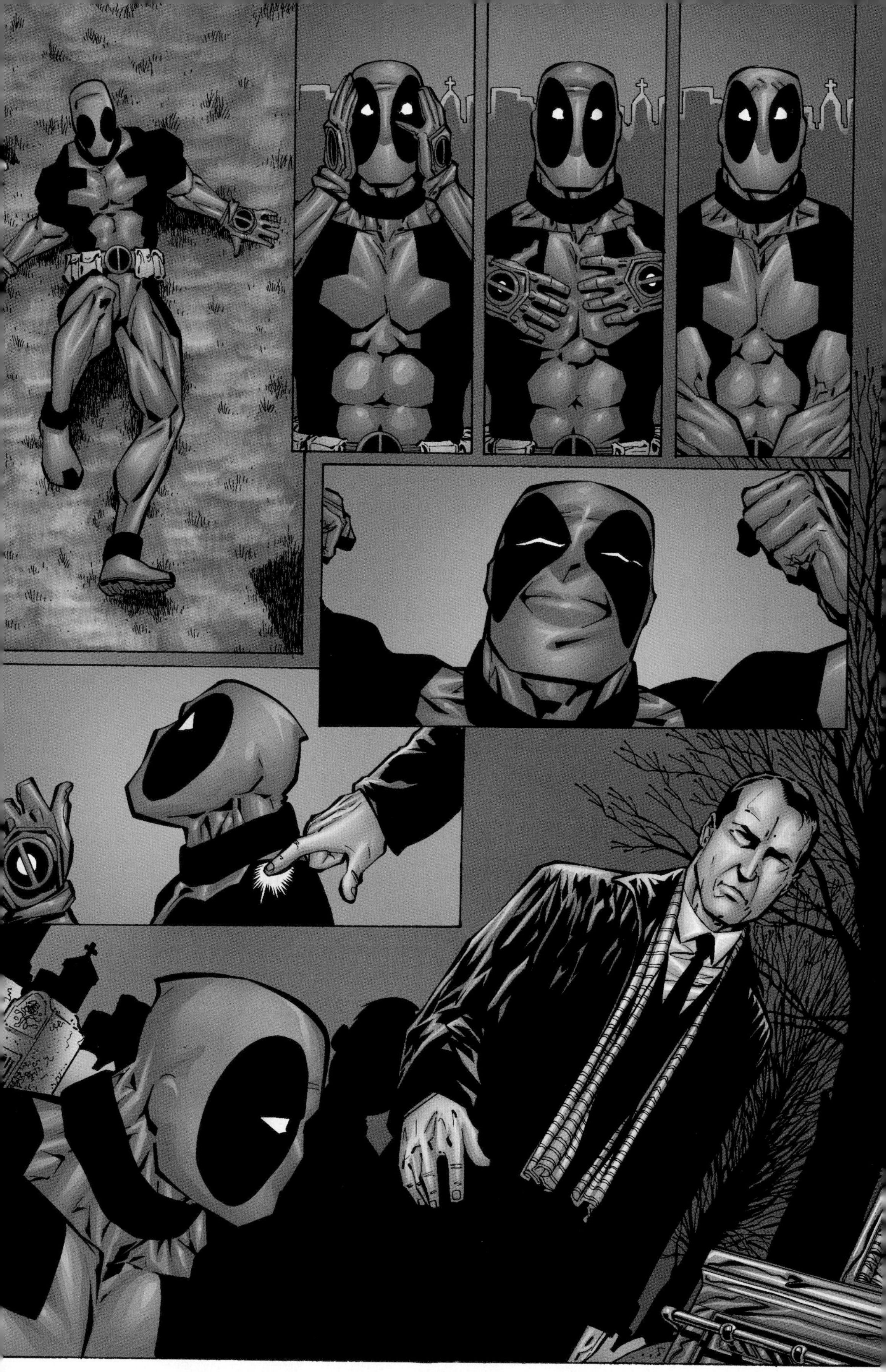

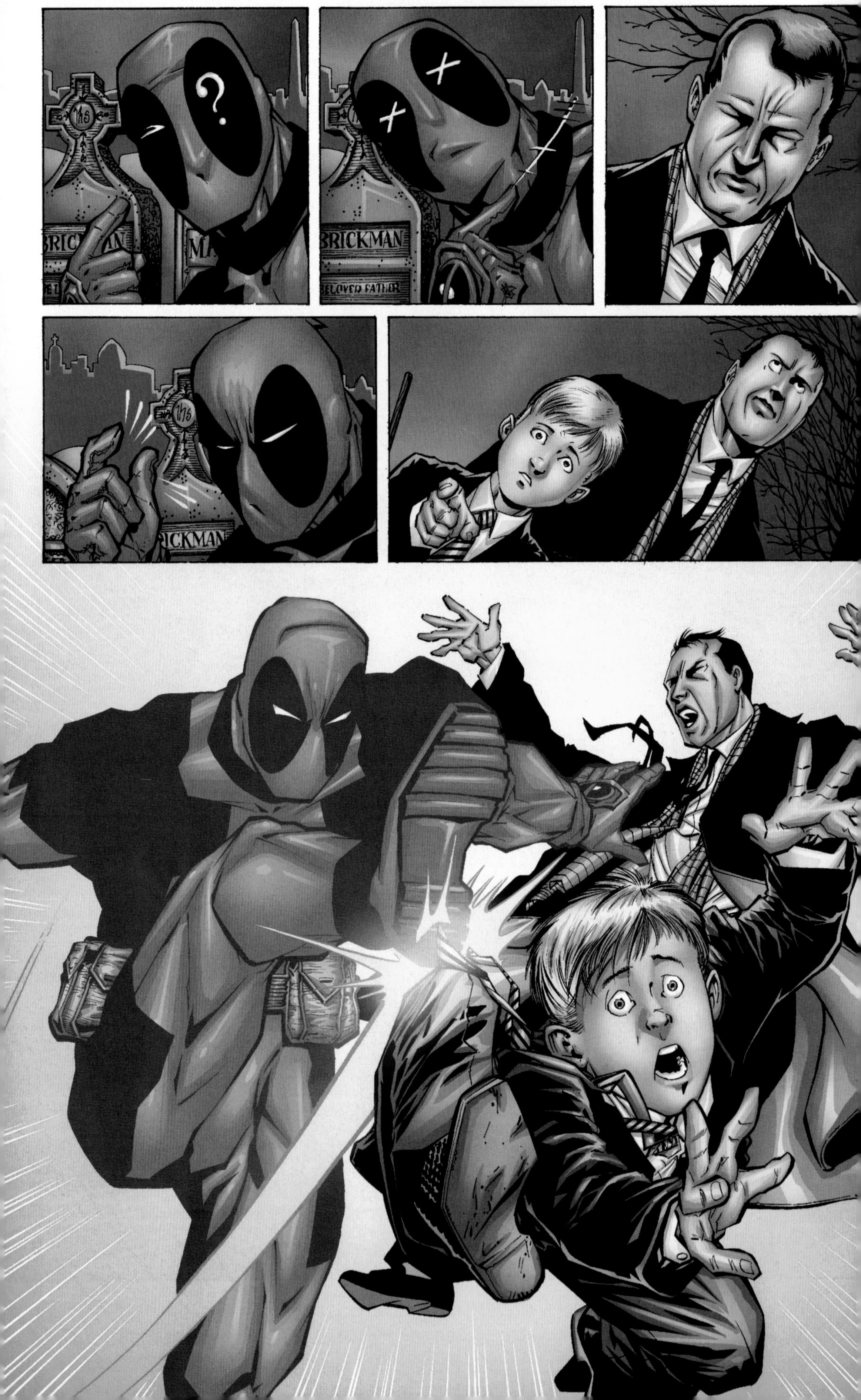

BRICKMAN
BELOVED FATHER

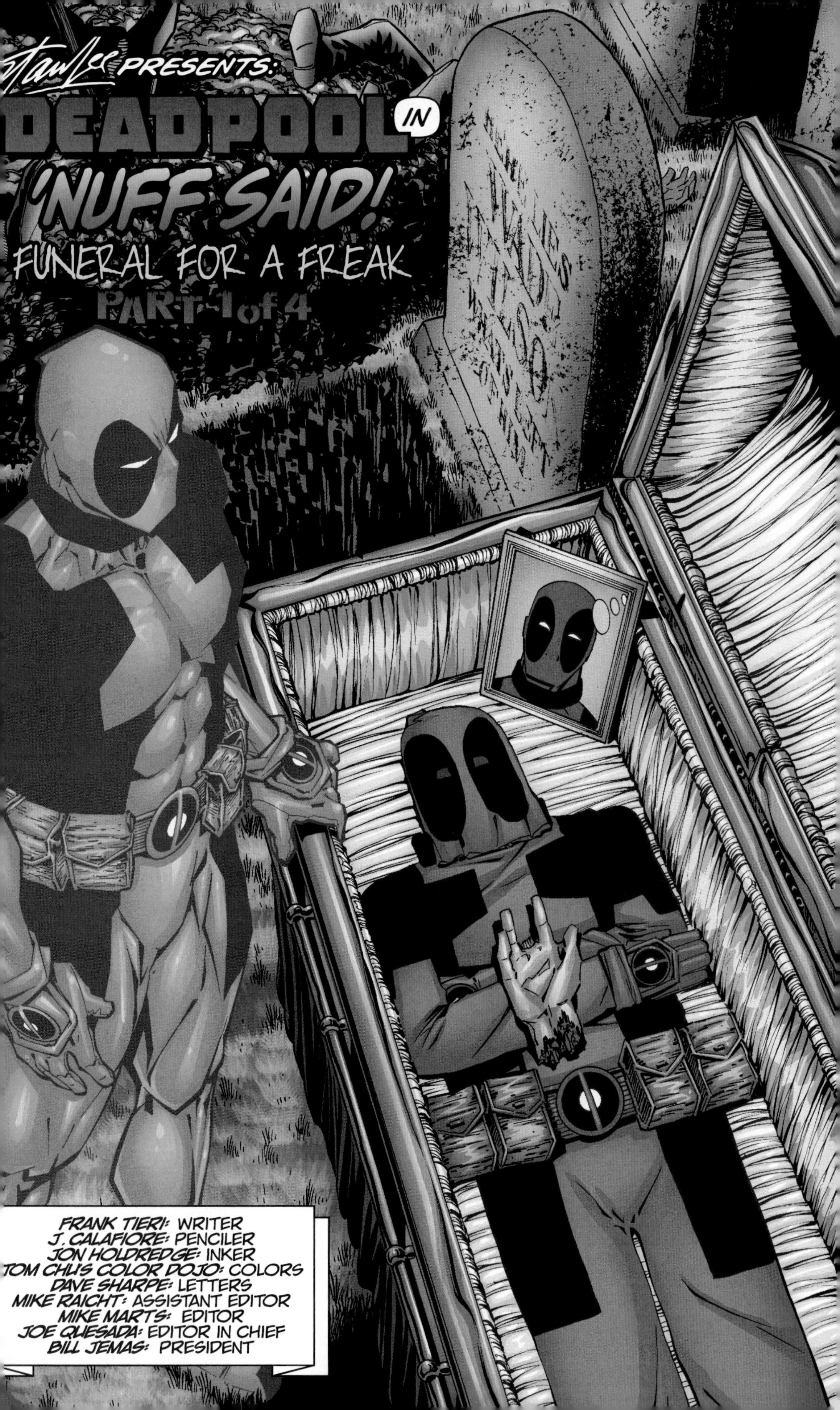

Stan Lee PRESENTS:
DEADPOOL IN
'NUFF SAID!
FUNERAL FOR A FREAK
PART 1 of 4
FRANK TIERI: WRITER
J. CALAFIORE: PENCILER
JON HOLDREDGE: INKER
TOM CHU'S COLOR DOJO: COLORS
DAVE SHARPE: LETTERS
MIKE RAICHT: ASSISTANT EDITOR
MIKE MARTS: EDITOR
JOE QUESADA: EDITOR IN CHIEF
BILL JEMAS: PRESIDENT

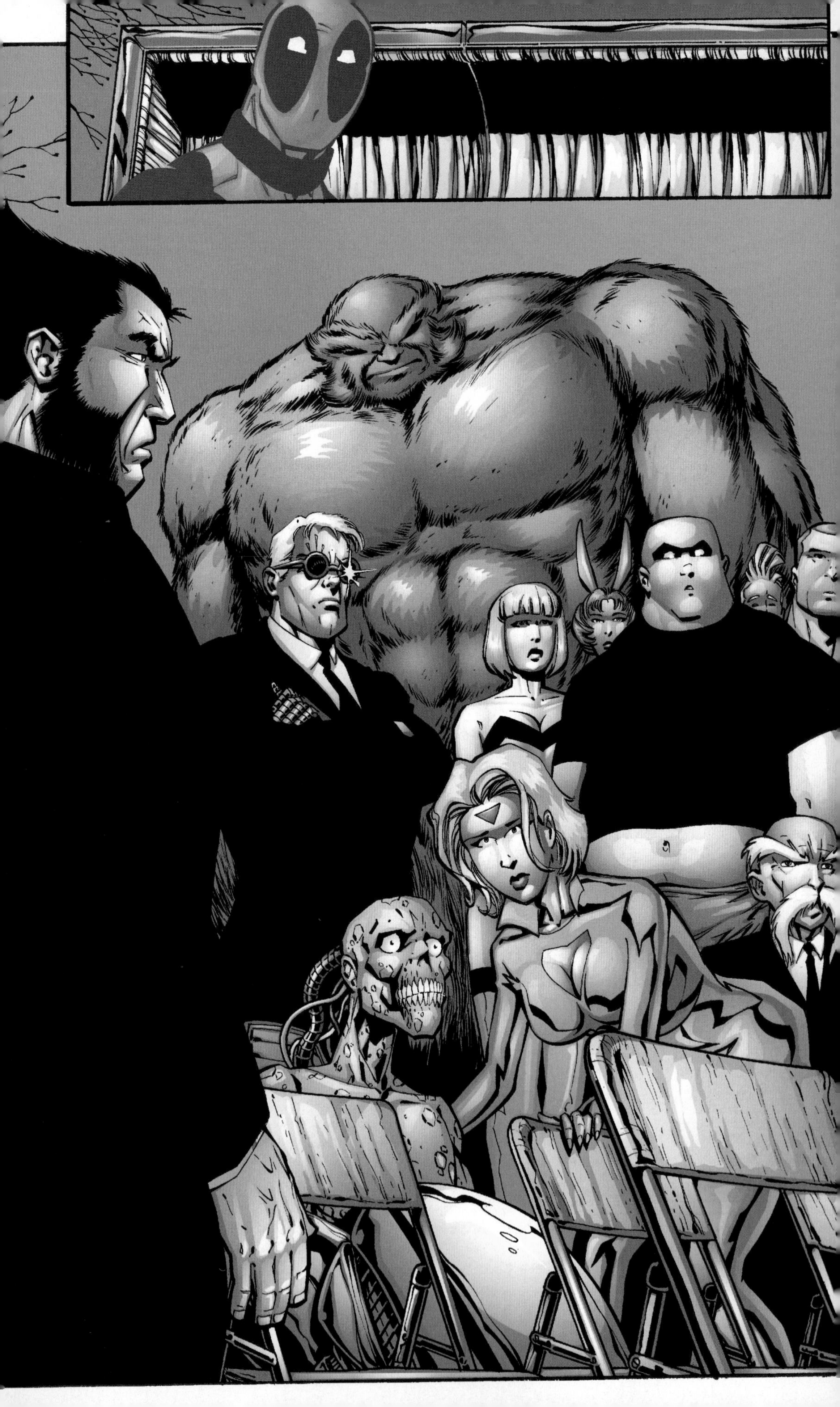

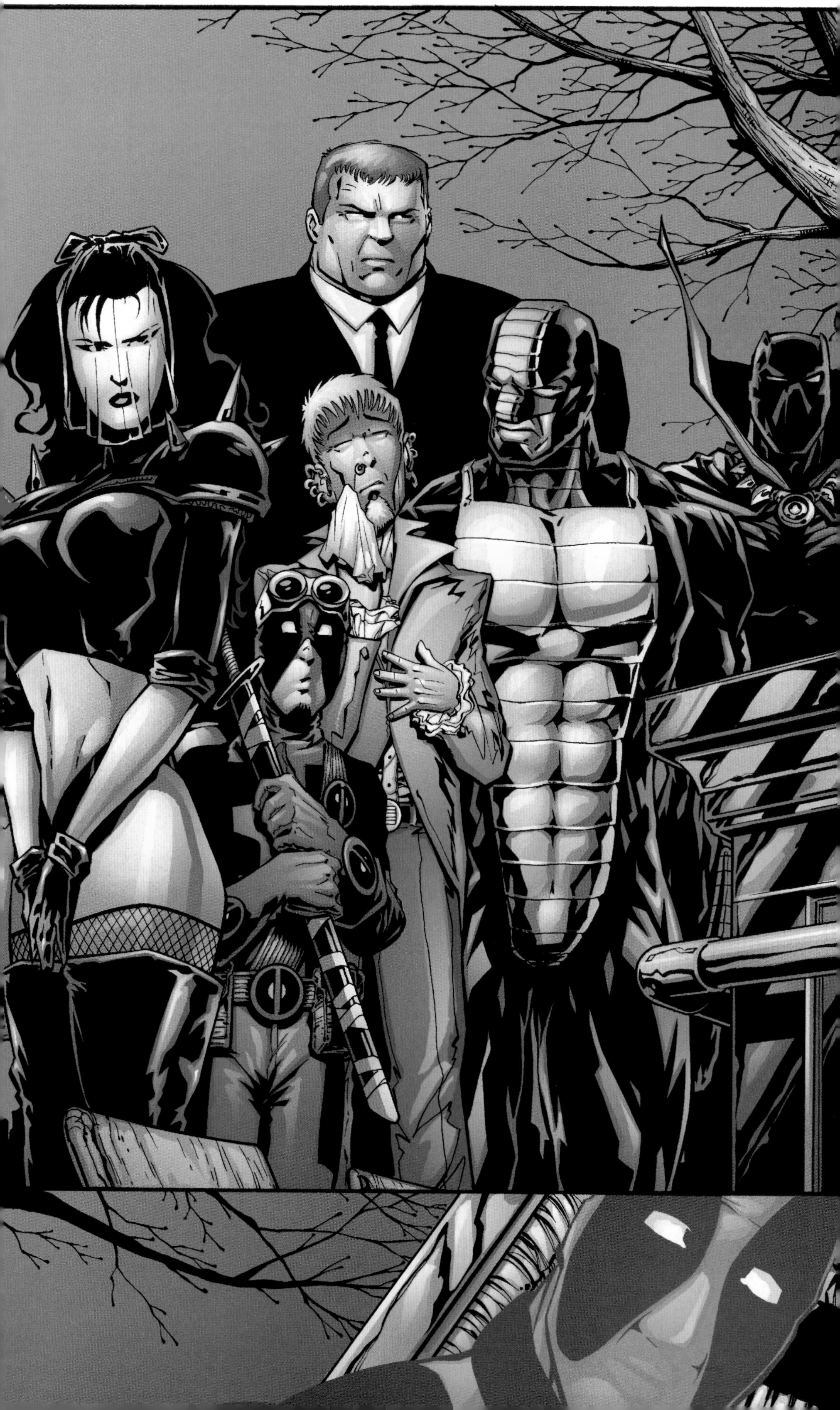

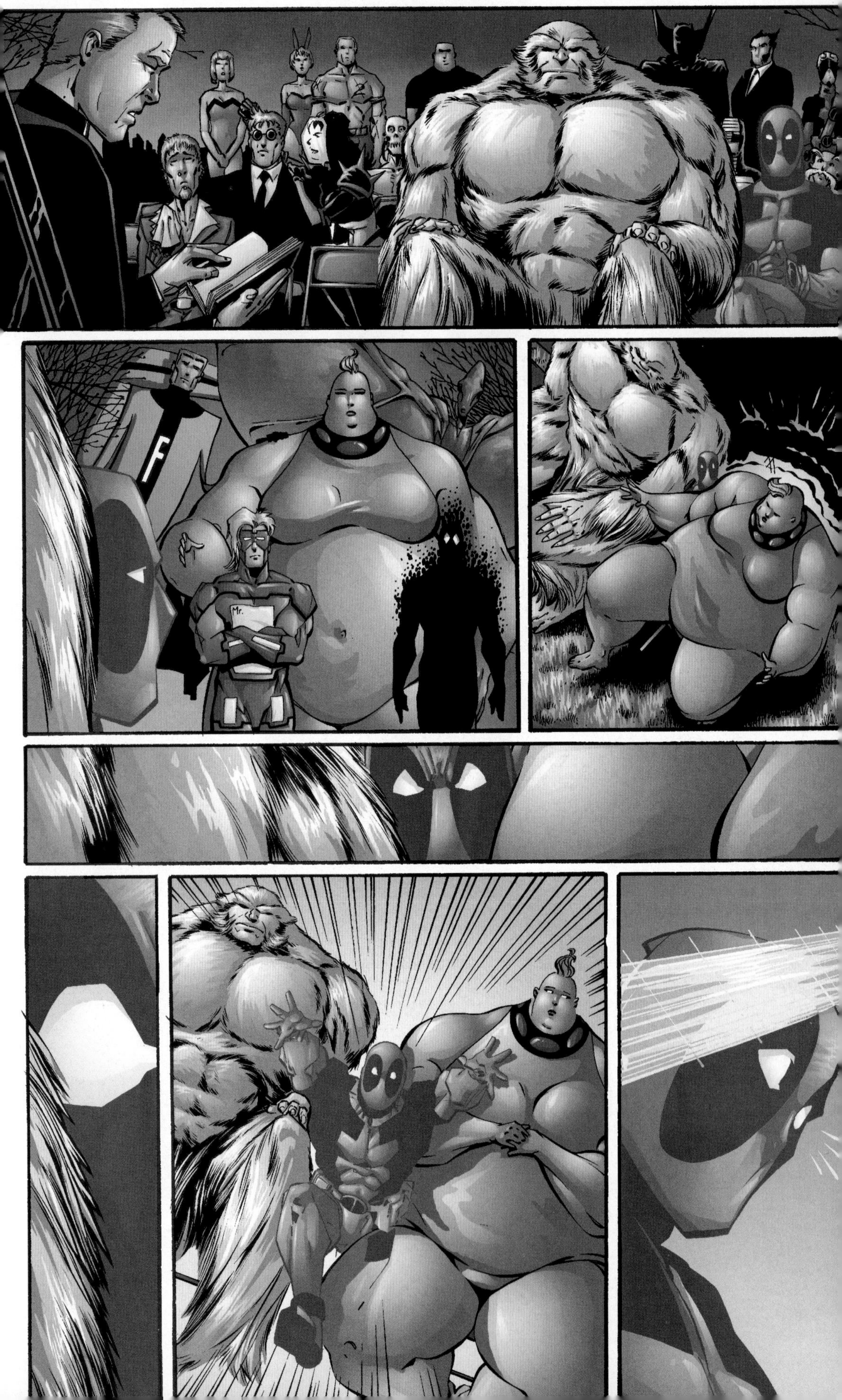

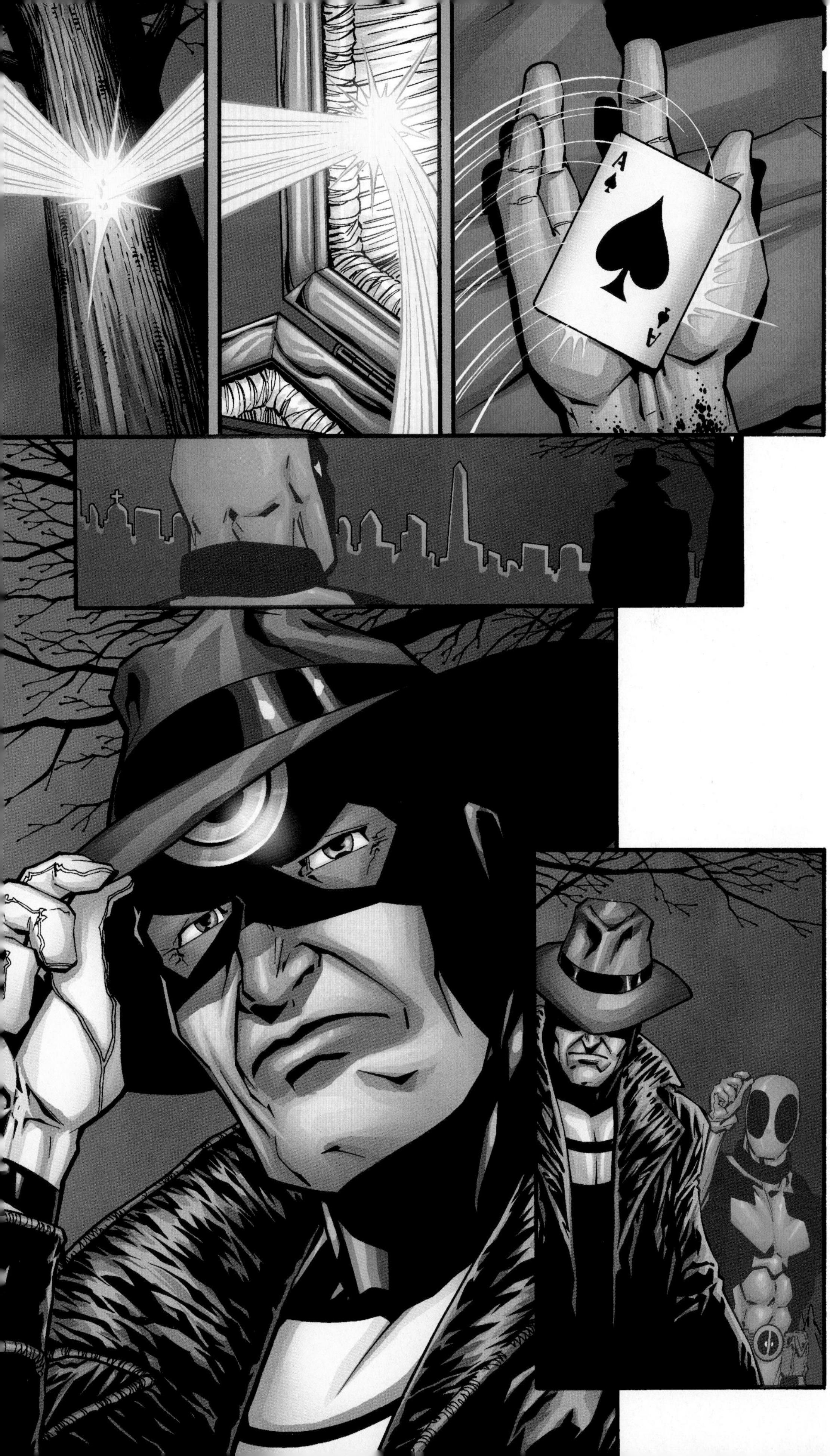
A

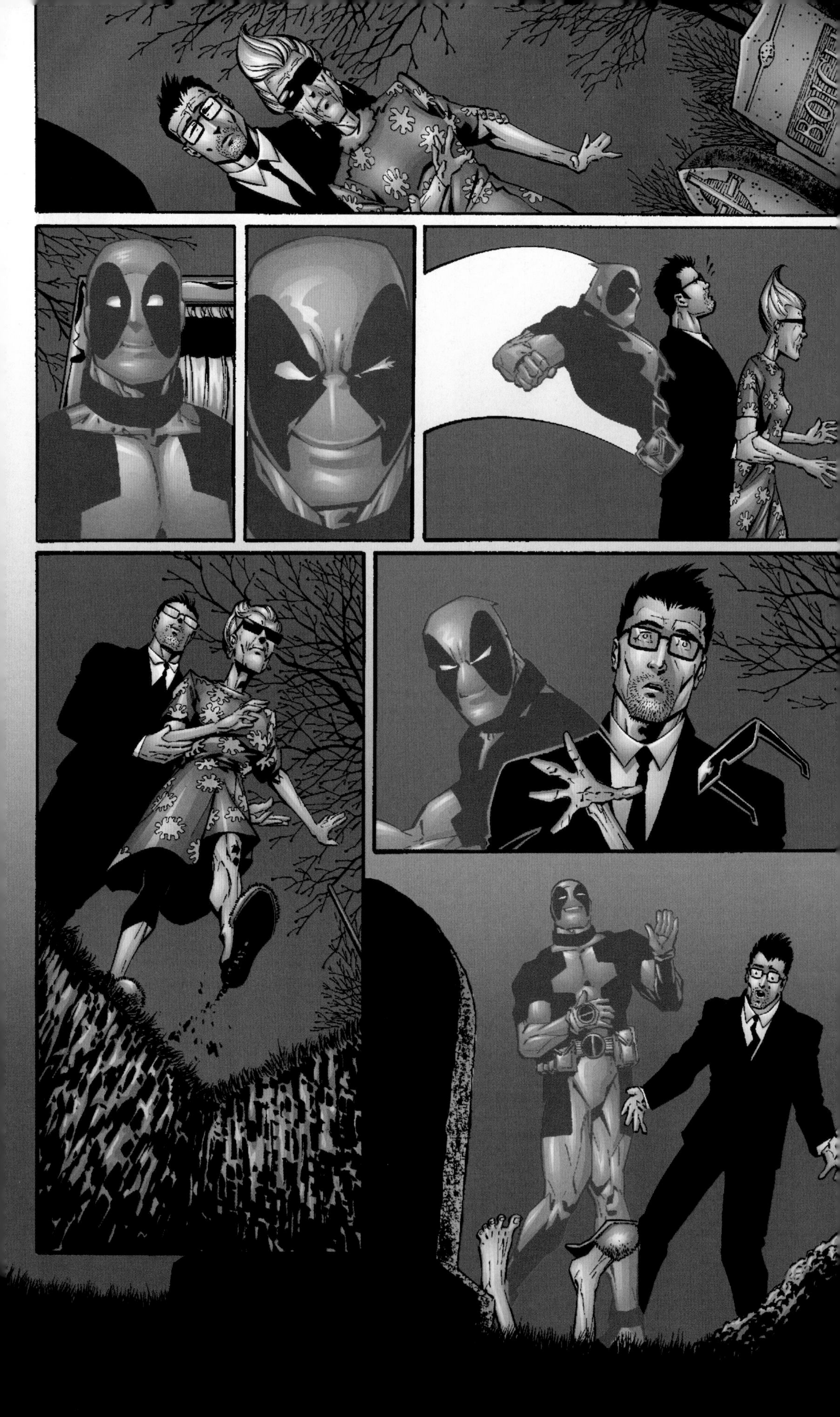

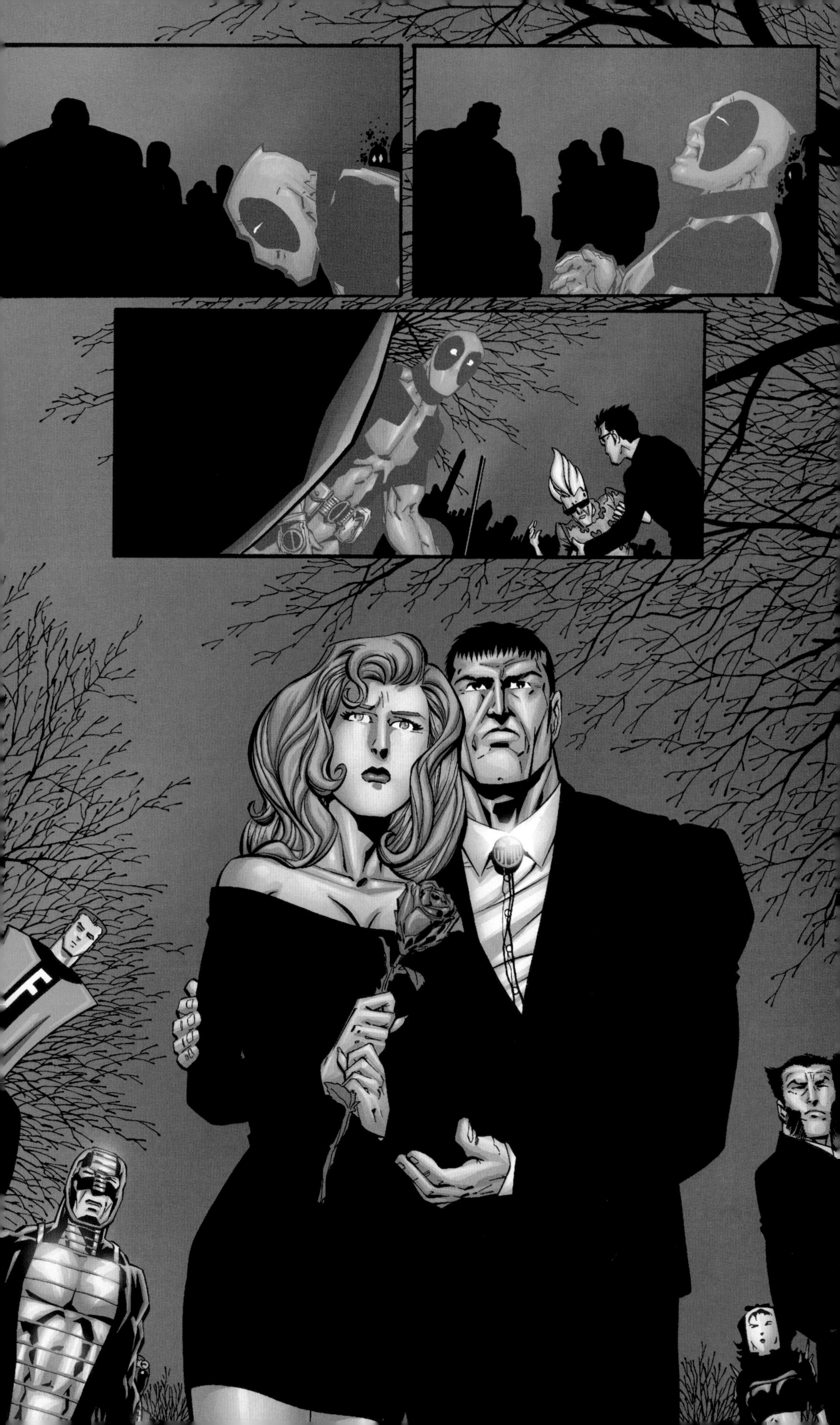

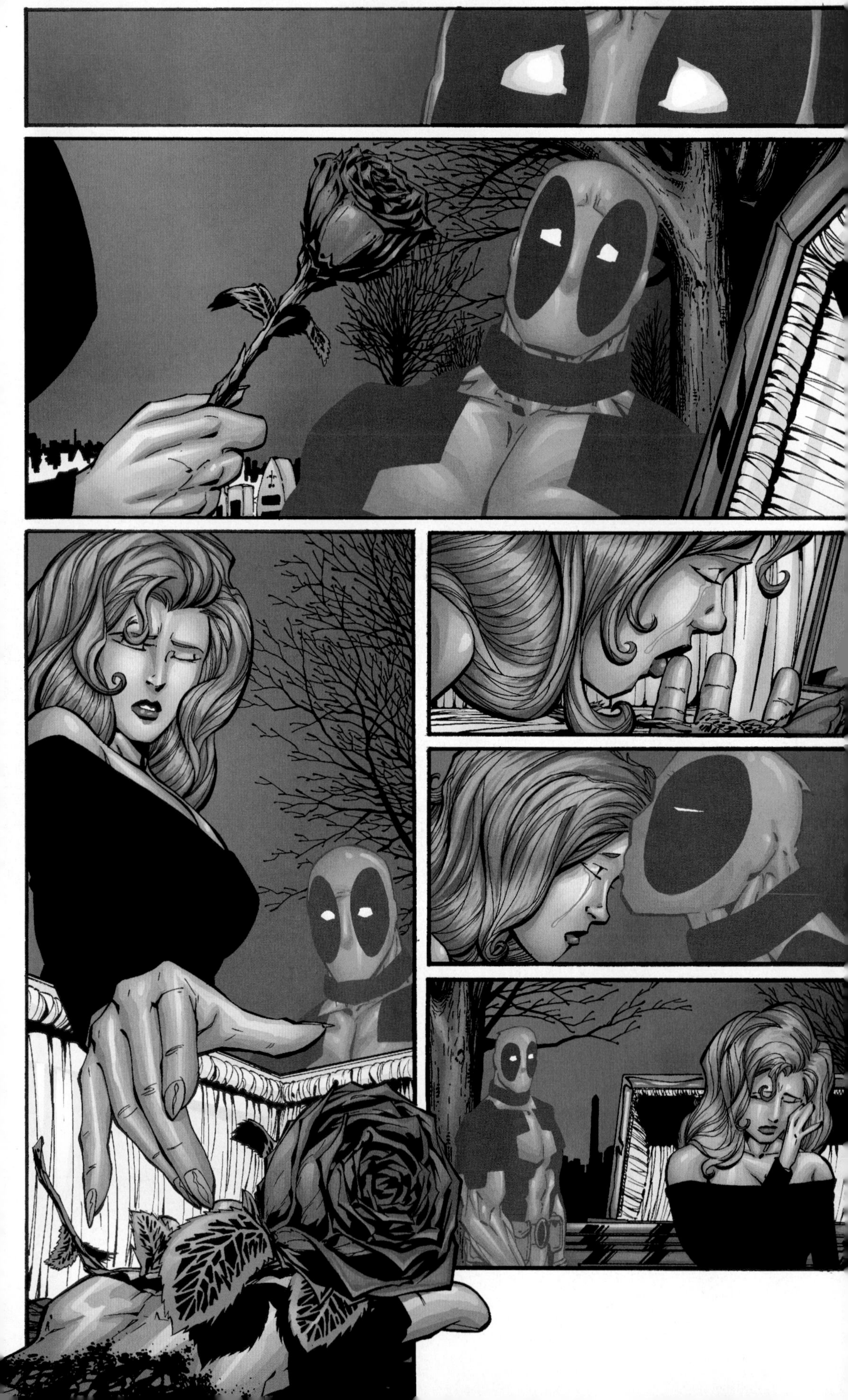

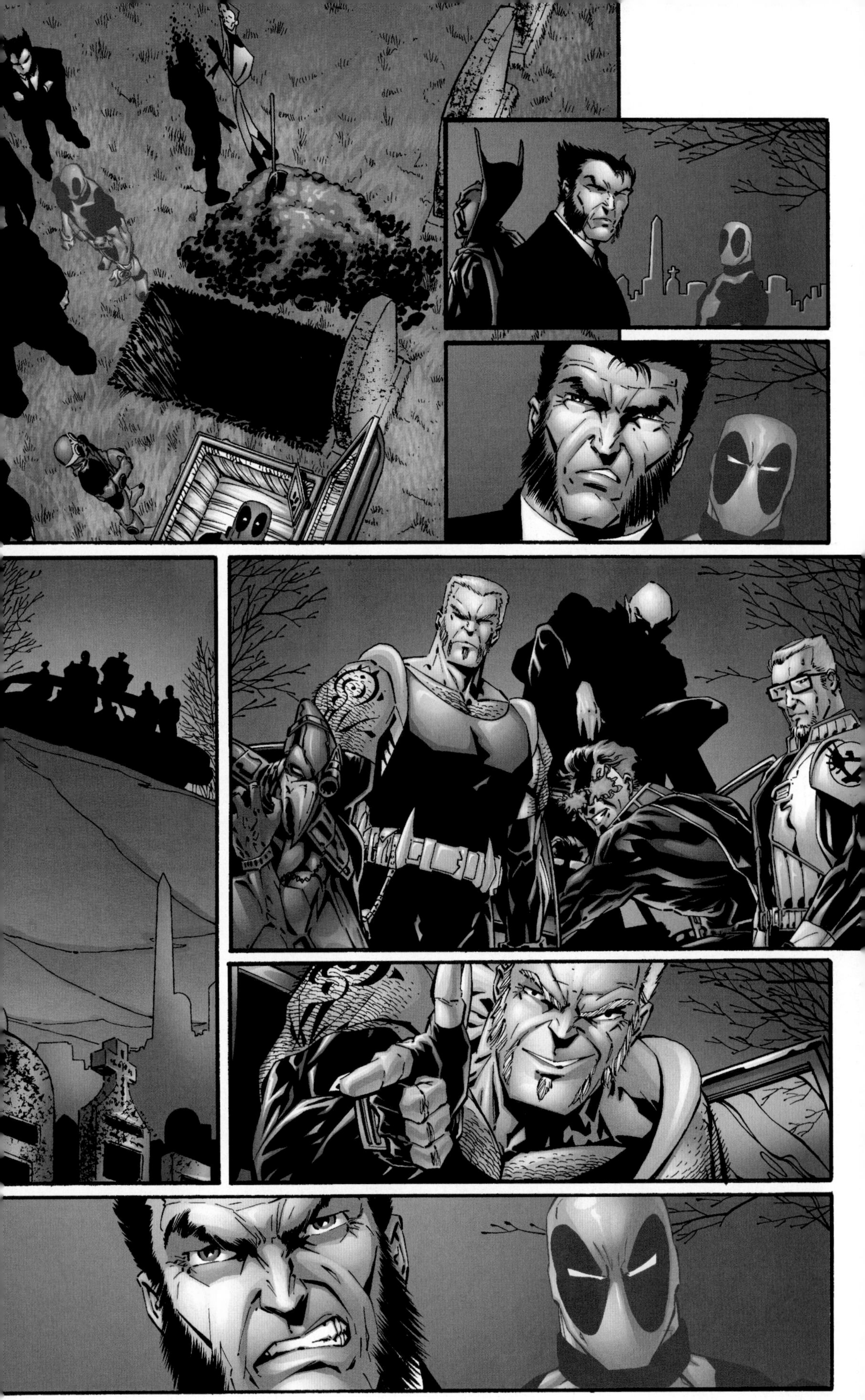

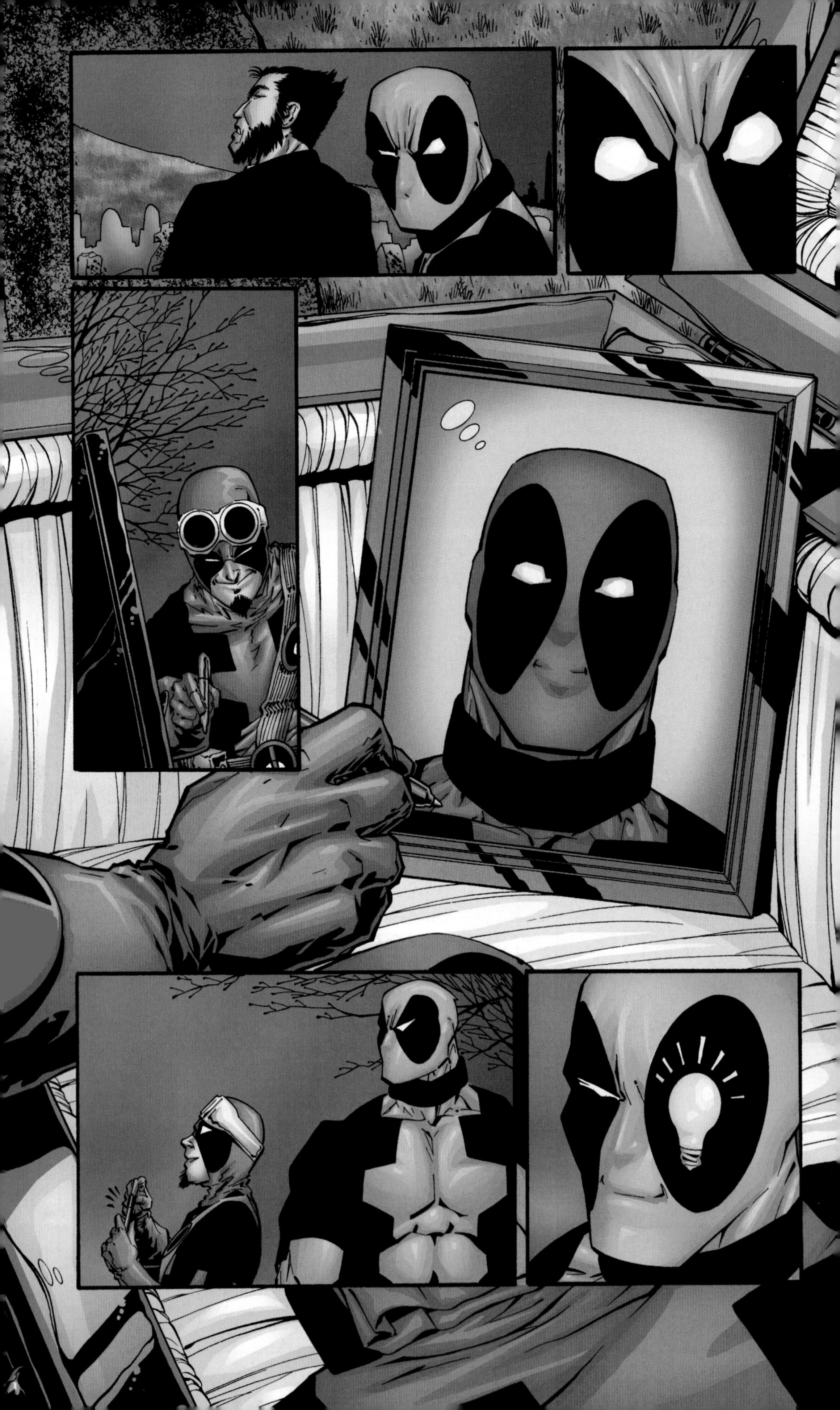

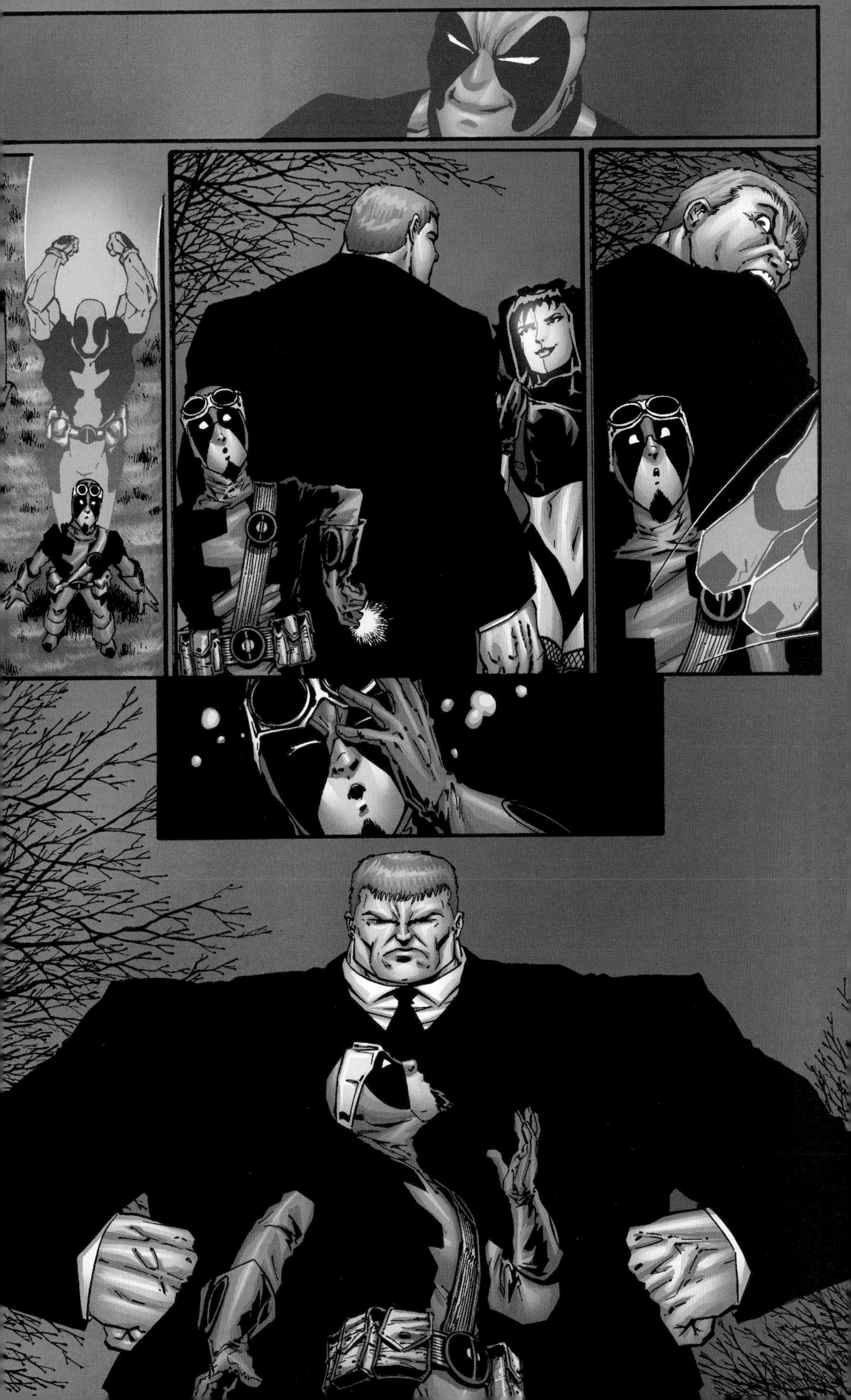

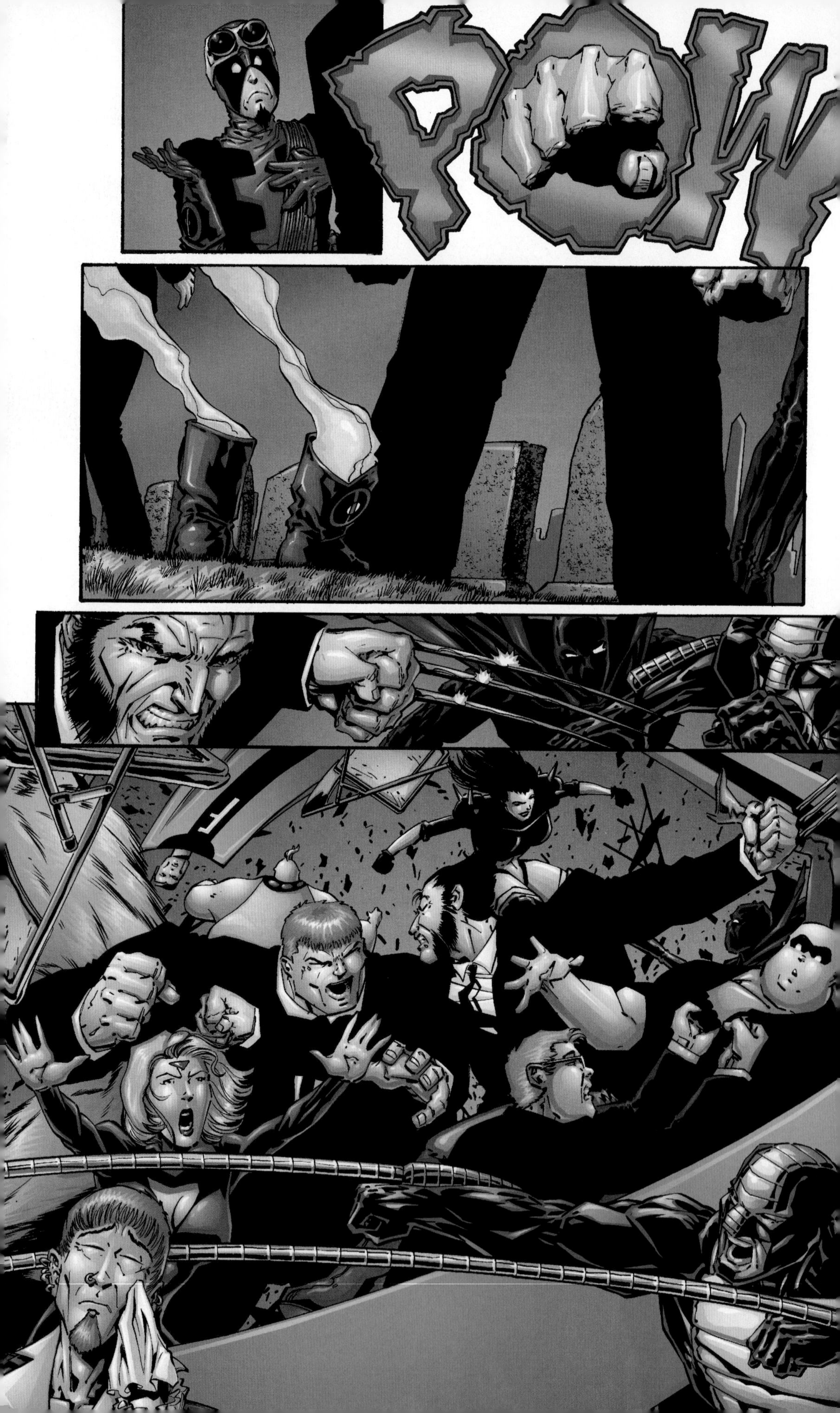
POW

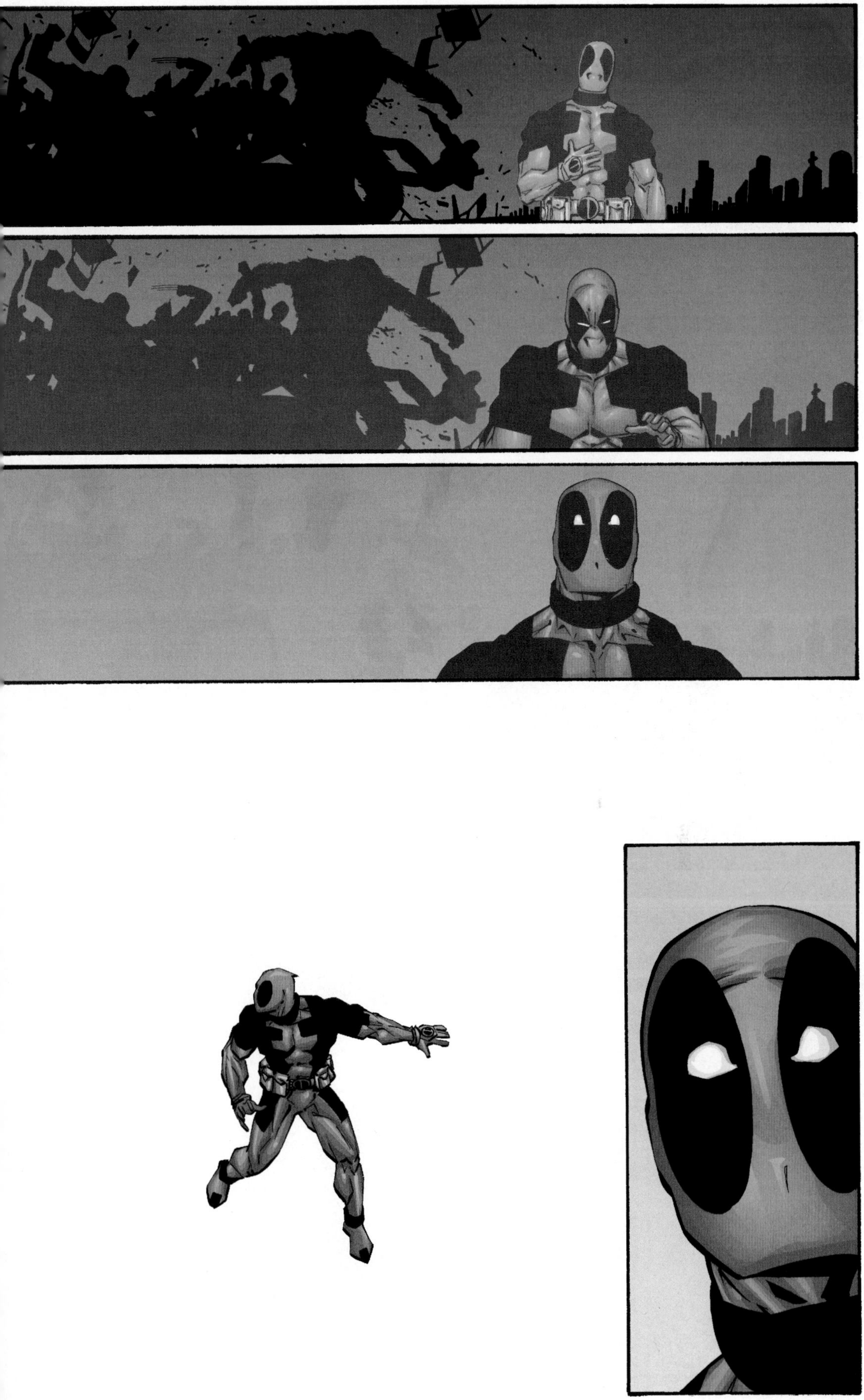

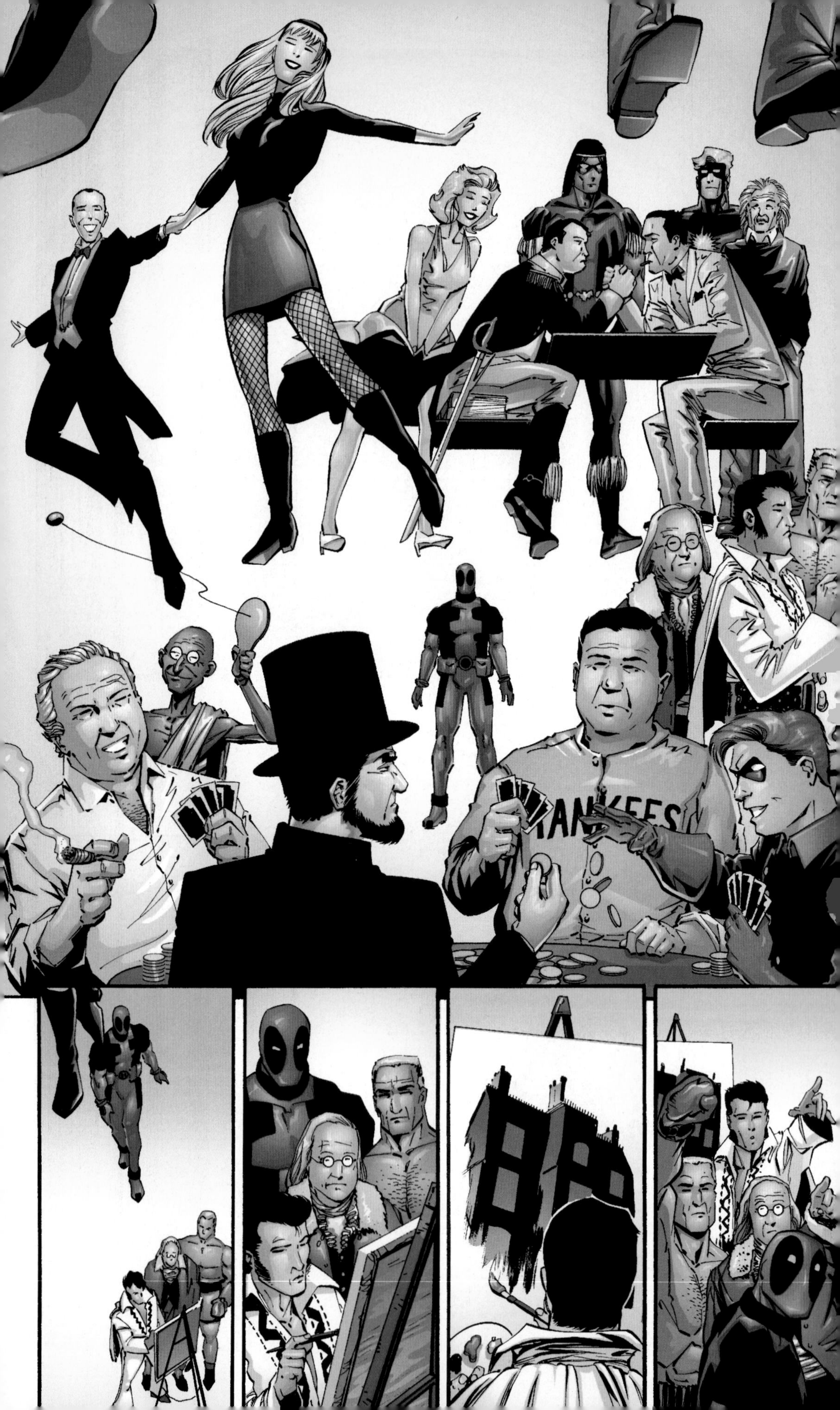

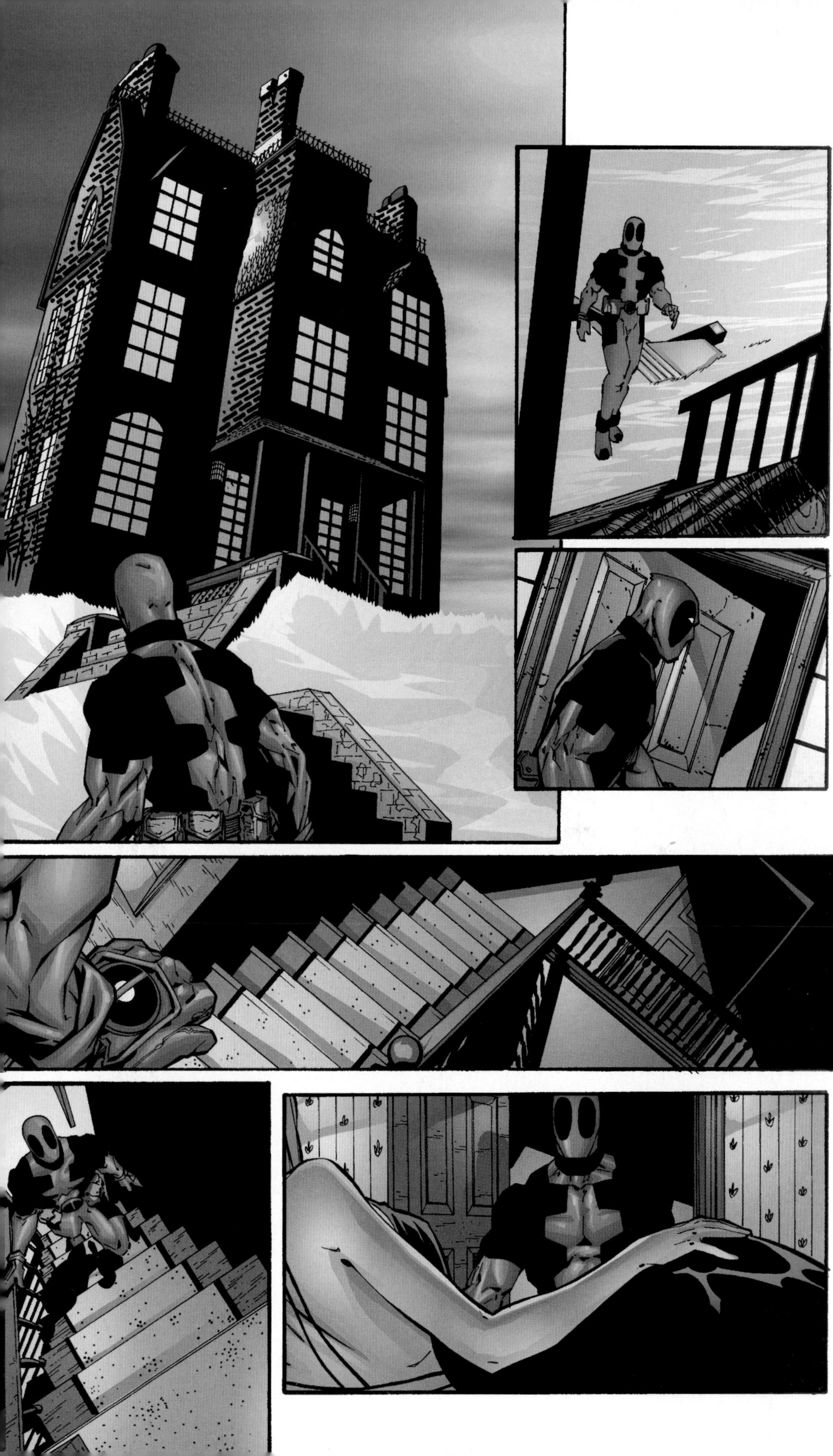

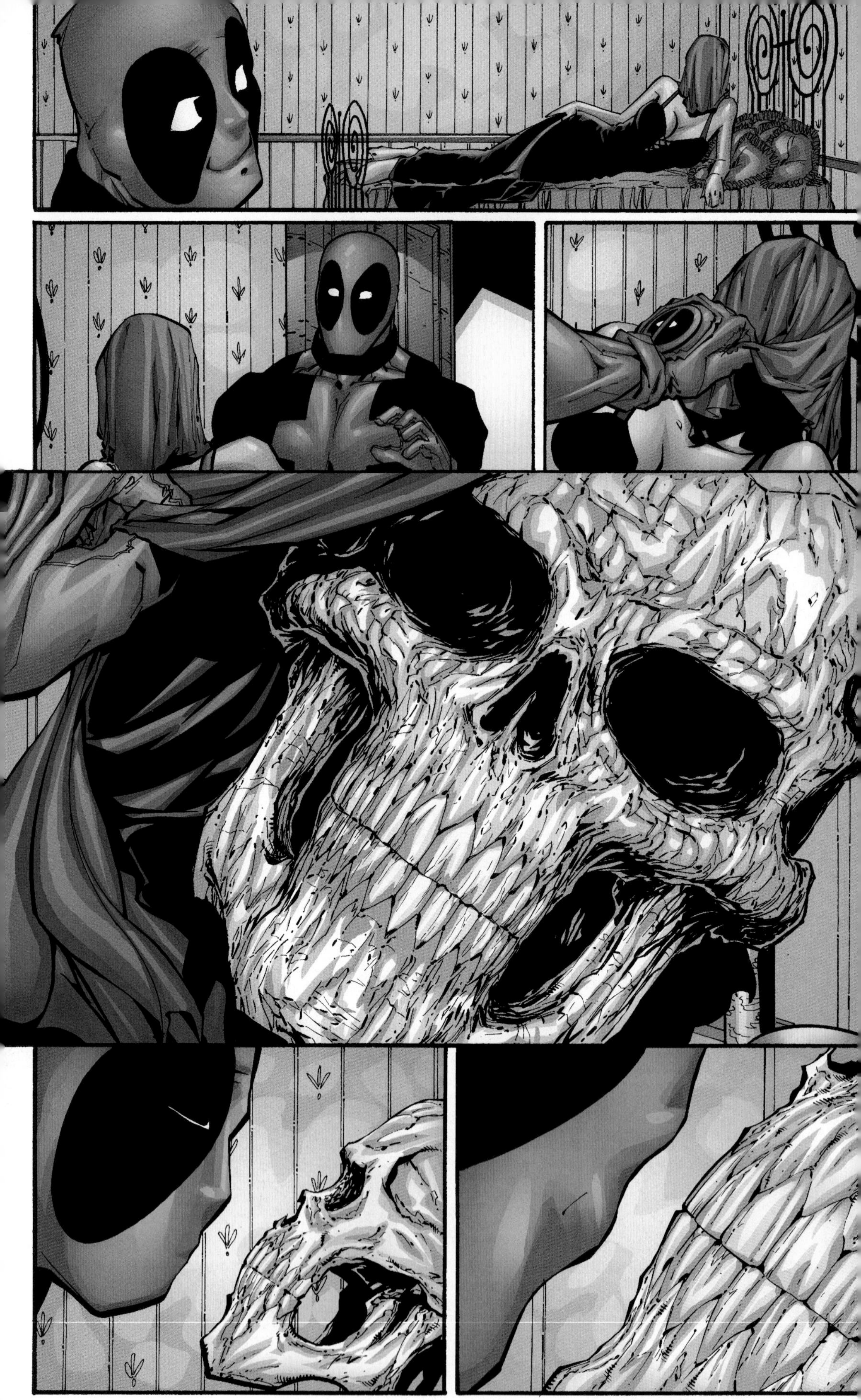

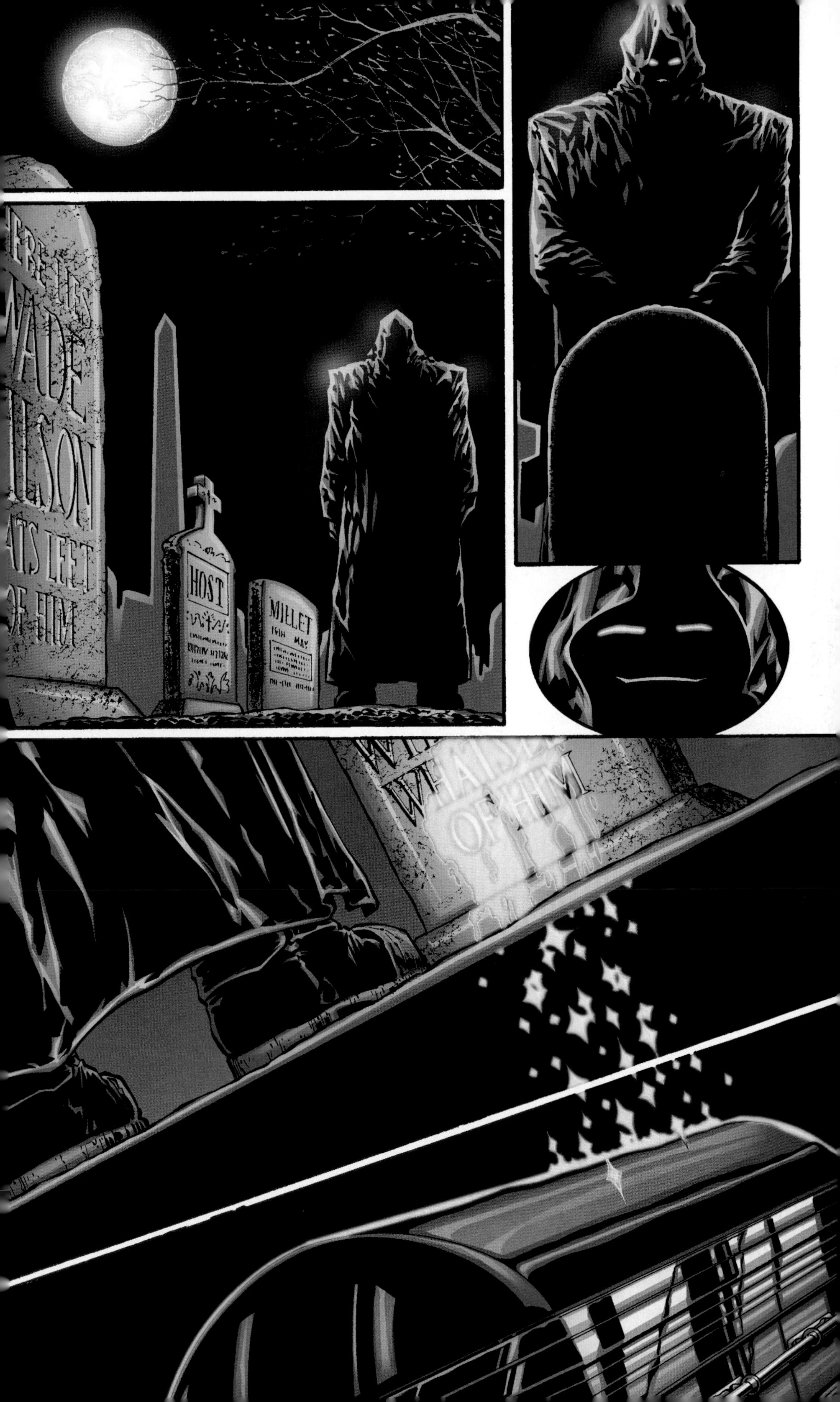

HOST
MILLET
OF HIM

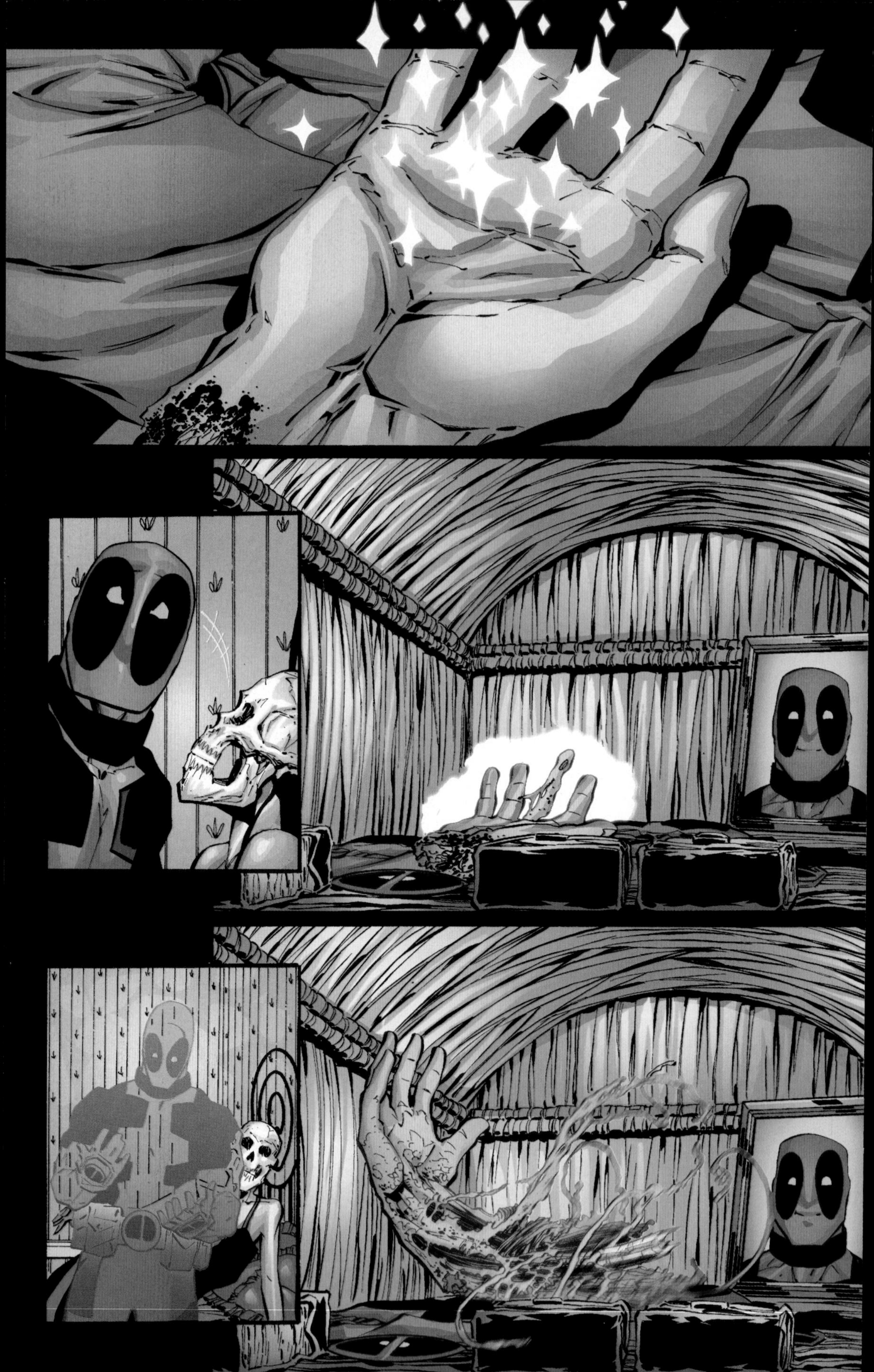

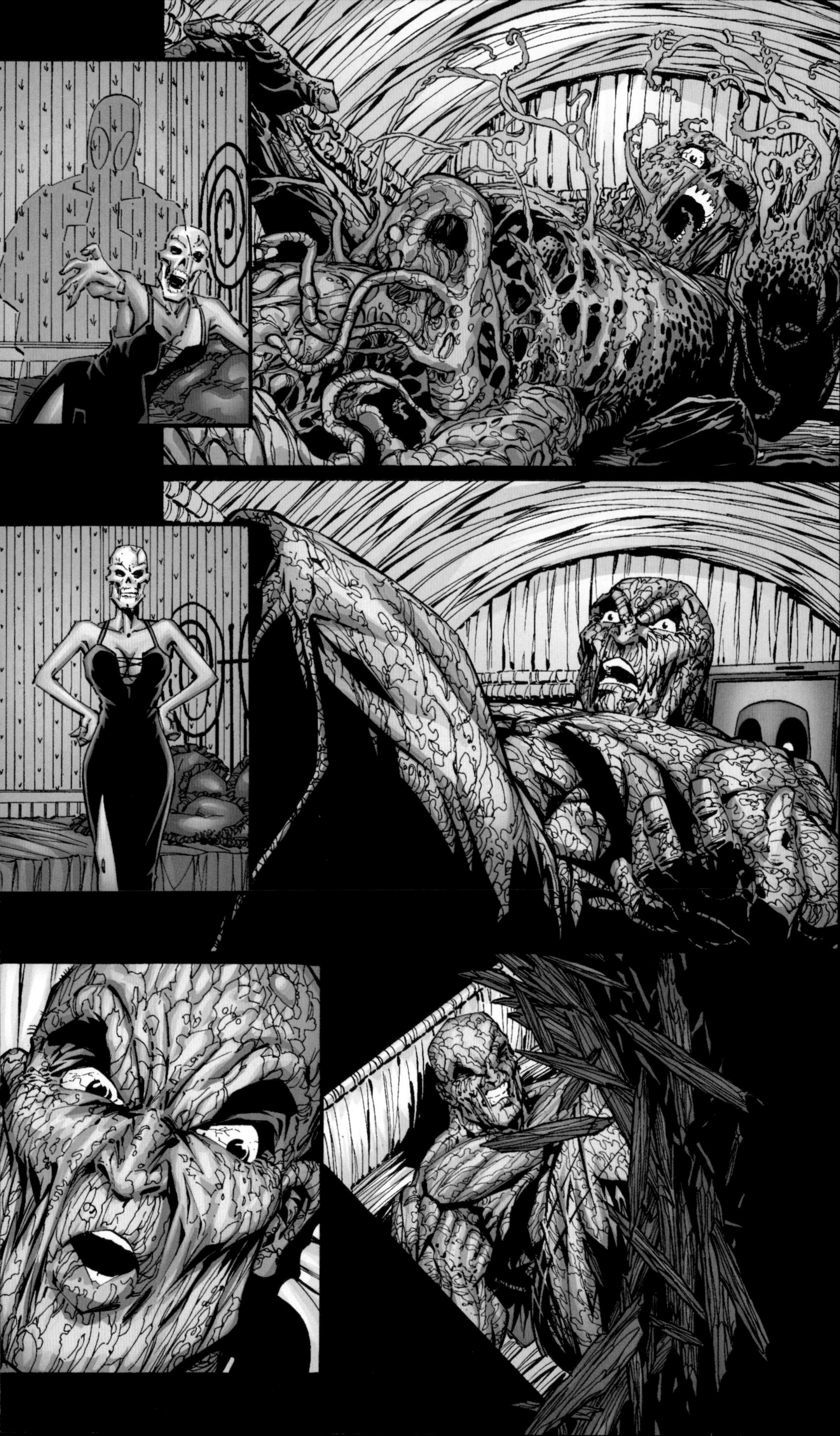

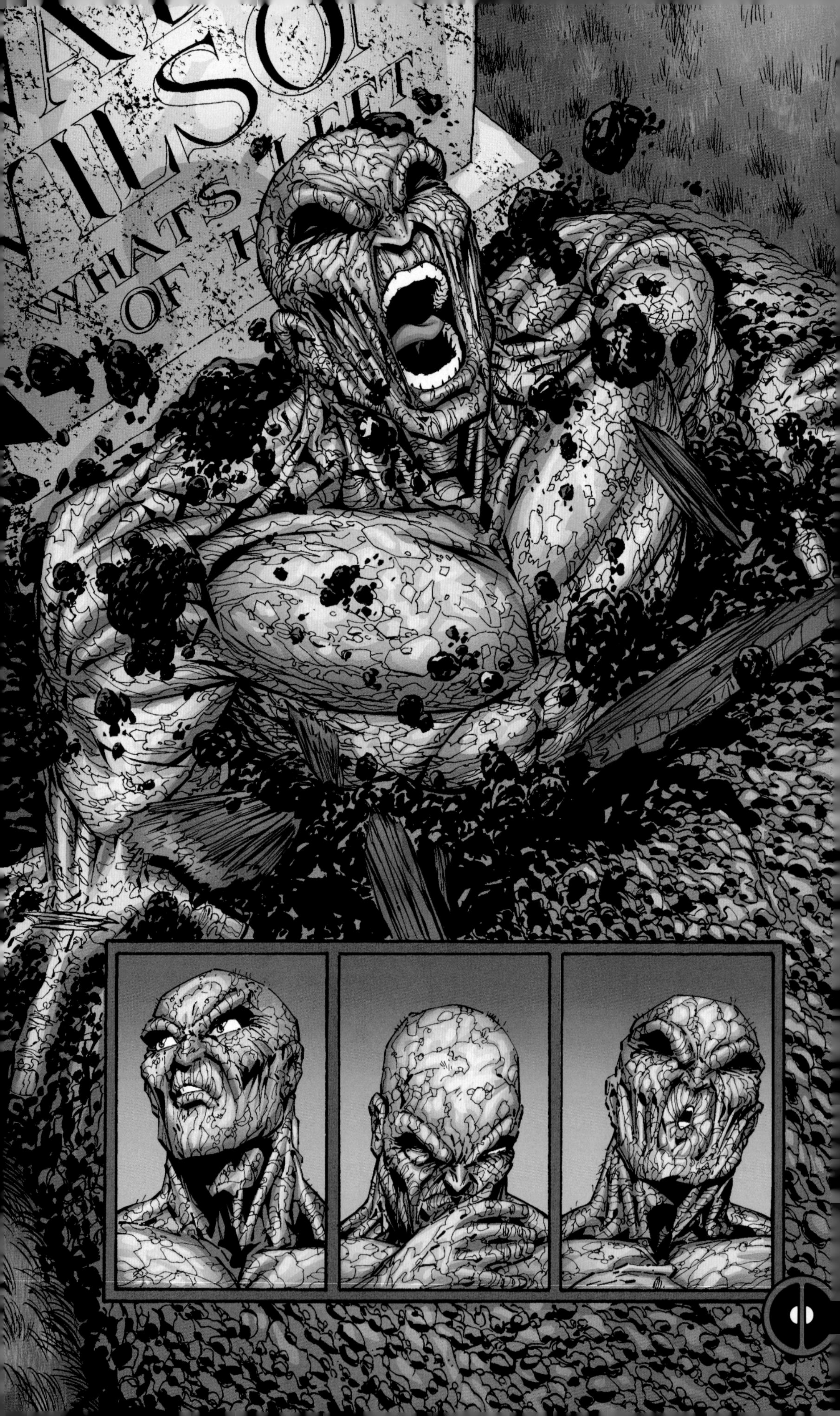
WHAT'S
OF

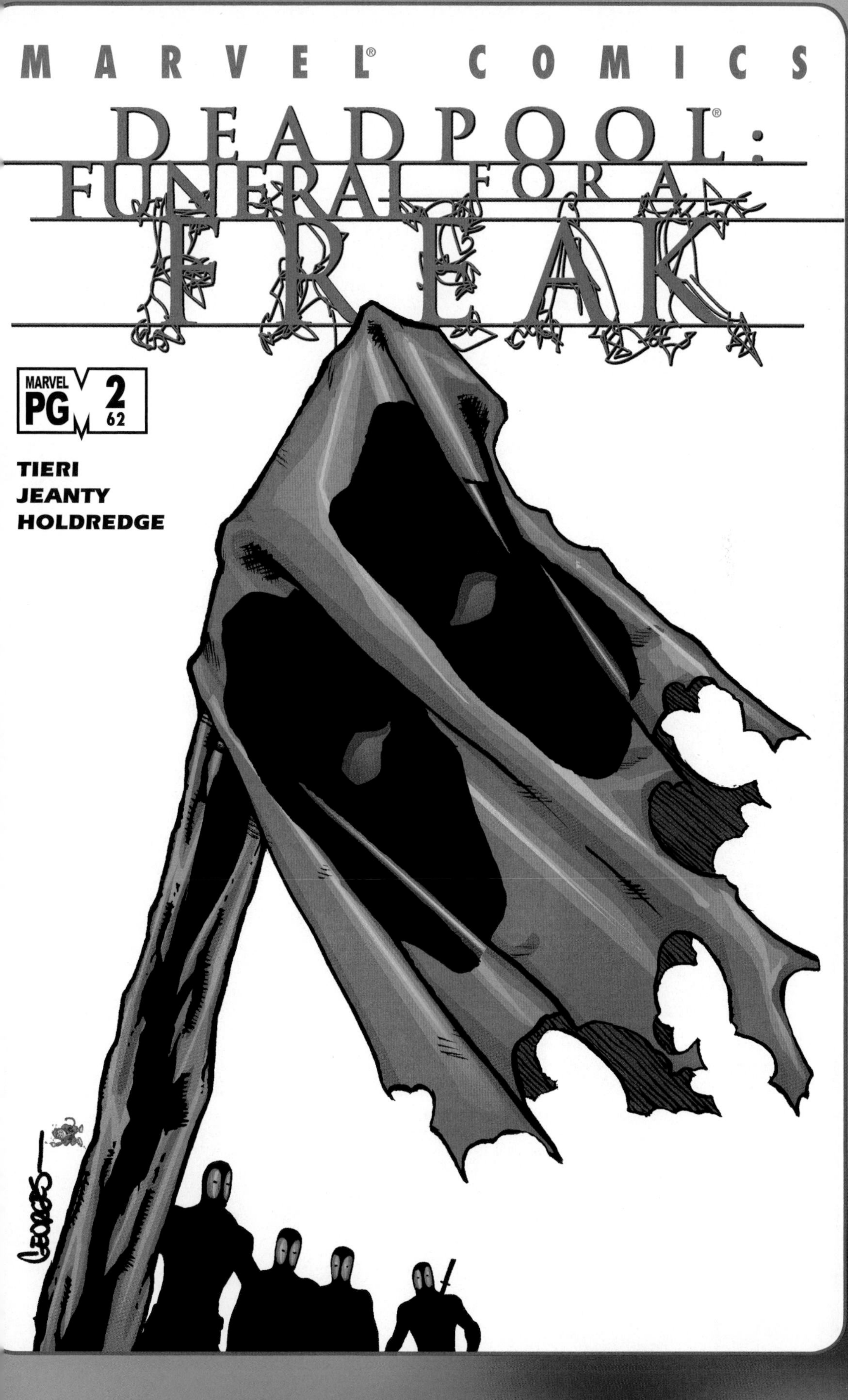
MARVEL® COMICS
DEADPOOL®: FUNERAL FOR A FREAK
MARVEL PG
2
62
TIERI
JEANTY
HOLDREDGE
GEORGES

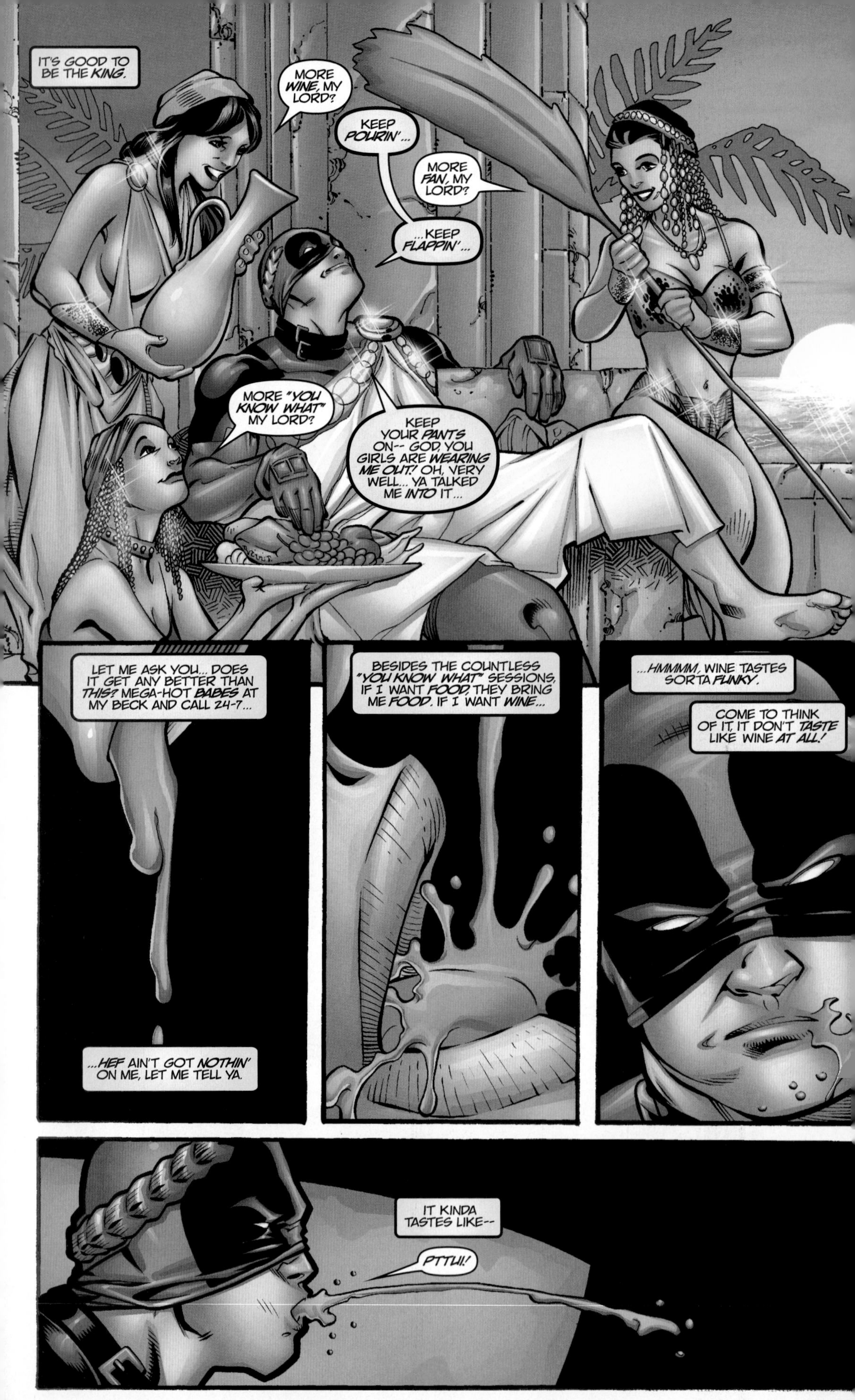
IT'S GOOD TO BE THE KING.
MORE WINE, MY LORD?
KEEP POURIN'...
MORE FAN, MY LORD?
...KEEP FLAPPIN'...
MORE "YOU KNOW WHAT" MY LORD?
KEEP YOUR PANTS ON-- GOD, YOU GIRLS ARE WEARING ME OUT! OH, VERY WELL... YA TALKED ME INTO IT...
LET ME ASK YOU... DOES IT GET ANY BETTER THAN THIS? MEGA-HOT BABES AT MY BECK AND CALL 24-7...
...HEF AIN'T GOT NOTHIN' ON ME, LET ME TELL YA.
BESIDES THE COUNTLESS "YOU KNOW WHAT" SESSIONS, IF I WANT FOOD, THEY BRING ME FOOD. IF I WANT WINE...
...HMMMM, WINE TASTES SORTA FUNKY.
COME TO THINK OF IT, IT DON'T TASTE LIKE WINE AT ALL!
IT KINDA TASTES LIKE--
PTTUI!

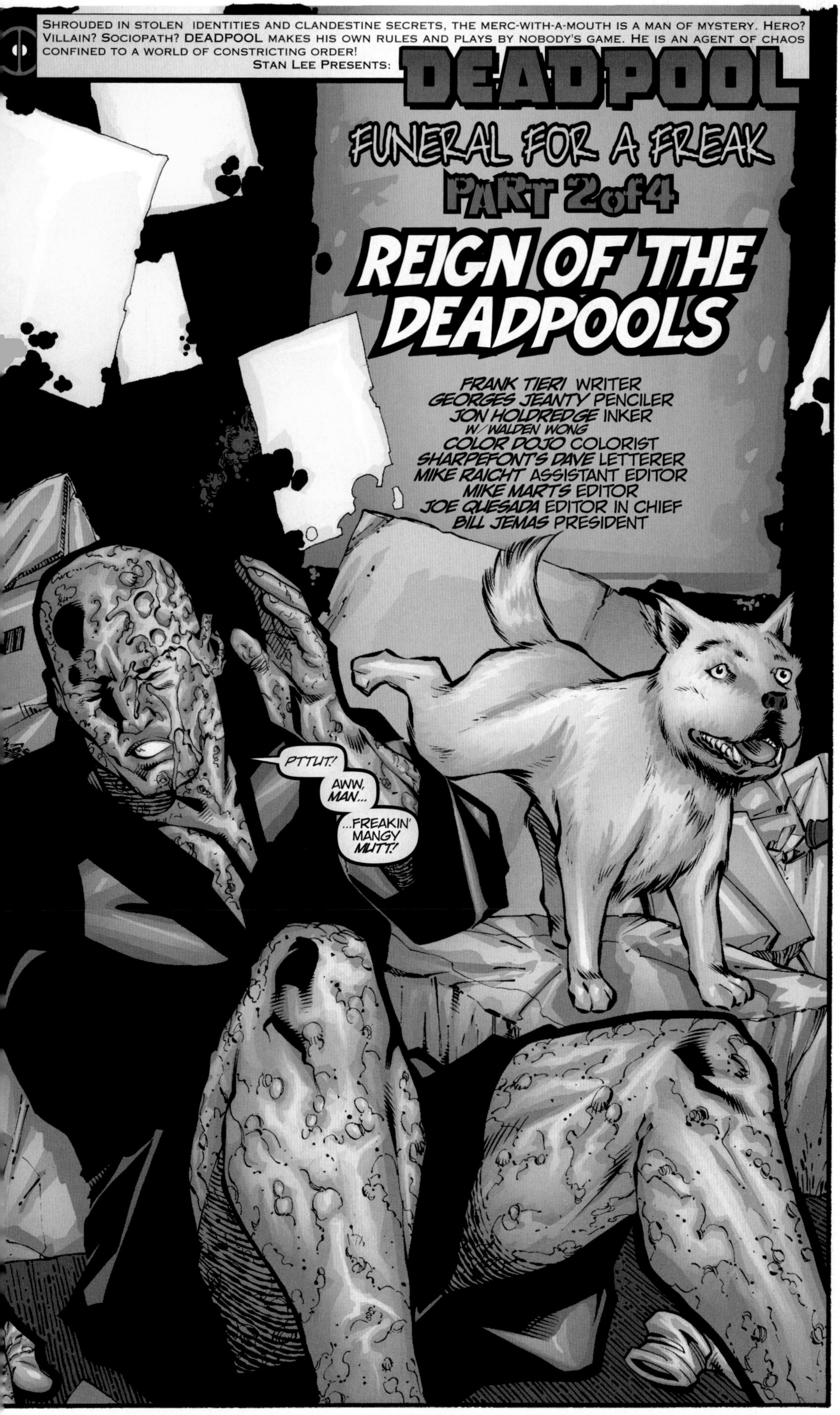

SHROUDED IN STOLEN IDENTITIES AND CLANDESTINE SECRETS, THE MERC-WITH-A-MOUTH IS A MAN OF MYSTERY. HERO? VILLAIN? SOCIOPATH? DEADPOOL MAKES HIS OWN RULES AND PLAYS BY NOBODY'S GAME. HE IS AN AGENT OF CHAOS CONFINED TO A WORLD OF CONSTRICTING ORDER!
STAN LEE PRESENTS:
DEADPOOL
FUNERAL FOR A FREAK
PART 2 OF 4
REIGN OF THE DEADPOOLS
FRANK TIERI WRITER
GEORGES JEANTY PENCILER
JON HOLDREDGE INKER
W/ WALDEN WONG
COLOR DOJO COLORIST
SHARPEFONT'S DAVE LETTERER
MIKE RAICHT ASSISTANT EDITOR
MIKE MARTS EDITOR
JOE QUESADA EDITOR IN CHIEF
BILL JEMAS PRESIDENT
PTTUT!
AWW, MAN...
...FREAKIN' MANGY MUTT!

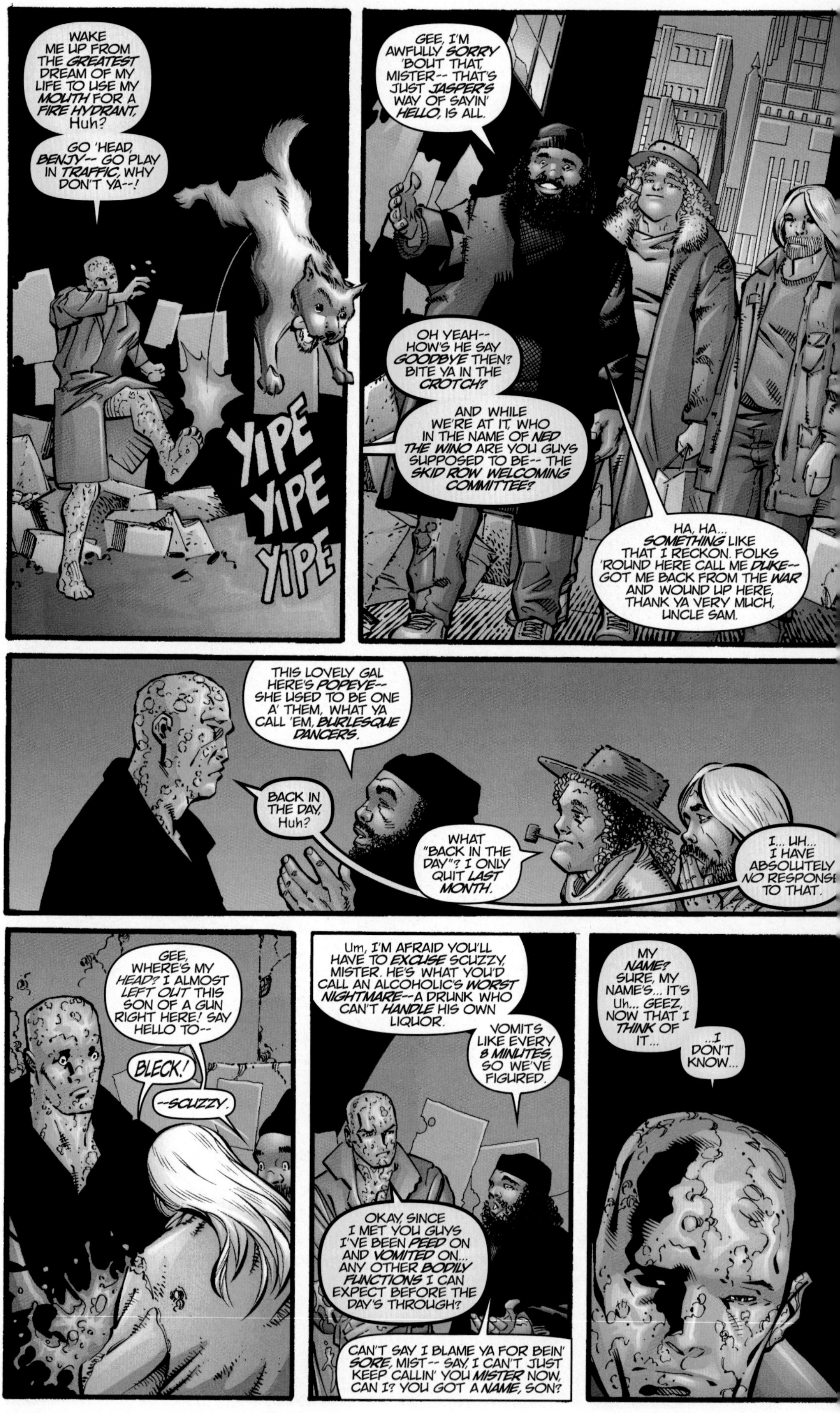

WAKE ME UP FROM THE GREATEST DREAM OF MY LIFE TO USE MY MOUTH FOR A FIRE HYDRANT, Huh?
GO 'HEAD, BENJY-- GO PLAY IN TRAFFIC, WHY DON'T YA--!
YIPE YIPE YIPE
GEE, I'M AWFULLY SORRY 'BOUT THAT, MISTER-- THAT'S JUST JASPER'S WAY OF SAYIN' HELLO, IS ALL.
OH YEAH-- HOW'S HE SAY GOODBYE THEN? BITE YA IN THE CROTCH?
AND WHILE WE'RE AT IT, WHO IN THE NAME OF NED THE WINO ARE YOU GUYS SUPPOSED TO BE-- THE SKID ROW WELCOMING COMMITTEE?
HA, HA... SOMETHING LIKE THAT I RECKON. FOLKS 'ROUND HERE CALL ME DUKE-- GOT ME BACK FROM THE WAR AND WOUND UP HERE, THANK YA VERY MUCH, UNCLE SAM.
THIS LOVELY GAL HERE'S POPEYE-- SHE USED TO BE ONE A' THEM, WHAT YA CALL 'EM, BURLESQUE DANCERS.
BACK IN THE DAY, Huh?
WHAT "BACK IN THE DAY"? I ONLY QUIT LAST MONTH.
I... UH... I HAVE ABSOLUTELY NO RESPONSE TO THAT.
GEE, WHERE'S MY HEAD? I ALMOST LEFT OUT THIS SON OF A GUN RIGHT HERE! SAY HELLO TO--
BLECK!
--SCUZZY.
Um, I'M AFRAID YOU'LL HAVE TO EXCUSE SCUZZY, MISTER. HE'S WHAT YOU'D CALL AN ALCOHOLIC'S WORST NIGHTMARE--A DRUNK WHO CAN'T HANDLE HIS OWN LIQUOR.
VOMITS LIKE EVERY 8 MINUTES, SO WE'VE FIGURED.
OKAY, SINCE I MET YOU GUYS I'VE BEEN PEED ON AND VOMITED ON... ANY OTHER BODILY FUNCTIONS I CAN EXPECT BEFORE THE DAY'S THROUGH?
CAN'T SAY I BLAME YA FOR BEIN' SORE, MIST-- SAY, I CAN'T JUST KEEP CALLIN' YOU MISTER NOW, CAN I? YOU GOT A NAME, SON?
MY NAME? SURE, MY NAME'S... IT'S Uh... GEEZ, NOW THAT I THINK OF IT...
...I DON'T KNOW...

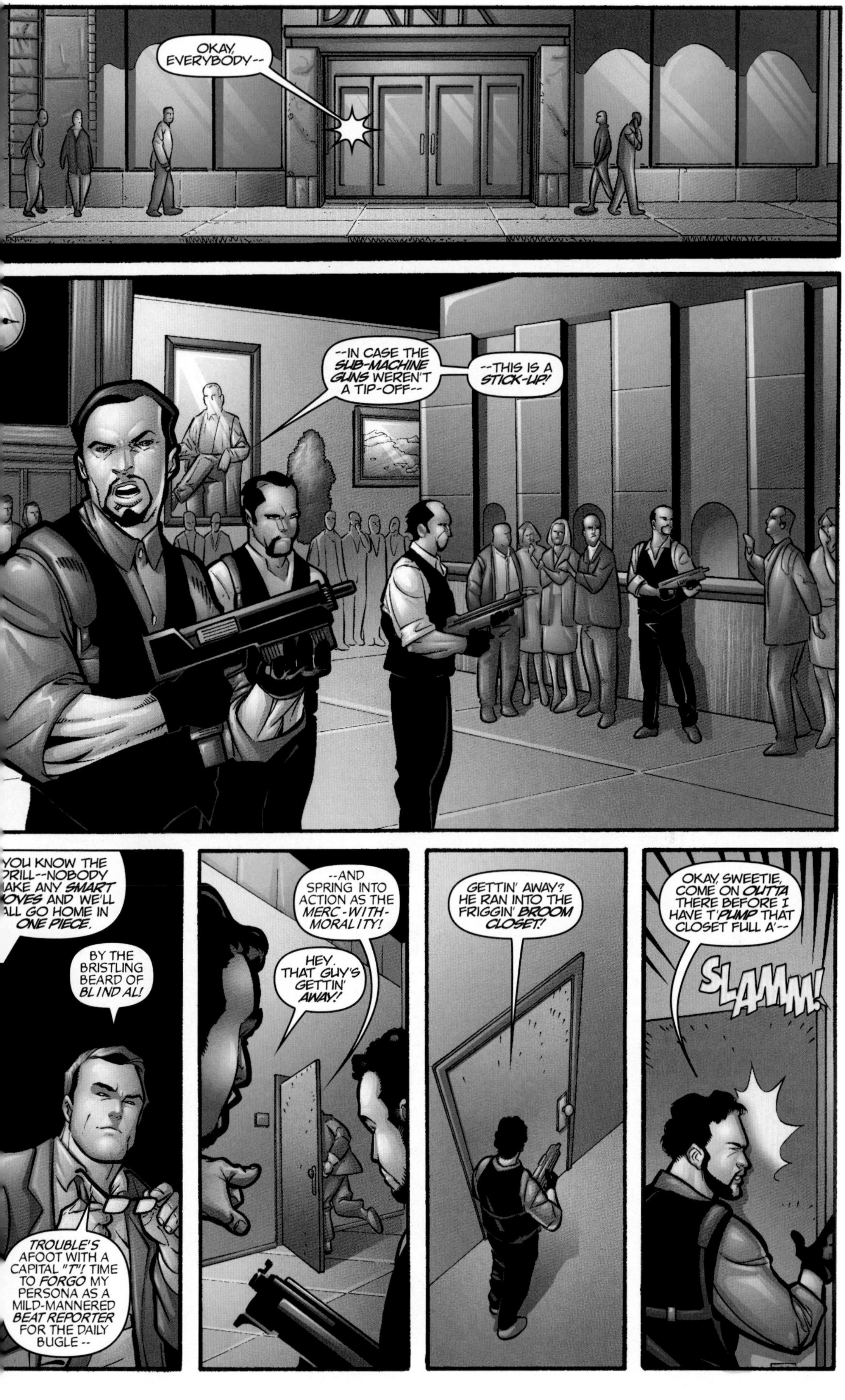

OKAY, EVERYBODY--
--IN CASE THE *SUB-MACHINE GUNS* WEREN'T A TIP-OFF--
--THIS IS A *STICK-UP!*
YOU KNOW THE RILL--NOBODY AKE ANY *SMART OVES* AND WE'LL ALL GO HOME IN *ONE PIECE*.
BY THE BRISTLING BEARD OF *BLIND AL!*
TROUBLE'S AFOOT WITH A CAPITAL *"T"!* TIME TO *FORGO* MY PERSONA AS A MILD-MANNERED *BEAT REPORTER* FOR THE DAILY BUGLE--
--AND SPRING INTO ACTION AS THE *MERC-WITH-MORALITY!*
HEY. THAT GUY'S GETTIN' *AWAY!*
GETTIN' AWAY? HE RAN INTO THE FRIGGIN' *BROOM CLOSET!*
OKAY, SWEETIE, COME ON *OUTTA* THERE BEFORE I HAVE T'*PUMP* THAT CLOSET FULL A'--
SLAMM!

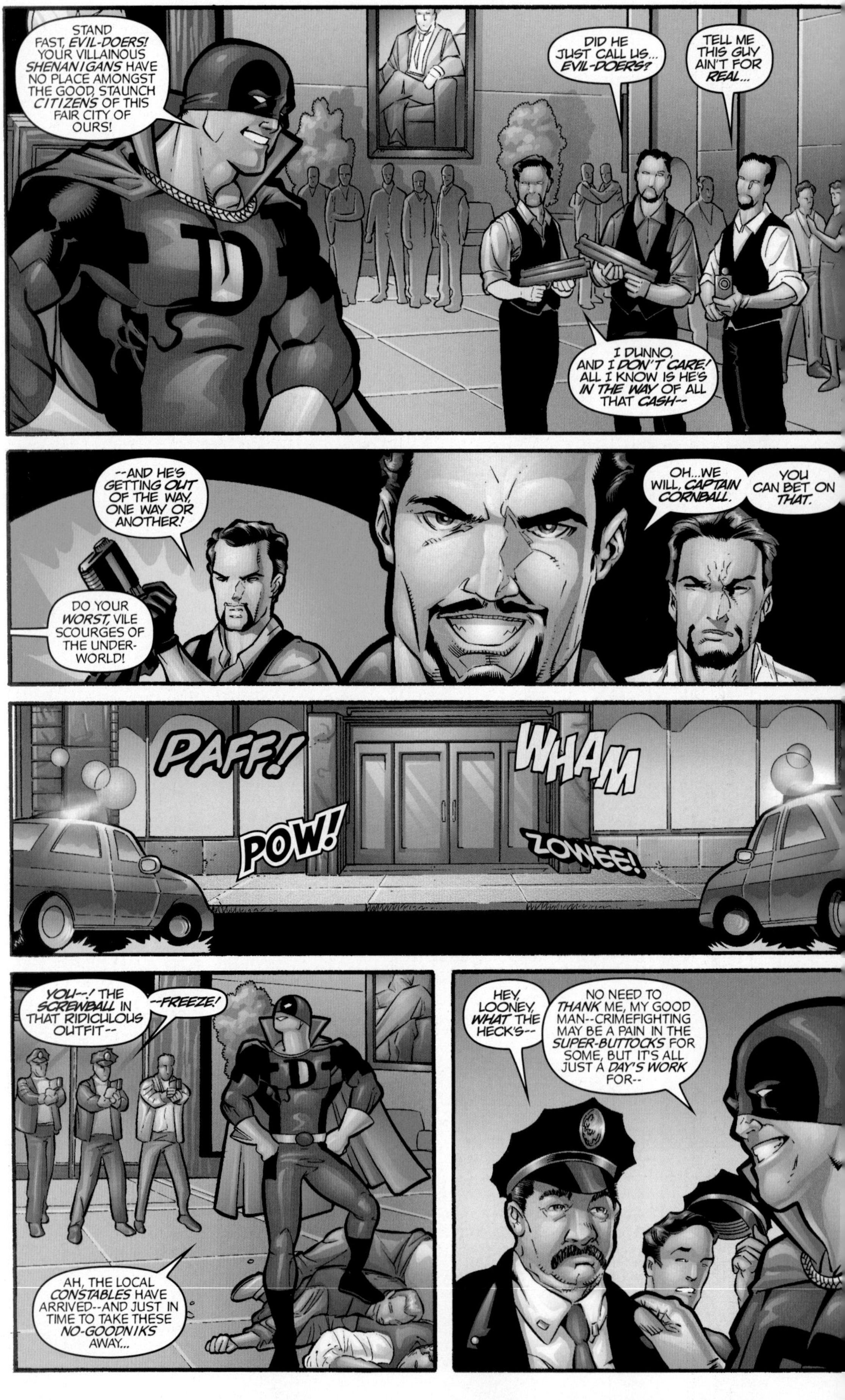
STAND FAST, EVIL-DOERS! YOUR VILLAINOUS SHENANIGANS HAVE NO PLACE AMONGST THE GOOD, STAUNCH CITIZENS OF THIS FAIR CITY OF OURS!
DID HE JUST CALL US... EVIL-DOERS?
TELL ME THIS GUY AIN'T FOR REAL...
I DUNNO, AND I DON'T CARE! ALL I KNOW IS HE'S IN THE WAY OF ALL THAT CASH--
--AND HE'S GETTING OUT OF THE WAY, ONE WAY OR ANOTHER!
OH...WE WILL, CAPTAIN CORNBALL.
YOU CAN BET ON THAT.
DO YOUR WORST, VILE SCOURGES OF THE UNDER-WORLD!
PAFF!
WHAM
POW!
ZOWEE!
YOU--! THE SCREWBALL IN THAT RIDICULOUS OUTFIT--
--FREEZE!
AH, THE LOCAL CONSTABLES HAVE ARRIVED--AND JUST IN TIME TO TAKE THESE NO-GOODNIKS AWAY...
HEY, LOONEY, WHAT THE HECK'S--
NO NEED TO THANK ME, MY GOOD MAN--CRIMEFIGHTING MAY BE A PAIN IN THE SUPER-BUTTOCKS FOR SOME, BUT IT'S ALL JUST A DAY'S WORK FOR--

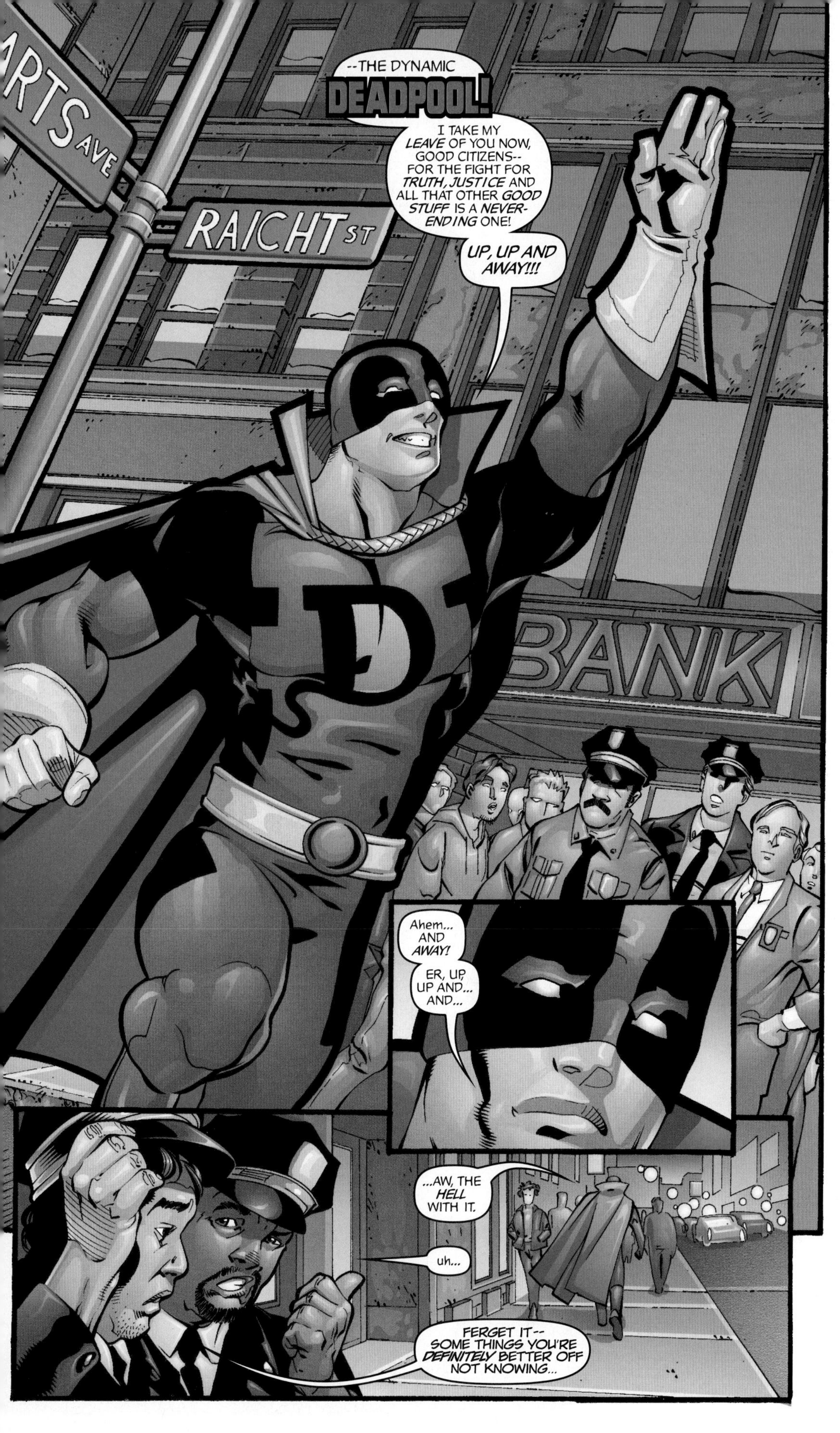

ARTS AVE
RAICHT ST
--THE DYNAMIC DEADPOOL!
I TAKE MY LEAVE OF YOU NOW, GOOD CITIZENS-- FOR THE FIGHT FOR TRUTH, JUSTICE AND ALL THAT OTHER GOOD STUFF IS A NEVER-ENDING ONE!
UP, UP AND AWAY!!!
BANK
Ahem... AND AWAY!
ER, UP, UP AND... AND...
...AW, THE HELL WITH IT.
uh...
FERGET IT-- SOME THINGS YOU'RE DEFINITELY BETTER OFF NOT KNOWING...

MAN, YOU'RE *LUCKY* YOU CAME ALONG BEFORE WE GOT TO *"FOOD SCROUNGIN' TIME"* -- BEST PART OF THE DAY IT IS!

YEAH, SOUNDS *GREAT.* SOMEBODY *SHOOT* ME NOW, PLEASE.

AWW, THAT'S JUST *NEWBIE* TALK, MISTER-- BELIEVE ME, YOU'LL GET USED TO THINGS QUICKER THAN YA *THINK.*

MIGHT HELP IF YA KNEW YOUR *NAME* AND HOW YA *GOT* HERE, THOUGH...

THAT'S THE *THING,* I HAVEN'T THE *FOGGIEST* IDEA HOW I GOT HERE-- JUST WOKE UP IN THE ALLEY WEARING THIS *OVERCOAT* WITH YOUR DOG GIVING ME A LITTLE *SHOWER...*

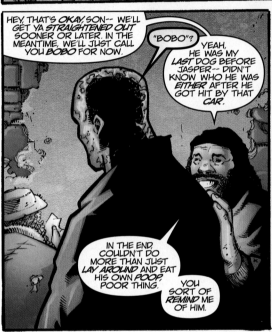

HEY, THAT'S *OKAY,* SON-- WE'LL GET YA *STRAIGHTENED OUT* SOONER OR LATER. IN THE MEANTIME, WE'LL JUST CALL YOU *BOBO* FOR NOW.

"BOBO"?

YEAH, HE WAS MY *LAST* DOG BEFORE JASPER-- DIDN'T KNOW WHO HE WAS *EITHER* AFTER HE GOT HIT BY THAT *CAR.*

IN THE END, COULDN'T DO MORE THAN JUST *LAY AROUND* AND EAT HIS OWN *POOP,* POOR THING.

YOU SORT OF *REMIND* ME OF HIM.

GEE... THANKS, THAT REALLY MAKES ME FEEL ALL *WARM* AND *FUZZY* INSIDE. NO, REALLY.

HEY, LOOKS LIKE SCUZZY'S *FOUND* SOMETHING!

OOOH, WE GOT *LUCKY* TODAY! MY FAVORITE-- *GOOP ON A STICK!* DON'T FIND *GOOD EATS* LIKE THAT TOO OFTEN!

LOOK, BOBO-- SCUZZY'S *OFFERIN* IT TO YA-- ONLY RIGHT YOU GETTIN' *FIRST DIBS* ON GRUB, BEIN' OUR *GUEST* AN' ALL.

W-WHAT?!

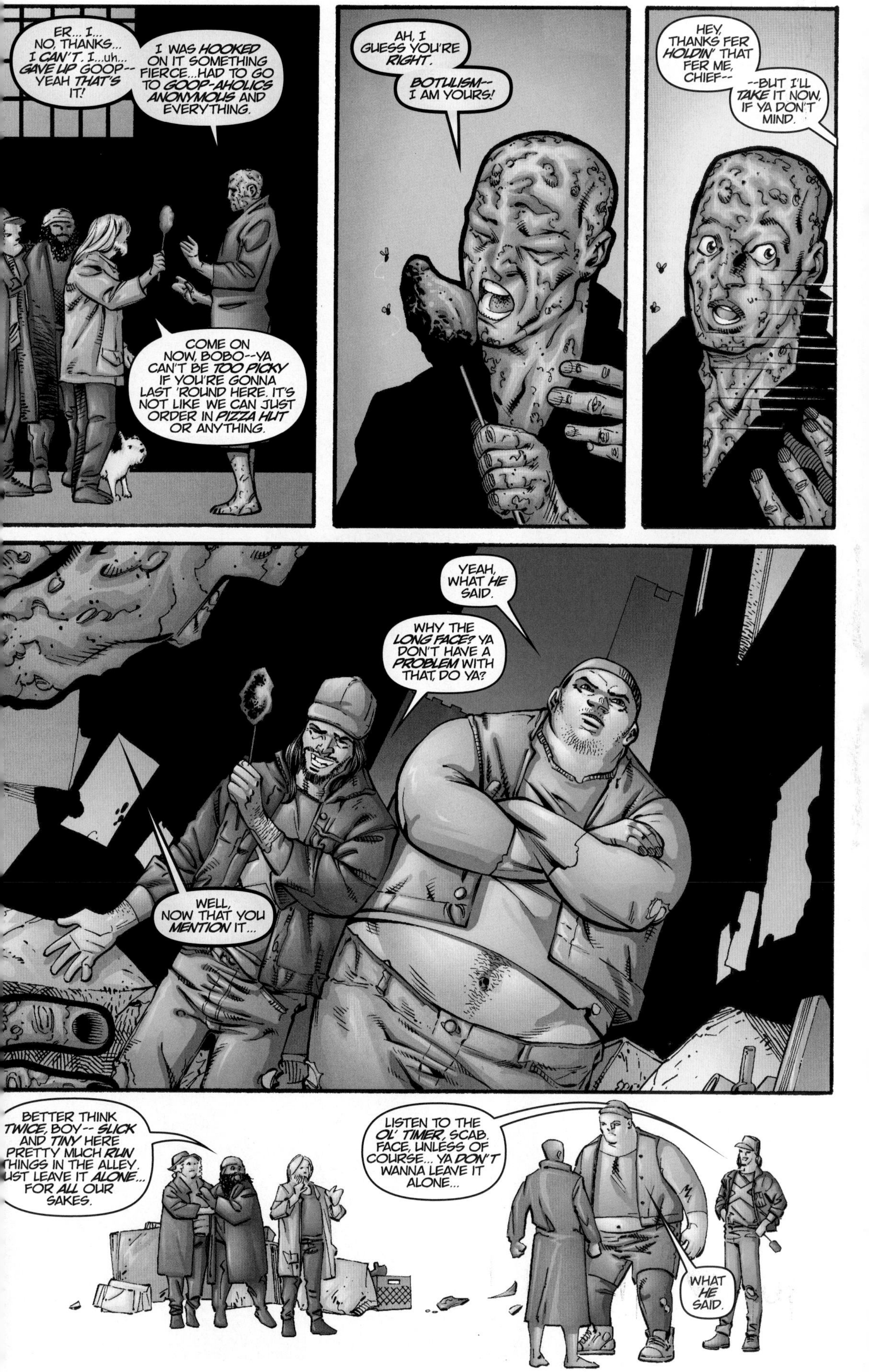
ER... I... NO, THANKS... I CAN'T. I...uh... GAVE UP GOOP-- YEAH THAT'S IT!
I WAS HOOKED ON IT SOMETHING FIERCE...HAD TO GO TO GOOP-AHOLICS ANONYMOUS AND EVERYTHING.
COME ON NOW, BOBO--YA CAN'T BE TOO PICKY IF YOU'RE GONNA LAST 'ROUND HERE. IT'S JUST NOT LIKE WE CAN JUST ORDER IN PIZZA HUT OR ANYTHING.
AH, I GUESS YOU'RE RIGHT.
BOTULISM-- I AM YOURS!
HEY, THANKS FER HOLDIN' THAT FER ME, CHIEF--
--BUT I'LL TAKE IT NOW, IF YA DON'T MIND.
YEAH, WHAT HE SAID.
WHY THE LONG FACE? YA DON'T HAVE A PROBLEM WITH THAT, DO YA?
WELL, NOW THAT YOU MENTION IT...
BETTER THINK TWICE, BOY-- SLICK AND TINY HERE PRETTY MUCH RUN THINGS IN THE ALLEY. JUST LEAVE IT ALONE... FOR ALL OUR SAKES.
LISTEN TO THE OL' TIMER, SCAB FACE, UNLESS OF COURSE... YA DON'T WANNA LEAVE IT ALONE...
WHAT HE SAID.

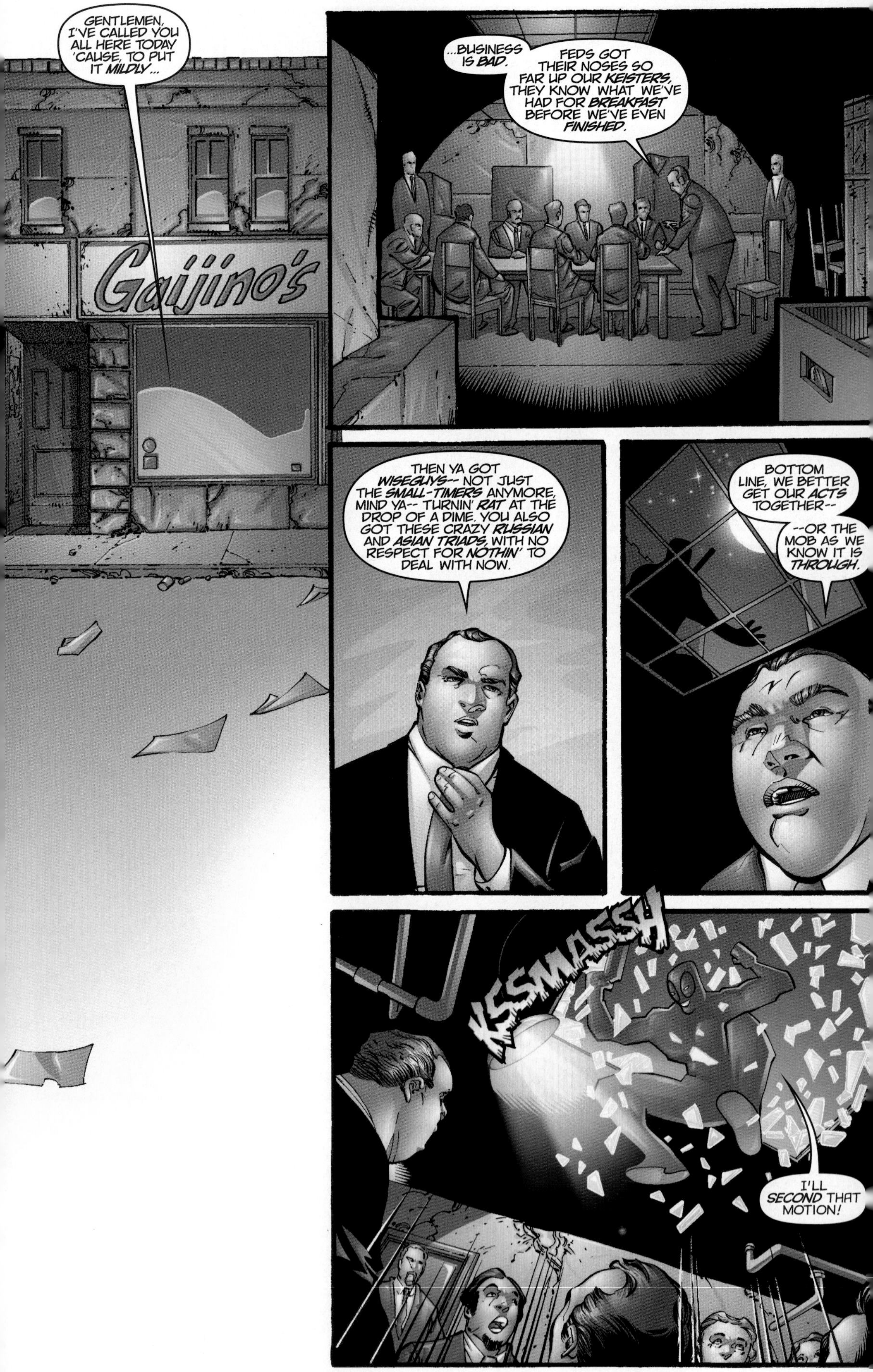

GENTLEMEN, I'VE CALLED YOU ALL HERE TODAY 'CAUSE, TO PUT IT MILDLY...
Gaijino's
...BUSINESS IS BAD.
FEDS GOT THEIR NOSES SO FAR UP OUR KEISTERS, THEY KNOW WHAT WE'VE HAD FOR BREAKFAST BEFORE WE'VE EVEN FINISHED.
THEN YA GOT WISEGUYS-- NOT JUST THE SMALL-TIMERS ANYMORE, MIND YA-- TURNIN' RAT AT THE DROP OF A DIME. YOU ALSO GOT THESE CRAZY RUSSIAN AND ASIAN TRIADS, WITH NO RESPECT FOR NOTHIN' TO DEAL WITH NOW.
BOTTOM LINE, WE BETTER GET OUR ACTS TOGETHER--
--OR THE MOB AS WE KNOW IT IS THROUGH.
KSSMASSH
I'LL SECOND THAT MOTION!

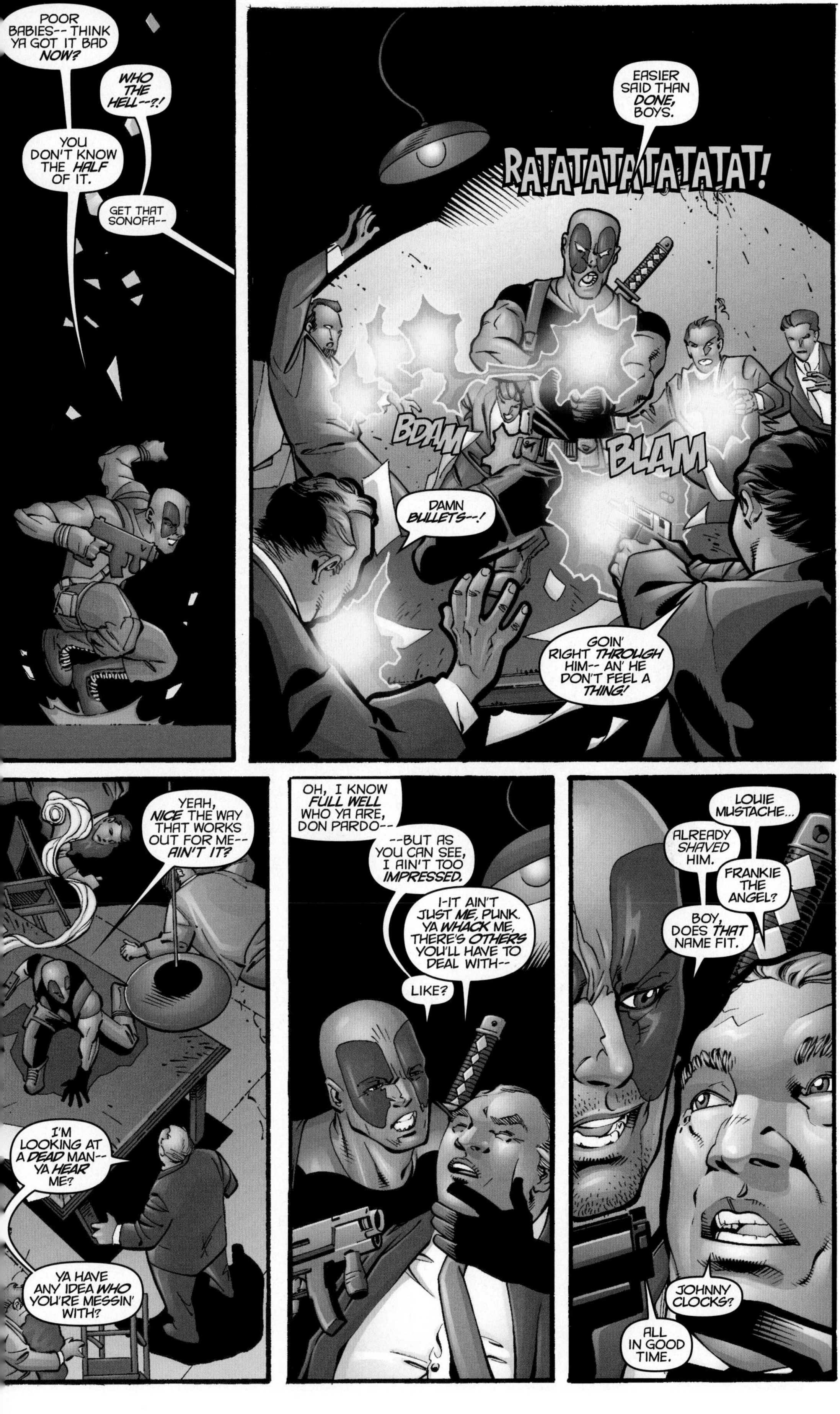

POOR BABIES-- THINK YA GOT IT BAD NOW?
WHO THE HELL--?!
YOU DON'T KNOW THE HALF OF IT.
GET THAT SONOFA--
EASIER SAID THAN DONE, BOYS.
RATATATATATATAT!
BDAM
BLAM
DAMN BULLETS--!
GOIN' RIGHT THROUGH HIM-- AN' HE DON'T FEEL A THING!
YEAH, NICE THE WAY THAT WORKS OUT FOR ME-- AIN'T IT?
I'M LOOKING AT A DEAD MAN-- YA HEAR ME?
YA HAVE ANY IDEA WHO YOU'RE MESSIN' WITH?
OH, I KNOW FULL WELL WHO YA ARE, DON PARDO--
--BUT AS YOU CAN SEE, I AIN'T TOO IMPRESSED.
I-IT AIN'T JUST ME, PUNK. YA WHACK ME, THERE'S OTHERS YOU'LL HAVE TO DEAL WITH--
LIKE?
LOUIE MUSTACHE...
ALREADY SHAVED HIM.
FRANKIE THE ANGEL?
BOY, DOES THAT NAME FIT.
JOHNNY CLOCKS?
ALL IN GOOD TIME.

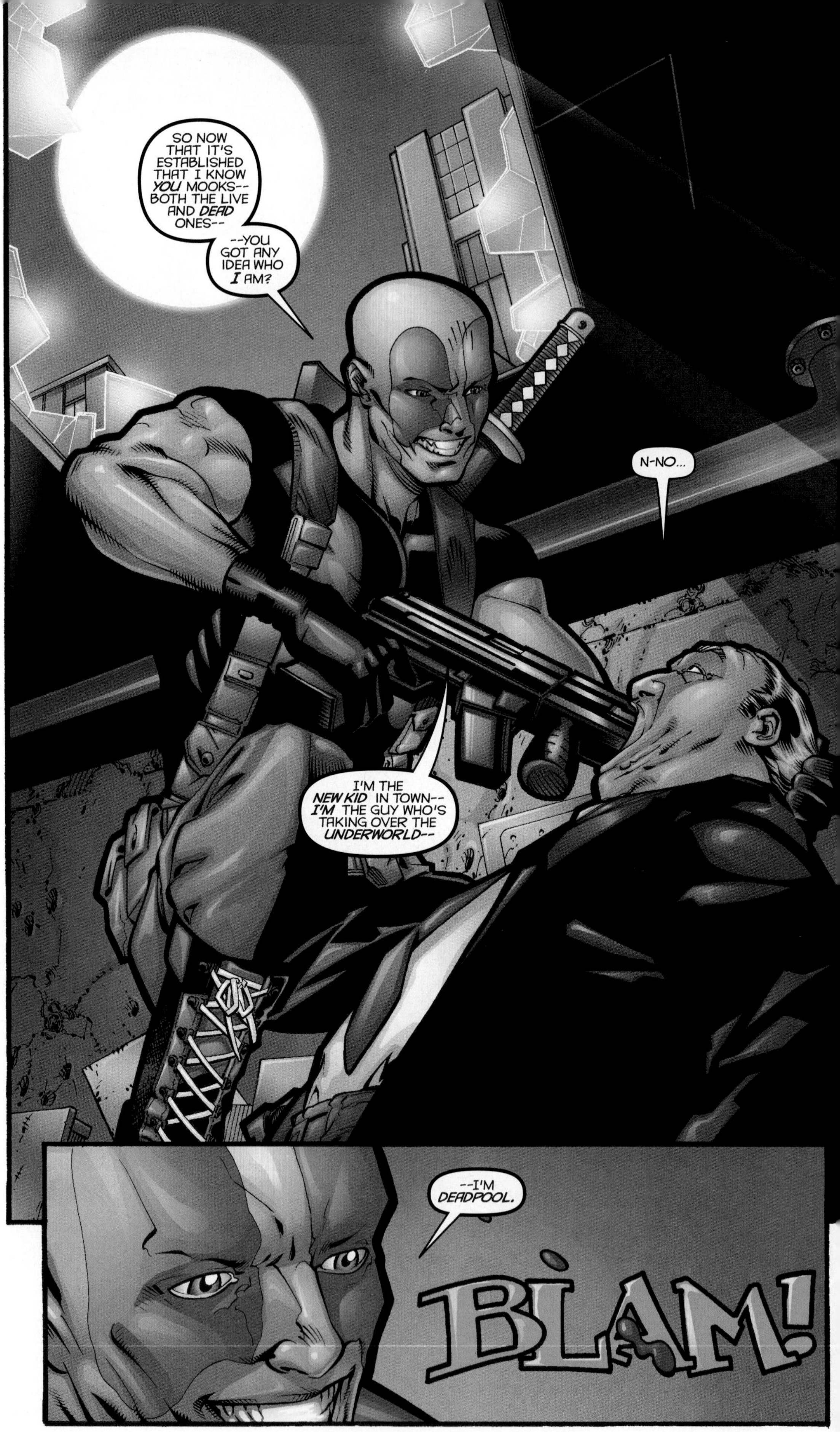
SO NOW THAT IT'S ESTABLISHED THAT I KNOW *YOU* MOOKS-- BOTH THE LIVE AND *DEAD* ONES--
--YOU GOT ANY IDEA WHO *I* AM?
N-NO...
I'M THE *NEW KID* IN TOWN-- *I'M* THE GUY WHO'S TAKING OVER THE *UNDERWORLD*--
--I'M *DEADPOOL.*
BLAM!

WHY DON'T YOU JUST LET US *BE*, SLICK? TAKE WHAT YOU CAME FOR... WE DON'T WANT ANY *TROUBLE*.

ACTUALLY, *TROUBLE'S* LOOKING REAL GOOD TO *ME* RIGHT ABOUT NOW.

DON'T WORRY, *WISE GUY*-- WE'LL GET TO YOU IN A *MINUTE*.

FIRST I WANNA KNOW WHY *SCUZZY* HERE WAS *EYE-BALLIN'* ME WHEN WE SHOWED.

URP.

OH, NO YA DON'T! YOU BETTER AIM THAT *PUKE* SOMEPLACE *ELSE* IF YA KNOW WHAT'S *GOOD* FOR YA!

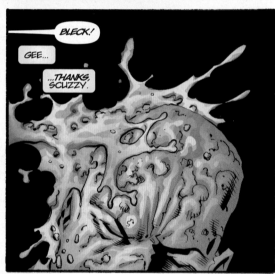

BLECK!

GEE...

...THANKS, SCUZZY.

BWAHAHAHAHAHA!

DID YOU *SEE* THAT?

YOU SEE *THAT*, BOYS?

POW

POW

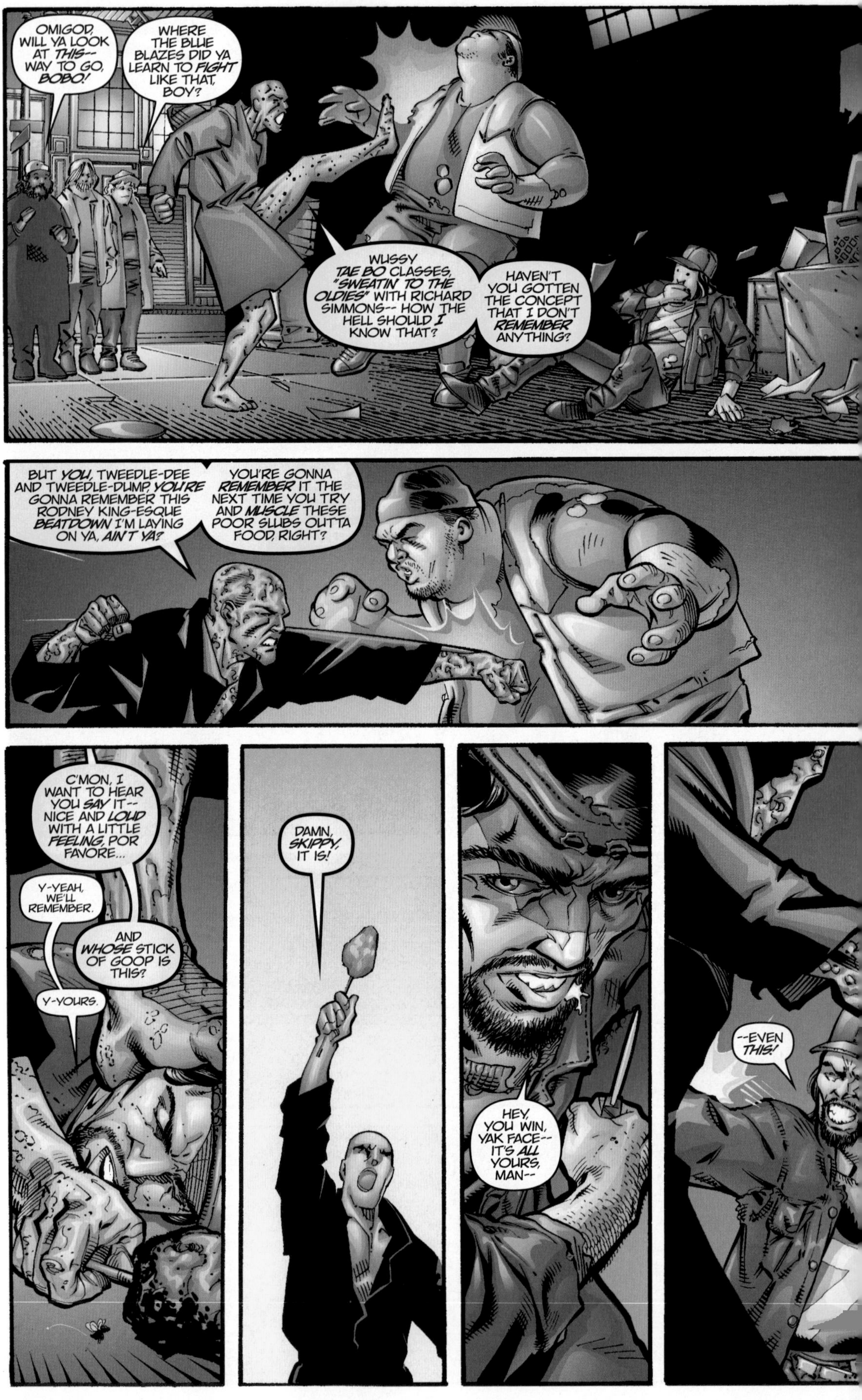
OMIGOD, WILL YA LOOK AT THIS-- WAY TO GO, BOBO!
WHERE THE BLUE BLAZES DID YA LEARN TO FIGHT LIKE THAT, BOY?
WUSSY TAE BO CLASSES, "SWEATIN' TO THE OLDIES" WITH RICHARD SIMMONS-- HOW THE HELL SHOULD I KNOW THAT?
HAVEN'T YOU GOTTEN THE CONCEPT THAT I DON'T REMEMBER ANYTHING?
BUT YOU, TWEEDLE-DEE AND TWEEDLE-DUMP, YOU'RE GONNA REMEMBER THIS RODNEY KING-ESQUE BEATDOWN I'M LAYING ON YA, AIN'T YA?
YOU'RE GONNA REMEMBER IT THE NEXT TIME YOU TRY AND MUSCLE THESE POOR SLUBS OUTTA FOOD, RIGHT?
C'MON, I WANT TO HEAR YOU SAY IT-- NICE AND LOUD WITH A LITTLE FEELING, POR FAVORE...
Y-YEAH, WE'LL REMEMBER.
AND WHOSE STICK OF GOOP IS THIS?
Y-YOURS.
DAMN, SKIPPY, IT IS!
HEY, YOU WIN, YAK FACE-- IT'S ALL YOURS, MAN--
--EVEN THIS!

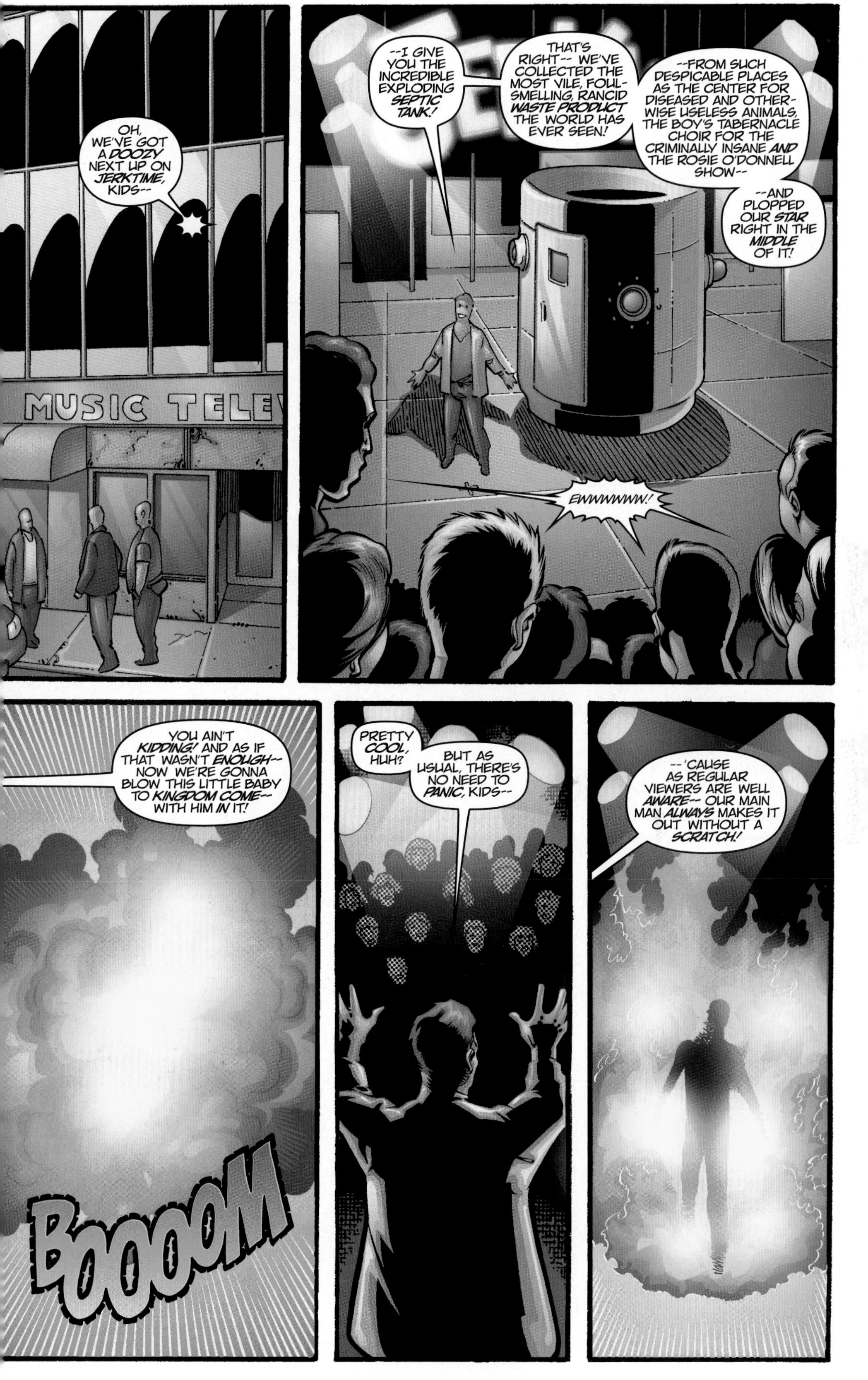
OH, WE'VE GOT A DOOZY NEXT UP ON JERKTIME, KIDS--
MUSIC TELEV
--I GIVE YOU THE INCREDIBLE EXPLODING SEPTIC TANK!
THAT'S RIGHT-- WE'VE COLLECTED THE MOST VILE, FOUL-SMELLING, RANCID WASTE PRODUCT THE WORLD HAS EVER SEEN!
--FROM SUCH DESPICABLE PLACES AS THE CENTER FOR DISEASED AND OTHER-WISE USELESS ANIMALS, THE BOY'S TABERNACLE CHOIR FOR THE CRIMINALLY INSANE AND THE ROSIE O'DONNELL SHOW--
--AND PLOPPED OUR STAR RIGHT IN THE MIDDLE OF IT!
EWWWWWW!
YOU AIN'T KIDDING! AND AS IF THAT WASN'T ENOUGH-- NOW WE'RE GONNA BLOW THIS LITTLE BABY TO KINGDOM COME-- WITH HIM IN IT!
BOOOOM
PRETTY COOL, HUH?
BUT AS USUAL, THERE'S NO NEED TO PANIC, KIDS--
--'CAUSE AS REGULAR VIEWERS ARE WELL AWARE-- OUR MAIN MAN ALWAYS MAKES IT OUT WITHOUT A SCRATCH!

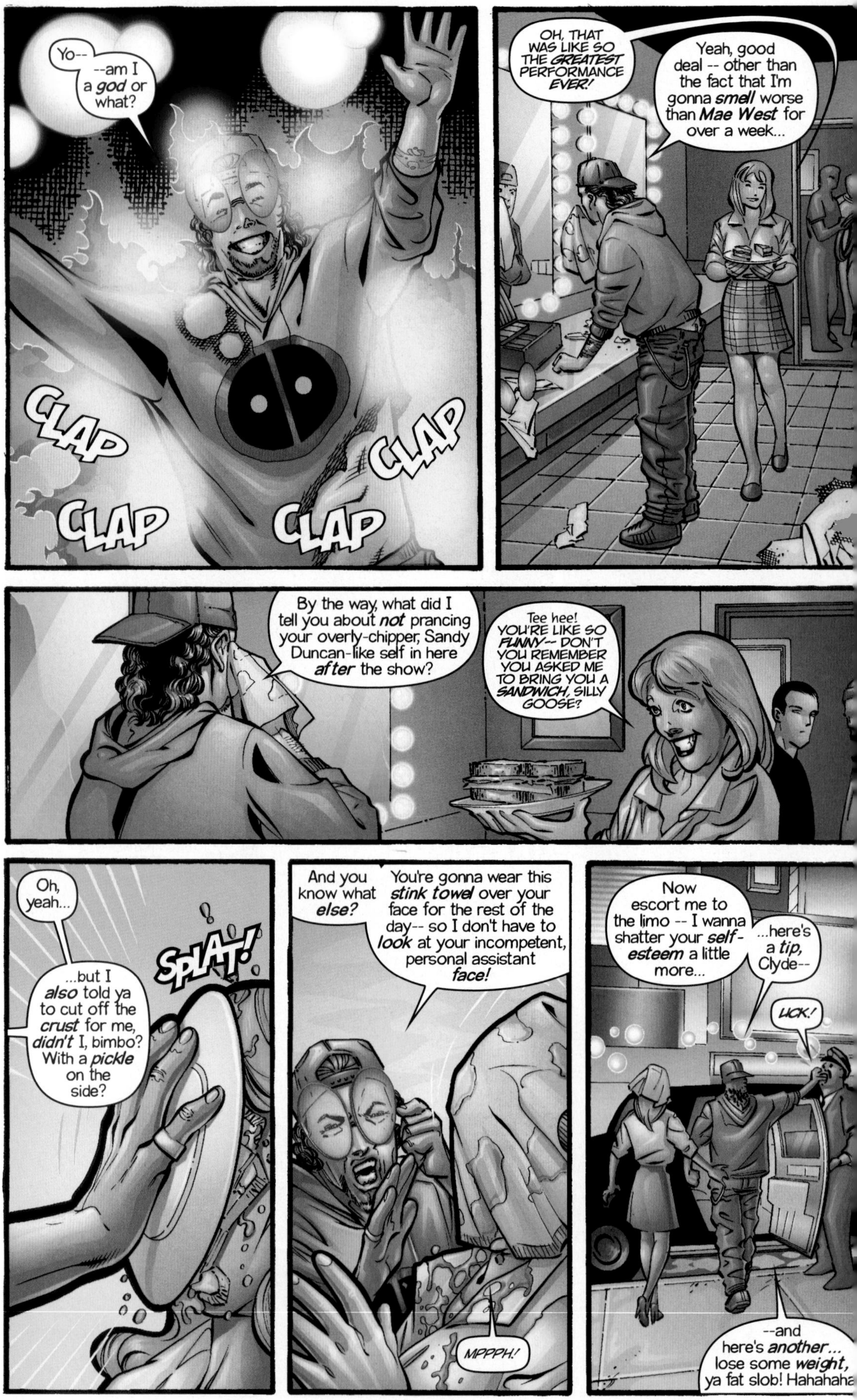
Yo--
--am I a god or what?
CLAP
CLAP
CLAP
CLAP
OH, THAT WAS LIKE SO THE GREATEST PERFORMANCE EVER!
Yeah, good deal -- other than the fact that I'm gonna smell worse than Mae West for over a week...
By the way, what did I tell you about not prancing your overly-chipper, Sandy Duncan-like self in here after the show?
Tee hee! YOU'RE LIKE SO FUNNY-- DON'T YOU REMEMBER YOU ASKED ME TO BRING YOU A SANDWICH, SILLY GOOSE?
Oh, yeah...
...but I also told ya to cut off the crust for me, didn't I, bimbo? With a pickle on the side?
SPLAT!
And you know what else?
You're gonna wear this stink towel over your face for the rest of the day-- so I don't have to look at your incompetent, personal assistant face!
MPPPH!
Now escort me to the limo -- I wanna shatter your self-esteem a little more...
...here's a tip, Clyde--
UCK!
--and here's another... lose some weight, ya fat slob! Hahahaha

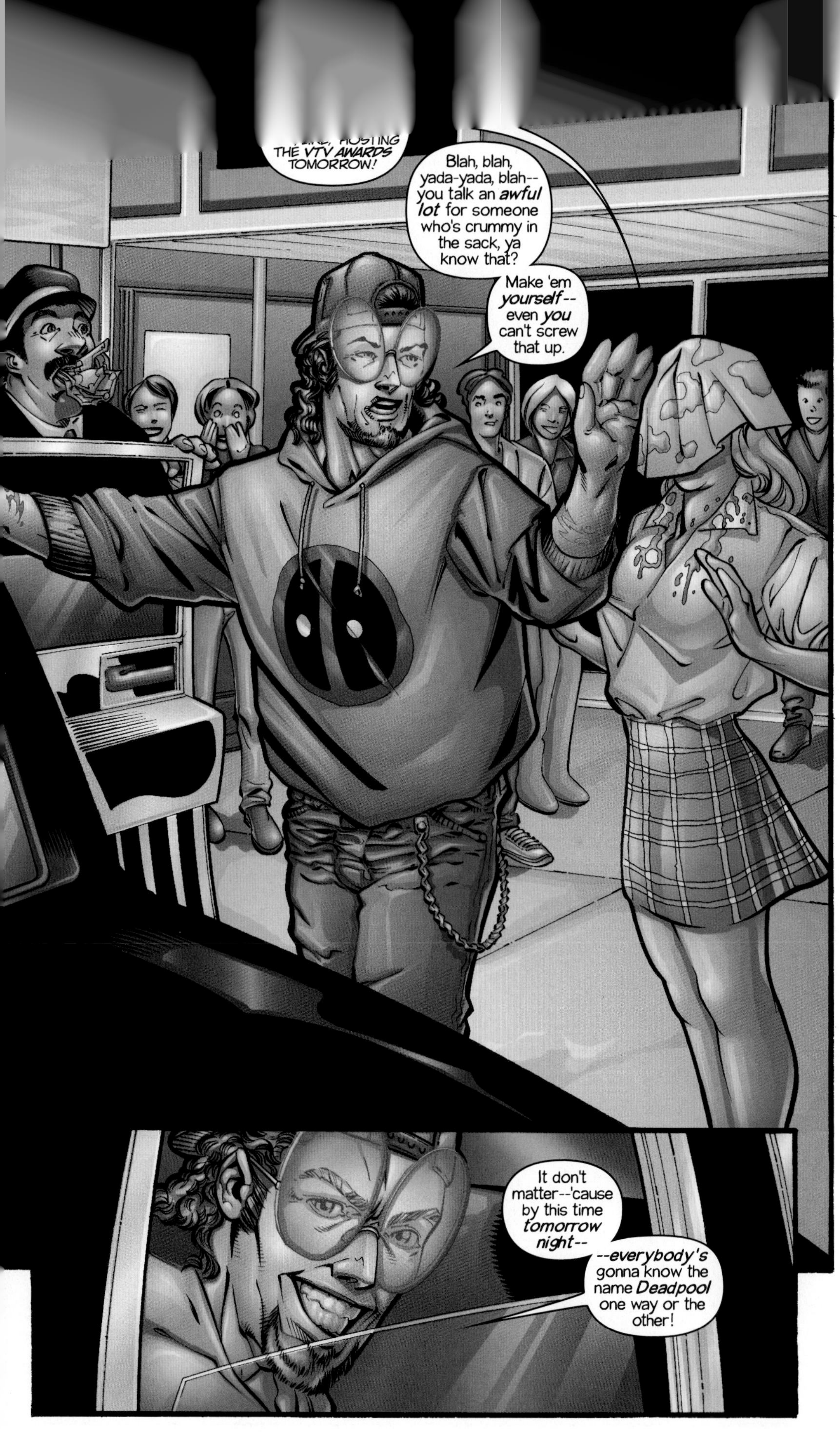

THE VTV AWARDS TOMORROW!
Blah, blah, yada-yada, blah-- you talk an awful lot for someone who's crummy in the sack, ya know that?
Make 'em yourself-- even you can't screw that up.
It don't matter--'cause by this time tomorrow night--
--everybody's gonna know the name Deadpool one way or the other!

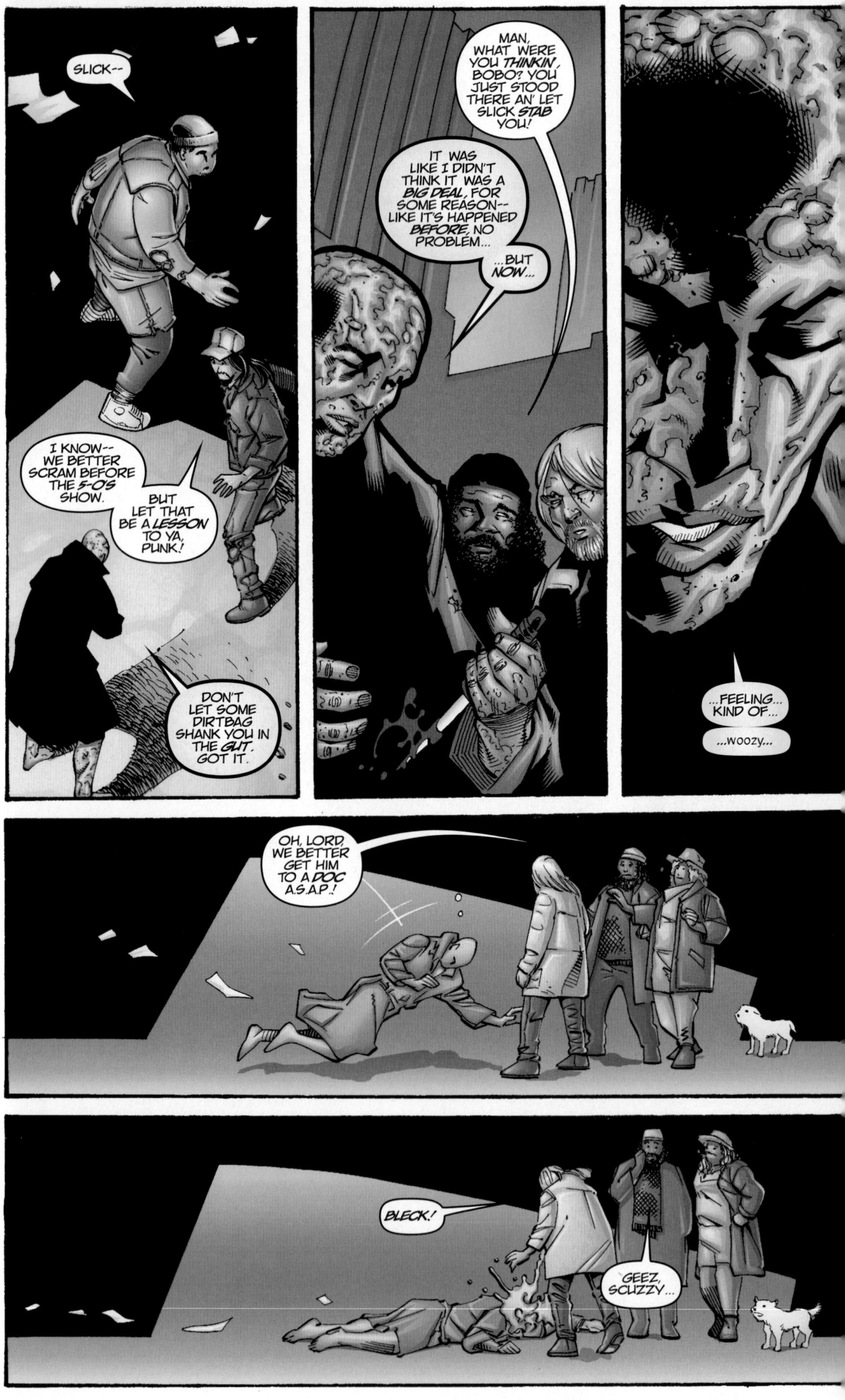
SLICK--
I KNOW-- WE BETTER SCRAM BEFORE THE 5-O'S SHOW.
BUT LET THAT BE A LESSON TO YA, PUNK!
DON'T LET SOME DIRTBAG SHANK YOU IN THE GUT. GOT IT.
MAN, WHAT WERE YOU THINKIN', BOBO? YOU JUST STOOD THERE AN' LET SLICK STAB YOU!
IT WAS LIKE I DIDN'T THINK IT WAS A BIG DEAL, FOR SOME REASON-- LIKE IT'S HAPPENED BEFORE, NO PROBLEM...
...BUT NOW...
...FEELING... KIND OF...
...woozy...
OH, LORD, WE BETTER GET HIM TO A DOC A.S.A.P.!
BLECK!
GEEZ, SCUZZY...

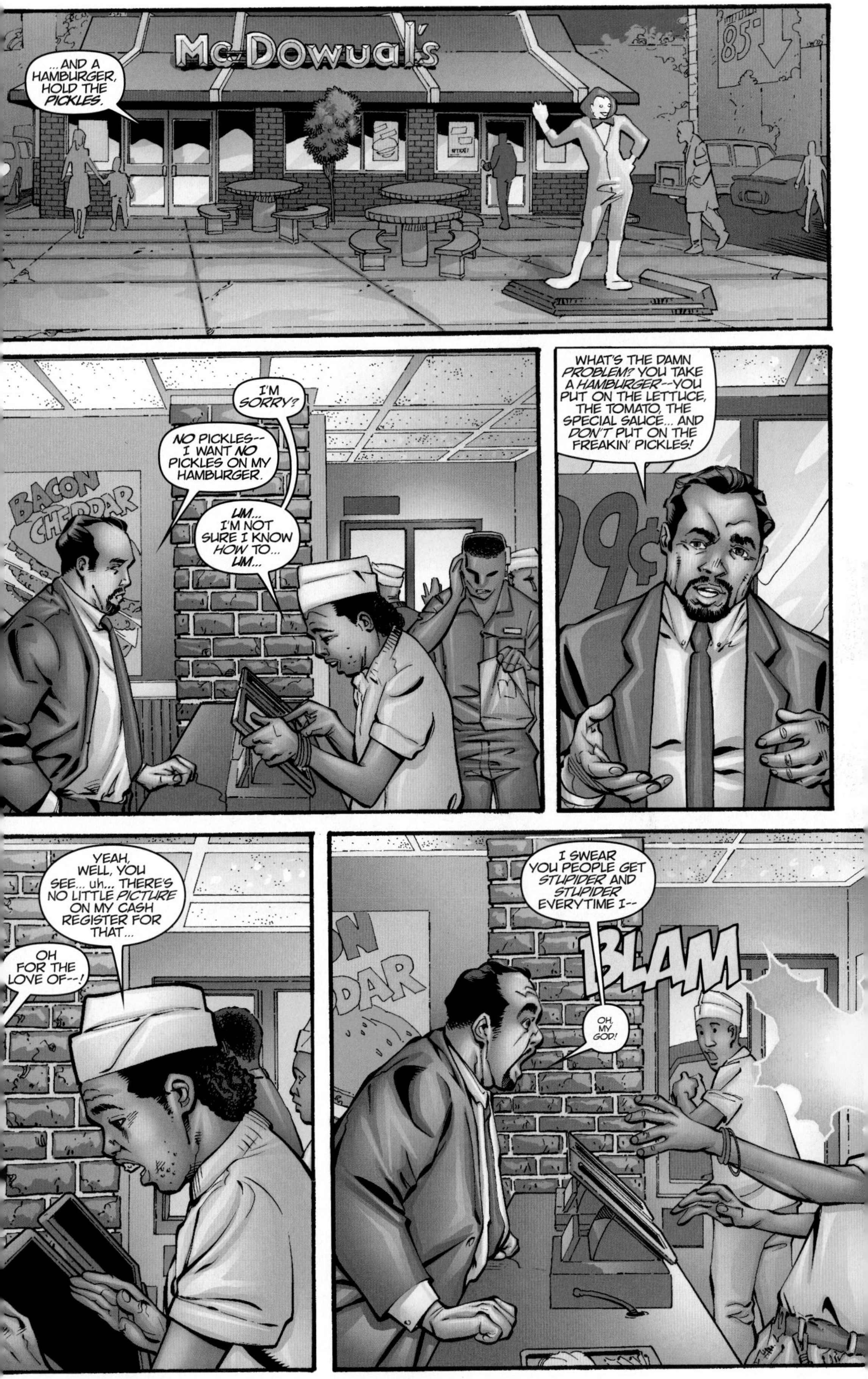
Mc-DOwual's
85¢
...AND A HAMBURGER, HOLD THE *PICKLES*.
I'M *SORRY*?
NO PICKLES-- I WANT *NO* PICKLES ON MY HAMBURGER.
UM... I'M NOT SURE I KNOW *HOW* TO... *UM*...
BACON CHEDDAR
WHAT'S THE DAMN *PROBLEM*? YOU TAKE A *HAMBURGER*--YOU PUT ON THE LETTUCE, THE TOMATO, THE SPECIAL SAUCE... AND *DON'T* PUT ON THE FREAKIN' PICKLES!
99¢
YEAH, WELL, YOU SEE... uh... THERE'S NO LITTLE *PICTURE* ON MY CASH REGISTER FOR THAT...
OH FOR THE LOVE OF--!
I SWEAR YOU PEOPLE GET *STUPIDER* AND *STUPIDER* EVERYTIME I--
BLAM
OH, MY GOD!

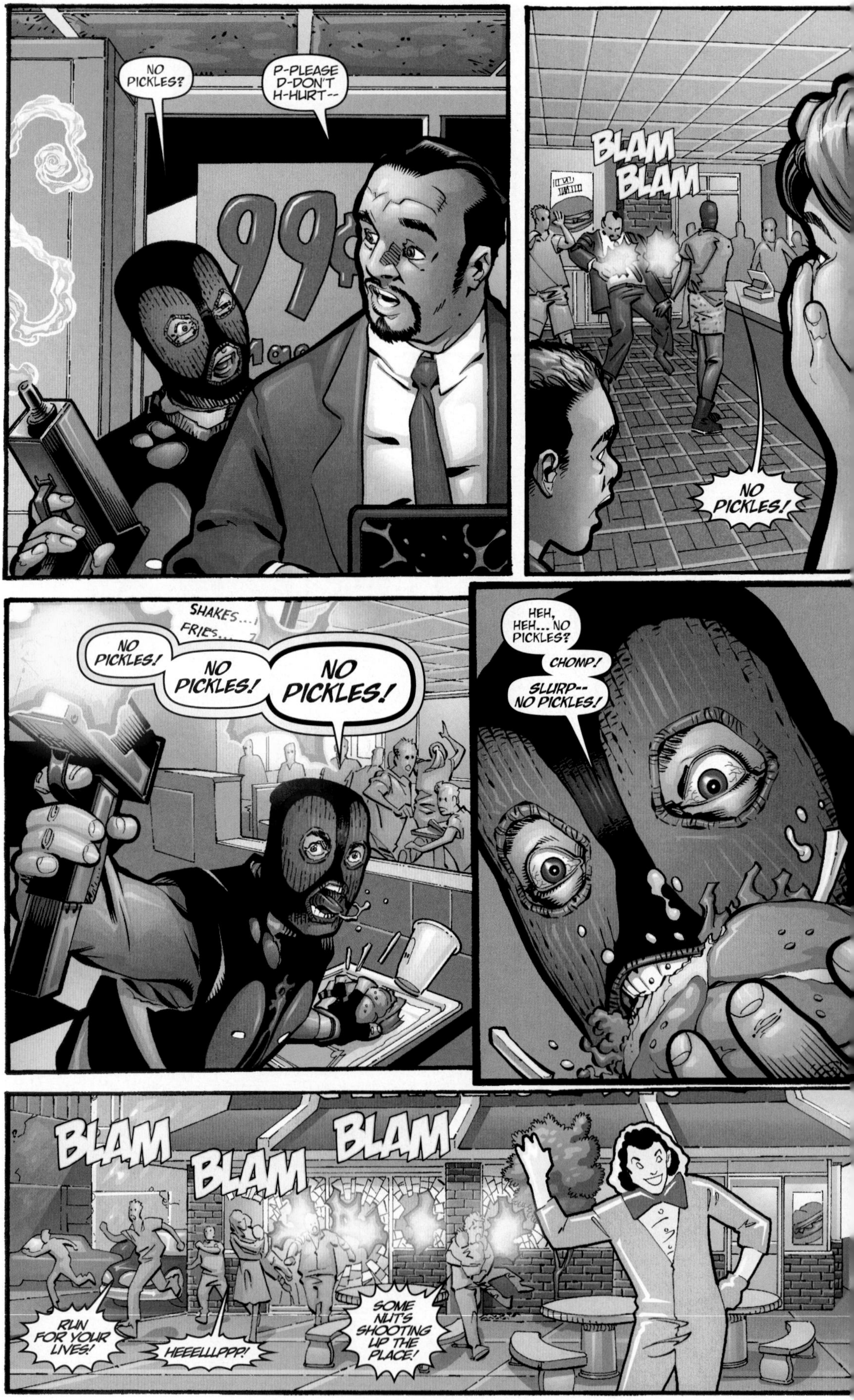
NO PICKLES?
P-PLEASE D-DON'T H-HURT--
BLAM BLAM
NO PICKLES!
SHAKES... FRIES...
NO PICKLES!
NO PICKLES!
NO PICKLES!
HEH, HEH... NO PICKLES?
CHOMP!
SLURP-- NO PICKLES!
BLAM
BLAM
BLAM
RUN FOR YOUR LIVES!
HEEELLLPPP!
SOME NUT'S SHOOTING UP THE PLACE!

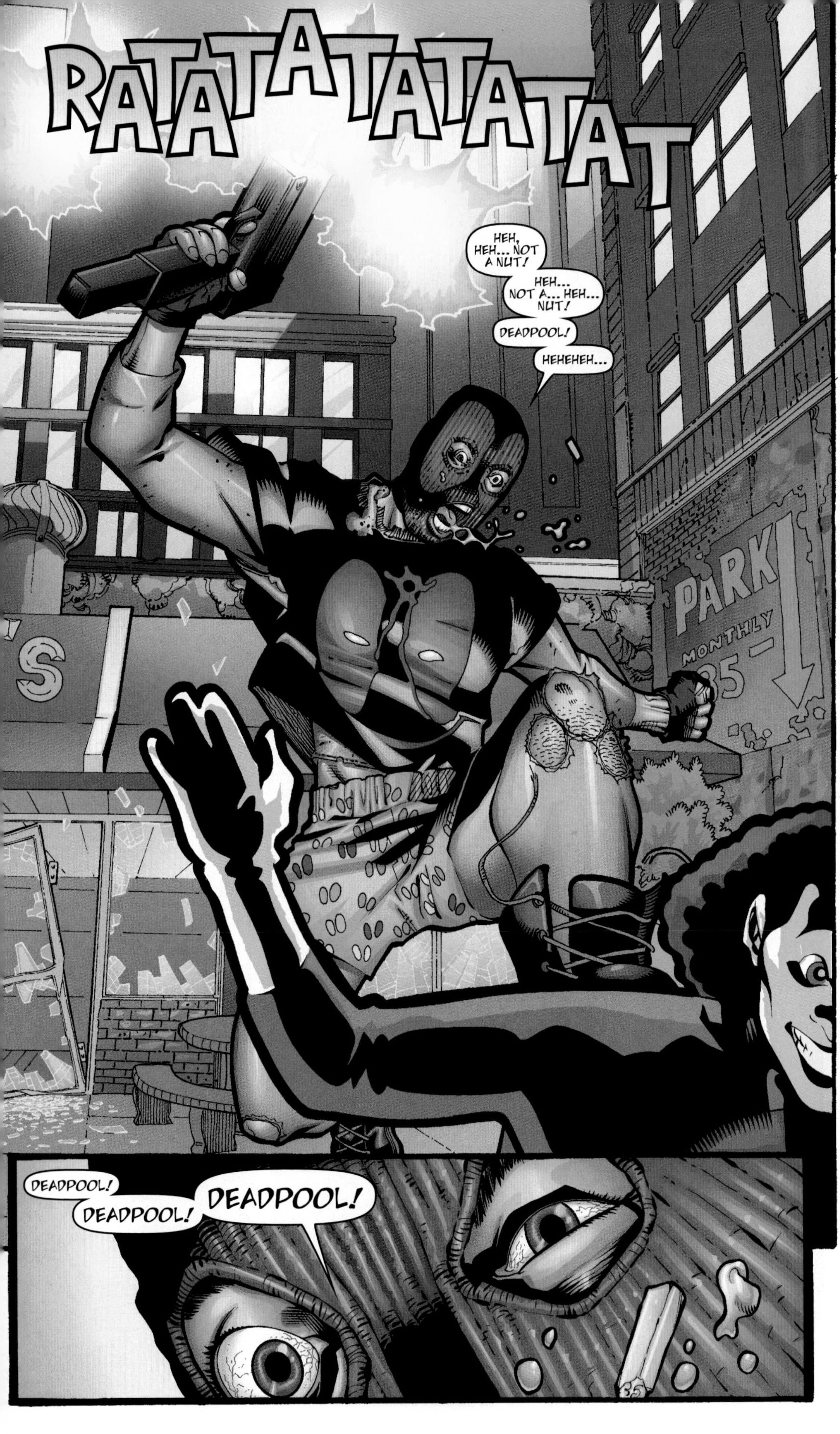
RATATATATATATAT
HEH, HEH... NOT A NUT!
HEH... NOT A... HEH... NUT!
DEADPOOL!
HEHEHEH...
PARK MONTHLY
DEADPOOL!
DEADPOOL!
DEADPOOL!

MAN, YOU SURE WERE LUCKY THAT *KNIFE* DIDN'T GO ANY DEEPER OR ELSE YOU'D A' BEEN A *GONER,* BOBO--

--WHAT THE BLAZES WAS ON YOUR *MIND?*

COULDN'T SAY... MUST'VE THOUGHT I WAS A *SUPER HERO* OR SOMETHING...

OR MAYBE YOU WAS *EXPERIMENTED* ON BY *ALIENS!* WE DIDN'T ASK YOU ABOUT YOUR *FACE* BEFORE-- YA KNOW, FIGURED YOU DIDN'T LIKE TO *TALK* 'BOUT IT-- BUT WITH A *KISSER* LIKE YOURS... *SOMETHING'S* GOT TO BE UP WITH THAT.

NEED MONEY FOR BOOZE-- HEY, AT LEAST I'M HONEST!

HERE YOU GO, PAL.

BLESS YOUR HEART, SONNY. ALTHOUGH... FOR A FEW DOLLARS *MORE,* I'D BE WILLIN' TO *EARN* THAT MONEY THE *RIGHT* WAY, IF YA KNOW WHAT I MEAN...

I... UH... DEAR GOD... UH...

NEED MONEY FOR BOOZE-- HEY, AT LEAST I'M HONEST!

BLECK!

HEY!!

SEE? IT *NEVER FAILS.* I TRY TO DO SOMETHING *NICE* AND I WIND UP GETTING VOMITED ON AND SOLICITED BY A SCRAGGLY OLD-- HUH?

WADE?

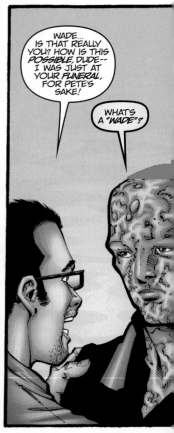

WADE... IS THAT REALLY YOU? HOW IS THIS *POSSIBLE,* DUDE-- I WAS JUST AT YOUR *FUNERAL,* FOR PETE'S SAKE!

WHAT'S A *"WADE"?*

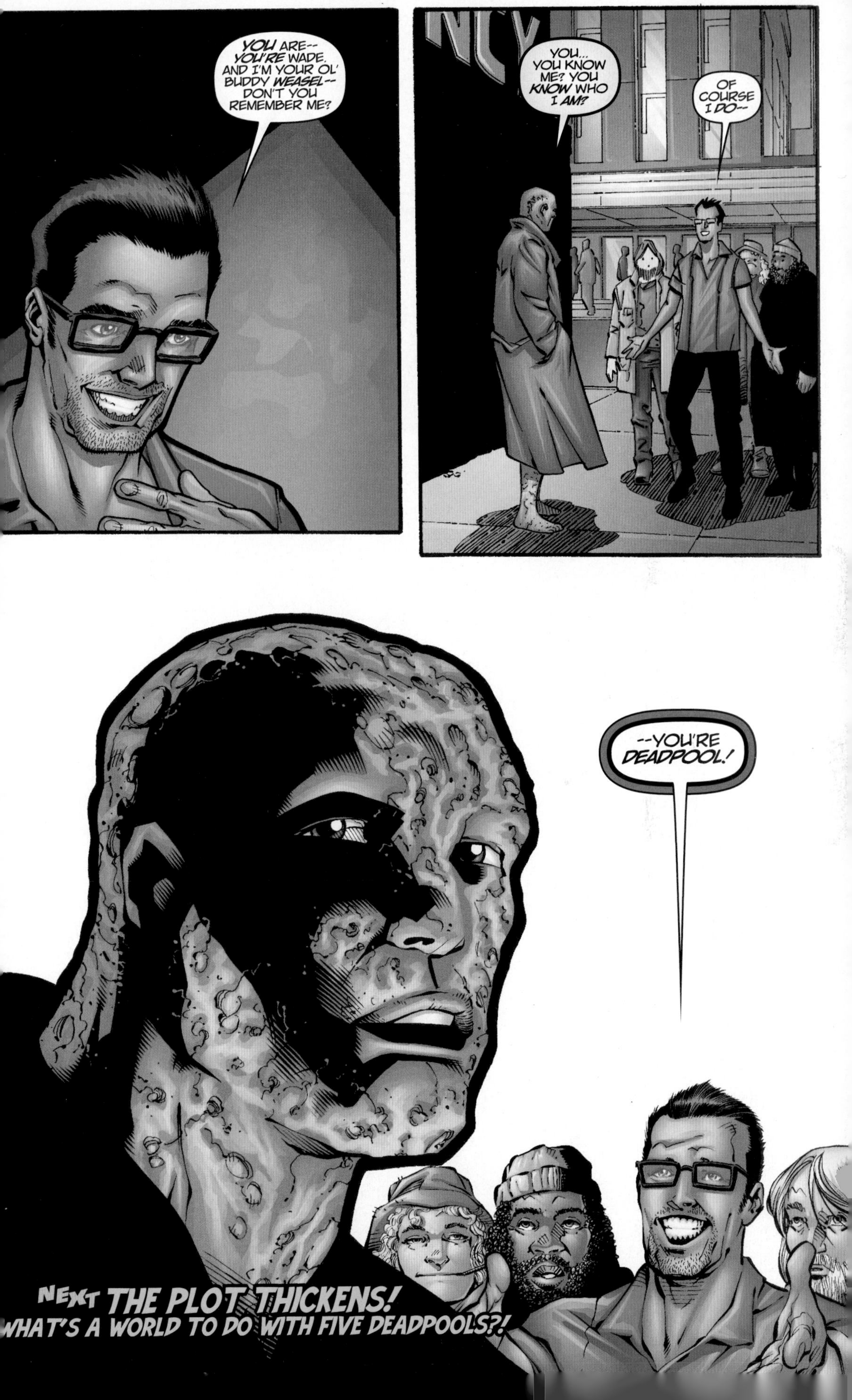
YOU ARE-- YOU'RE WADE. AND I'M YOUR OL' BUDDY WEASEL-- DON'T YOU REMEMBER ME?
YOU... YOU KNOW ME? YOU KNOW WHO I AM?
OF COURSE I DO--
--YOU'RE DEADPOOL!
NEXT THE PLOT THICKENS!
WHAT'S A WORLD TO DO WITH FIVE DEADPOOLS?!

MARVEL® COMICS
DEADPOOL®:
FUNERAL FOR A
FREAK
MARVEL PG
3
63
TIERI
JEANTY
HOLDREDGE

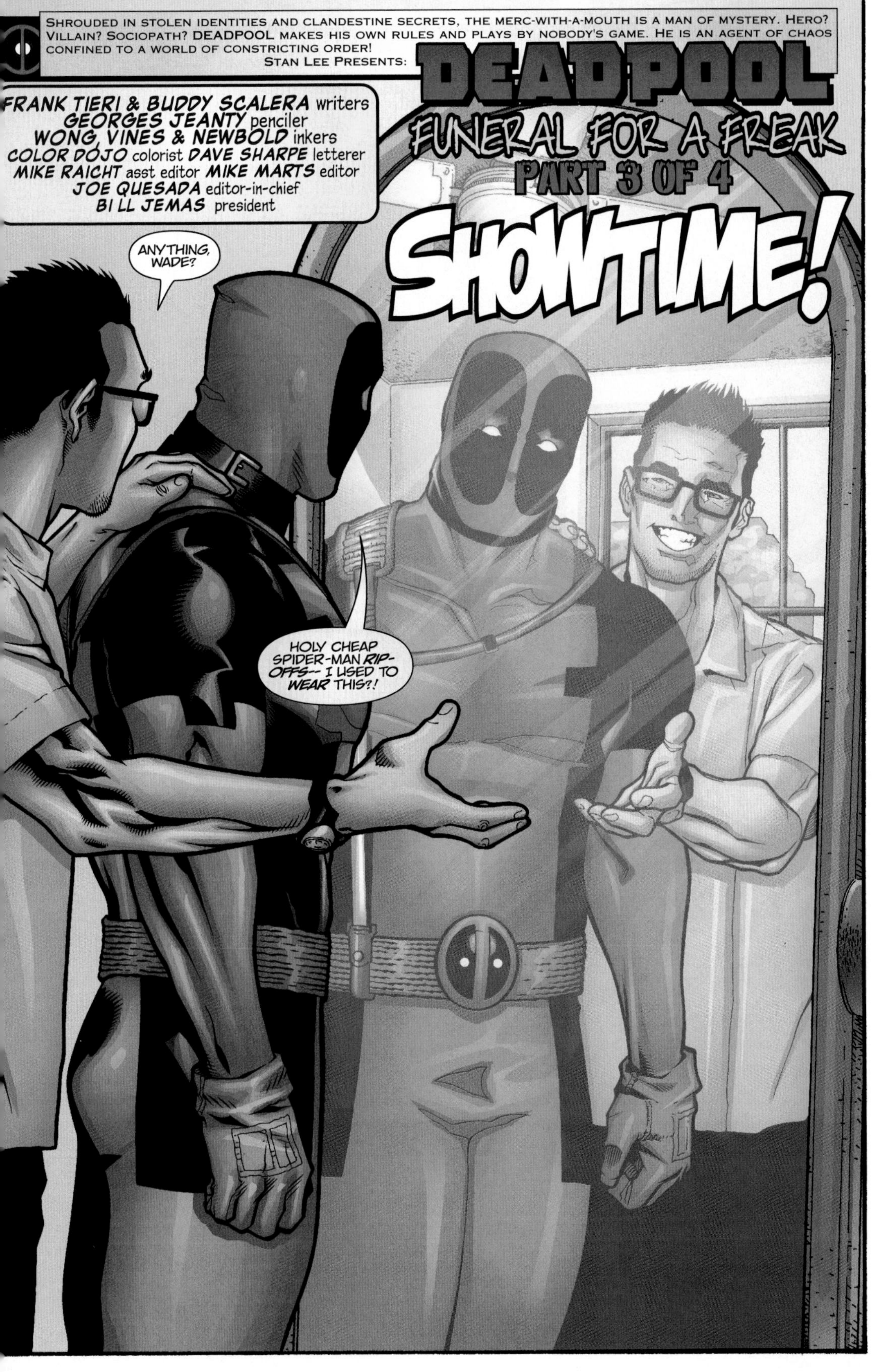

SHROUDED IN STOLEN IDENTITIES AND CLANDESTINE SECRETS, THE MERC-WITH-A-MOUTH IS A MAN OF MYSTERY. HERO? VILLAIN? SOCIOPATH? DEADPOOL MAKES HIS OWN RULES AND PLAYS BY NOBODY'S GAME. HE IS AN AGENT OF CHAOS CONFINED TO A WORLD OF CONSTRICTING ORDER!
STAN LEE PRESENTS:
DEADPOOL
FUNERAL FOR A FREAK
PART 3 OF 4
SHOWTIME!
FRANK TIERI & BUDDY SCALERA writers
GEORGES JEANTY penciler
WONG, VINES & NEWBOLD inkers
COLOR DOJO colorist DAVE SHARPE letterer
MIKE RAICHT asst editor MIKE MARTS editor
JOE QUESADA editor-in-chief
BILL JEMAS president
ANYTHING, WADE?
HOLY CHEAP SPIDER-MAN RIP-OFFS-- I USED TO WEAR THIS?!

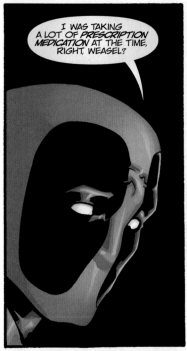

I WAS TAKING A LOT OF *PRESCRIPTION MEDICATION* AT THE TIME, RIGHT, WEASEL?

AW, C'MON, WADE...IT'S NOT LIKE WEARING *BLUE TIGHTS* WITH *LITTLE RED BOOTIES* AND A *CAPE* OR SOMETHING FRUITY LIKE THAT.

OH WELL... BACK TO *SQUARE ONE.* ALTHOUGH I REALLY THOUGHT PUTTING ON YOUR OLD *DEADPOOL* COSTUME WOULD SHAKE SOMETHING *LOOSE...*

YEAH, IT DID -- MY *INNARDS.*

HEY, DON'T YA *FRET* NONE, *BOBO* --YOU'LL GET ALL YER *MARBLES* BACK IN NO TIME FLAT, YOU'LL SEE.

GREAT... PEP TALKS FROM THE *HYGIENICALLY CHALLENGED.*

THAT'S *ALL* I NEED RIGHT NOW.

Hmmm... I SEE YOU HAVEN'T FORGOTTEN HOW TO BE *CRUMMY* TO YOUR *FRIENDS,* AT LEAST.

SPEAKING OF WHICH, DID I EVER GO OVER WHY WE *STOPPED TALKING* FOR A WHILE?

GLUG!

SHOE POLISH

GLUG!

YEAH, YEAH, YEAH--ONLY LIKE A *HUNDRED* TIMES. I WAS LIKE *GEORGE STEINBRENNER* IN SPANDEX. I GOT IT.

NOW WHAT'S *THIS?*

THIS, WADE WILSON--

--THIS IS *YOUR LIFE!* OR TO BE PRECISE, IT'S *STUFF* THAT YOU'VE STOLEN/COLLECTED/SLICED PEOPLE'S ACHILLES TENDONS FOR OVER THE YEARS...

...NOW LET'S SEE HERE...

...DOC DOOM'S MASK, AMELIA EARHART'S PILOT'S LICENSE, BLIND AL'S ULCER PILLS, THAT YODA PUPPET YOU SWIPED OFF OF MARK HAMILL, JIMMY HOFFA'S HEAD...

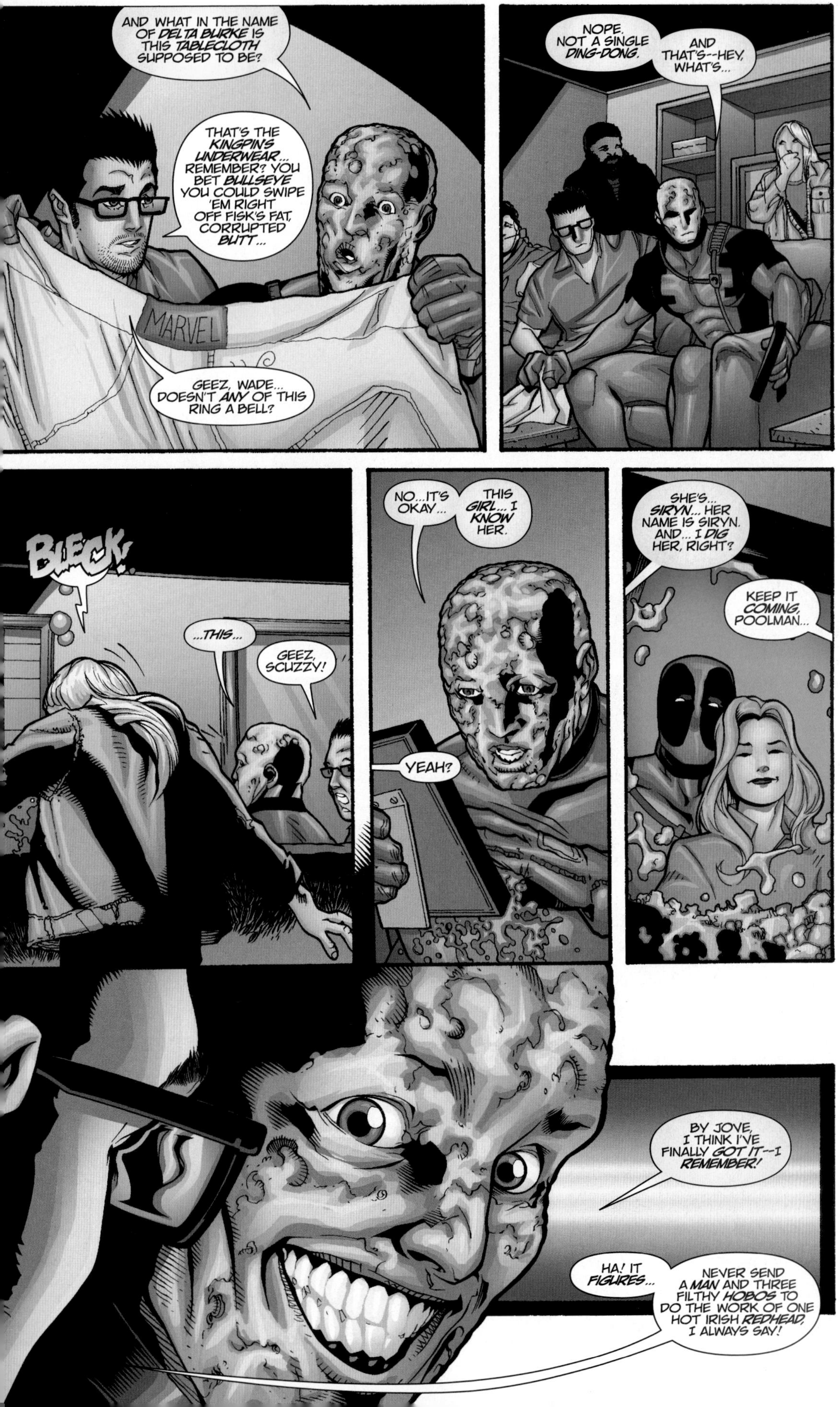
AND WHAT IN THE NAME OF DELTA BURKE IS THIS TABLECLOTH SUPPOSED TO BE?
THAT'S THE KINGPINS UNDERWEAR... REMEMBER? YOU BET BULLSEYE YOU COULD SWIPE 'EM RIGHT OFF FISK'S FAT, CORRUPTED BUTT...
MARVEL
GEEZ, WADE... DOESN'T ANY OF THIS RING A BELL?
NOPE. NOT A SINGLE DING-DONG.
AND THAT'S--HEY, WHAT'S...
BLECK!
...THIS...
GEEZ, SCUZZY!
NO...IT'S OKAY...
THIS GIRL... I KNOW HER.
YEAH?
SHE'S... SIRYN... HER NAME IS SIRYN. AND... I DIG HER, RIGHT?
KEEP IT COMING, POOLMAN...
BY JOVE, I THINK I'VE FINALLY GOT IT--I REMEMBER!
HA! IT FIGURES...
NEVER SEND A MAN AND THREE FILTHY HOBOS TO DO THE WORK OF ONE HOT IRISH REDHEAD, I ALWAYS SAY!

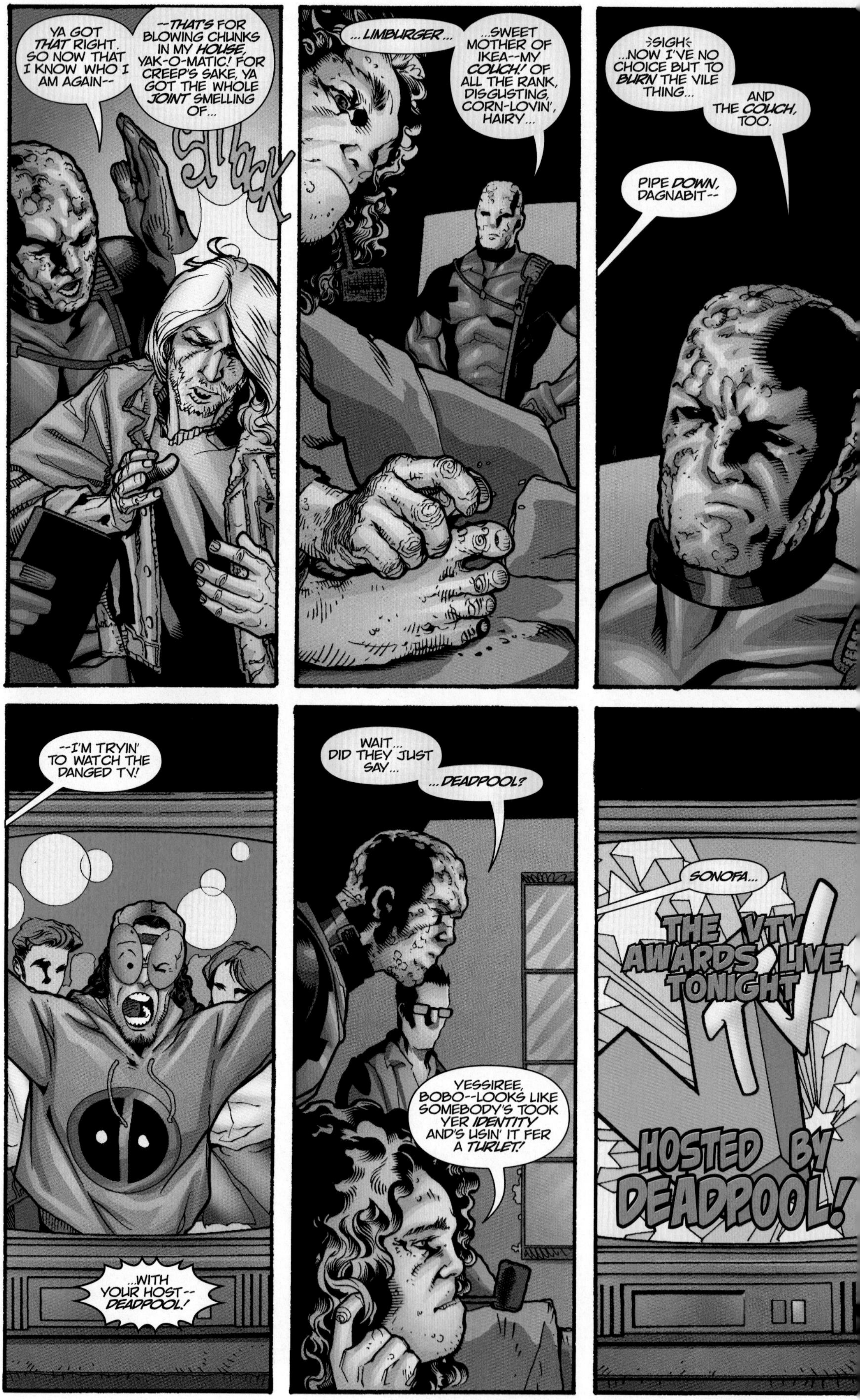
YA GOT THAT RIGHT. SO NOW THAT I KNOW WHO I AM AGAIN--
--THAT'S FOR BLOWING CHUNKS IN MY HOUSE, YAK-O-MATIC! FOR CREEP'S SAKE, YA GOT THE WHOLE JOINT SMELLING OF...
SMACK
...LIMBURGER...
...SWEET MOTHER OF IKEA--MY COUCH! OF ALL THE RANK, DISGUSTING, CORN-LOVIN', HAIRY...
SIGH ...NOW I'VE NO CHOICE BUT TO BURN THE VILE THING...
AND THE COUCH, TOO.
PIPE DOWN, DAGNABIT--
--I'M TRYIN' TO WATCH THE DANGED TV!
...WITH YOUR HOST--DEADPOOL!
WAIT... DID THEY JUST SAY...
...DEADPOOL?
YESSIREE, BOBO--LOOKS LIKE SOMEBODY'S TOOK YER IDENTITY AND'S USIN' IT FER A TURLET!
SONOFA...
THE VTV AWARDS LIVE TONIGHT
HOSTED BY DEADPOOL!

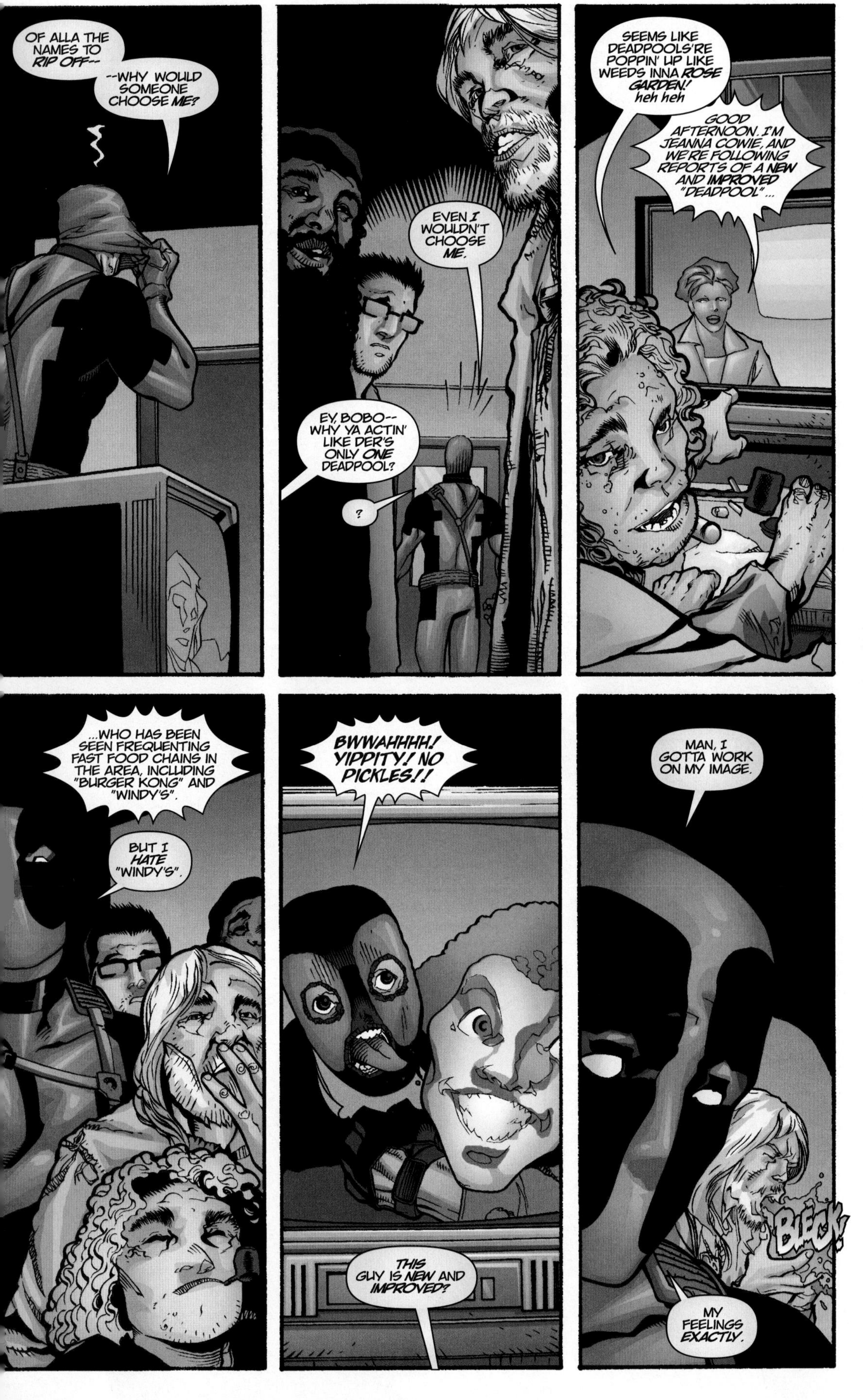
OF ALLA THE NAMES TO RIP OFF--
--WHY WOULD SOMEONE CHOOSE ME?
EVEN I WOULDN'T CHOOSE ME.
EY, BOBO-- WHY YA ACTIN' LIKE DER'S ONLY ONE DEADPOOL?
?
SEEMS LIKE DEADPOOLS'RE POPPIN' UP LIKE WEEDS INNA ROSE GARDEN! heh heh
GOOD AFTERNOON. I'M JEANNA COWIE, AND WE'RE FOLLOWING REPORTS OF A NEW AND IMPROVED "DEADPOOL"...
...WHO HAS BEEN SEEN FREQUENTING FAST FOOD CHAINS IN THE AREA, INCLUDING "BURGER KONG" AND "WINDY'S".
BUT I HATE "WINDY'S".
BWWAHHHH! YIPPITY! NO PICKLES!!
THIS GUY IS NEW AND IMPROVED?
MAN, I GOTTA WORK ON MY IMAGE.
BLECK
MY FEELINGS EXACTLY.

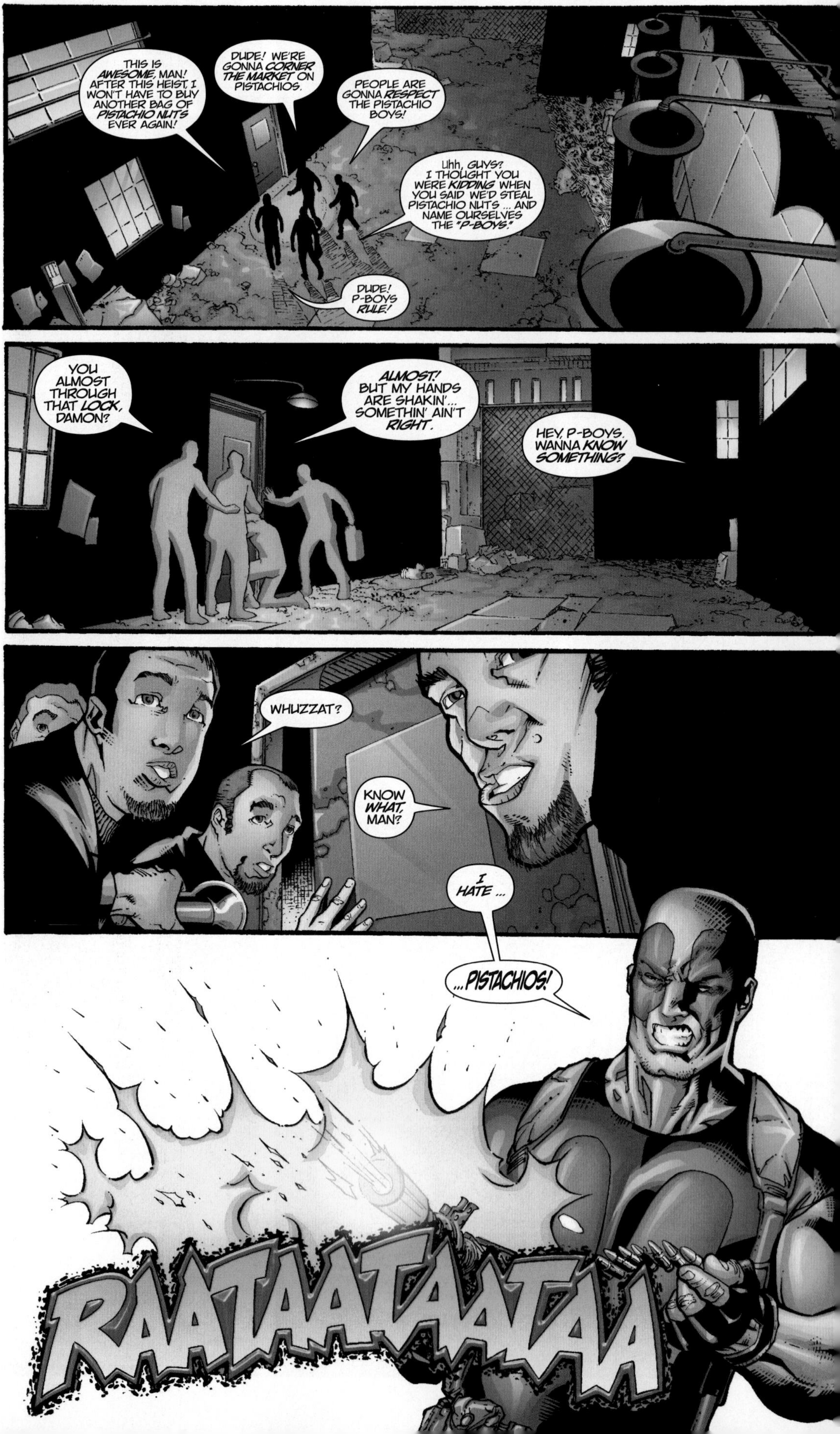

THIS IS AWESOME, MAN! AFTER THIS HEIST, I WON'T HAVE TO BUY ANOTHER BAG OF PISTACHIO NUTS EVER AGAIN!
DUDE! WE'RE GONNA CORNER THE MARKET ON PISTACHIOS.
PEOPLE ARE GONNA RESPECT THE PISTACHIO BOYS!
Uhh, GUYS? I THOUGHT YOU WERE KIDDING WHEN YOU SAID WE'D STEAL PISTACHIO NUTS ... AND NAME OURSELVES THE "P-BOYS."
DUDE! P-BOYS RULE!
YOU ALMOST THROUGH THAT LOCK, DAMON?
ALMOST! BUT MY HANDS ARE SHAKIN'... SOMETHIN' AIN'T RIGHT.
HEY, P-BOYS, WANNA KNOW SOMETHING?
WHUZZAT?
KNOW WHAT, MAN?
I HATE ...
...PISTACHIOS!
RAATAATAATAA

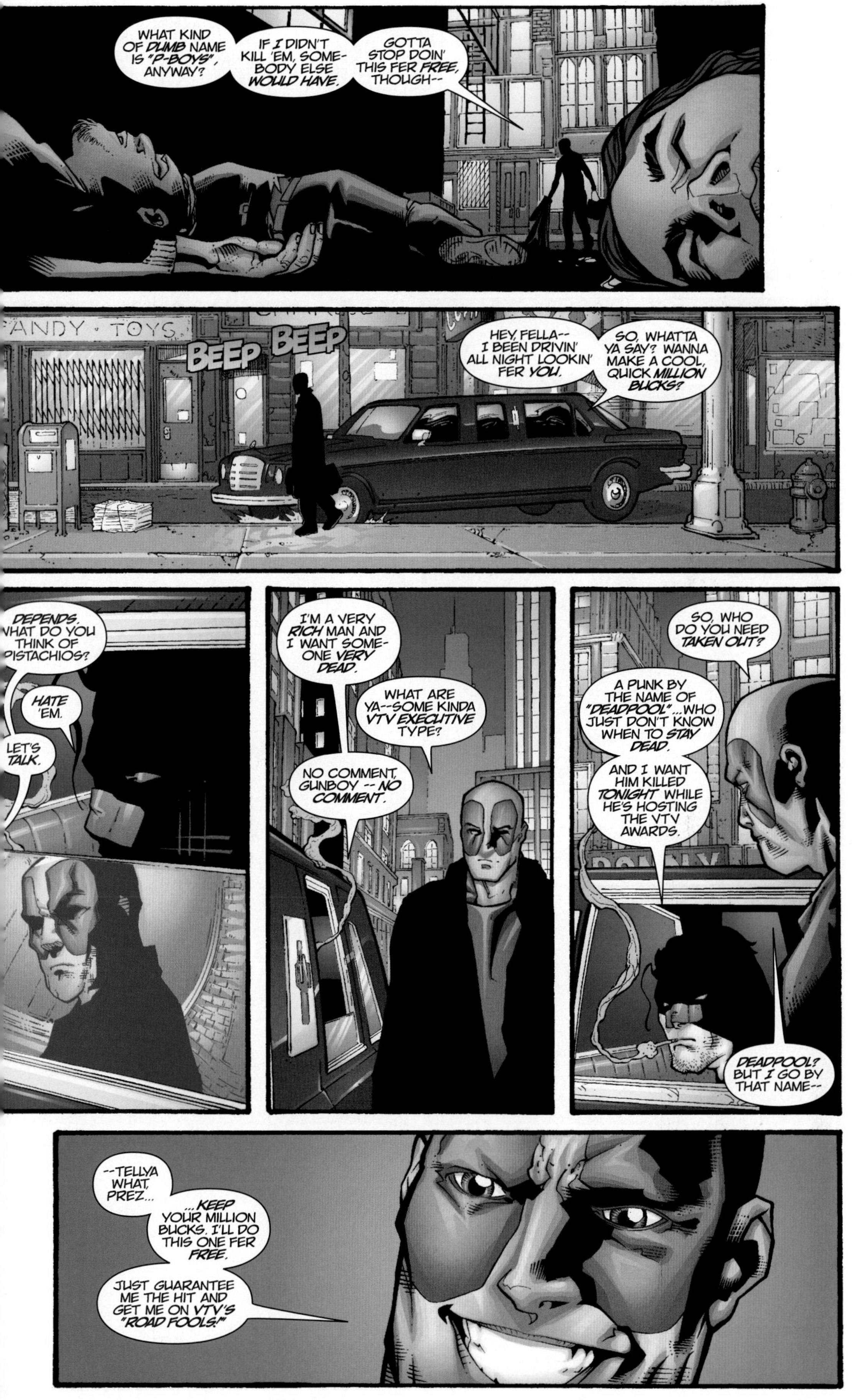
WHAT KIND OF DUMB NAME IS "P-BOYS", ANYWAY?
IF I DIDN'T KILL 'EM, SOMEBODY ELSE WOULD HAVE.
GOTTA STOP DOIN' THIS FER FREE, THOUGH--
FANDY • TOYS
BEEP BEEP
HEY, FELLA-- I BEEN DRIVIN' ALL NIGHT LOOKIN' FER YOU.
SO, WHATTA YA SAY? WANNA MAKE A COOL, QUICK MILLION BUCKS?
DEPENDS. WHAT DO YOU THINK OF PISTACHIOS?
HATE 'EM.
LET'S TALK.
I'M A VERY RICH MAN AND I WANT SOME-ONE VERY DEAD.
WHAT ARE YA--SOME KINDA VTV EXECUTIVE TYPE?
NO COMMENT, GUNBOY -- NO COMMENT.
SO, WHO DO YOU NEED TAKEN OUT?
A PUNK BY THE NAME OF "DEADPOOL"...WHO JUST DON'T KNOW WHEN TO STAY DEAD.
AND I WANT HIM KILLED TONIGHT WHILE HE'S HOSTING THE VTV AWARDS.
DEADPOOL? BUT I GO BY THAT NAME--
--TELLYA WHAT, PREZ...
...KEEP YOUR MILLION BUCKS. I'LL DO THIS ONE FER FREE.
JUST GUARANTEE ME THE HIT AND GET ME ON VTV'S "ROAD FOOLS!"

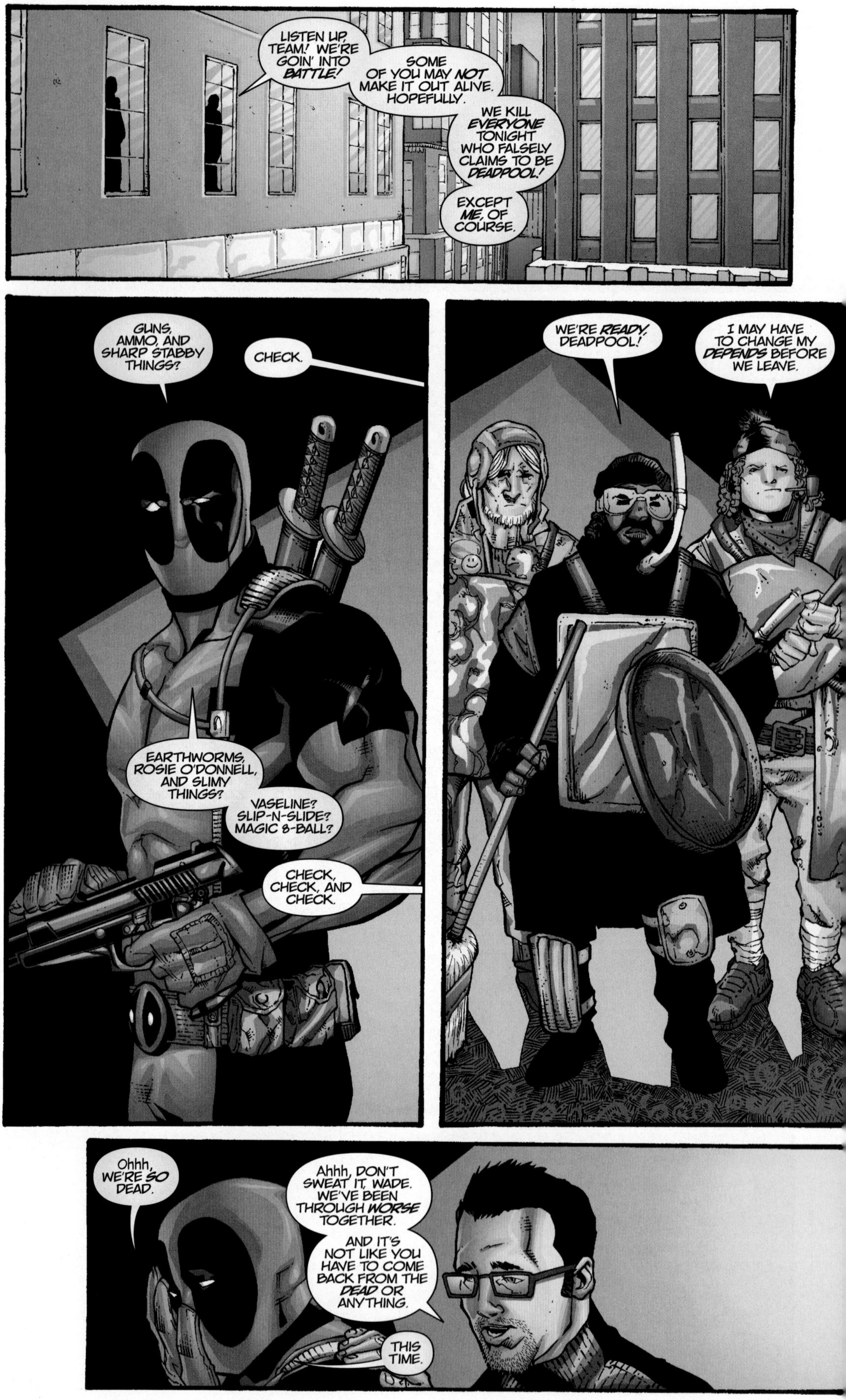
LISTEN UP, TEAM! WE'RE GOIN' INTO BATTLE!
SOME OF YOU MAY NOT MAKE IT OUT ALIVE. HOPEFULLY.
WE KILL EVERYONE TONIGHT WHO FALSELY CLAIMS TO BE DEADPOOL!
EXCEPT ME, OF COURSE.
GUNS, AMMO, AND SHARP STABBY THINGS?
CHECK.
EARTHWORMS, ROSIE O'DONNELL, AND SLIMY THINGS?
VASELINE? SLIP-N-SLIDE? MAGIC 8-BALL?
CHECK, CHECK, AND CHECK.
WE'RE READY, DEADPOOL!
I MAY HAVE TO CHANGE MY DEPENDS BEFORE WE LEAVE.
Ohhh, WE'RE SO DEAD.
Ahhh, DON'T SWEAT IT, WADE. WE'VE BEEN THROUGH WORSE TOGETHER.
AND IT'S NOT LIKE YOU HAVE TO COME BACK FROM THE DEAD OR ANYTHING.
THIS TIME.

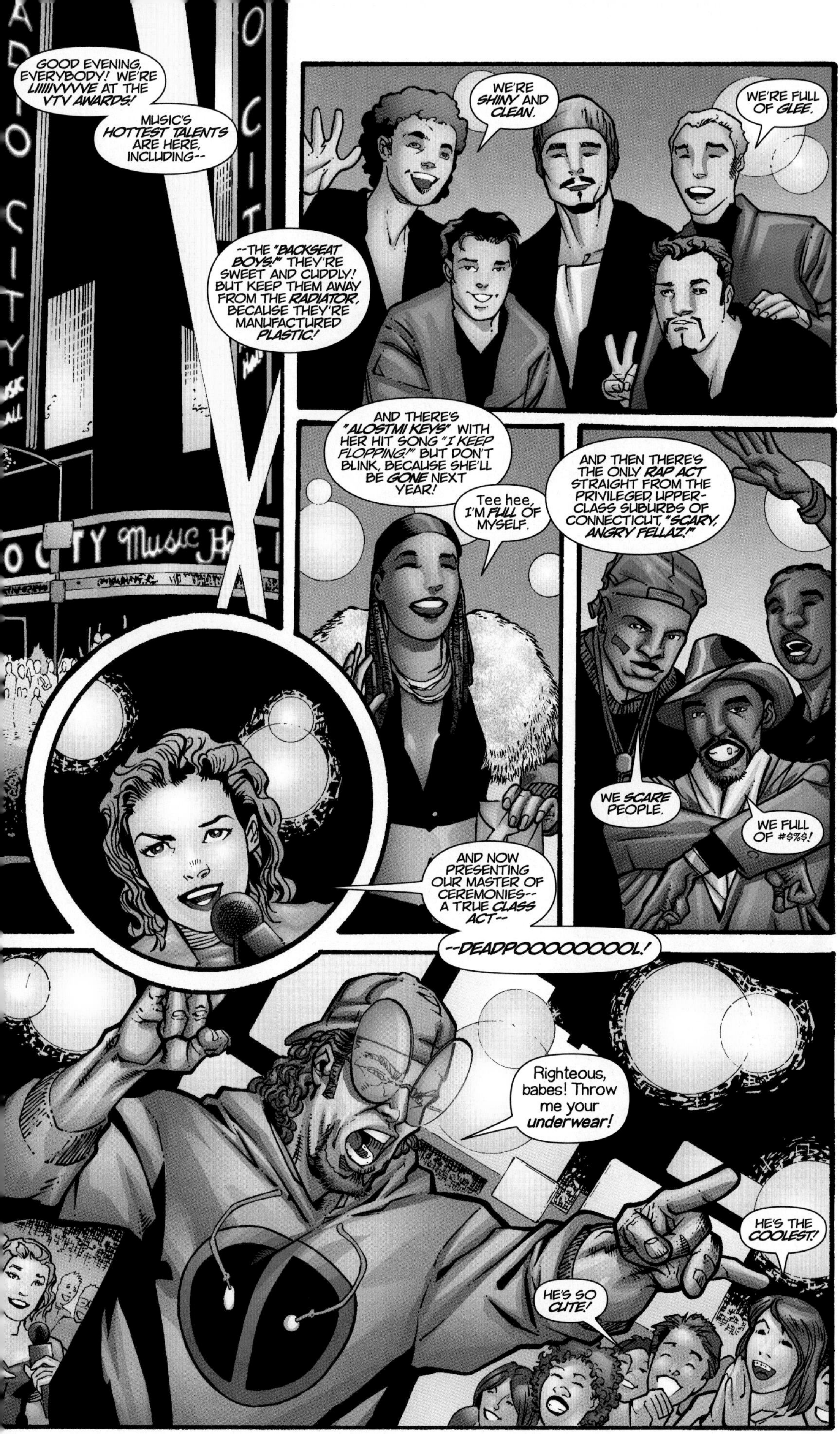
GOOD EVENING, EVERYBODY! WE'RE LIIIIIVVVVE AT THE VTV AWARDS!
MUSIC'S HOTTEST TALENTS ARE HERE, INCLUDING--
WE'RE SHINY AND CLEAN.
WE'RE FULL OF GLEE.
--THE "BACKSEAT BOYS!" THEY'RE SWEET AND CUDDLY! BUT KEEP THEM AWAY FROM THE RADIATOR, BECAUSE THEY'RE MANUFACTURED PLASTIC!
AND THERE'S "ALOSTMI KEYS" WITH HER HIT SONG "I KEEP FLOPPING!" BUT DON'T BLINK, BECAUSE SHE'LL BE GONE NEXT YEAR!
Tee hee, I'M FULL OF MYSELF.
AND THEN THERE'S THE ONLY RAP ACT STRAIGHT FROM THE PRIVILEGED UPPER-CLASS SUBURBS OF CONNECTICUT, "SCARY, ANGRY FELLAZ!"
WE SCARE PEOPLE.
WE FULL OF #$%$!
AND NOW PRESENTING OUR MASTER OF CEREMONIES-- A TRUE CLASS ACT--
--DEADPOOOOOOOOOL!
Righteous, babes! Throw me your underwear!
HE'S THE COOLEST!
HE'S SO CUTE!

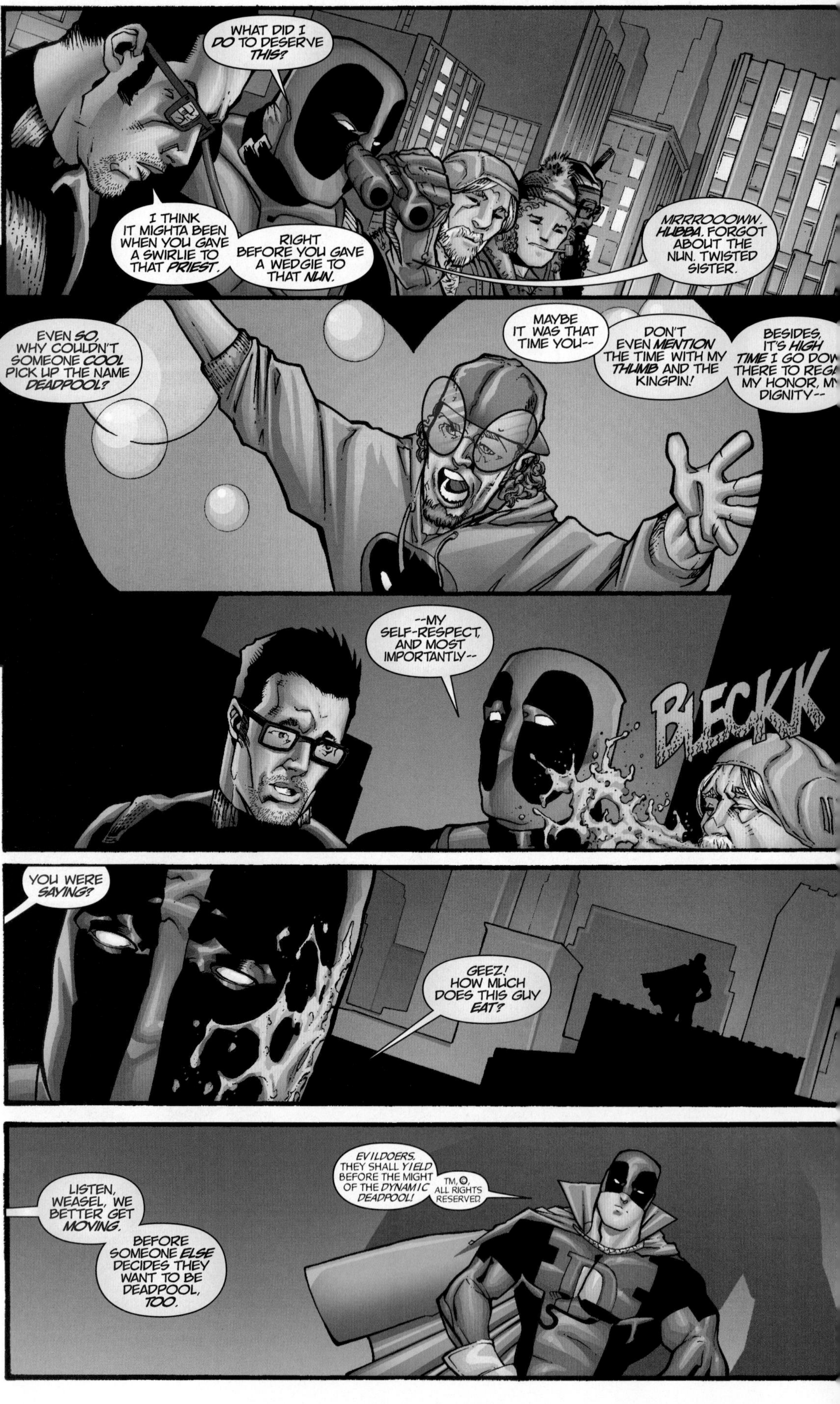
WHAT DID I DO TO DESERVE THIS?
I THINK IT MIGHTA BEEN WHEN YOU GAVE A SWIRLIE TO THAT PRIEST.
RIGHT BEFORE YOU GAVE A WEDGIE TO THAT NUN.
MRRROOOWN. HUBBA. FORGOT ABOUT THE NUN. TWISTED SISTER.
EVEN SO, WHY COULDN'T SOMEONE COOL PICK UP THE NAME DEADPOOL?
MAYBE IT WAS THAT TIME YOU--
DON'T EVEN MENTION THE TIME WITH MY THUMB AND THE KINGPIN!
BESIDES, IT'S HIGH TIME I GO DOW THERE TO REGA MY HONOR, M DIGNITY--
--MY SELF-RESPECT, AND MOST IMPORTANTLY--
BLECKK
YOU WERE SAYING?
GEEZ! HOW MUCH DOES THIS GUY EAT?
LISTEN, WEASEL, WE BETTER GET MOVING.
BEFORE SOMEONE ELSE DECIDES THEY WANT TO BE DEADPOOL, TOO.
EVILDOERS, THEY SHALL YIELD BEFORE THE MIGHT OF THE DYNAMIC DEADPOOL!
TM, ©, ALL RIGHTS RESERVED

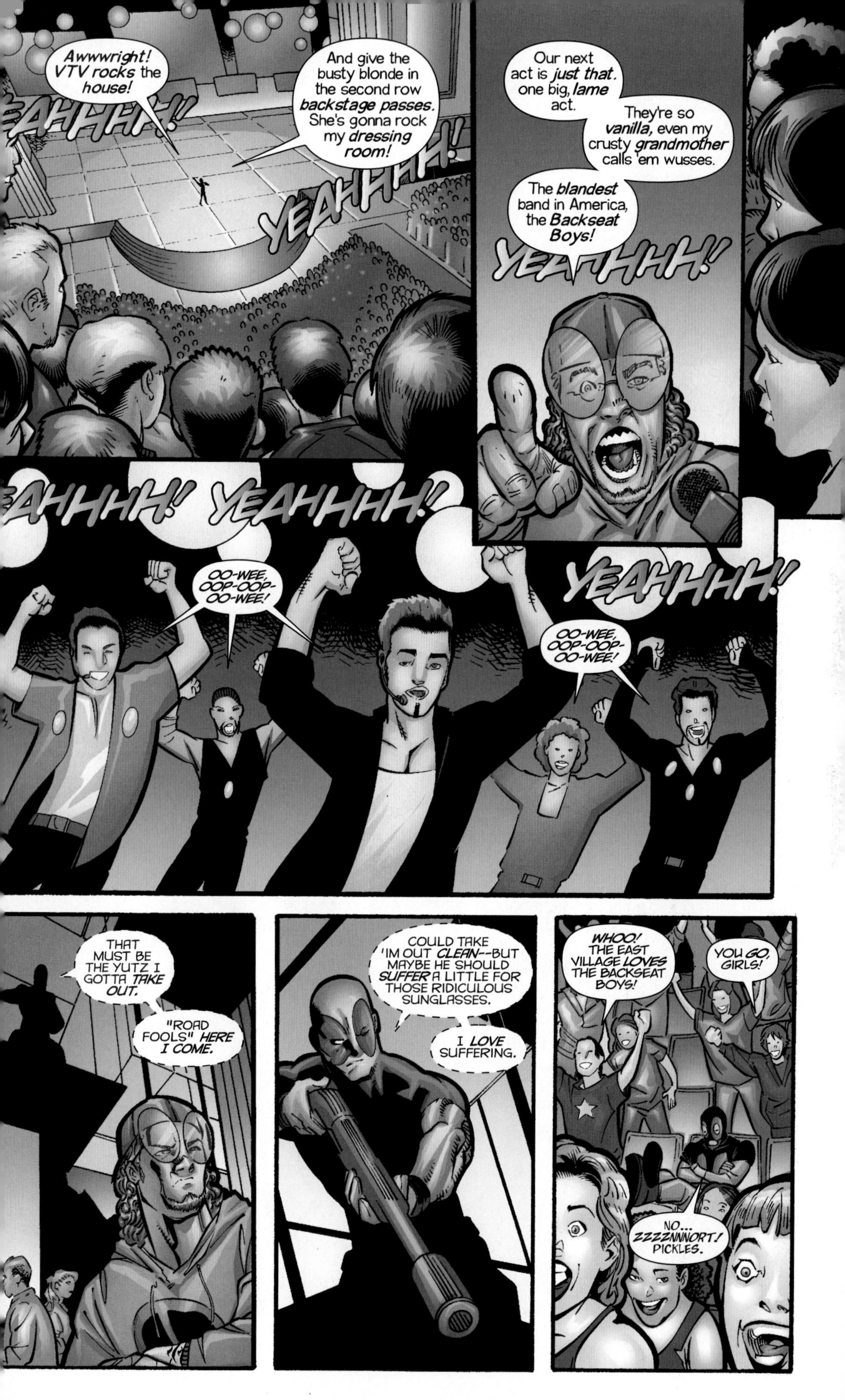
Awwwright! VTV rocks the house!
YEAHHHH!
And give the busty blonde in the second row backstage passes. She's gonna rock my dressing room!
YEAHHHH!
Our next act is just that. one big, lame act.
They're so vanilla, even my crusty grandmother calls 'em wusses.
The blandest band in America, the Backseat Boys!
YEAHHHH!
EAHHHH! YEAHHHH!
OO-WEE, OOP-OOP-OO-WEE!
YEAHHHH!
OO-WEE, OOP-OOP-OO-WEE!
THAT MUST BE THE YUTZ I GOTTA TAKE OUT.
"ROAD FOOLS" HERE I COME.
COULD TAKE 'IM OUT CLEAN--BUT MAYBE HE SHOULD SUFFER A LITTLE FOR THOSE RIDICULOUS SUNGLASSES.
I LOVE SUFFERING.
WHOO! THE EAST VILLAGE LOVES THE BACKSEAT BOYS!
YOU GO, GIRLS!
NO... ZZZZNNNORT! PICKLES.

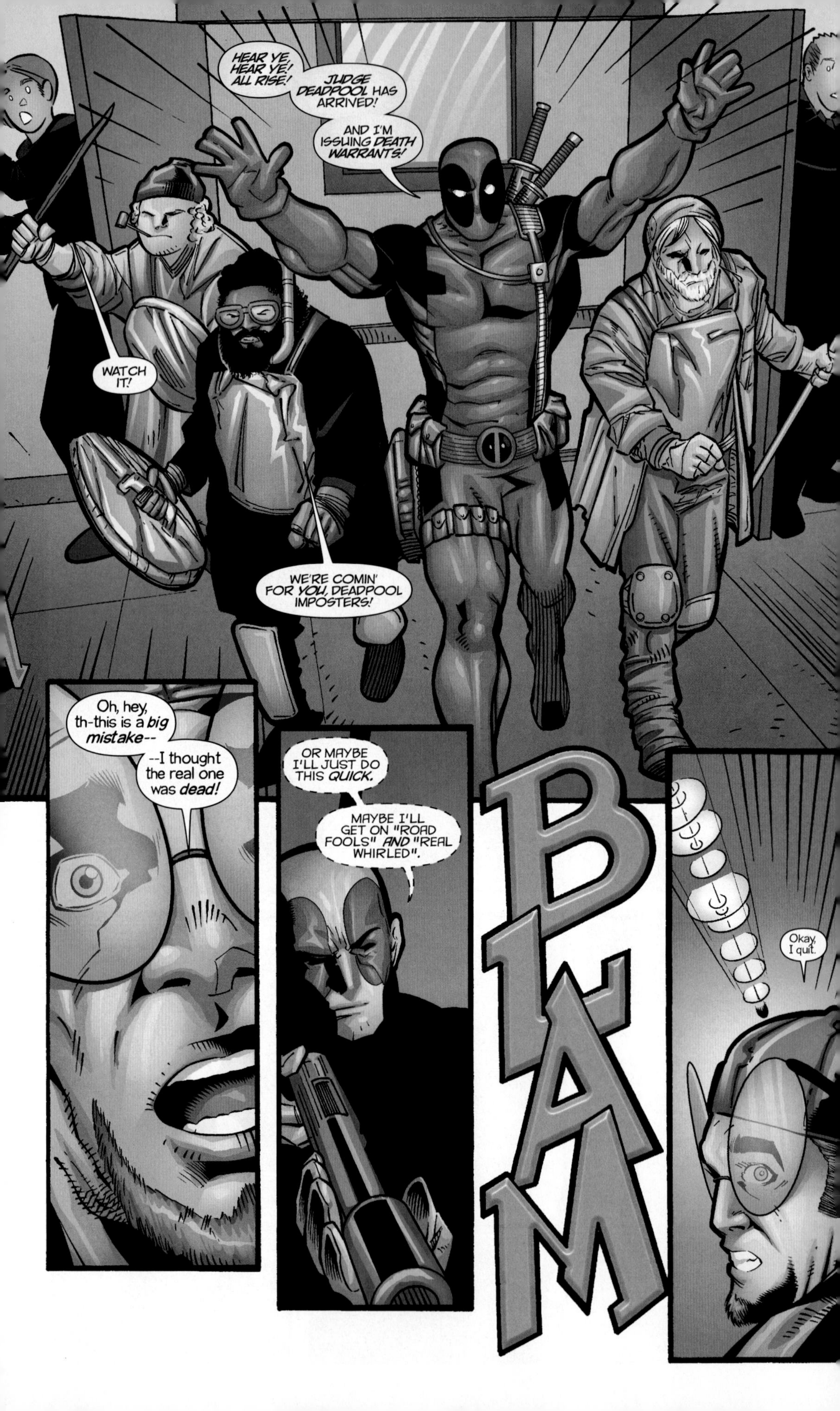
HEAR YE, HEAR YE! ALL RISE!
JUDGE DEADPOOL HAS ARRIVED!
AND I'M ISSUING DEATH WARRANTS!
WATCH IT!
WE'RE COMIN' FOR YOU, DEADPOOL IMPOSTERS!
Oh, hey, th-this is a big mistake--
--I thought the real one was dead!
OR MAYBE I'LL JUST DO THIS QUICK.
MAYBE I'LL GET ON "ROAD FOOLS" AND "REAL WHIRLED".
BLAM
Okay, I quit.

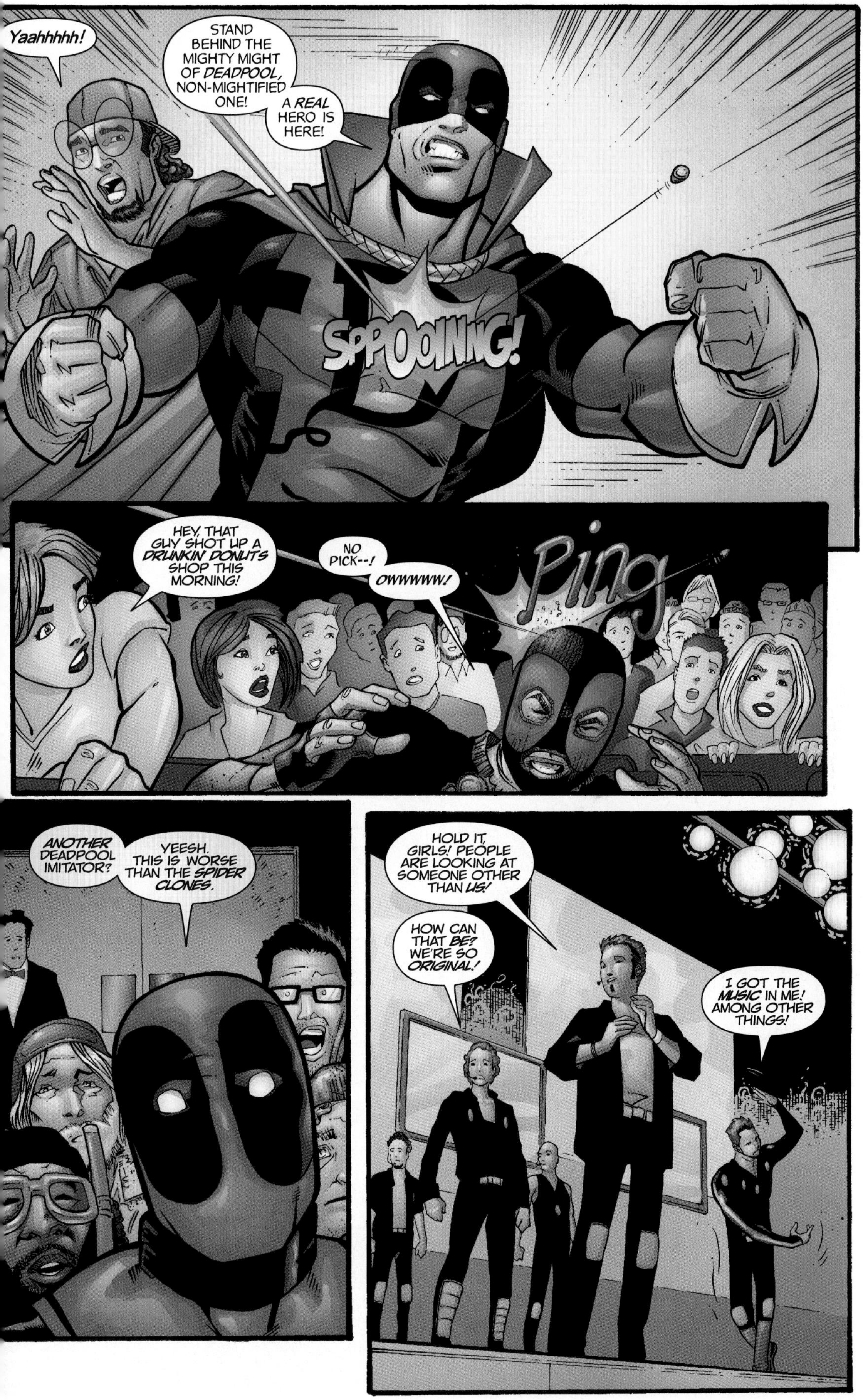

Yaahhhhh!
STAND BEHIND THE MIGHTY MIGHT OF DEADPOOL, NON-MIGHTIFIED ONE!
A REAL HERO IS HERE!
SPPOOINNG!
HEY, THAT GUY SHOT UP A DRUNKIN DONUTS SHOP THIS MORNING!
NO PICK--!
OWWWWW!
Ping
ANOTHER DEADPOOL IMITATOR?
YEESH. THIS IS WORSE THAN THE SPIDER CLONES.
HOLD IT, GIRLS! PEOPLE ARE LOOKING AT SOMEONE OTHER THAN US!
HOW CAN THAT BE? WE'RE SO ORIGINAL!
I GOT THE MUSIC IN ME! AMONG OTHER THINGS!

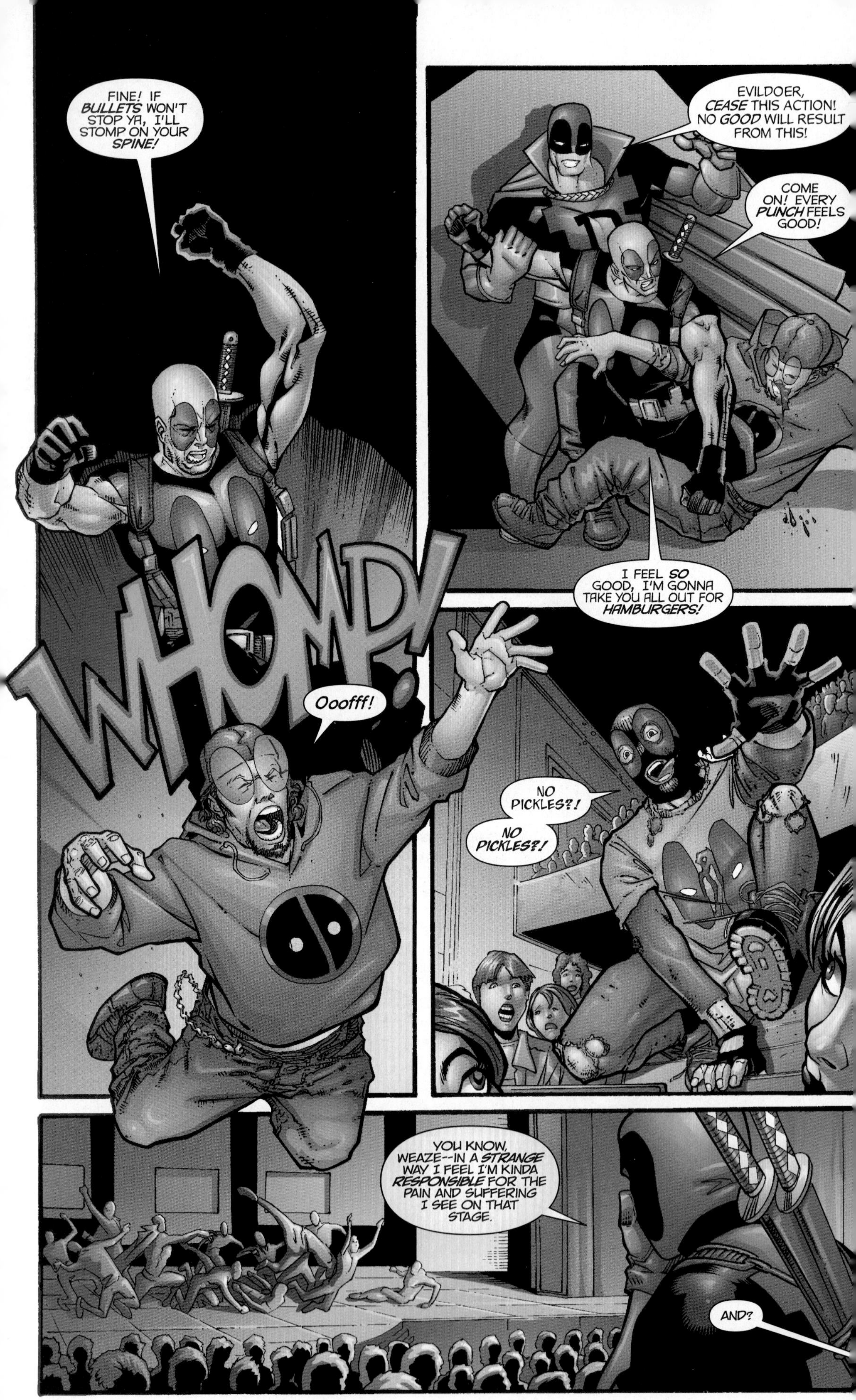
FINE! IF BULLETS WON'T STOP YA, I'LL STOMP ON YOUR SPINE!
WHOMP!
Ooofff!
EVILDOER, CEASE THIS ACTION! NO GOOD WILL RESULT FROM THIS!
COME ON! EVERY PUNCH FEELS GOOD!
I FEEL SO GOOD, I'M GONNA TAKE YOU ALL OUT FOR HAMBURGERS!
NO PICKLES?!
NO PICKLES?!
YOU KNOW, WEAZE--IN A STRANGE WAY I FEEL I'M KINDA RESPONSIBLE FOR THE PAIN AND SUFFERING I SEE ON THAT STAGE.
AND?

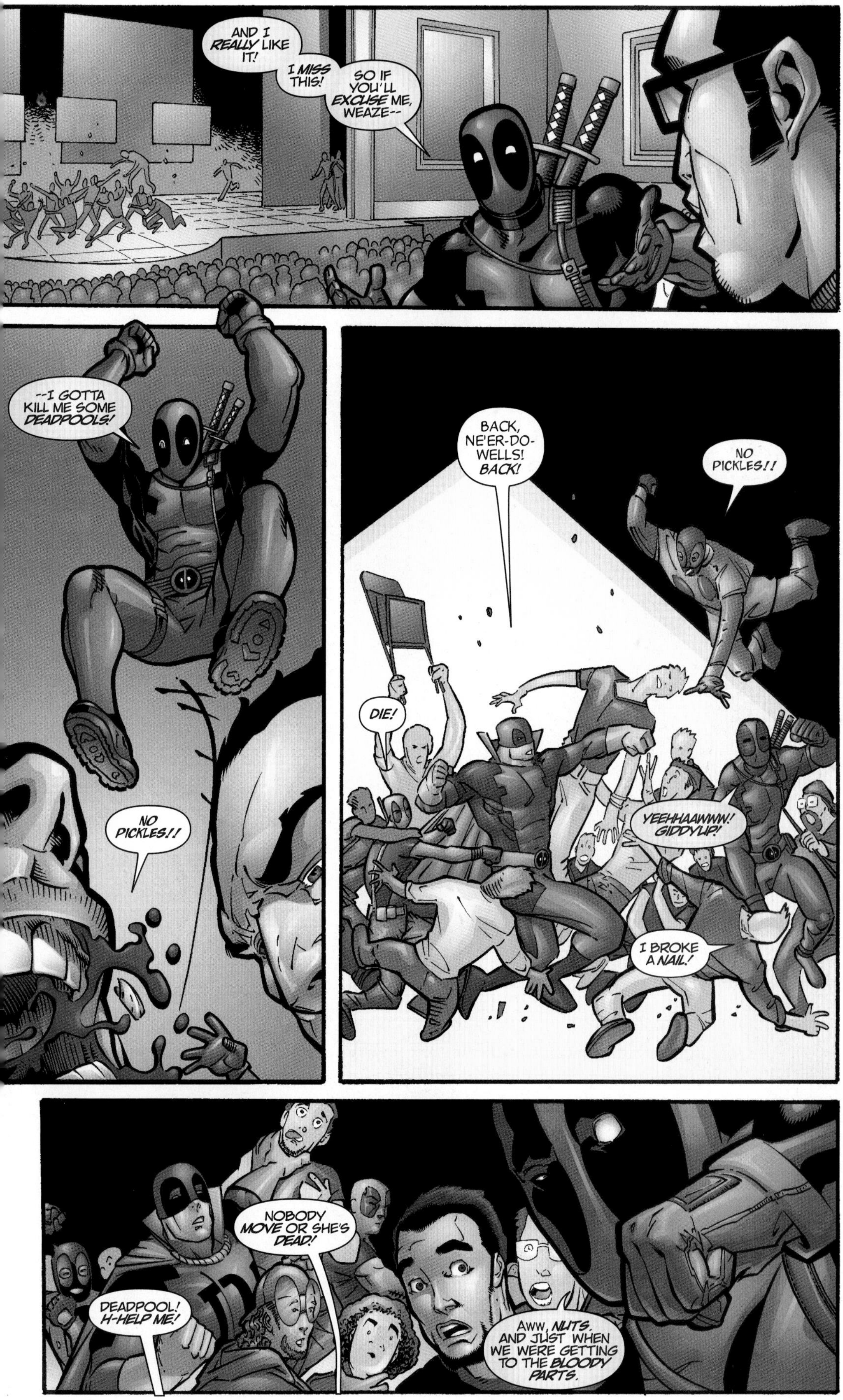
AND I REALLY LIKE IT!
I MISS THIS!
SO IF YOU'LL EXCUSE ME, WEAZE--
--I GOTTA KILL ME SOME DEADPOOLS!
NO PICKLES!!
BACK, NE'ER-DO-WELLS! BACK!
NO PICKLES!!
DIE!
YEEHHAAWWN! GIDDYUP!
I BROKE A NAIL!
NOBODY MOVE OR SHE'S DEAD!
DEADPOOL! H-HELP ME!
AWW, NUTS. AND JUST WHEN WE WERE GETTING TO THE BLOODY PARTS.

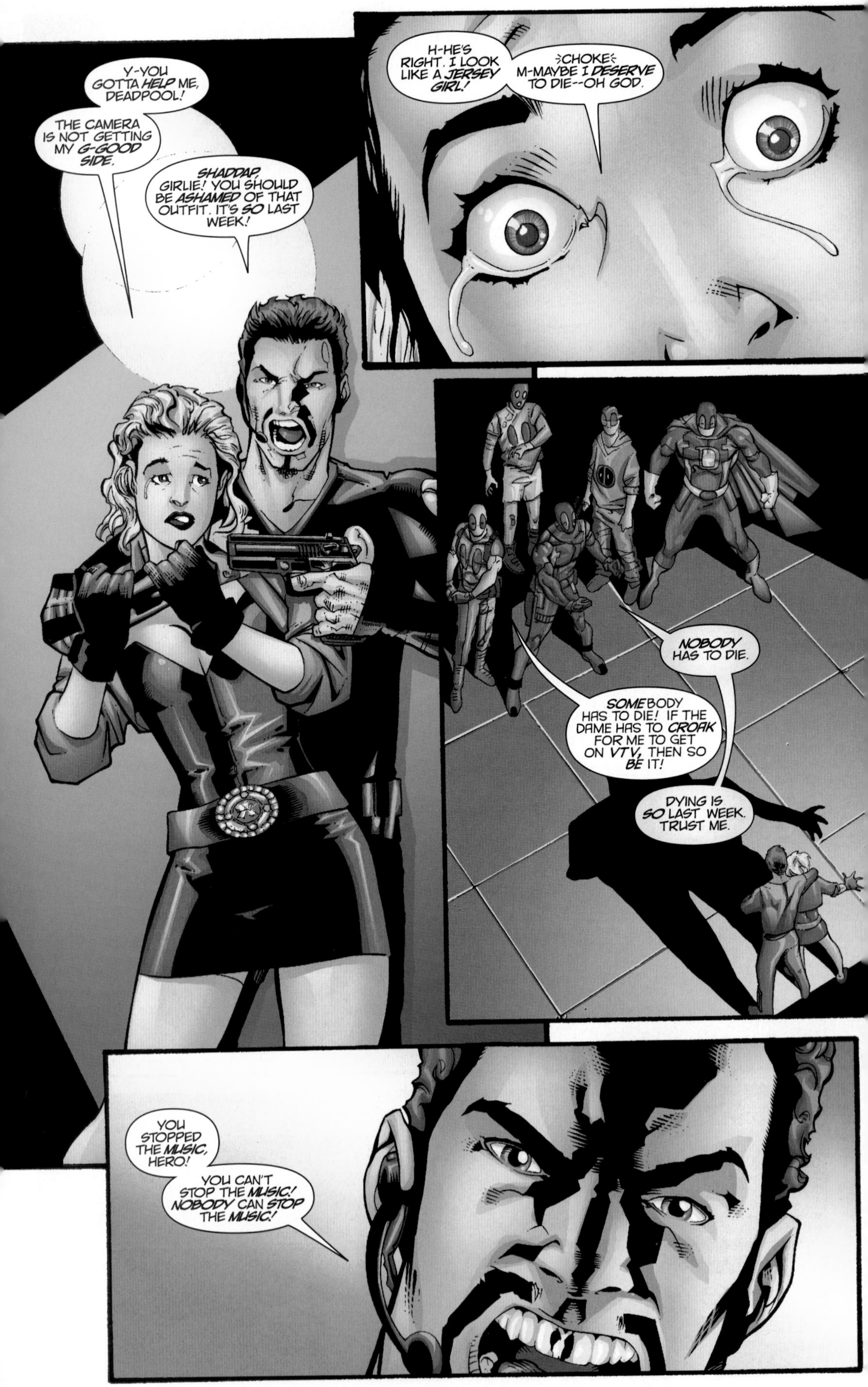
Y-YOU GOTTA HELP ME, DEADPOOL!
THE CAMERA IS NOT GETTING MY G-GOOD SIDE.
SHADDAP, GIRLIE! YOU SHOULD BE ASHAMED OF THAT OUTFIT. IT'S SO LAST WEEK!
H-HE'S RIGHT. I LOOK LIKE A JERSEY GIRL!
CHOKE M-MAYBE I DESERVE TO DIE--OH GOD.
NOBODY HAS TO DIE.
SOMEBODY HAS TO DIE! IF THE DAME HAS TO CROAK FOR ME TO GET ON VTV, THEN SO BE IT!
DYING IS SO LAST WEEK. TRUST ME.
YOU STOPPED THE MUSIC, HERO!
YOU CAN'T STOP THE MUSIC! NOBODY CAN STOP THE MUSIC!

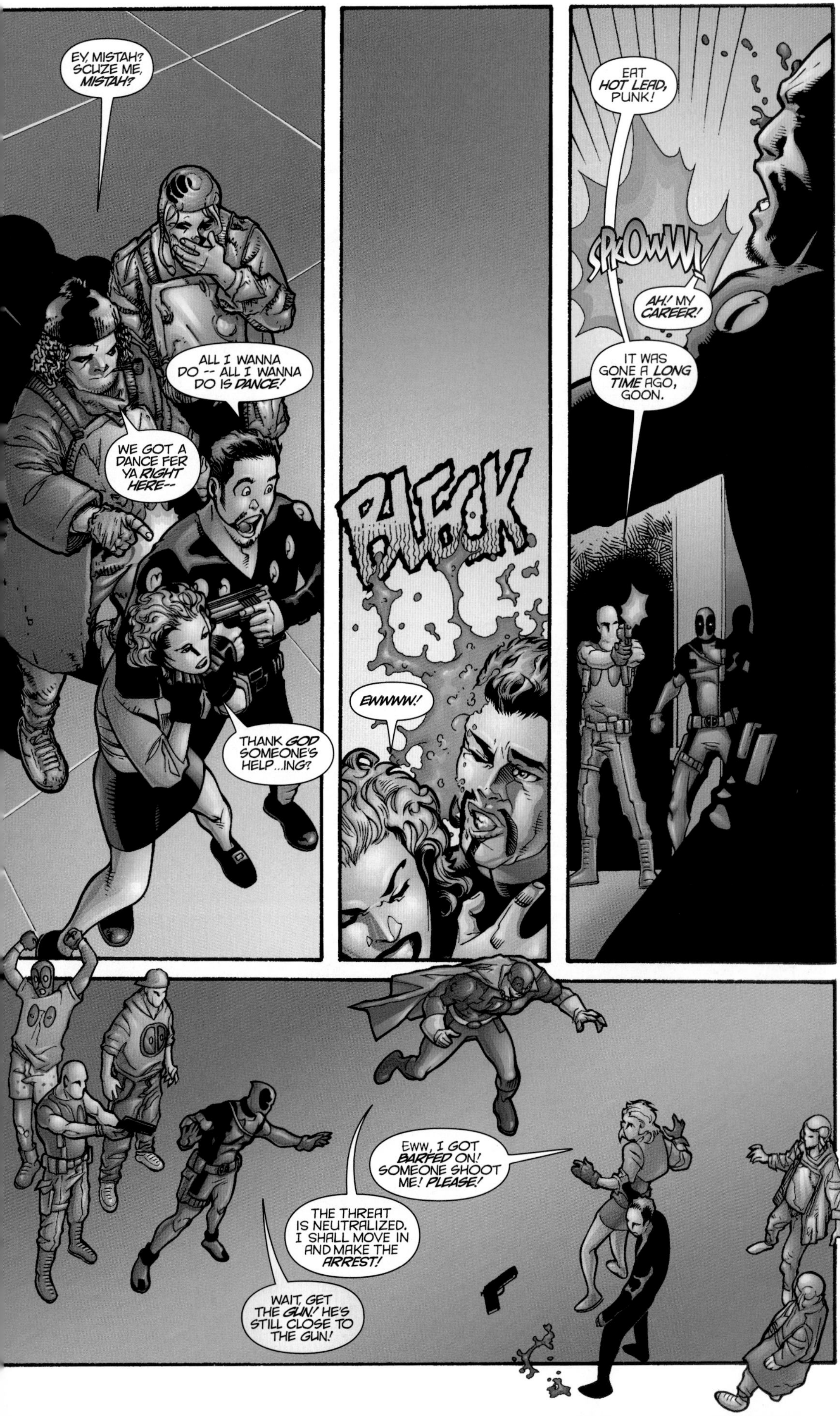
EY, MISTAH? SCUZE ME, MISTAH?
ALL I WANNA DO -- ALL I WANNA DO IS DANCE!
WE GOT A DANCE FER YA RIGHT HERE--
THANK GOD SOMEONE'S HELP...ING?
PAK
EWWWW!
EAT HOT LEAD, PUNK!
SPKOWW!
AH! MY CAREER!
IT WAS GONE A LONG TIME AGO, GOON.
EWW, I GOT BARFED ON! SOMEONE SHOOT ME! PLEASE!
THE THREAT IS NEUTRALIZED. I SHALL MOVE IN AND MAKE THE ARREST!
WAIT, GET THE GUN! HE'S STILL CLOSE TO THE GUN!

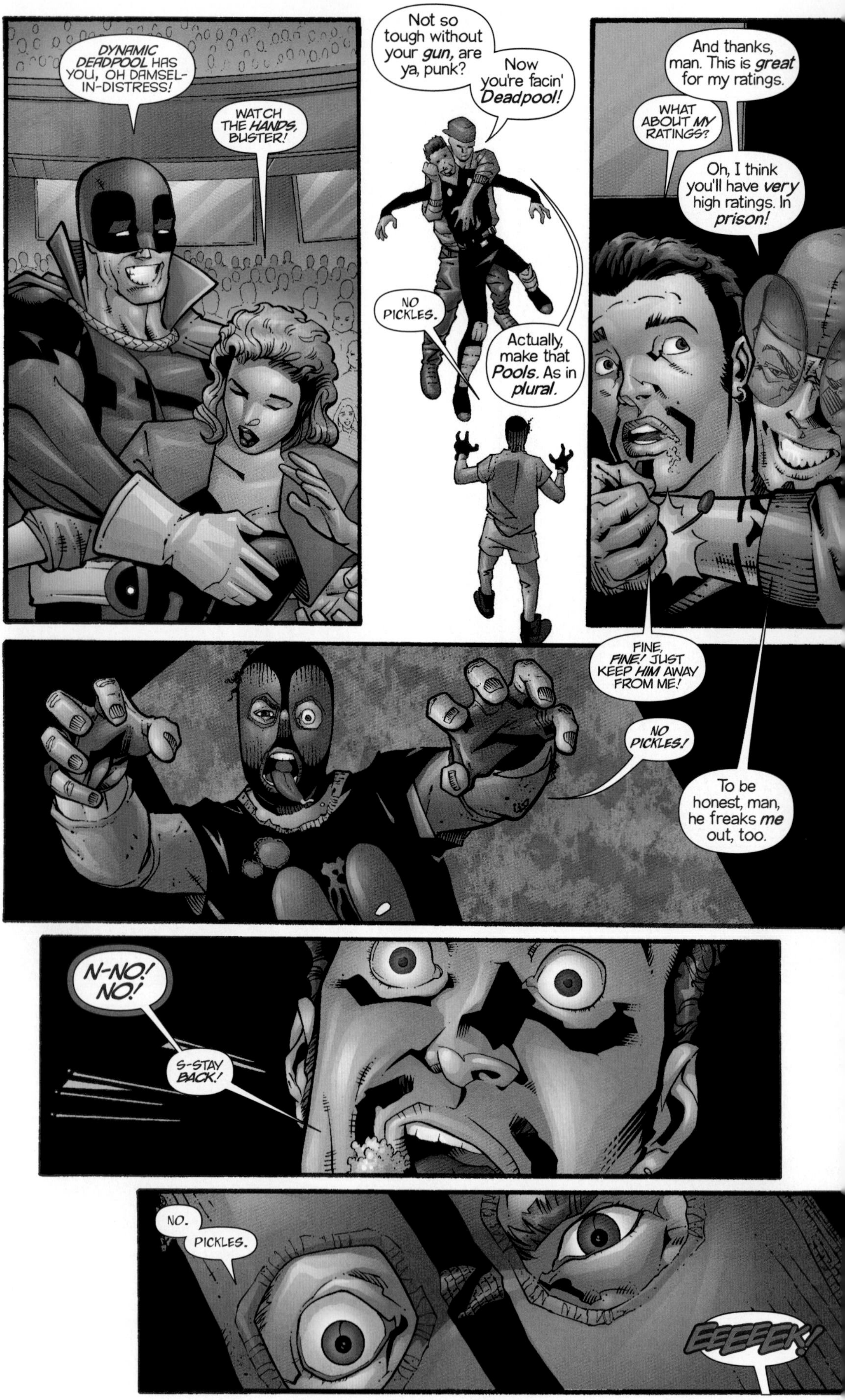
DYNAMIC DEADPOOL HAS YOU, OH DAMSEL-IN-DISTRESS!
WATCH THE HANDS, BUSTER!
Not so tough without your gun, are ya, punk?
Now you're facin' Deadpool!
NO PICKLES.
Actually, make that Pools. As in plural.
And thanks, man. This is great for my ratings.
WHAT ABOUT MY RATINGS?
Oh, I think you'll have very high ratings. In prison!
FINE, FINE! JUST KEEP HIM AWAY FROM ME!
NO PICKLES!
To be honest, man, he freaks me out, too.
N-NO! NO!
S-STAY BACK!
NO.
PICKLES.
EEEEEK!

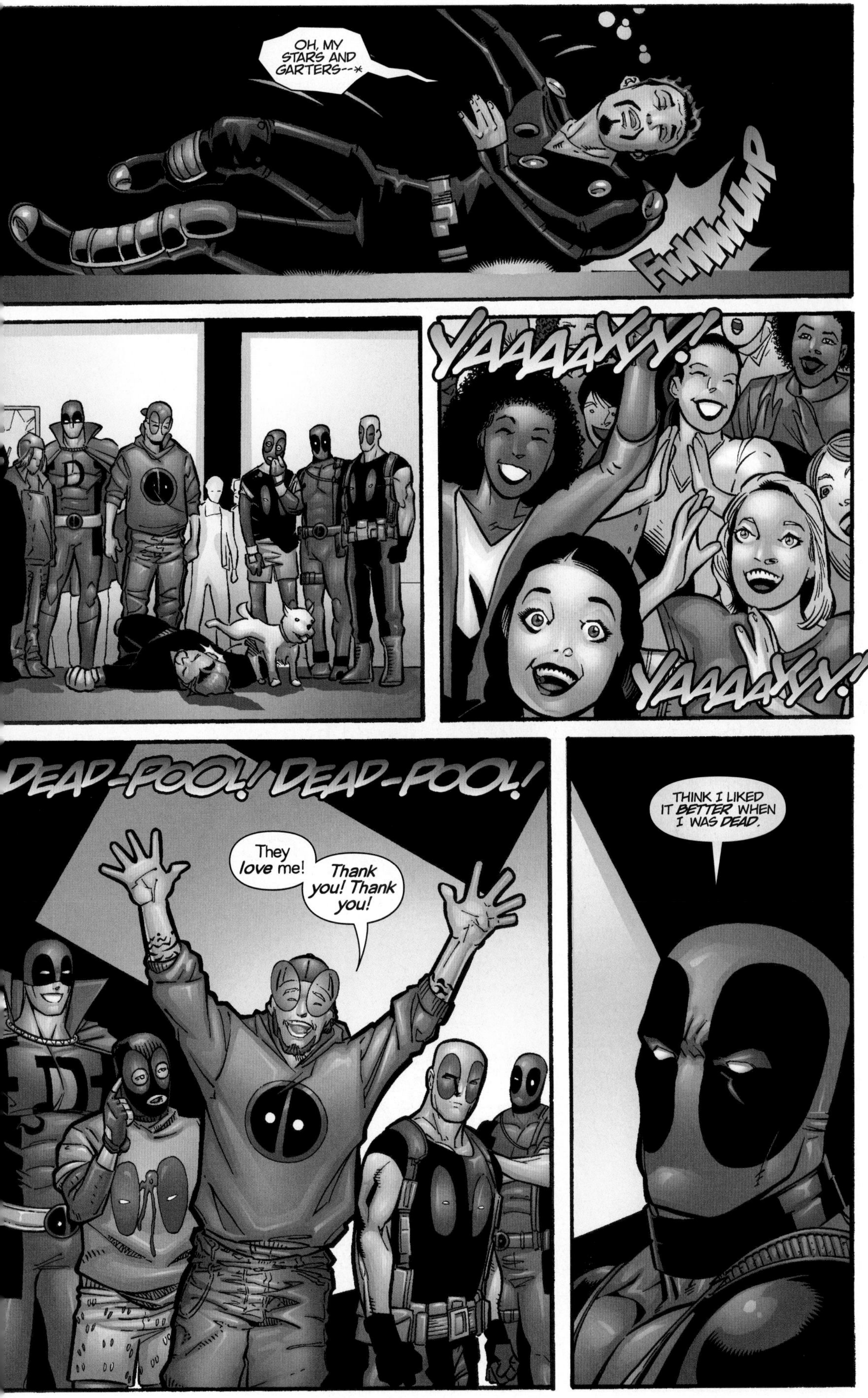

OH, MY STARS AND GARTERS--*
FWWWUMP
YAAAAAYY!
YAAAAAYY!
DEAD-POOL! DEAD-POOL!
They love me!
Thank you! Thank you!
THINK I LIKED IT BETTER WHEN I WAS DEAD.

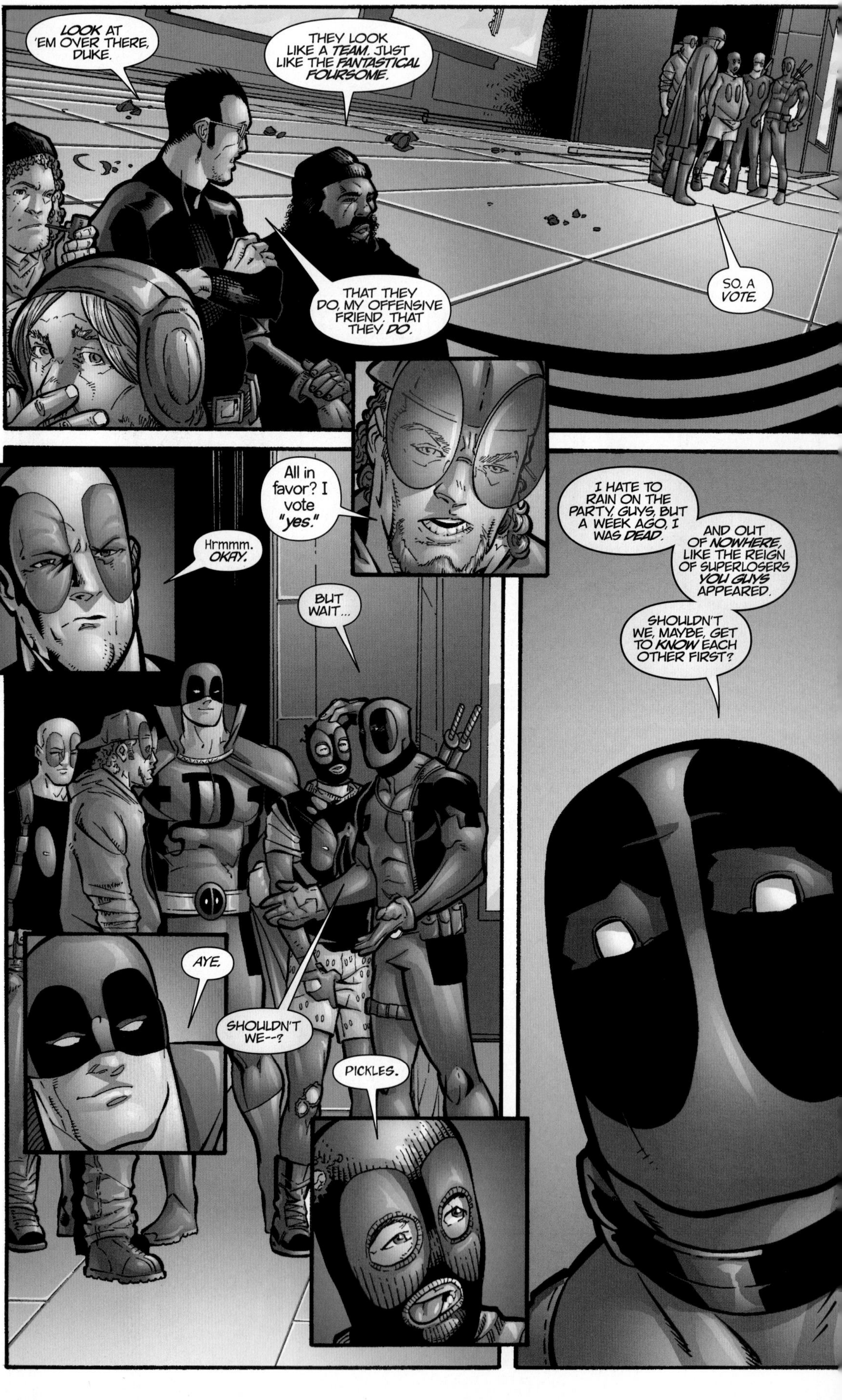
LOOK AT 'EM OVER THERE, DUKE.
THEY LOOK LIKE A TEAM. JUST LIKE THE FANTASTICAL FOURSOME.
THAT THEY DO, MY OFFENSIVE FRIEND. THAT THEY DO.
SO, A VOTE.
All in favor? I vote "yes."
Hrmmm. OKAY.
BUT WAIT...
AYE.
SHOULDN'T WE--?
PICKLES.
I HATE TO RAIN ON THE PARTY, GUYS, BUT A WEEK AGO, I WAS DEAD.
AND OUT OF NOWHERE, LIKE THE REIGN OF SUPERLOSERS YOU GUYS APPEARED.
SHOULDN'T WE, MAYBE, GET TO KNOW EACH OTHER FIRST?

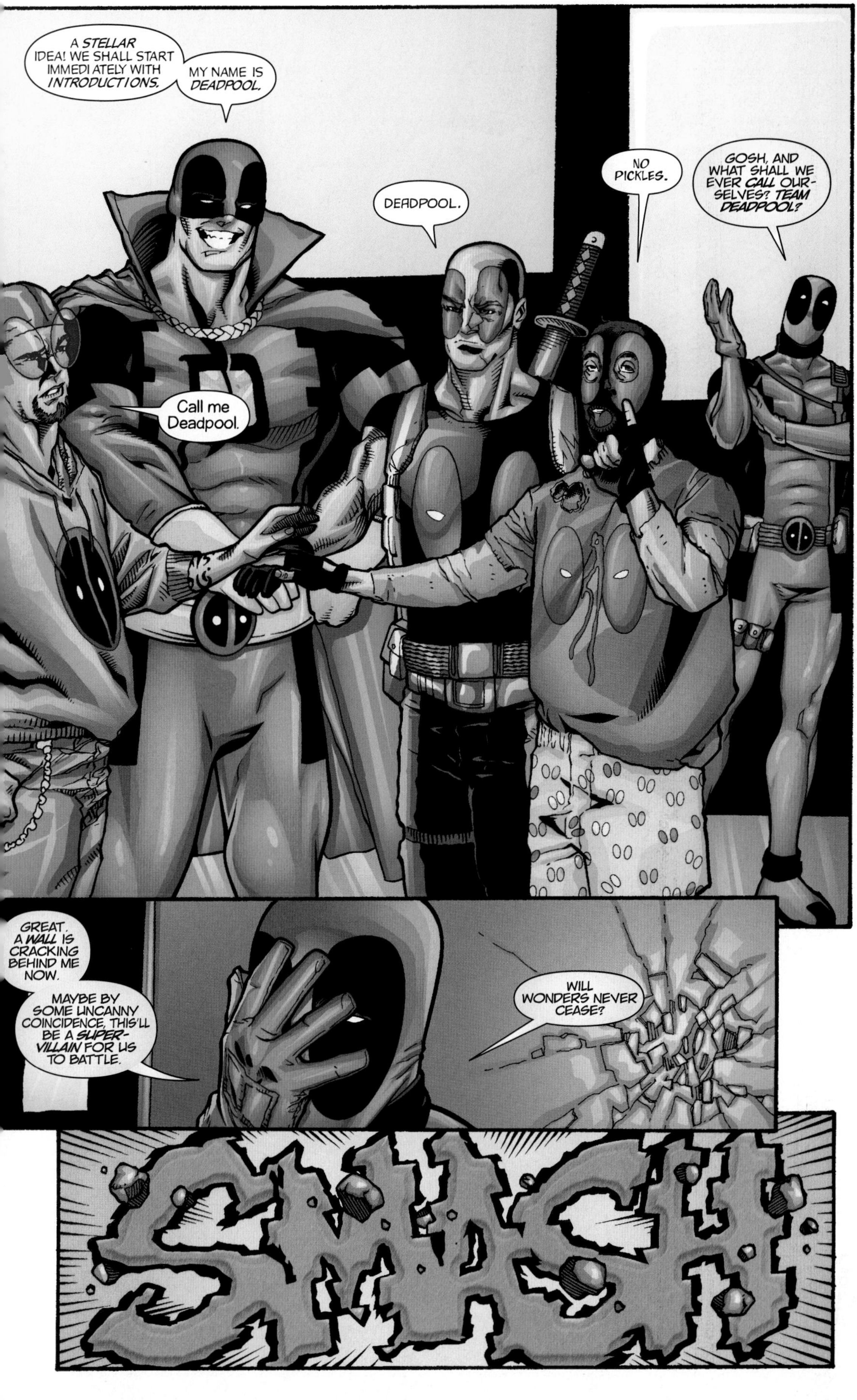

A STELLAR IDEA! WE SHALL START IMMEDIATELY WITH INTRODUCTIONS.
MY NAME IS DEADPOOL.
Call me Deadpool.
DEADPOOL.
NO PICKLES.
GOSH, AND WHAT SHALL WE EVER CALL OURSELVES? TEAM DEADPOOL?
GREAT. A WALL IS CRACKING BEHIND ME NOW.
MAYBE BY SOME UNCANNY COINCIDENCE, THIS'LL BE A SUPER-VILLAIN FOR US TO BATTLE.
WILL WONDERS NEVER CEASE?
SMASH

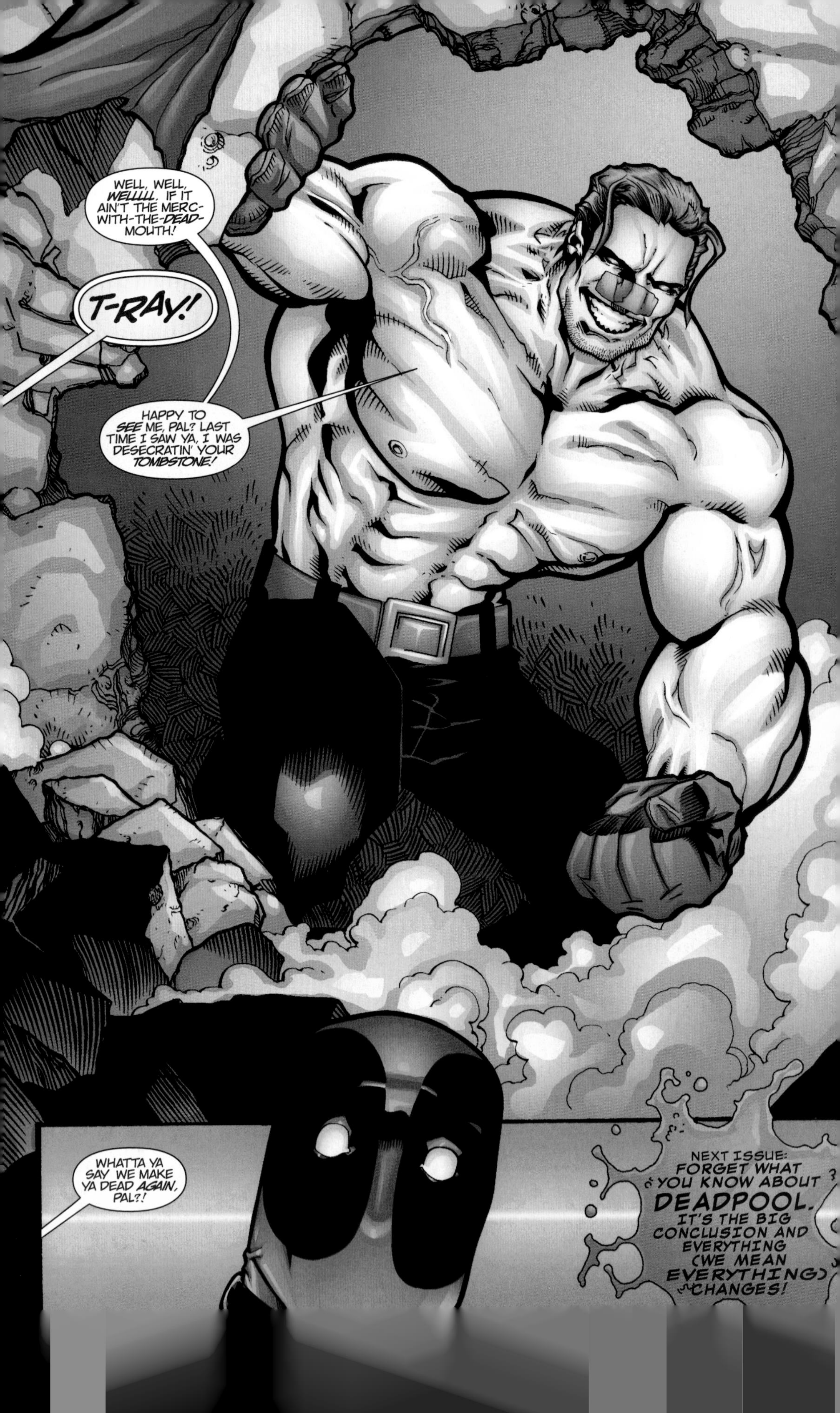
WELL, WELL, WELLLLL. IF IT AIN'T THE MERC-WITH-THE-DEAD-MOUTH!
T-RAY!
HAPPY TO SEE ME, PAL? LAST TIME I SAW YA, I WAS DESECRATIN' YOUR TOMBSTONE!
WHATTA YA SAY WE MAKE YA DEAD AGAIN, PAL?!
NEXT ISSUE: FORGET WHAT YOU KNOW ABOUT DEADPOOL. IT'S THE BIG CONCLUSION AND EVERYTHING (WE MEAN EVERYTHING) CHANGES!

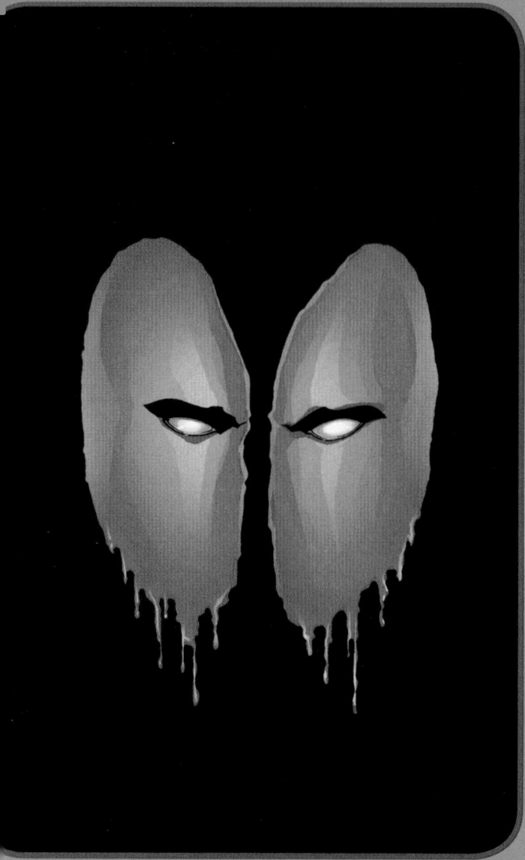

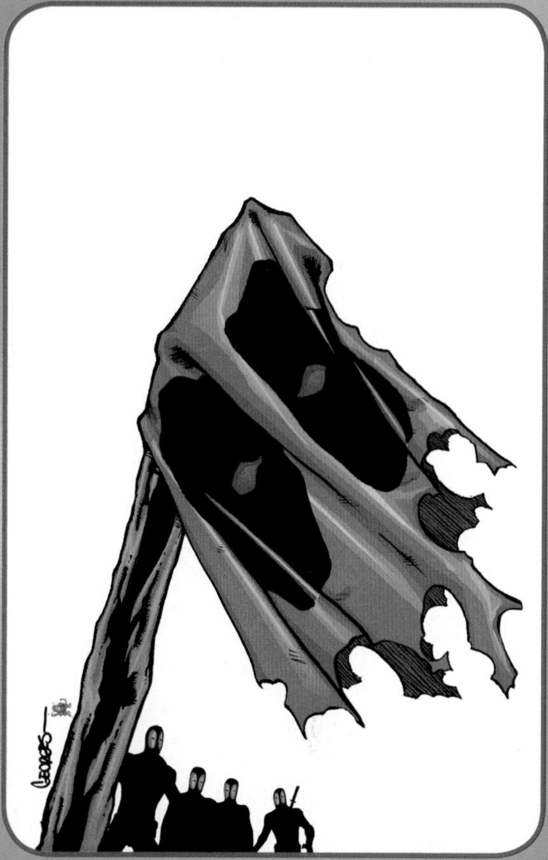

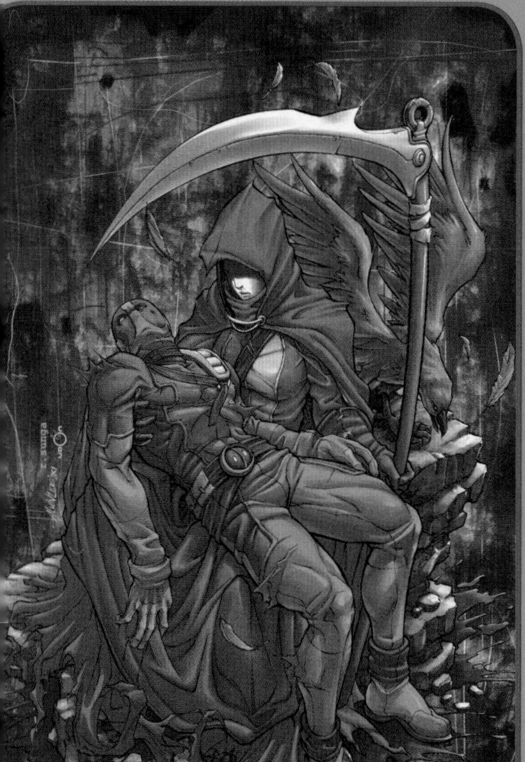

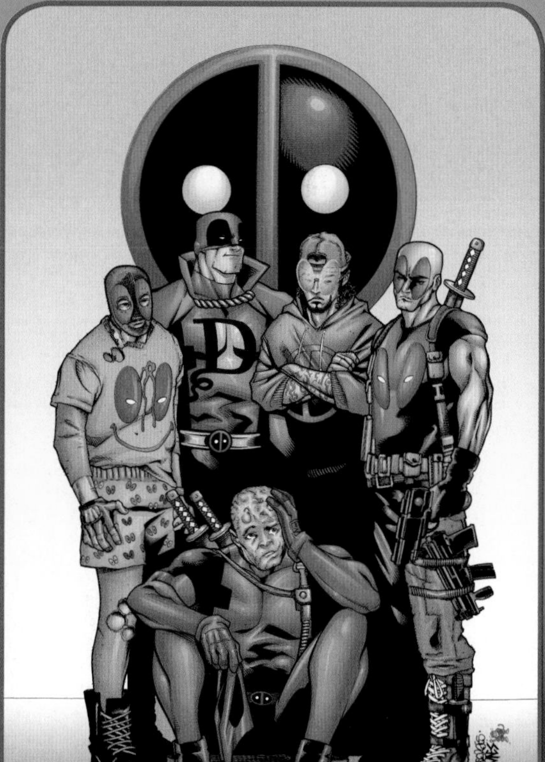

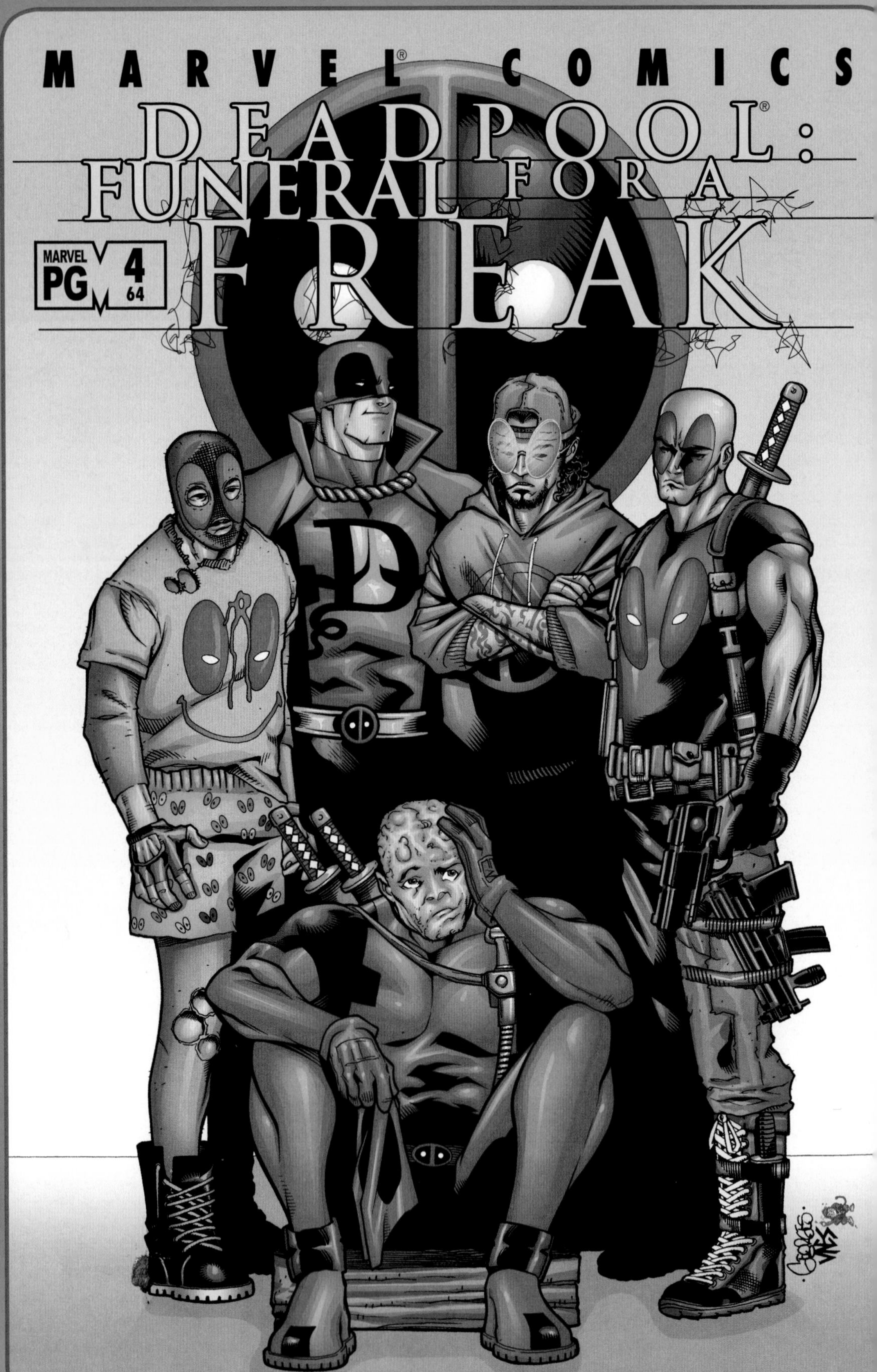

MARVEL® COMICS
DEADPOOL®:
FUNERAL FOR A
FREAK
MARVEL PG
4
64

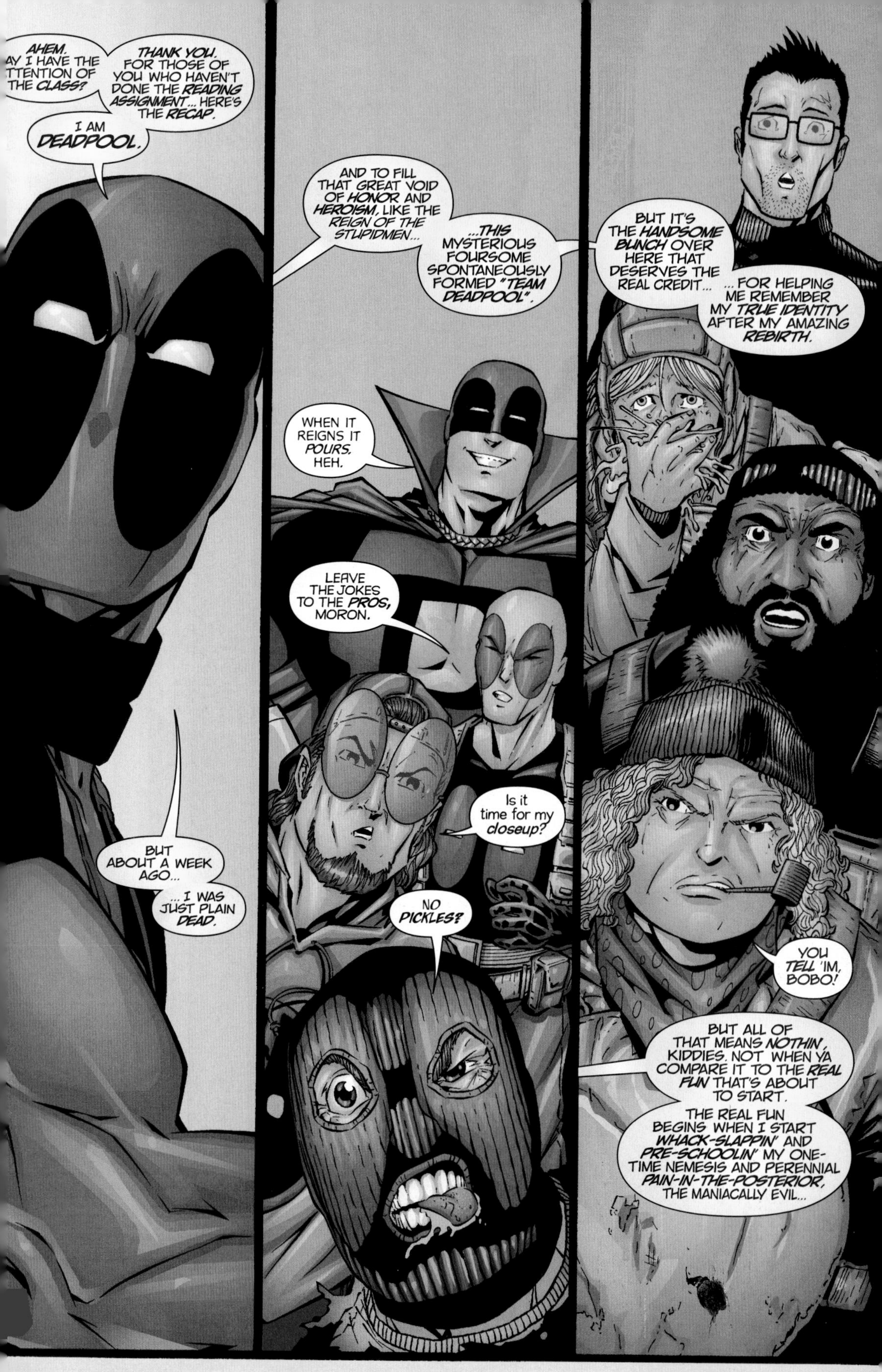AHEM. ...AY I HAVE THE ...TTENTION OF THE CLASS?
THANK YOU. FOR THOSE OF YOU WHO HAVEN'T DONE THE READING ASSIGNMENT... HERE'S THE RECAP.
I AM DEADPOOL.
AND TO FILL THAT GREAT VOID OF HONOR AND HEROISM, LIKE THE REIGN OF THE STUPIDMEN...
...THIS MYSTERIOUS FOURSOME SPONTANEOUSLY FORMED "TEAM DEADPOOL".
BUT IT'S THE HANDSOME BUNCH OVER HERE THAT DESERVES THE REAL CREDIT...
...FOR HELPING ME REMEMBER MY TRUE IDENTITY AFTER MY AMAZING REBIRTH.
WHEN IT REIGNS IT POURS. HEH.
LEAVE THE JOKES TO THE PROS, MORON.
Is it time for my closeup?
NO PICKLES?
BUT ABOUT A WEEK AGO...
...I WAS JUST PLAIN DEAD.
YOU TELL 'IM, BOBO!
BUT ALL OF THAT MEANS NOTHIN, KIDDIES. NOT WHEN YA COMPARE IT TO THE REAL FUN THAT'S ABOUT TO START.
THE REAL FUN BEGINS WHEN I START WHACK-SLAPPIN' AND PRE-SCHOOLIN' MY ONE-TIME NEMESIS AND PERENNIAL PAIN-IN-THE-POSTERIOR, THE MANIACALLY EVIL...

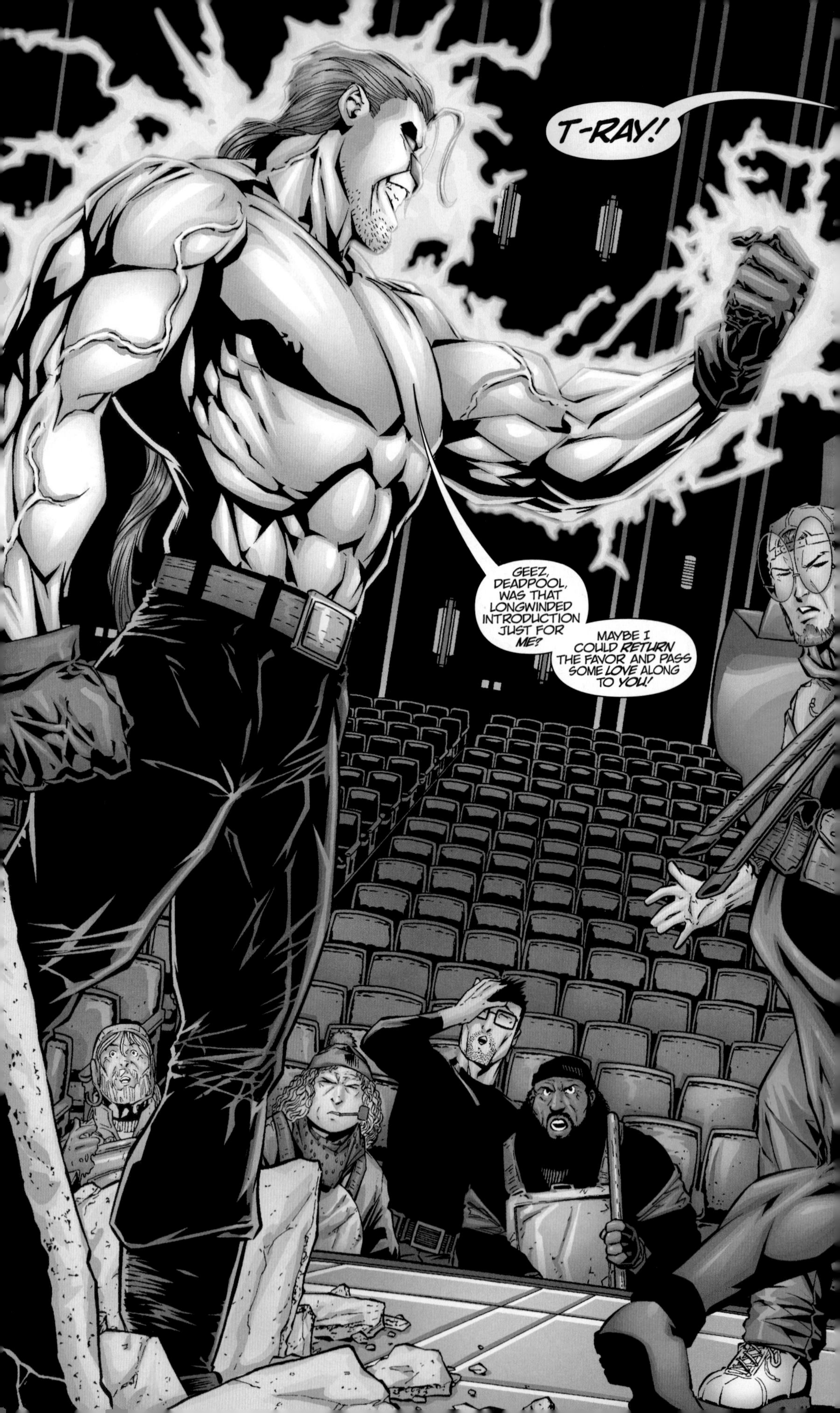
T-RAY!
GEEZ, DEADPOOL, WAS THAT LONGWINDED INTRODUCTION JUST FOR ME?
MAYBE I COULD RETURN THE FAVOR AND PASS SOME LOVE ALONG TO YOU!

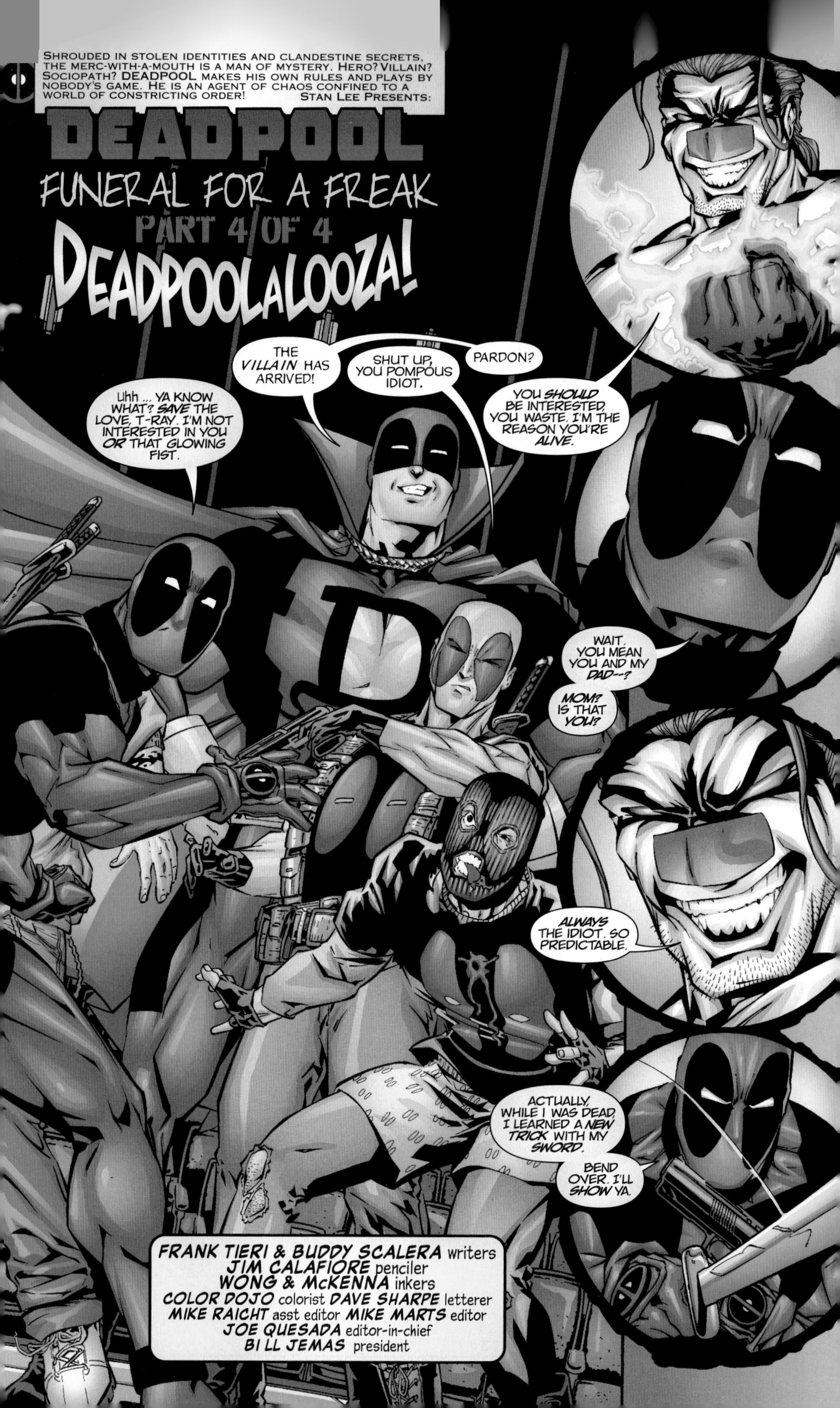

SHROUDED IN STOLEN IDENTITIES AND CLANDESTINE SECRETS, THE MERC-WITH-A-MOUTH IS A MAN OF MYSTERY. HERO? VILLAIN? SOCIOPATH? DEADPOOL MAKES HIS OWN RULES AND PLAYS BY NOBODY'S GAME. HE IS AN AGENT OF CHAOS CONFINED TO A WORLD OF CONSTRICTING ORDER! STAN LEE PRESENTS:
DEADPOOL
FUNERAL FOR A FREAK
PART 4 OF 4
DEADPOOLALOOZA!
THE VILLAIN HAS ARRIVED!
SHUT UP, YOU POMPOUS IDIOT.
PARDON?
UHH ... YA KNOW WHAT? SAVE THE LOVE, T-RAY. I'M NOT INTERESTED IN YOU OR THAT GLOWING FIST.
YOU SHOULD BE INTERESTED, YOU WASTE. I'M THE REASON YOU'RE ALIVE.
WAIT. YOU MEAN YOU AND MY DAD--?
MOM? IS THAT YOU?
ALWAYS THE IDIOT. SO PREDICTABLE.
ACTUALLY, WHILE I WAS DEAD, I LEARNED A NEW TRICK WITH MY SWORD.
BEND OVER. I'LL SHOW YA.
FRANK TIERI & BUDDY SCALERA writers
JIM CALAFIORE penciler
WONG & McKENNA inkers
COLOR DOJO colorist DAVE SHARPE letterer
MIKE RAICHT asst editor MIKE MARTS editor
JOE QUESADA editor-in-chief
BILL JEMAS president

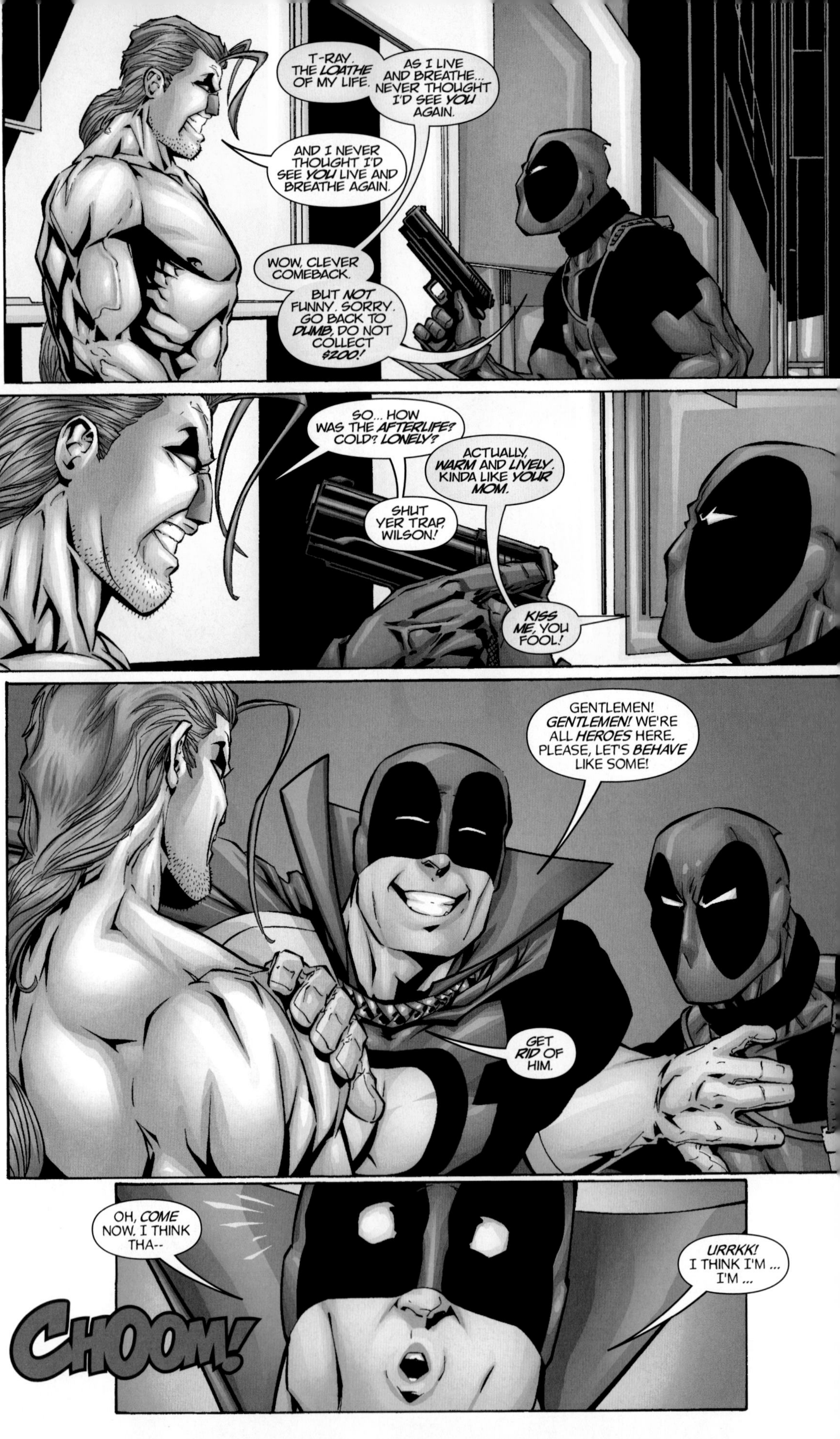

T-RAY. THE LOATHE OF MY LIFE.
AS I LIVE AND BREATHE... NEVER THOUGHT I'D SEE YOU AGAIN.
AND I NEVER THOUGHT I'D SEE YOU LIVE AND BREATHE AGAIN.
WOW, CLEVER COMEBACK.
BUT NOT FUNNY. SORRY. GO BACK TO DUMB, DO NOT COLLECT $200!
SO... HOW WAS THE AFTERLIFE? COLD? LONELY?
ACTUALLY, WARM AND LIVELY. KINDA LIKE YOUR MOM.
SHUT YER TRAP, WILSON!
KISS ME, YOU FOOL!
GENTLEMEN! GENTLEMEN! WE'RE ALL HEROES HERE. PLEASE, LET'S BEHAVE LIKE SOME!
GET RID OF HIM.
OH, COME NOW. I THINK THA--
CHOOM!
URRKK! I THINK I'M ... I'M ...

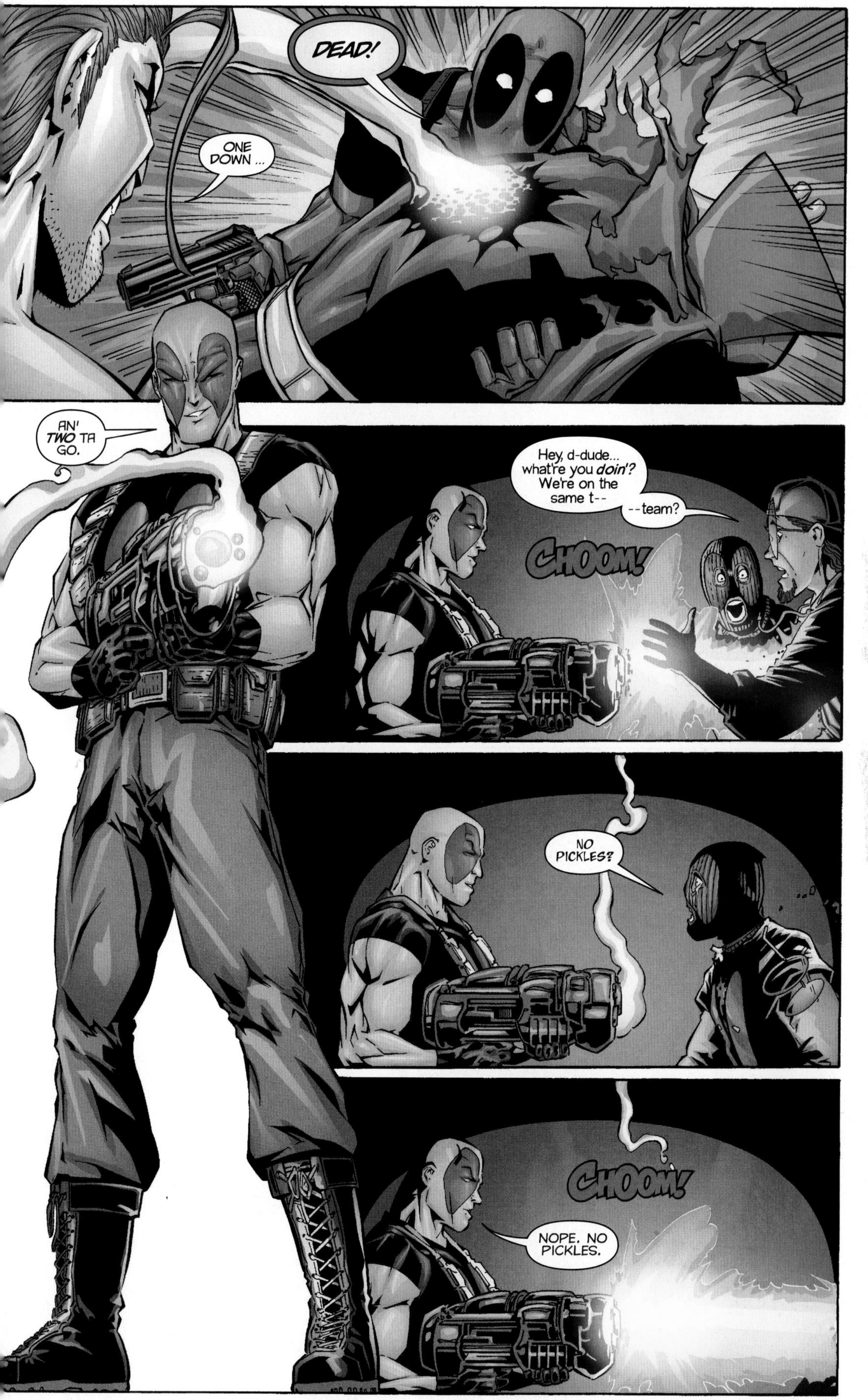
DEAD!
ONE DOWN ...
AN' TWO TA GO.
Hey, d-dude... what're you doin'? We're on the same t--
--team?
CHOOM!
NO PICKLES?
CHOOM!
NOPE. NO PICKLES.

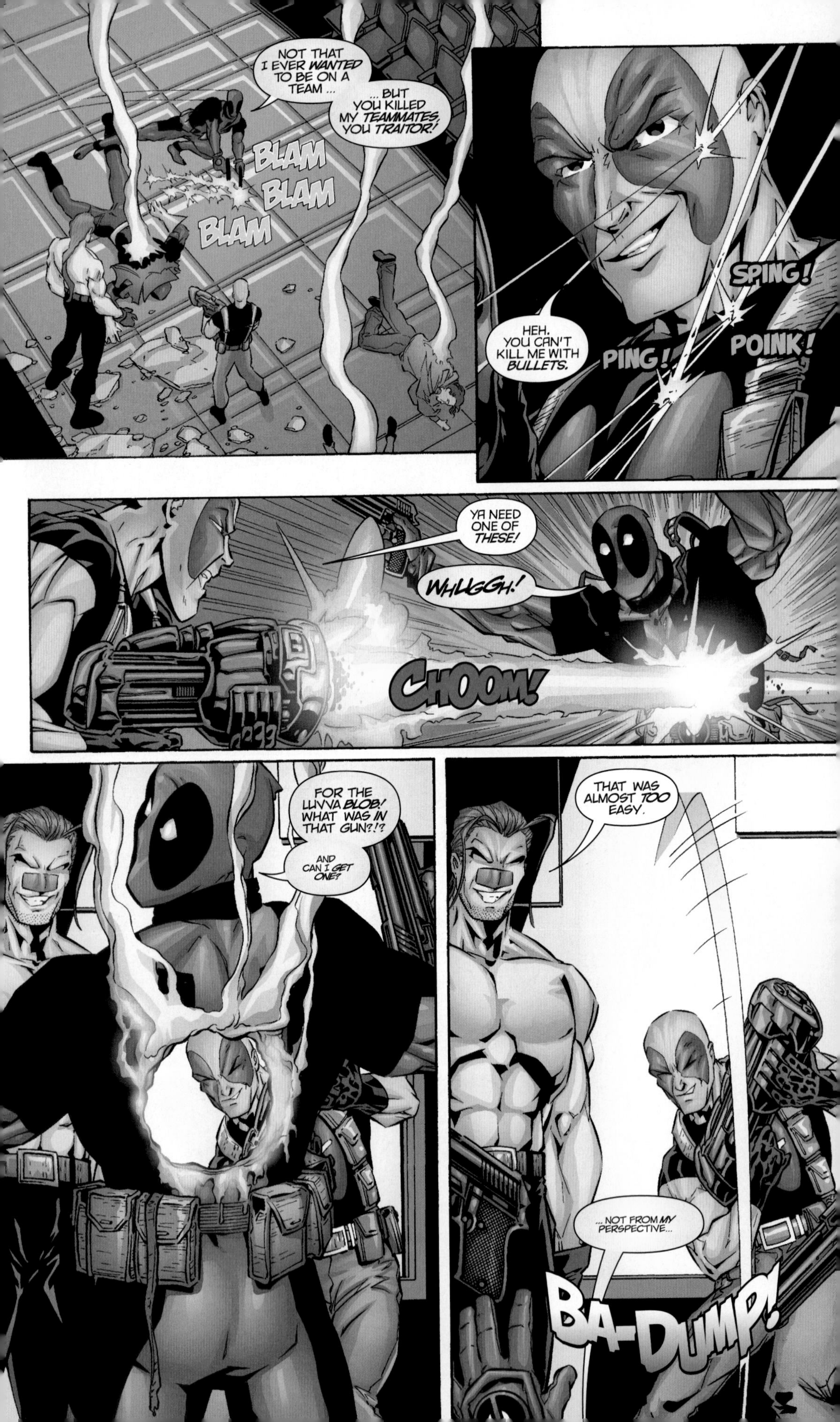
NOT THAT I EVER WANTED TO BE ON A TEAM ...
... BUT YOU KILLED MY TEAMMATES, YOU TRAITOR!
BLAM
BLAM
BLAM
HEH. YOU CAN'T KILL ME WITH BULLETS.
SPING!
POINK!
PING!
YA NEED ONE OF THESE!
WHUGGH!
CHOOM!
FOR THE LUVVA BLOB! WHAT WAS IN THAT GUN?!?
AND CAN I GET ONE?
THAT WAS ALMOST TOO EASY.
...NOT FROM MY PERSPECTIVE...
BA-DUMP!

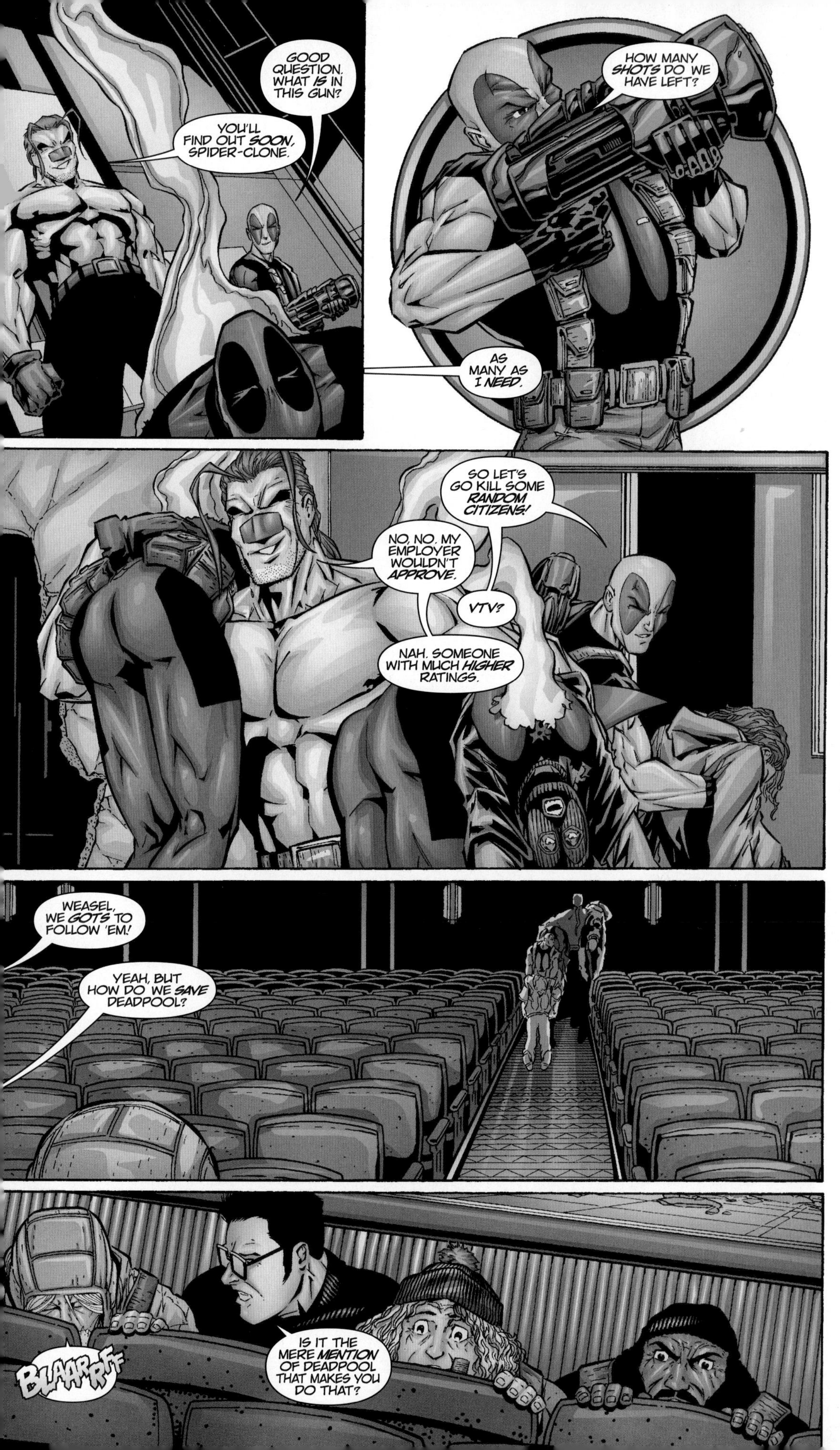
GOOD QUESTION. WHAT IS IN THIS GUN?
YOU'LL FIND OUT SOON, SPIDER-CLONE.
HOW MANY SHOTS DO WE HAVE LEFT?
AS MANY AS I NEED.
SO LET'S GO KILL SOME RANDOM CITIZENS!
NO, NO. MY EMPLOYER WOULDN'T APPROVE.
VTV?
NAH. SOMEONE WITH MUCH HIGHER RATINGS.
WEASEL, WE GOTS TO FOLLOW 'EM!
YEAH, BUT HOW DO WE SAVE DEADPOOL?
BLAARRFF
IS IT THE MERE MENTION OF DEADPOOL THAT MAKES YOU DO THAT?

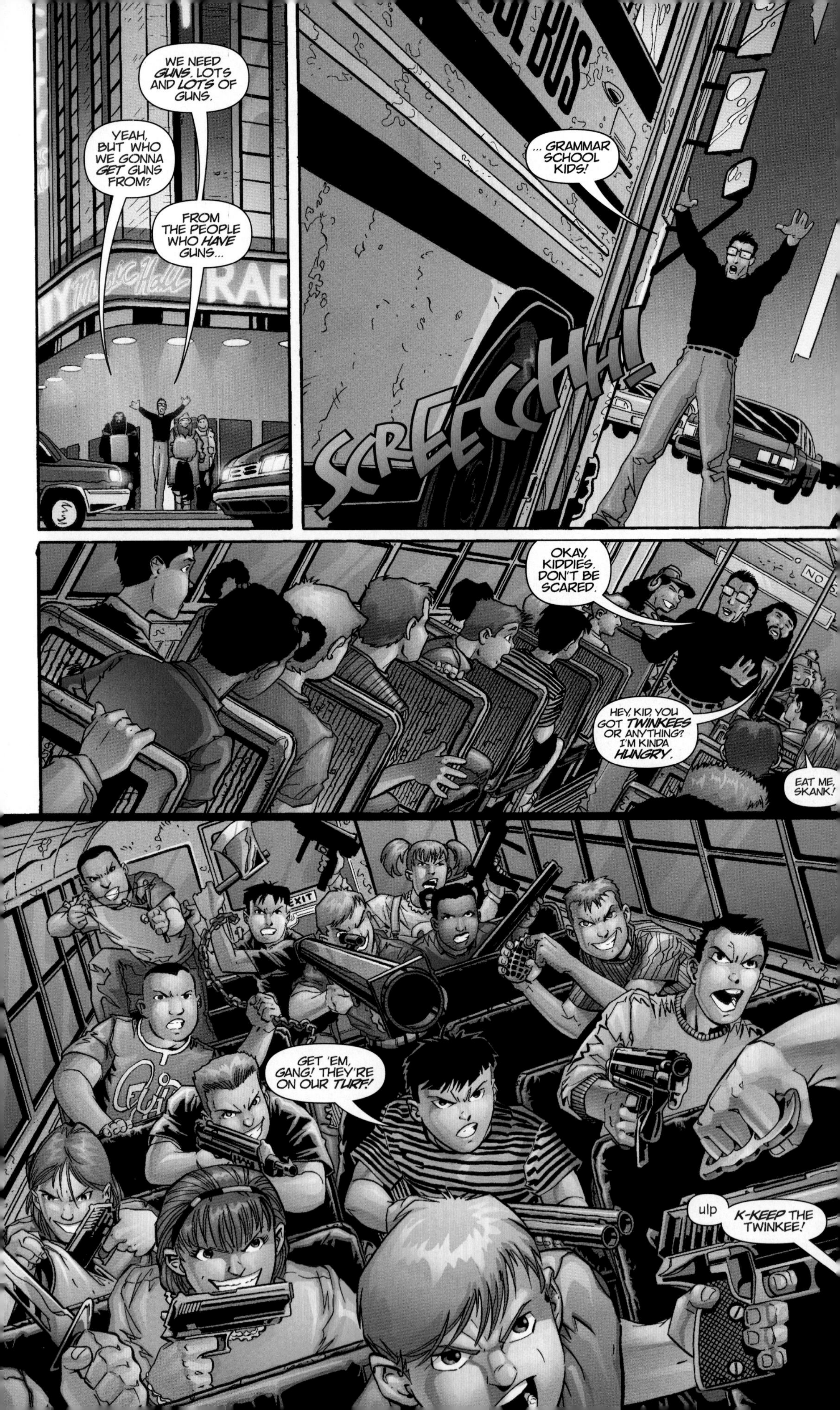

WE NEED GUNS. LOTS AND LOTS OF GUNS.
YEAH, BUT WHO WE GONNA GET GUNS FROM?
FROM THE PEOPLE WHO HAVE GUNS...
... GRAMMAR SCHOOL KIDS!
SCREEECCHH!
OKAY, KIDDIES. DON'T BE SCARED.
HEY, KID, YOU GOT TWINKEES OR ANYTHING? I'M KINDA HUNGRY.
EAT ME, SKANK!
GET 'EM, GANG! THEY'RE ON OUR TURF!
ulp
K-KEEP THE TWINKEE!

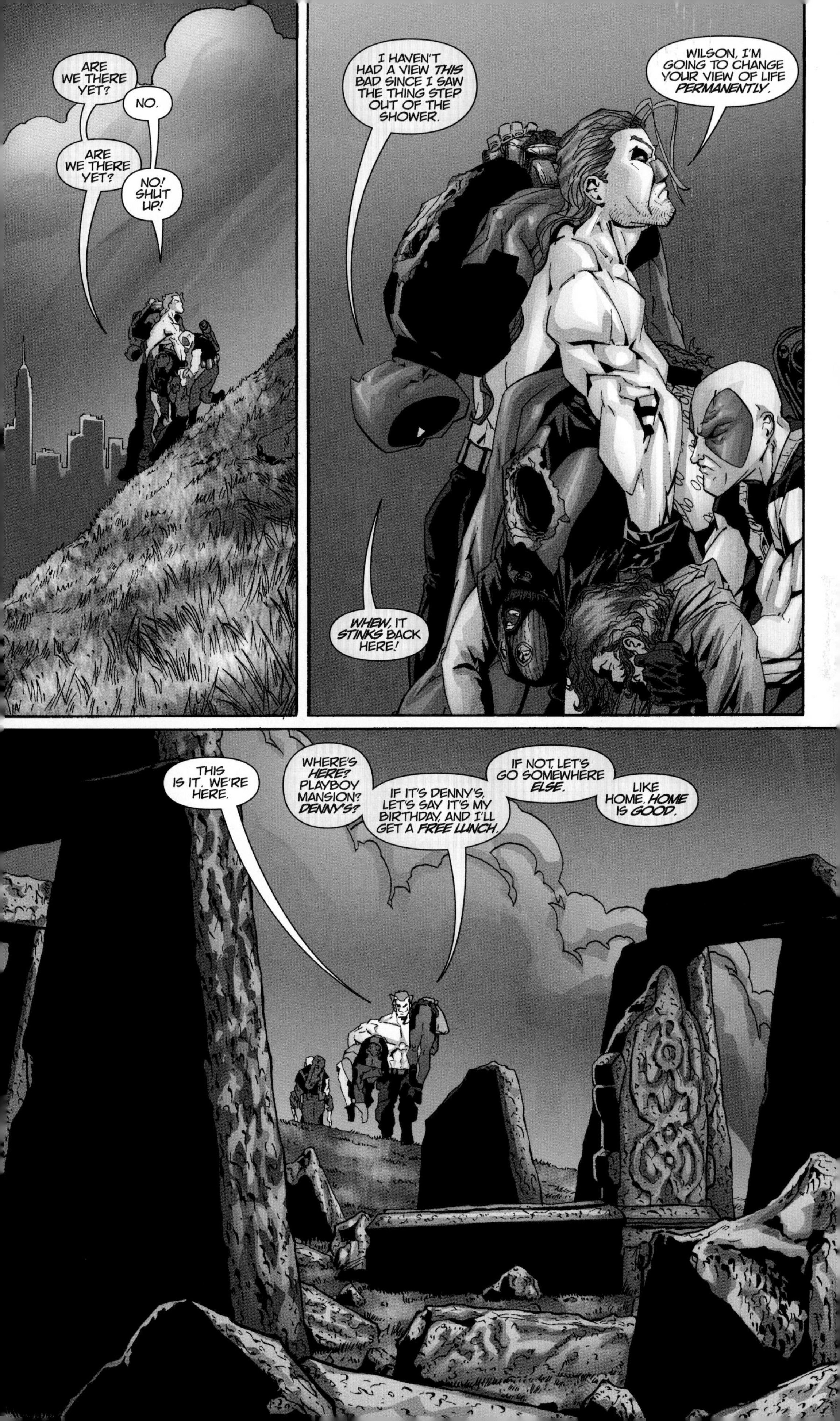
ARE WE THERE YET?
NO.
ARE WE THERE YET?
NO! SHUT UP!
I HAVEN'T HAD A VIEW THIS BAD SINCE I SAW THE THING STEP OUT OF THE SHOWER.
WILSON, I'M GOING TO CHANGE YOUR VIEW OF LIFE PERMANENTLY.
WHEW, IT STINKS BACK HERE!
THIS IS IT. WE'RE HERE.
WHERE'S HERE? PLAYBOY MANSION? DENNY'S?
IF IT'S DENNY'S, LET'S SAY IT'S MY BIRTHDAY, AND I'LL GET A FREE LUNCH.
IF NOT, LET'S GO SOMEWHERE ELSE.
LIKE HOME. HOME IS GOOD.

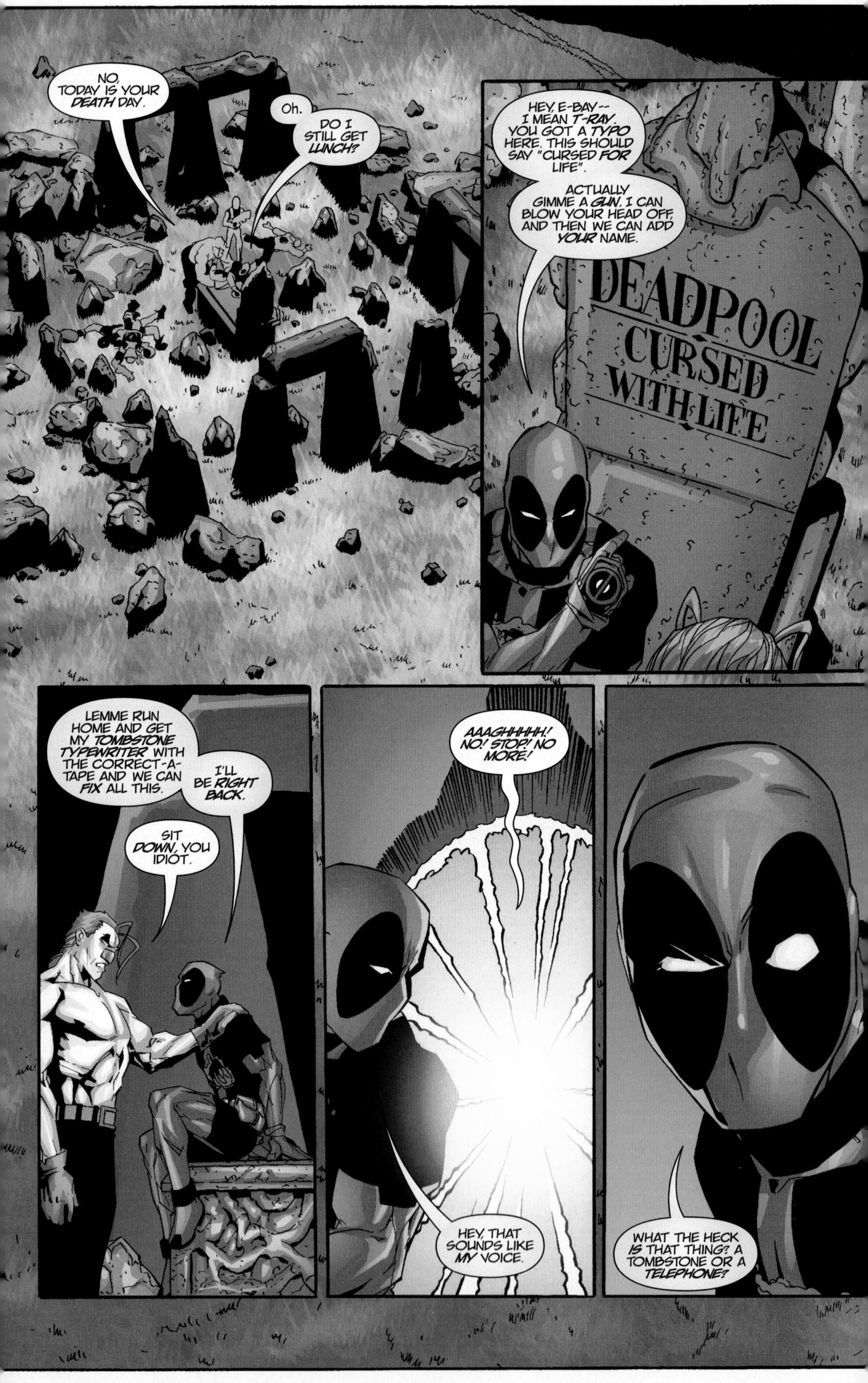
NO, TODAY IS YOUR DEATH DAY.
Oh.
DO I STILL GET LUNCH?
HEY, E-BAY-- I MEAN T-RAY. YOU GOT A TYPO HERE. THIS SHOULD SAY "CURSED FOR LIFE".
ACTUALLY GIMME A GUN. I CAN BLOW YOUR HEAD OFF, AND THEN WE CAN ADD YOUR NAME.
DEADPOOL
CURSED WITH LIFE
LEMME RUN HOME AND GET MY TOMBSTONE TYPEWRITER WITH THE CORRECT-A-TAPE AND WE CAN FIX ALL THIS.
I'LL BE RIGHT BACK.
SIT DOWN, YOU IDIOT.
AAAGHHHH! NO! STOP! NO MORE!
HEY, THAT SOUNDS LIKE MY VOICE.
WHAT THE HECK IS THAT THING? A TOMBSTONE OR A TELEPHONE?

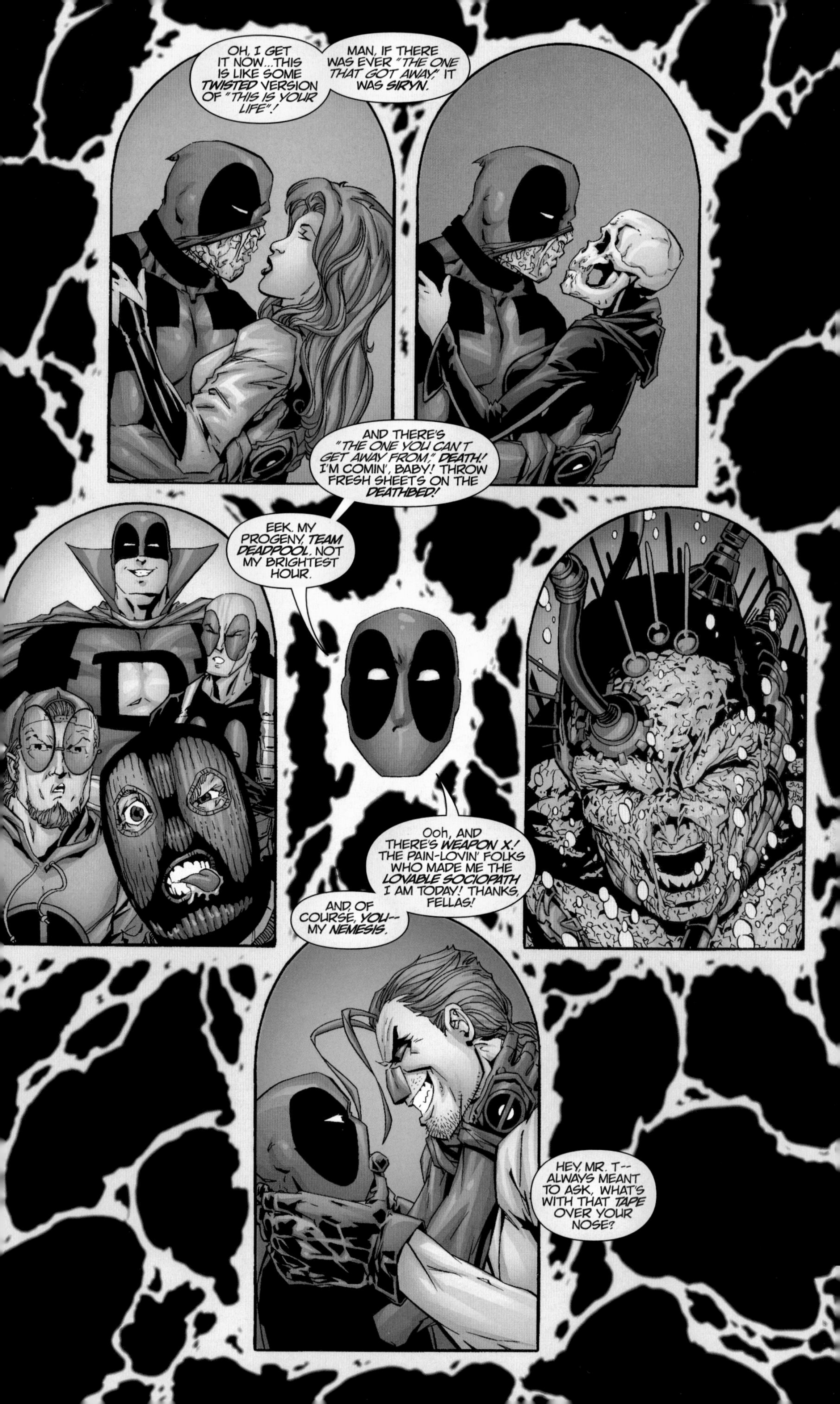

OH, I GET IT NOW...THIS IS LIKE SOME TWISTED VERSION OF "THIS IS YOUR LIFE"!
MAN, IF THERE WAS EVER "THE ONE THAT GOT AWAY," IT WAS SIRYN.
AND THERE'S "THE ONE YOU CAN'T GET AWAY FROM," DEATH! I'M COMIN', BABY! THROW FRESH SHEETS ON THE DEATHBED!
EEK. MY PROGENY, TEAM DEADPOOL. NOT MY BRIGHTEST HOUR.
Ooh, AND THERE'S WEAPON X! THE PAIN-LOVIN' FOLKS WHO MADE ME THE LOVABLE SOCIOPATH I AM TODAY! THANKS, FELLAS!
AND OF COURSE, YOU-- MY NEMESIS.
HEY, MR. T-- ALWAYS MEANT TO ASK, WHAT'S WITH THAT TAPE OVER YOUR NOSE?

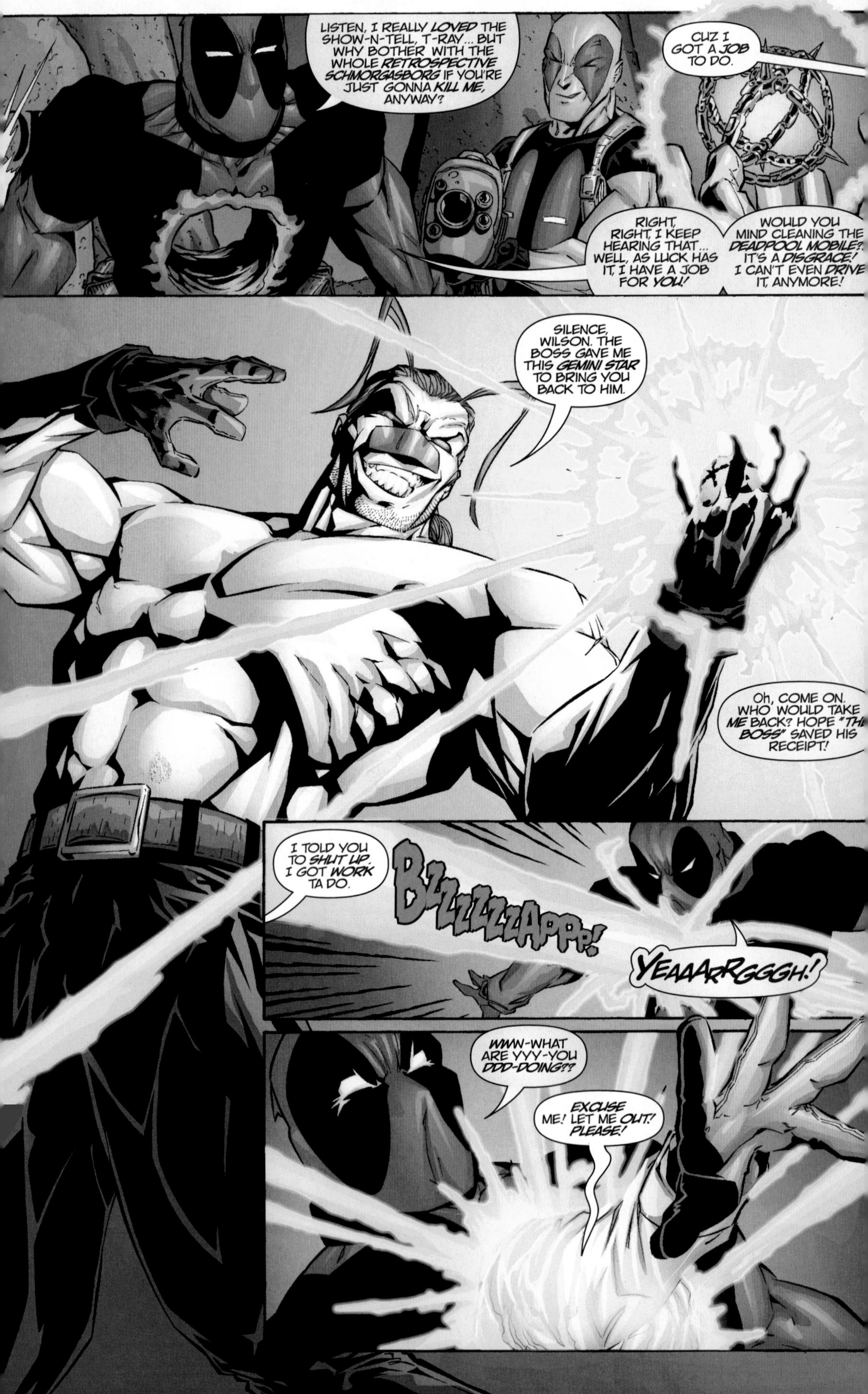
LISTEN, I REALLY LOVED THE SHOW-N-TELL, T-RAY... BUT WHY BOTHER WITH THE WHOLE RETROSPECTIVE SCHMORGASBORG IF YOU'RE JUST GONNA KILL ME, ANYWAY?
CUZ I GOT A JOB TO DO.
RIGHT, RIGHT, I KEEP HEARING THAT... WELL, AS LUCK HAS IT, I HAVE A JOB FOR YOU!
WOULD YOU MIND CLEANING THE DEADPOOL MOBILE? IT'S A DISGRACE! I CAN'T EVEN DRIVE IT, ANYMORE!
SILENCE, WILSON. THE BOSS GAVE ME THIS GEMINI STAR TO BRING YOU BACK TO HIM.
Oh, COME ON. WHO WOULD TAKE ME BACK? HOPE "THE BOSS" SAVED HIS RECEIPT!
I TOLD YOU TO SHUT UP. I GOT WORK TA DO.
BZZZZZZZAPPP!
YEAAARRGGGH!
WWW-WHAT ARE YYY-YOU DDD-DOING??
EXCUSE ME! LET ME OUT! PLEASE!

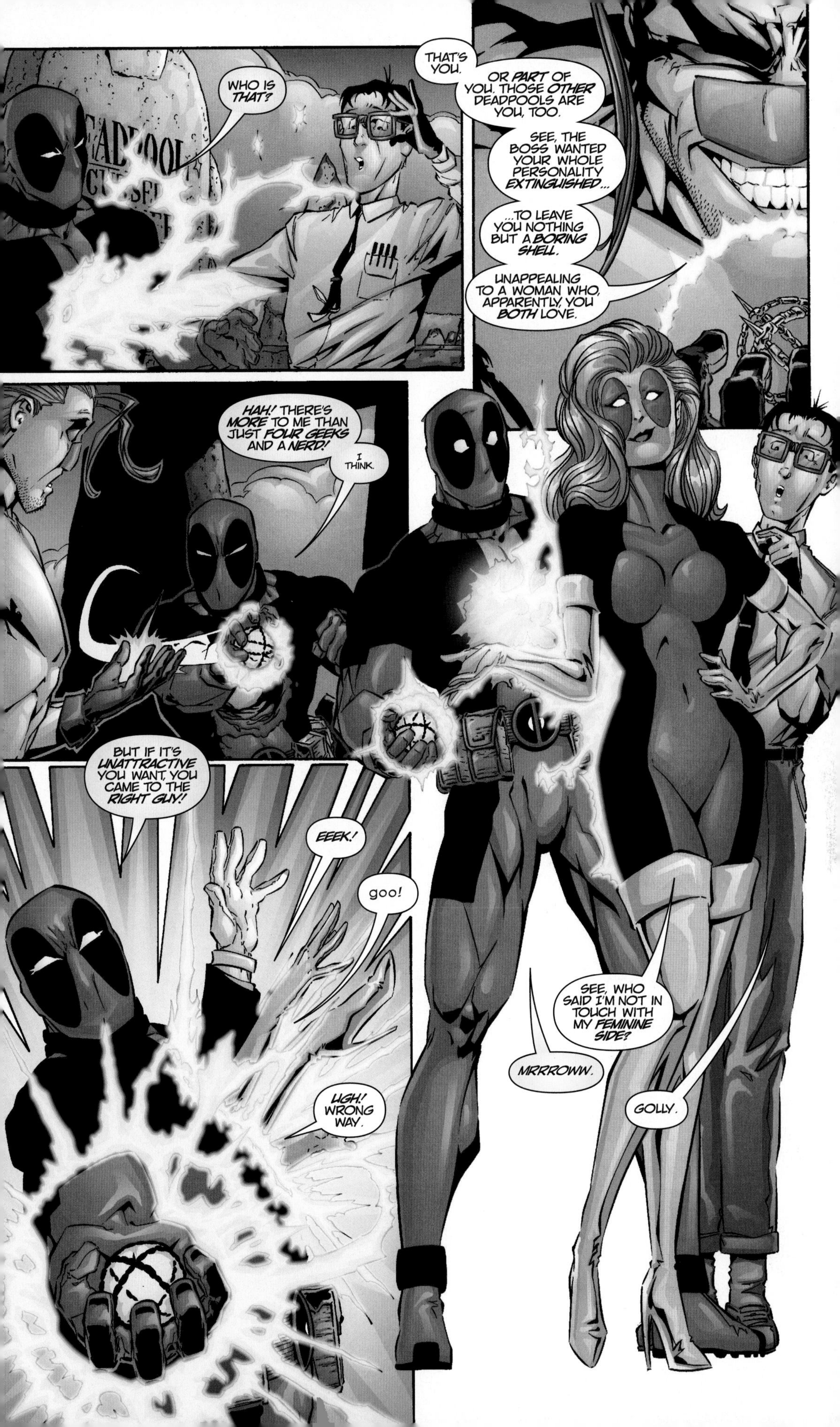
WHO IS THAT?
THAT'S YOU.
OR PART OF YOU. THOSE OTHER DEADPOOLS ARE YOU, TOO.
SEE, THE BOSS WANTED YOUR WHOLE PERSONALITY EXTINGUISHED...
...TO LEAVE YOU NOTHING BUT A BORING SHELL.
UNAPPEALING TO A WOMAN WHO, APPARENTLY, YOU BOTH LOVE.
HAH! THERE'S MORE TO ME THAN JUST FOUR GEEKS AND A NERD!
I THINK.
BUT IF IT'S UNATTRACTIVE YOU WANT, YOU CAME TO THE RIGHT GUY!
EEEK!
goo!
UGH! WRONG WAY.
SEE, WHO SAID I'M NOT IN TOUCH WITH MY FEMININE SIDE?
MRRROWN.
GOLLY.

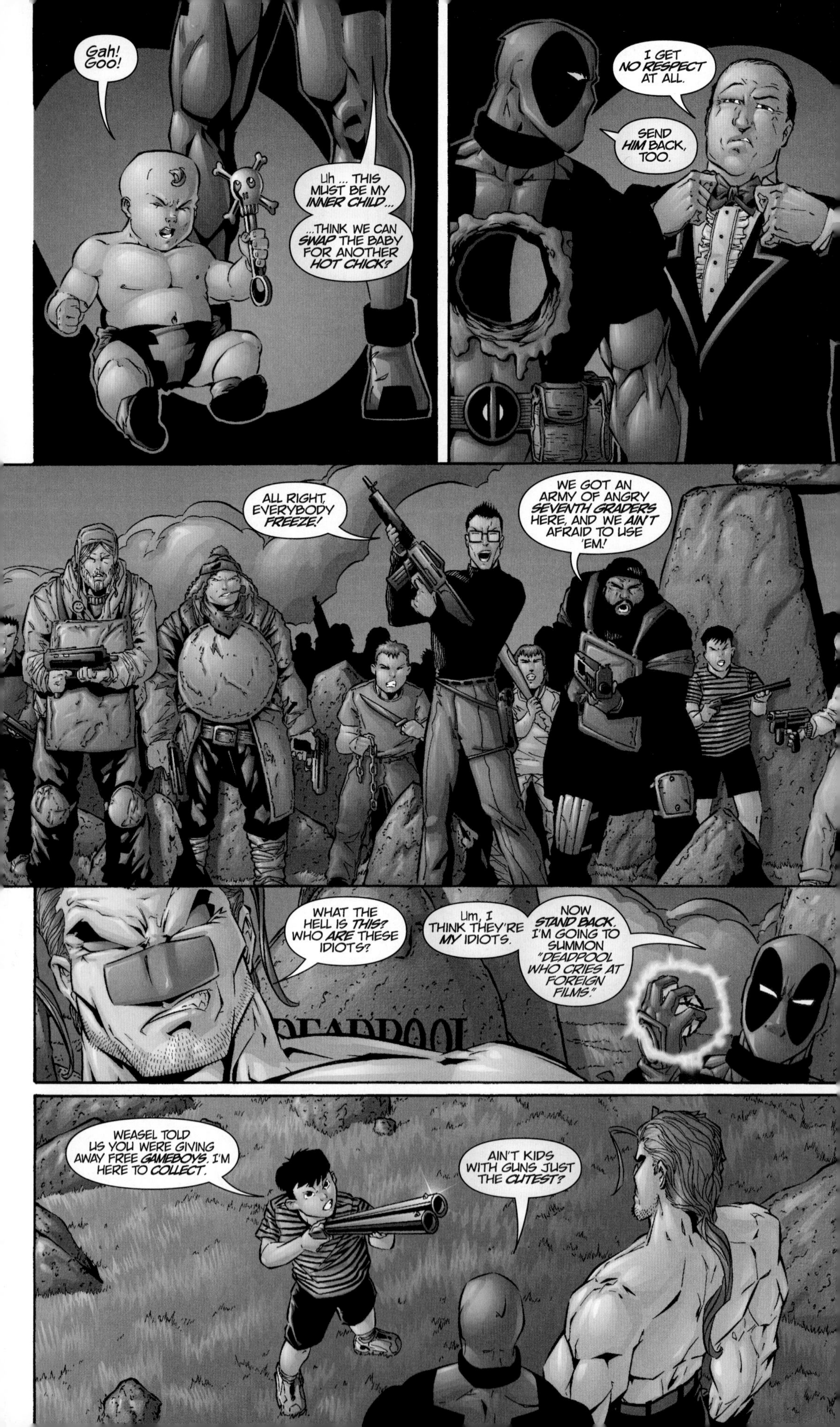
Gah! Goo!
Uh ... THIS MUST BE MY INNER CHILD...
...THINK WE CAN SWAP THE BABY FOR ANOTHER HOT CHICK?
I GET NO RESPECT AT ALL.
SEND HIM BACK, TOO.
ALL RIGHT, EVERYBODY FREEZE!
WE GOT AN ARMY OF ANGRY SEVENTH GRADERS HERE, AND WE AIN'T AFRAID TO USE 'EM!
WHAT THE HELL IS THIS? WHO ARE THESE IDIOTS?
Um, I THINK THEY'RE MY IDIOTS.
NOW STAND BACK. I'M GOING TO SUMMON "DEADPOOL WHO CRIES AT FOREIGN FILMS."
DEADPOOL
WEASEL TOLD US YOU WERE GIVING AWAY FREE GAMEBOYS. I'M HERE TO COLLECT.
AIN'T KIDS WITH GUNS JUST THE CUTEST?

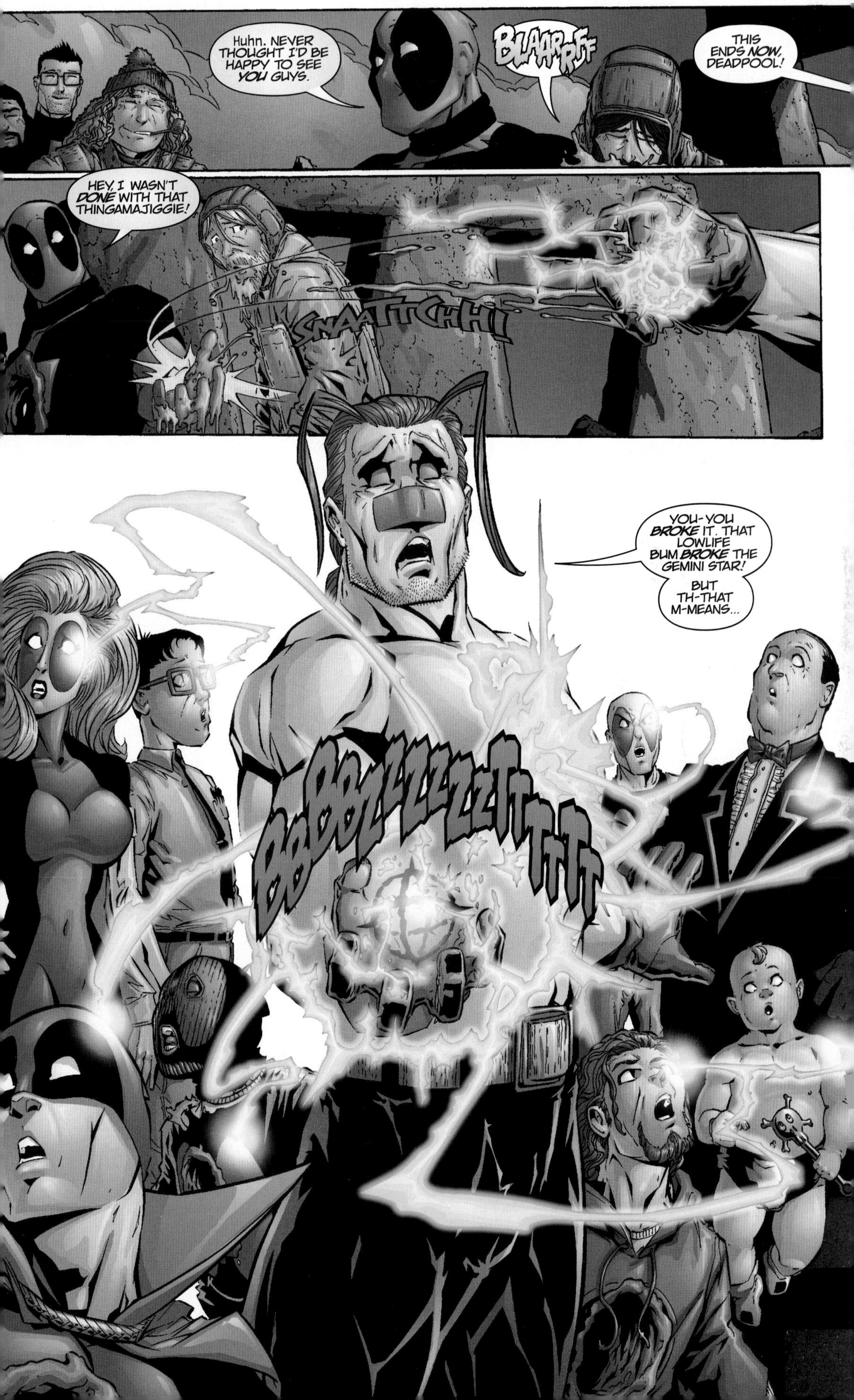
Huhn. NEVER THOUGHT I'D BE HAPPY TO SEE *YOU* GUYS.
BLAARRFF
THIS ENDS *NOW*, DEADPOOL!
HEY, I WASN'T *DONE* WITH THAT THINGAMAJIGGIE!
SNAATTCHH!
YOU-YOU *BROKE* IT. THAT LOWLIFE BUM *BROKE* THE GEMINI STAR!
BUT TH-THAT M-MEANS...
BBBZZZZZZTTTTTT

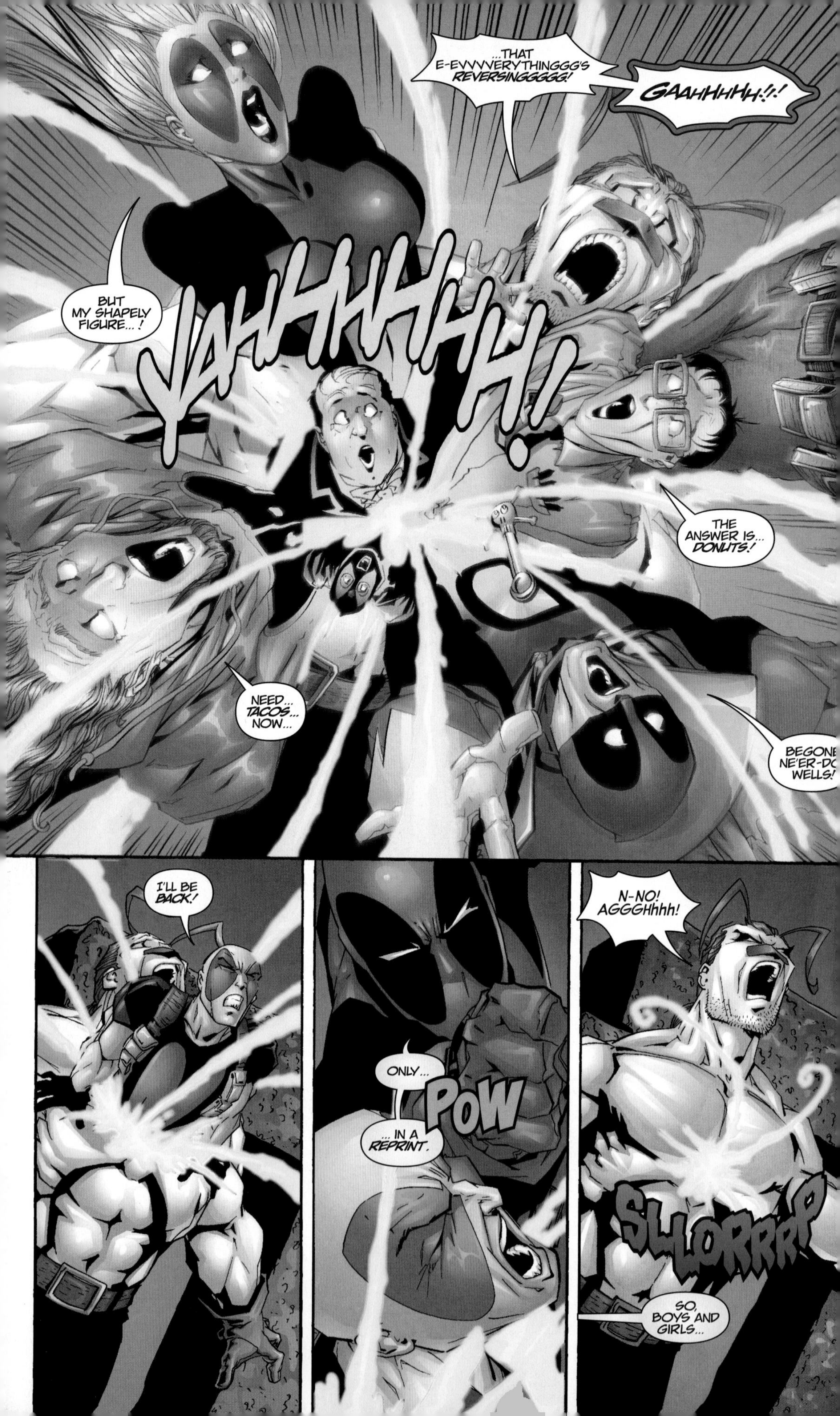
...THAT E-EVVVVERYTHINGGG'S REVERSINGGGGG!
GAAHHHHH!!!
BUT MY SHAPELY FIGURE...!
YAHHHHHH!
THE ANSWER IS... DONUTS!
NEED... TACOS... NOW...
BEGONE NE'ER-DO WELLS!
I'LL BE BACK!
ONLY...
POW
...IN A REPRINT.
N-NO! AGGGHhhh!
SLLORRRP
SO, BOYS AND GIRLS...

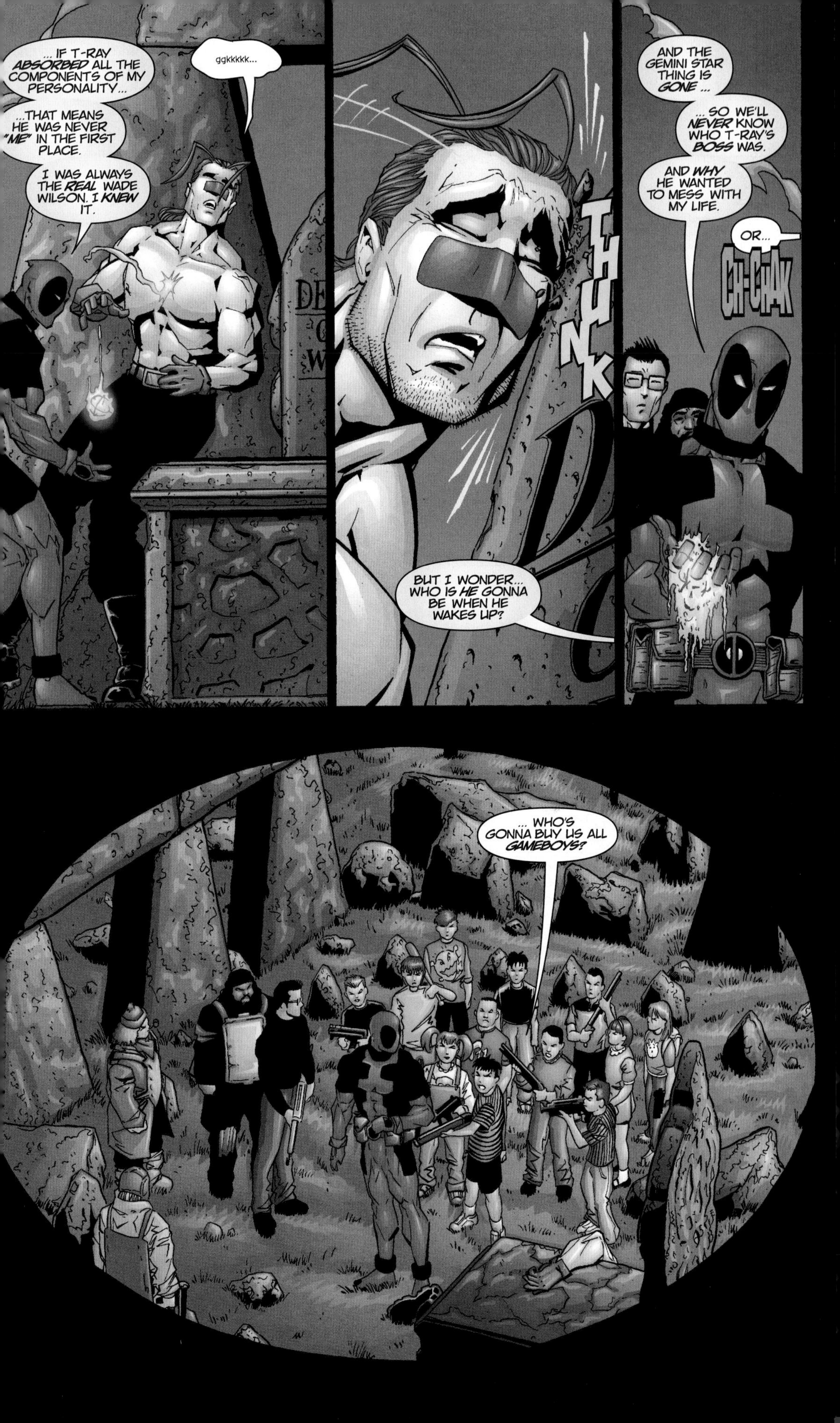
... IF T-RAY ABSORBED ALL THE COMPONENTS OF MY PERSONALITY...
...THAT MEANS HE WAS NEVER "ME" IN THE FIRST PLACE.
I WAS ALWAYS THE REAL WADE WILSON. I KNEW IT.
ggkkkkk...
THUNK
BUT I WONDER... WHO IS HE GONNA BE WHEN HE WAKES UP?
AND THE GEMINI STAR THING IS GONE ...
... SO WE'LL NEVER KNOW WHO T-RAY'S BOSS WAS.
AND WHY HE WANTED TO MESS WITH MY LIFE.
OR...
CH-CHAK
... WHO'S GONNA BUY US ALL GAMEBOYS?

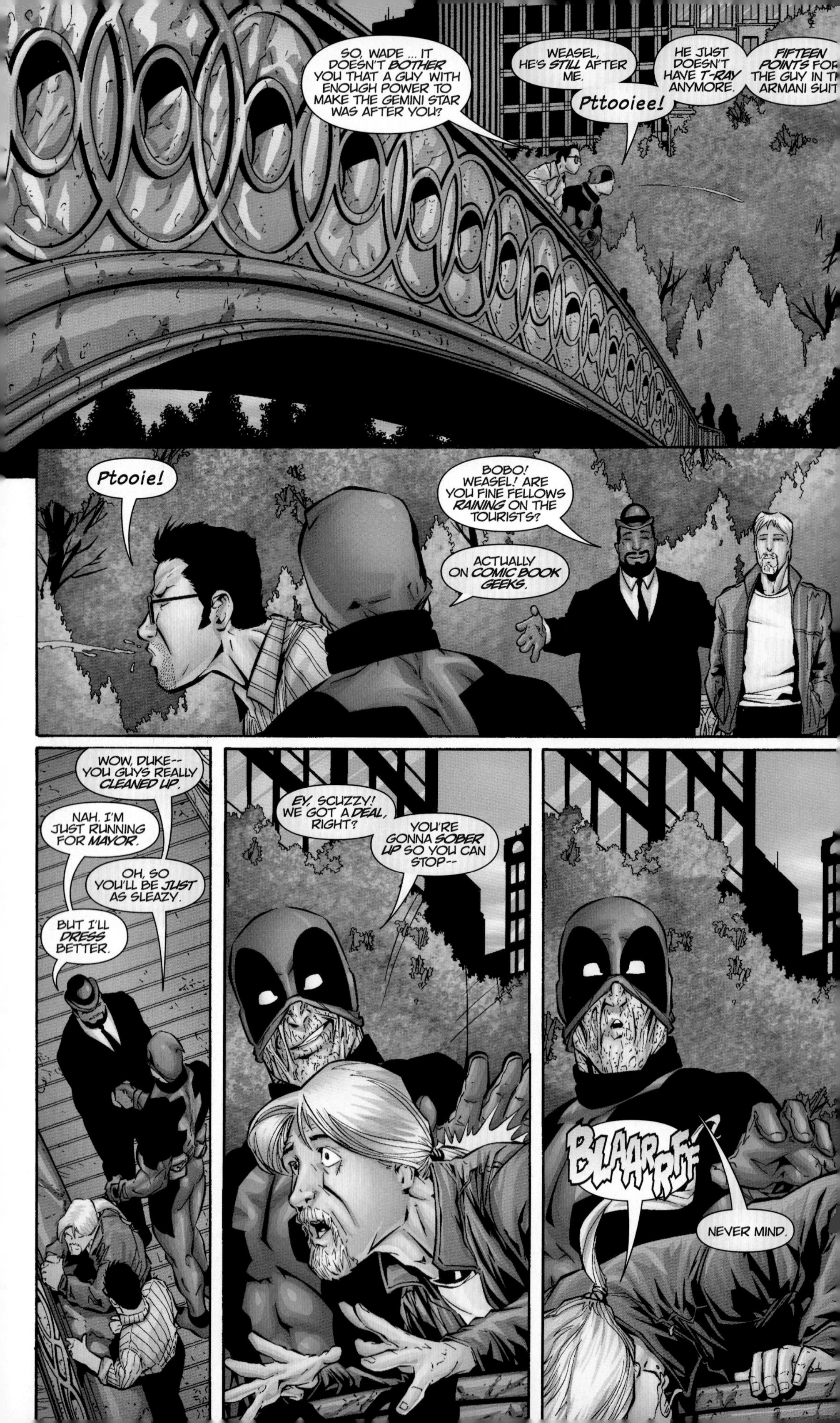
SO, WADE ... IT DOESN'T BOTHER YOU THAT A GUY WITH ENOUGH POWER TO MAKE THE GEMINI STAR WAS AFTER YOU?
WEASEL, HE'S STILL AFTER ME.
Pttooiee!
HE JUST DOESN'T HAVE T-RAY ANYMORE.
FIFTEEN POINTS FOR THE GUY IN THE ARMANI SUIT
Ptooie!
BOBO! WEASEL! ARE YOU FINE FELLOWS RAINING ON THE TOURISTS?
ACTUALLY ON COMIC BOOK GEEKS.
WOW, DUKE-- YOU GUYS REALLY CLEANED UP.
NAH. I'M JUST RUNNING FOR MAYOR.
OH, SO YOU'LL BE JUST AS SLEAZY.
BUT I'LL DRESS BETTER.
EY, SCUZZY! WE GOT A DEAL, RIGHT?
YOU'RE GONNA SOBER UP SO YOU CAN STOP--
BLAARRFF
NEVER MIND.

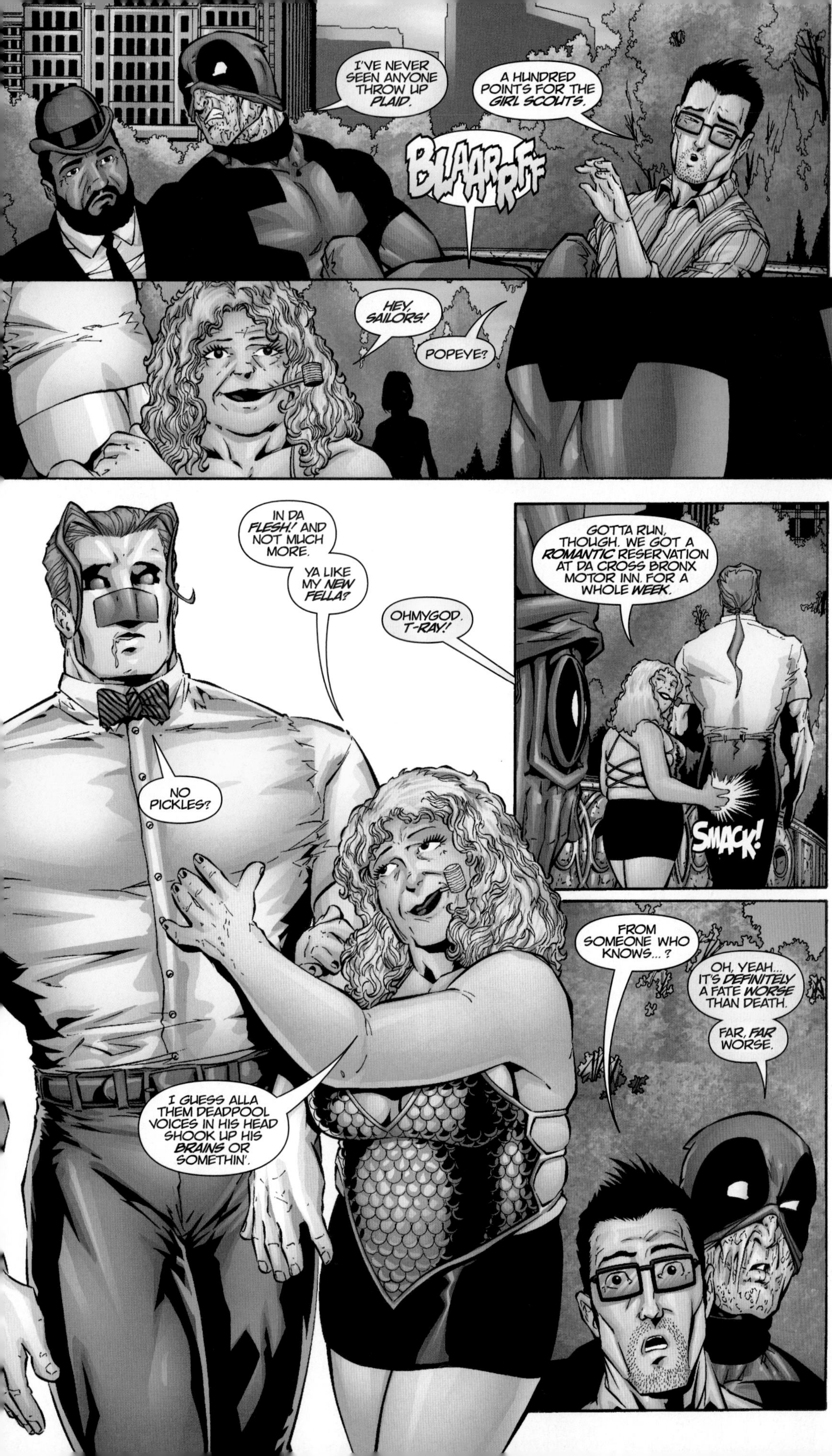
I'VE NEVER SEEN ANYONE THROW UP PLAID.
A HUNDRED POINTS FOR THE GIRL SCOUTS.
BLAARRFF
HEY, SAILORS!
POPEYE?
IN DA FLESH! AND NOT MUCH MORE.
YA LIKE MY NEW FELLA?
OHMYGOD. T-RAY!
NO PICKLES?
I GUESS ALLA THEM DEADPOOL VOICES IN HIS HEAD SHOOK UP HIS BRAINS OR SOMETHIN'.
GOTTA RUN, THOUGH. WE GOT A ROMANTIC RESERVATION AT DA CROSS BRONX MOTOR INN. FOR A WHOLE WEEK.
SMACK!
FROM SOMEONE WHO KNOWS...?
OH, YEAH... IT'S DEFINITELY A FATE WORSE THAN DEATH.
FAR, FAR WORSE.

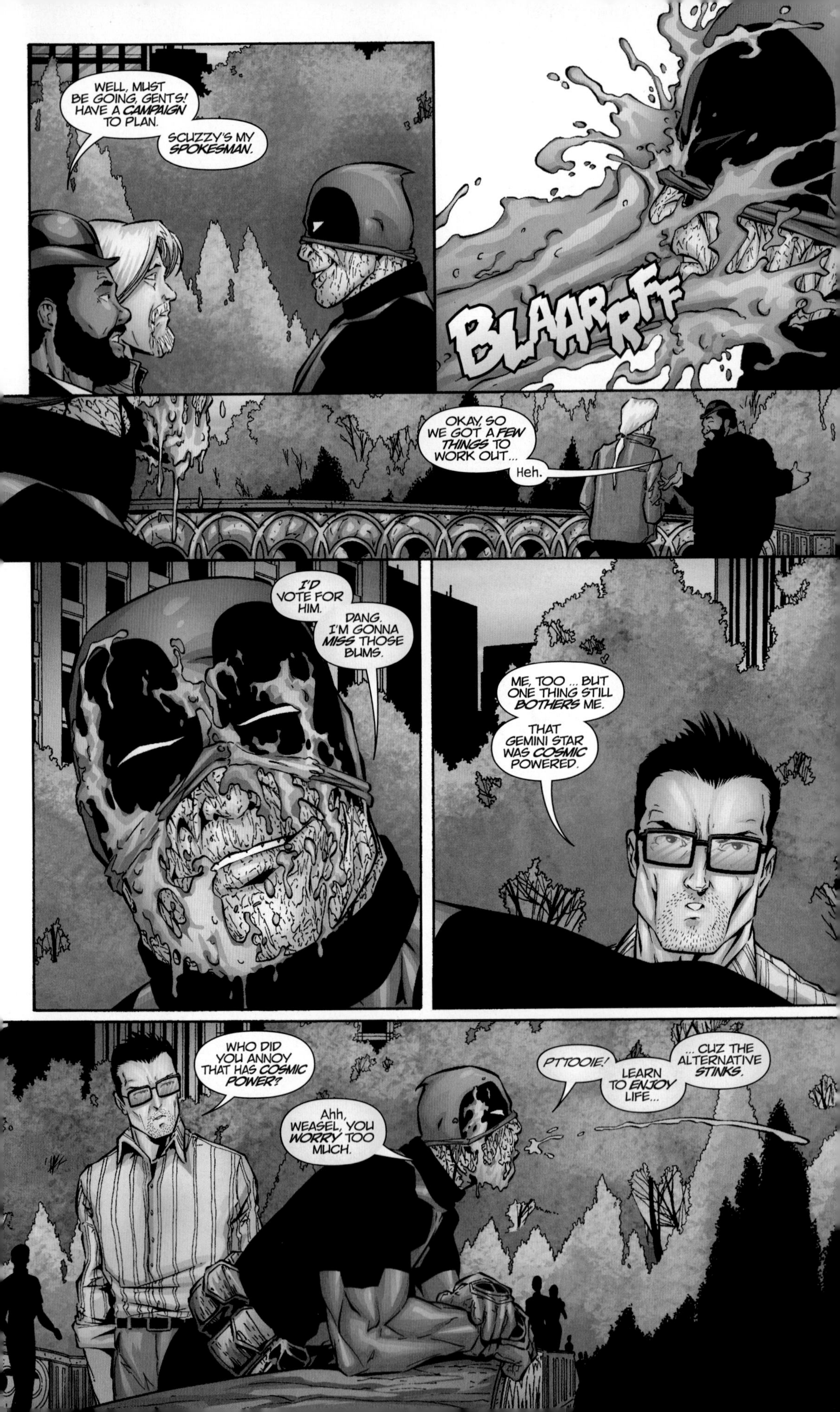
WELL, MUST BE GOING, GENTS! HAVE A CAMPAIGN TO PLAN.
SCUZZY'S MY SPOKESMAN.
BLAARRFF
OKAY, SO WE GOT A FEW THINGS TO WORK OUT...
Heh.
I'D VOTE FOR HIM.
DANG. I'M GONNA MISS THOSE BUMS.
ME, TOO ... BUT ONE THING STILL BOTHERS ME.
THAT GEMINI STAR WAS COSMIC POWERED.
WHO DID YOU ANNOY THAT HAS COSMIC POWER?
Ahh, WEASEL, YOU WORRY TOO MUCH.
PTTOOIE!
LEARN TO ENJOY LIFE...
... CUZ THE ALTERNATIVE STINKS.

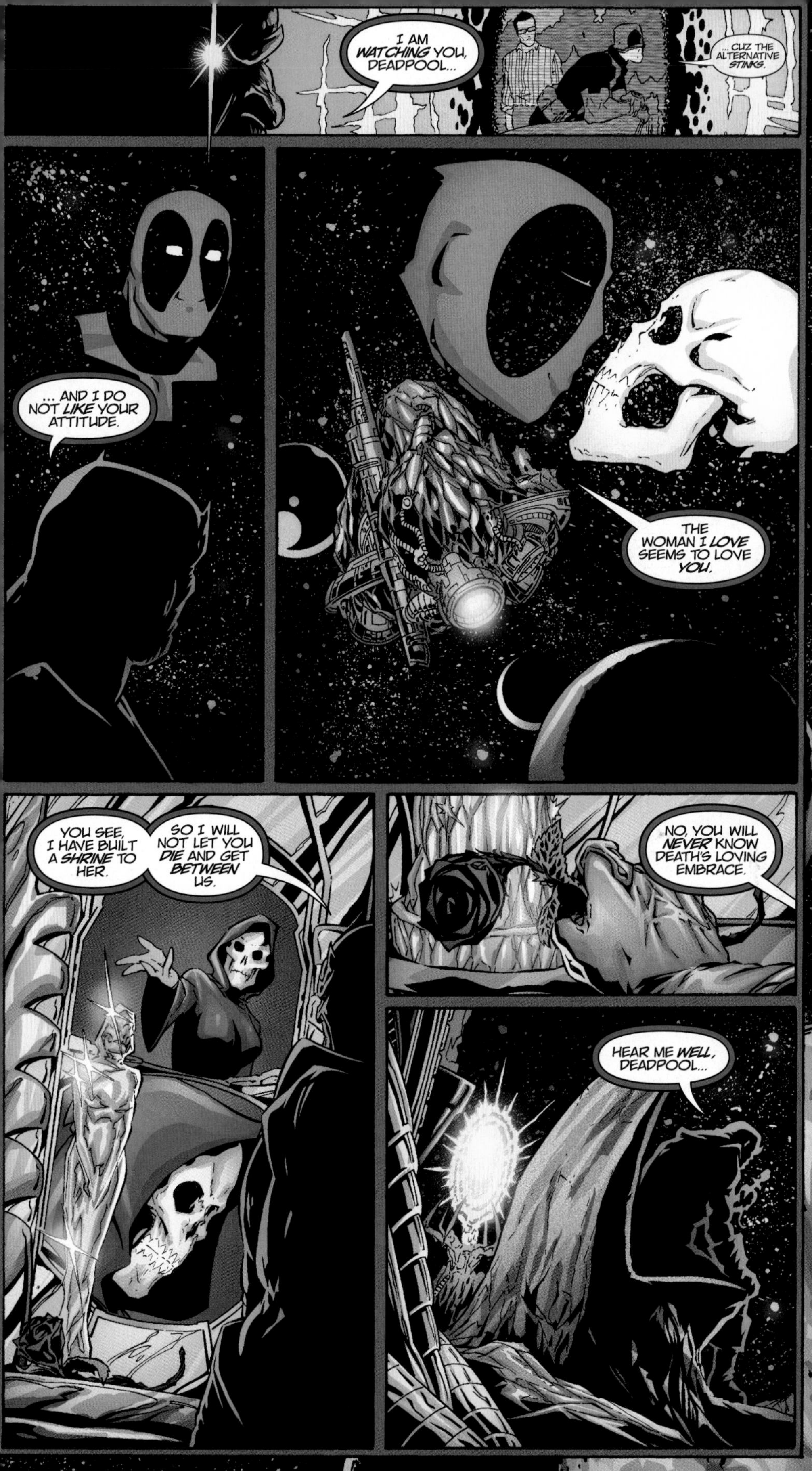
I AM *WATCHING* YOU, DEADPOOL...
... CUZ THE ALTERNATIVE *STINKS*.
... AND I DO NOT *LIKE* YOUR ATTITUDE.
THE WOMAN I *LOVE* SEEMS TO LOVE *YOU*.
YOU SEE, I HAVE BUILT A *SHRINE* TO HER.
SO I WILL NOT LET YOU *DIE* AND GET *BETWEEN* US.
NO, YOU WILL *NEVER* KNOW DEATH'S LOVING EMBRACE.
HEAR ME *WELL*, DEADPOOL...

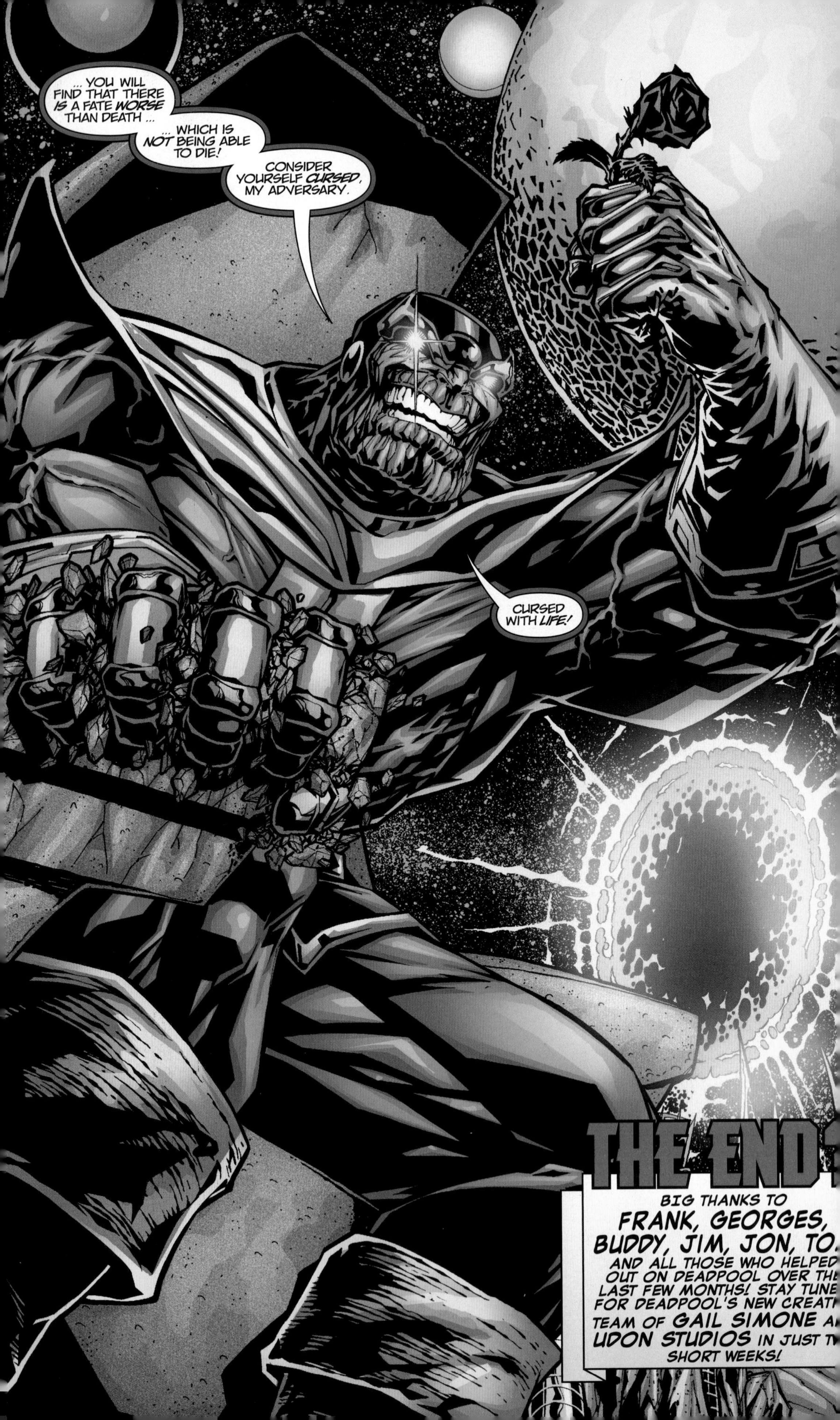
... YOU WILL FIND THAT THERE IS A FATE WORSE THAN DEATH ...
... WHICH IS NOT BEING ABLE TO DIE!
CONSIDER YOURSELF CURSED, MY ADVERSARY.
CURSED WITH LIFE!
THE END
BIG THANKS TO
FRANK, GEORGES,
BUDDY, JIM, JON, TO
AND ALL THOSE WHO HELPED OUT ON DEADPOOL OVER TH LAST FEW MONTHS! STAY TUNE FOR DEADPOOL'S NEW CREATI TEAM OF GAIL SIMONE A UDON STUDIOS IN JUST T SHORT WEEKS!

We dared them.

That's right, almost a year ago, Marvel Prez Bill Jemas and EIC Joe Quesada hatched a test for the Mighty Marvel Maestros: Since you are the best artists and writers in the biz, we challenge you to tell a story using visuals only. After all, if a picture is worth a thousand words, then a comic book filled with images only would be worth... well, more words than the Collector could count!

And if you think creating a story with no words is half the work, think again, True Believer! The writer has to craft a story using no dialogue or caption boxes to communicate information — and pencilers have to make sure their storytelling is so clear that text isn't needed to explain what's going on.

Just to show you how our Mighty Marvel Maestros met the challenge, and to give you a unique peek behind the curtain, here's the plot to the very story you just read! Just compare it to the art and you'll see how the dare was done!

PAGE 1

DP (in full classic costume) lying on the floor, just coming to.

He gets up, he's touching his chest in disbelief ... he can't believe he's still alive.

He lets out a "woo hoo!", thinking he's alive.

Suddenly, he gets tapped on the shoulder.

He turns to see Bruce Willis from the Sixth Sense.

PAGE 2

DP, quizzically points to himself ...

Then makes the slashing "I'm dead" sign with his finger across his neck—he also tilts his head back, closes his eyes and sticks his tongue out the side of his mouth as he does this.

Bruce Willis nods "yes".

DP makes snaps his fingers, saying "drats!".

Frank Tieri
Deadpool #61

Then he notices Halley Joel Osmet is pointing at him—Bruce Willis is rolling his eyes like "here we go again".

DP gets mad—kicks Osmet in the butt and shoves Willis from behind away from him.

PAGE 3

Walks over to his coffin

Splash—we see the full view of the coffin. There's a hand in there (all that was left of him), his classic costume (it's draped in the coffin with the hand on top of it) and a picture of DP smirking (with costume). There's also a tombstone that says "here lies Wade Wilson ... at least what's left of him".

PAGE 4 and 5

This should act like a Double Page spread of panels: 12 panels, either 4 down and three across or 3 down and 4 across.
DP turns (Jim, at this point I'm thinking maybe we should have DP appear somewhat ghostly for the rest of the issue. But maybe this is more of a colorist thing. --Mike)

The people have started to arrive (everyone's pretty much in suits and appropriate funeral garb), Wolverine first ...

Then Sasquatch ...

Typhoid Mary (wearing a veil, but we can see she has that two face painted thing underneath) ...

Constrictor and that flamboyant landlord (you drew him in issue 44-45, Jim) ...

The gang from the Hellhouse ...

Zoe Culloden and Monty ...

Poolboy (in costume) ...

Juggernaut ...

Black Panther ...

Cable ...

DP forces a smile—seeing all these people show up sort of gets to him.

Frank Tieri
Deadpool #61

PAGE 6

A priest stands by the coffin, overseeing the ceremony. There are rows of chairs in front of the coffin where the people have seated (Typhoid Mary is hitting on Cable, who's not interested. In fact, everytime we see her in the background, she should be hitting on a different man, Wolvie, Juggernaut, Constrictor, Sasquatch) others have remained standing. DP, smiling nodding in approval as if to say it's a good turn out for his funeral, sits down in an empty seat next to Sasquatch.

Shot of the Great Lakes Avengers arriving

Big Bertha comes and sits in Wade's seat, squashing him up against Sasquatch.

Close on Wade—his left cheek is covered in Sasquatch's fur, his right in Bertha's fat.

DP jumps up from in between them like a swimmer coming up for air.

Suddenly, something whizzes by his head ...

PAGE 7

... ricochets off a nearby tree ...

... bounces off the open lid of the coffin ...

... and flops into the hand in the coffin—we now see it's the ace of spades.

DP looks to see a man standing several feet behind all the people and chairs—he's wearing an overcoat and hat.

Closer on him, and we see it's Bullseye—he's tipping his hat.

He turns to walk off—DP tips his "hat" to him, too (he makes the motion as if he had a hat).

Page 8

Now Blind Al and Weasel arrive, Weasel is holding her arm, helping her along.

DP smiles as he sees them.

And then smirks an evil smile as he gets a mischievous idea.

He jumps into Weasel's body.

And has Weasel lead Blind Al into the open grave. He jumps out of Weasel's body right when the old lady's on the edge of the grave.

She falls in—all we can see is her feet as the rest of her is in the grave. Weasel is in a state of disbelief at what he's done. But DP's spirit is laughing hysterically.

Page 9

The tone of the next two pages will get decidedly serious. The crowd suddenly begins to part ...

DP looks over, wondering why—in the background, Weasel should be helping the annoyed Blind Al out of the grave.

Big panel as we see it's Siryn, being helped by her teammate, Thunderbird (James Proudstar)—she's deeply sad, and holds a rose in her hand.

PAGE 10

DP 's face suddenly gets sad, too, as he sees her

She walks towards the coffin. DP, with much emotion in his face, looks on (I wouldn't make him actually cry though—it just ain't his thing).

Shot of her crying, she's putting the rose in the coffin on top of the hand—DP looks on, right behind her.

She kisses the hand.

He kisses her forehead ...

... and watches her lovingly as she goes to sit down.

PAGE 11

Shot of everyone, they're all together, talking by the gravesite—it's almost like a party (but obviously not as festive).

Suddenly, Wolvie turns his attention from the crowd, but only DP has noticed.

He starts to sniff in the air—still only DP notices.

Frank Tieri
Deadpool #61

He looks in the distance to a hill overlooking the funeral—we see the shadowy figures of the Weapon X gang—Sabes, the Director, Agent Jackson, Sauron, Mesmero, Wildchild, and Kane.

Closer on them—they've noticed Wolvie has seen them, they're all got a sinister smile on as they get into a nearby limo—Sabes even winks at Wolvie and does the gun sign with his hand.

Shot of Wolvie and DP—they've got the same exact angry look on their faces.

PAGE 12

DP still angry, but his eyes have turned the other way as if something else has caught his attention.

Then suddenly, he has a look of disbelief on his face.

We now see what it is—unnoticed by anyone, Poolboy stands snickering near the coffin, having defaced DP's picture with a magic marker—(he's drawn in some missing teeth, put a mustache on him, stuff like that.

DP is steaming as he watches Poolboy nonchalantly walk back into the crowd.

Suddenly, an idea comes to him (lightbulb! above his head).

PAGE 13

Shot of DP with a sinister smile on his face—he'll get revenge on that kid.

He jumps into Poolboy's body.

And grabs the Juggernaut's rear—(Juggie was in the midst of a conversation with someone).

DP then jumps out of Poolboy's body—Poolboy is disoriented.

Shot of Poolboy, frightened as he looks up at the enraged Juggernaut.

PAGE 14

Poolboy shrugs and points to himself, like "what did I do?"

Shot of Juggie's fist slugging Poolboy—Poolboy's knocked out of his shoes.

Now everyone in the crowd turns their attention to this—Wolvie pops his claws.

All hell breaks loose. There's some pushing and shoving, some people trying to break things up.

Big Shot as it all erupts.

PAGE 15

Shot of DP laughing to himself as he walks away from the melee—in the background the fight rages on.

He's still walking, laughing and doesn't notice everything starting to fade away.

Now he does—everything around him is blank.

He turns behind him—everything behind him is blank, too.

He turns back again and there's a surprised look on his face.

PAGE 16

Big panel—only this time there's a very surreal scene, with dead celebrities and famous dead people all around doing things (everything else though is still white, blank space). There's a card game going on between Archie Bunker, Bucky, Babe Ruth and Abe Lincoln. Fred Astaire is waltzing with Gwen Stacy. Ghandi is playing ping-pong with Baron Zemo. Elvis is painting a picture, Ben Franklin and Battlin' Jack Murdock look on. Humphrey Bogart and Napoleon are at a table arm wresting — looking on is Marilyn Monroe, Captain Marvel, Thunderbird and Einstein.

DP is walking through this scene looking at all these people in like a daze—where the hell is he?

Then he comes upon Elvis painting the picture with Ben Franklin and Battlin' Jack looking on.

We now see it's a picture of a house.

Everyone now stops what they're doing and points to something we can't see yet—DP looks at what they're all pointing at.

Frank Tieri
Deadpool #61

PAGE 17

Big panel as we see it's a big, white Norman Bates looking house—it's as if it appeared out of nowhere in this nothingness.

DP, like in a trance, starts to walk towards it.

He opens the door.

We see stairs leading upstairs and another door right at the top of the steps—the door is slightly open and a white light emanates from inside.

He slowly starts to walk upstairs.

He enters the door— a beautiful woman dressed in lingerie with a veil on lies seductively on the bed—the room is otherwise white, and fairly sterile.

PAGE 18

DP looks at the audience, smirks and raises his eyebrow as if to say "hubba-hubba".

He approaches the woman on the bed.

He pulls back her veil.

Big panel—and we see the unmistakably skull face of Death.

Shot of DP about to kiss Death.

PAGE 19

Shot of the graveyard at night, particularly DP's grave.

We see a mysterious cloaked figure is there.

He approaches the grave, standing on it.

PAGE 20

Shot inside the casket.

Back to the house—DP's face jolts, like something happened. He was just about to kiss Death, too.

The grave—suddenly, the hand starts moving.

The house—DP's looking at his hands and body as he begins to fade—Death is sitting up, alarmed.

The grave—it begins to grow out as an arm starts to form.

PAGE 21

The house—DP's almost completely faded out—Death reaches up to grab him.

The grave—more now, a torso and a head and legs are beginning to form.

The house—there's dead space where DP used to be, Death is standing there, annoyed.

The grave—shot of DP.

He's looking around, confused at where he is.

He puts his two legs through the roof of the coffin.

PAGE 22

DP, from the waist up, emerges from his grave (remember he has no costume—so he should be all scaly and scarred again).

He sniffs around—something smells funny.

He sniffs himself .

He makes a face of "ewwww" as he realizes it's him.

END.

Frank Tieri
Deadpool #61